A History of Shiʿi Islam

The Institute of Ismaili Studies
Shiʿi Heritage Series, 1

Editorial Board: Farhad Daftary (general editor), Maria De Cillis (managing editor), Gurdofarid Miskinzoda (managing editor), Mohammad-Ali Amir-Moezzi, Hermann Landolt, Wilferd Madelung, Andrew Newman, Sabine Schmidtke, Paul E. Walker

Farhad Daftary is the Co-Director of The Institute of Ismaili Studies, London, and Head of the Institute's Department of Academic Research and Publications. Since the mid-1960s, when he was completing his doctoral studies at the University of California, Berkeley, he has cultivated his interest in Shiʿi studies, with special reference to its Ismaili tradition, on which he is an authority. As well as serving on various editorial boards, Dr Daftary is a consulting editor of *Encyclopaedia Iranica*, co-editor (with W. Madelung) of *Encyclopaedia Islamica*, and the general editor of the 'Ismaili Heritage Series' and the 'Ismaili Texts and Translations Series'. He is the author and editor of numerous publications, including *The Ismāʿīlīs* (1990; 2nd ed., 2007), *The Assassin Legends* (1994), *A Short History of the Ismailis* (1998), *Intellectual Traditions in Islam* (2000), *Ismaili Literature* (2004), *A Modern History of the Ismailis* (2011), as well as many articles and encyclopaedia entries. Dr Daftary's books have been translated into Arabic, Persian, Turkish, Urdu, Gujarati, Chinese and various European languages.

A History of Shiʿi Islam

by
Farhad Daftary

I.B.Tauris *Publishers*
LONDON • NEW YORK
in association with
The Institute of Ismaili Studies
LONDON, 2013

Published in 2013 by I.B.Tauris & Co. Ltd
6 Salem Road, London W2 4BU
175 Fifth Avenue, New York NY 10010
www.ibtauris.com

in association with The Institute of Ismaili Studies
210 Euston Road, London NW1 2DA
www.iis.ac.uk

Distributed in the United States and Canada Exclusively by
Palgrave Macmillan, 175 Fifth Avenue, New York NY 10010

ISBN: 978 1 78076 841 0

A full CIP record for this book is available from the British Library
A full CIP record is available from the Library of Congress

Library of Congress Catalog Card Number: available

Typeset in Minion Tra for The Institute of Ismaili Studies

Printed and bound in Great Britain by T.J. International, Padstow, Cornwall

FSC www.fsc.org MIX Paper from responsible sources FSC® C013056

The Institute of Ismaili Studies

The Institute of Ismaili Studies was established in 1977 with the object of promoting scholarship and learning on Islam, in the historical as well as contemporary contexts, and a better understanding of its relationship with other societies and faiths.

The Institute's programmes encourage a perspective which is not confined to the theological and religious heritage of Islam, but seeks to explore the relationship of religious ideas to broader dimensions of society and culture. The programmes thus encourage an interdisciplinary approach to the materials of Islamic history and thought. Particular attention is also given to issues of modernity that arise as Muslims seek to relate their heritage to the contemporary situation.

Within the Islamic tradition, the Institute's programmes promote research on those areas which have, to date, received relatively little attention from scholars. These include the intellectual and literary expressions of Shiʿism in general, and Ismailism in particular.

In the context of Islamic societies, the Institute's programmes are informed by the full range and diversity of cultures in which Islam is practised today, from the Middle East, South and Central Asia, and Africa to the industrialised societies of the West, thus taking into consideration the variety of contexts that shape the ideals, beliefs and practices of the faith.

These objectives are realised through concrete programmes and activities organised and implemented by various departments of the Institute. The Institute also collaborates periodically, on a programme-specific basis, with other institutions of learning in the United Kingdom and abroad.

The Institute's academic publications fall into a number of inter-related categories:

1. Occasional papers or essays addressing broad themes of the relationship between religion and society, with special reference to Islam.
2. Works exploring specific aspects of Islamic faith and culture, or the contributions of individual Muslim thinkers or writers.
3. Editions or translations of significant primary or secondary texts.
4. Translations of poetic or literary texts that illustrate the rich heritage of spiritual, devotional and symbolic expressions in Muslim history.
5. Works on Ismaili history and thought, and the relationship of the Ismailis to other traditions, communities and schools of thought in Islam.
6. Proceedings of conferences and seminars sponsored by the Institute.
7. Bibliographical works and catalogues that document manuscripts, printed texts and other source materials.

This book falls into category two listed above.

In facilitating these and other publications, the Institute's sole aim is to encourage original research and analysis of relevant issues. While every effort is made to ensure that the publications are of a high academic standard, there is naturally bound to be a diversity of views, ideas and interpretations. As such, the opinions expressed in these publications must be understood as belonging to their authors alone.

Shiʿi Heritage Series

Shiʿi Muslims, with their rich intellectual and cultural heritage, have contributed significantly to the fecundity and diversity of the Islamic traditions throughout the centuries, enabling Islam to evolve and flourish both as a major religion and also as a civilisation. In spite of this, Shiʿi Islam has received little scholarly attention in the West, in medieval as well modern times. It is only in recent decades that academic interest has focused increasingly on Shiʿi Islam within the wider study of Islam.

The principal objective of the *Shiʿi Heritage Series*, launched by The Institute of Ismaili Studies, is to enhance general knowledge of Shiʿi Islam and promote a better understanding of its history, doctrines and practices in their historical and contemporary manifestations. Addressing all Shiʿi communities, the series also aims to engage in discussions on theoretical and methodological issues, while inspiring further research in the field.

Works published in this series will include monographs, collective volumes, editions and translations of primary texts, and bibliographical projects, bringing together some of the most significant themes in the study of Shiʿi Islam through an interdisciplinary approach, and making them accessible to a wide readership.

Table of Contents

Genealogical Tables and Lists xiii
Preface xv
Note on Transliteration and Dates xvii
Abbreviations xix

1. Introduction: Progress in the Study of Shiʿi Islam 1
    Diversity in early Islam 3
    Medieval Sunni perceptions 5
    Medieval European perceptions 7
    Orientalist perspectives 16
    Modern scholarship on Shiʿi Islam 18

2. The Origins and Early History of Shiʿi Islam 25
    Origins of Shiʿism 25
    The early Shiʿa 29
    The Kaysaniyya 37
    The *ghulat* 40
    The early Imamiyya 43
    The Imami Shiʿi doctrine of the imamate 53

3. The Ithnaʿasharis or Twelvers 57
    The later Twelver imams and the hidden Mahdi 58
    From the occultation of the twelfth imam to the Mongol invasions 67
    From Nasir al-Din al-Tusi to the advent of the Safawids 74
    From the Safawids to early modern times 81
    From around 1215/1800 to the present 89

4. The Ismailis 105
    The early Ismailis 106
    The Fatimid phase in Ismaili history 115

The Tayyibi Ismailis: The Yamani and Indian phases 125
The Nizari Ismailis: The Alamut phase 130
Later developments in Nizari Ismaili history 136
The Anjudan revival 138
The modern period 141

5. The Zaydis 145
The early Zaydis 145
The Zaydis of the Caspian region in Persia 151
The Zaydis of Yaman 162

6. The Nusayris or ʿAlawis 175
Nusayri studies 176
History of the Nusayris 179
The Nusayri-ʿAlawi doctrines 185

Glossary 191
Notes 211
Bibliography 249
Index 283

Genealogical Tables and Lists

2.1	The Hashimids and Early Shiʿi Imams	52
3.1	Imams of the Twelver Shiʿis	66
4.1	Fatimid Caliph-Imams (297–567/909–1171)	116
4.2	Nizari Ismaili Rulers at Alamut (483–654/1090–1256)	131
4.3	Nizari Ismaili Imams of Modern Times	142

Preface

I have been conducting research into the history and doctrines of the Ismailis since the mid-1960s, when I was completing my doctoral studies at the University of California, Berkeley. This field of Shiʿi studies was still relatively new, with a handful of scholars making original contributions on the basis of the recently recovered Ismaili manuscript sources. Meanwhile, in 1988 I had joined The Institute of Ismaili Studies in London, where I have maintained my interest in Shiʿi studies, with special reference to its Ismaili tradition.

Much progress has been made in understanding the true nature of the history and teachings of the Ismailis, who have been misrepresented throughout the centuries for a variety of reasons. However, the Ismailis constitute only one of the major Shiʿi communities, second in size to the Twelvers, or Ithnaʿasharis, who are dominant in Iran, Iraq and certain other regions of the Middle East. It is, indeed, a fact that Shiʿi communities of all traditions still continue to be variously misunderstood and misrepresented, whether by other Muslims or by non-Muslims as well. In recognition of these realities I embarked, several years ago, on studying more inclusively all the major Shiʿi Muslim communities and their distinctive traditions. The result is the present book, which draws on the scattered findings of modern scholarship in the field. I have attempted here to explain the formative era of Shiʿi Islam, when a multitude of Muslim groups and schools of thought were elaborating their doctrinal positions; I then devote separate chapters to the history of the Twelvers, the Ismailis, the Zaydis and the Nusayris, who are now more commonly known as the ʿAlawis. These four communities account for almost the entirety of the Shiʿi Muslim population of the world. I have striven to produce a survey of Shiʿi Islam that can serve as an accessible work of reference for both academics and broader non-specialist readers. I hope I have achieved this goal, at least to some extent.

It remains for me to express my deepest gratitude to Professor Wilferd Madelung, the foremost contemporary authority in Shiʿi studies, for having kindly read the entire typescript of this book; his invaluable comments and suggestions have improved the final product. I would also like to thank Tara Woolnough for her keen editorial work, and Nadia Holmes for meticulously preparing the various drafts of the typescript. Finally, I should like to record my unique debt of gratitude to The Institute of Ismaili Studies and its esteemed patron for providing a congenial intellectual space that enables scholars to pursue their academic activities with unparalleled institutional support.

FD
June 2013

Note on Transliteration and Dates

The system of transliteration used in this book for the Arabic and Persian scripts is essentially that adopted in the third edition of *The Encyclopaedia of Islam*. In the text and the endnotes, diacritical marks are dispensed with, except those for *ʿayn* and *hamza*, but they are fully retained in the Glossary and the Bibliography. However, dynastic, geographical and community names that occur frequently in the book have not been transliterated.

The lunar years of the Islamic calendar are generally followed throughout the text and endnotes (with the exception of Chapter 1) by the corresponding Gregorian solar years (for example, 11/632). The years of the Islamic era, initiated by the emigration (*hijra*) of the Prophet Muhammad from Mecca to Medina in September 622, commonly abbreviated in the Latin form AH (*Anno Hegirae*), have been converted to the corresponding dates of the Christian era, abbreviated as AD (*Anno Domini*), on the basis of the conversion tables given in Greville S. P. Freeman-Grenville, *The Muslim and Christian Calendars* (London, 1963). In Iran (called Persia in the West until 1936), a solar Islamic calendar was officially adopted in the 1920s. The Islamic dates of the sources published in modern Iran are, therefore, solar (Persian, Shamsi; abbreviated to Sh. in the endnotes and the Bibliography), coinciding with the corresponding Christian years starting on 21 March.

Abbreviations

The following abbreviations are used for certain periodicals and encyclopaedias cited frequently in the Notes and Bibliography:

BSOAS	*Bulletin of the School of Oriental and African Studies*
EI	*The Encyclopaedia of Islam*, 1st edition
EI2	*The Encyclopaedia of Islam*, new (second) edition
EI3	*The Encyclopaedia of Islam, Three*
EIR	*Encyclopaedia Iranica*
EIS	*Encyclopaedia Islamica*
IJMES	*International Journal of Middle East Studies*
JAOS	*Journal of the American Oriental Society*
JRAS	*Journal of the Royal Asiatic Society*

1

Introduction: Progress in the Study of Shiʿi Islam

Islam is a civilisation as well as a major world religion, with some 1.3 billion Muslims scattered across almost every region of the globe, especially in the Middle East (the birthplace of Islam), Asia and Africa. Currently, around 15 per cent of the Muslim population of the world belong to various communities or branches of Shiʿi Islam, with the Ithnaʿasharis (or Twelvers) accounting for the largest numbers.

Twelver Shiʿism has remained the official religion of Iran (Persia) since the beginning of the 16th century. The bulk, more than 95 per cent, of Iran's current population of 78 million adhere to the Twelver branch of Shiʿi Islam, and there are almost as many Twelvers in South Asia, across Pakistan, India and Bangladesh. The Twelver Shiʿis also form majority communities in Iraq and Bahrayn. Twelver communities of various sizes may be found in every other country of the Middle East, notably in Lebanon, Saudi Arabia and the United Arab Emirates, as well as in Afghanistan and the Central Asian republics.

The Ismailis of various branches, numbering at least 10 million according to official estimates, account for the second largest Shiʿi community in the world. Dispersed as religious minorities in more than thirty countries of Asia, the Middle East, Africa, Europe and North America, at the present time the majority of the Ismaili Shiʿi population of the world, belonging to the Nizari branch and acknowledging the Aga Khan as their spiritual leader, are concentrated in Afghanistan, Tajikistan, Pakistan, India and Syria. In South Asia, the Nizari Ismailis have been designated as Khojas, while the Tayyibis, representing the other dominant branch of Ismaili Shiʿism, are known as Bohras there. Another important Tayyibi Ismaili community is located in Yaman, with adherents also living in Saudi Arabia.

The Zaydis represent another significant Shiʿi community. In medieval times, important Zaydi communities existed in Persia, but in modern times the Zaydi Shiʿis are concentrated almost exclusively in Yaman, where they account for around 20–40 per cent of the country's total population of about 24 million. In addition, perhaps another one million Zaydis live within the present boundaries of Saudi Arabia. There are also the ʿAlawi Shiʿis, known more generally in earlier times as Nusayris. The ʿAlawis are concentrated in the north-western province of Latakia in Syria, where they account for around 10 per cent of the country's total population of 22 million. ʿAlawi Shiʿis are also to be found in northern Lebanon and in southern Turkey.

To arrive at the total Shiʿi Muslim population of the world, one also needs to take account of those communities and lesser groupings who do not always openly acknowledge their particular Shiʿi or Shiʿi-related identity, such as the Bektashis of Turkey. Furthermore, there are those communities, like the Druzes of the Middle East, who split from the Ismailis and are no longer affiliated to any of the Shiʿi communities, nor do they regard themselves theologically as specifically Shiʿi Muslims. The Bahais, whose origins may be traced to Twelver Shiʿism in Persia, may also belong to this latter category, as Bahaism is considered a new religion by its adherents. However, in this book we shall concentrate on the major Shiʿi communities, notably the Ithnaʿasharis, Ismailis, Zaydis and ʿAlawis.

In addition to their significant number (ca. 200 million), Shiʿi Muslims have played a crucial role, proportionally greater than their relative size, in furthering the intellectual and artistic achievements of the Islamic civilisation. Indeed, the Shiʿi scholars and literati of various branches and regions, including scientists, philosophers, theologians, jurists and poets, have made seminal contributions to Islamic thought and culture. There have also been numerous Shiʿi dynasties, families or individual rulers who patronised scholars, poets and artists as well as various institutions of learning in Islam. Amongst such Shiʿi dynasties, particular mention may be made of the Buyids, the Fatimids, the Hamdanids and the Safawids as well as a host of lesser or local Shiʿi dynasties of North Africa, the Middle East and India. All in all, the Shiʿi Muslims have contributed significantly over the entire course of Islamic history to the richness and diversity of the Islamic traditions, enabling Islam to evolve and flourish not merely as a religion, but also as a major world civilisation. In spite of its relative significance, however, Shiʿi Islam has received very little scholarly attention in the West, both in medieval and modern times. And when it has been discussed, whether in general or in terms of some of its subdivisions, it has normally been treated marginally as a 'sect', a 'heterodoxy' or even a 'heresy', echoing the attitude of Sunni Muslims who have always accounted for the majority share of Muslim society.

Diversity in early Islam

The Prophet Muhammad, under what Muslims accept as divine guidance, laid the foundations of a new religion, which was propagated as the seal of the great monotheistic religions of the Abrahamic tradition. Thus, it was claimed that Islam had superseded the revealed messages of Judaism and Christianity, whose adherents from early on received a special status amongst Muslims as the 'people of the book' (*ahl al-kitab*). Be that as it may, the nascent Muslim community, or *umma*, itself soon split into numerous rival factions and lesser groups, as Muslims continued to disagree on a host of fundamental issues after the death of the Prophet Muhammad in the year 11/632.

Modern scholarship has shown that during at least the first three centuries of their history, marking the formative period of Islam, Muslims lived in an intellectually dynamic and fluid milieu characterised by a multiplicity of communities of interpretation and schools of thought with a diversity of views on a wide range of religio-political issues. The early Muslims were confronted by many gaps in their religious knowledge and understanding of the Islamic revelation, which revolved around issues such as the attributes of God, the nature of authority and definitions of true believers and sinners, amongst other theological concerns. It was during this formative period that different groups and movements began to elaborate their doctrinal positions and gradually acquire the distinctive identities and designations that often encapsulated central aspects of their belief systems. In this effervescent ambience, Muslims engaged in lively discourses and disputations on a variety of theological, juristic and political issues, while ordinary Muslims as well as their scholars moved rather freely amongst different communities and schools of thought. In terms of political loyalties, which remained closely linked to theological perspectives, pluralism in early Islam ranged from the stances of those Muslims, later designated as Sunnis, who endorsed the historical caliphate and the authority-power structure that had actually emerged in the Muslim society, to various religio-political communities or 'communities of interpretation', notably the Shiʿis and the Kharijis, who aspired towards the establishment of new social orders and leadership structures.

In this emerging partisan context, the Sunni Muslims' medieval religious scholars (*ʿulama*) painted a picture that is at great variance with the findings of modern scholarship on the subject. According to this Sunni perspective, endorsed unwittingly by the earlier generations of orientalists, Islam was from the begining a monolithic phenomenon with a well-defined doctrinal basis from which different groups then deviated over time. Thus, Sunni Islam was portrayed by its exponents as the 'true' interpretation of Islam, while all non-Sunni Muslim communities, especially the Shiʿa among them, who had supposedly 'deviated' from the right path, were accused of heresy (*ilhad*), innovation (*bidʿa*) or even unbelief (*kufr*).

By the same token the Shiʿa, too, it should be noted, had elaborated their own paradigmatic model of 'true Islam', rooted in a particular interpretation of early Islamic history and a distinctive conception of religious authority vested in the Prophet Muhammad's family, or the *ahl al-bayt*. The Shiʿa, whose own medieval scholars, similarly to the Sunni ones, did not generally allow for doctrinal evolution, soon disagreed among themselves regarding the identity of the legitimate spiritual leaders or imams of the community. As a result, the Shiʿa themselves in the course of their history subdivided into a number of major communities, notably the Ithnaʿasharis (or Twelvers), the Ismailis and Zaydis, as well as several minor groupings. There were also those Shiʿi communities, such as the Kaysaniyya, who did not survive even though they occupied important positions during the formative phase of Shiʿi Islam. At any rate, each Shiʿi community has elaborated a distinct self-image and perception of its earliest history, rationalising its own claims and legitimising the authority of its leadership and line of imams to the exclusion of similar claims propounded by other Shiʿi communities.

In such a milieu of theological pluralism and diversity of communal interpretations and political loyalties, abundantly reflected in the heresiographical tradition of the Muslims, obviously a general consensus could not be attained for designating any single interpretation of Islam as 'true Islam'. To make matters more complicated, different regimes lent their support to particular doctrinal positions that were legitimised in their state by their *ʿulama* who, in turn, were accorded a privileged social status in the society. It cannot be over-emphasised that many of the original and fundamental disagreements among Sunnis, Shiʿis and other Muslims will in all likelihood never be satisfactorily explained and resolved, mainly because of a lack of reliable sources, especially from the earliest centuries of Islamic history. As is well known, almost no written records, with the major exception of the text of the Qurʾan, representing the sacred scripture of Islam, have survived from those early centuries, while the later writings of the historians, theologians, heresiographers and other categories of Muslim authors, display variegated 'sectarian' biases. The perceptions and receptions of the Shiʿi Muslims by others, in both Muslim and Christian domains, as well as modern developments in the study of Shiʿi Islam, have seen their own fascinating evolution. In addition to what we have already said, we shall now turn to further salient points regarding these topics.

Medieval Sunni perceptions

Sunni authors belonging to different schools and literary traditions had, for the most part, no interest in collecting accurate information on Shiʿi Islam and its internal divisions, as they treated all Shiʿi interpretations of Islam as deviations from the true interpretation and thus amounting to heresies. They were particularly harsh in their forceful evaluation of the Ismaili Shiʿis, who had organised themselves into a revolutionary movement challenging the authority and legitimacy of the Sunni Abbasid order. Indeed, the Ismailis represented the most politically active wing of Shiʿism, with a religio-political agenda that strove to uproot the Abbasids and restore the caliphate to the particular line of ʿAlid imams recognised by their Shiʿi community. Their revolutionary message was disseminated widely throughout the Islamic lands, especially from the middle of the 3rd/9th century.

Under such circumstances, the Ismailis from early on aroused the hostility of the Sunni establishment. With the foundation of the Fatimid caliphate, ruled by the Ismaili imams, in 297/909, the Ismaili challenge to the established order was actualised, eliciting intensified Sunni reactions. Almost immediately, the Sunni Abbasids and their

ʿ*ulama* launched a widespread anti-Ismaili literary campaign. The overall aim of this prolonged campaign of invective was to discredit the Ismaili community from its very origins so that the Ismailis might be condemned by other Muslims as 'heretics' on doctrinal grounds. Numerous Sunni polemicists now began systematically to fabricate the necessary evidence that would lend support to the condemnation and refutation of the Ismailis on specific theological grounds. These polemicists, starting with a certain Ibn Rizam who lived in Baghdad during the first half of the 4th/10th century, cleverly concocted intricate accounts of the alleged sinister teachings and practices of the Ismailis, while refuting the ʿAlid genealogy of their imams. The anti-Ismaili polemics provided a major source of 'information' for Sunni heresiographers, such as al-Baghdadi (d. 429/1037),[1] who produced another sizeable collection of writings against the Ismailis and other Shiʿi Muslim communities and groups. By contrast, the Imami Shiʿi heresiographers, such as al-Nawbakhti (d. after 300/912), who were few in number but better informed than their Sunni counterparts on the internal divisions of Shiʿism and their doctrines, were notably less hostile towards the Ismaili Shiʿis even though they supported a different line of imams.[2]

By engaging in what might be viewed as a highly energetic medieval version of a propaganda campaign, the anti-Ismaili authors, in fact, produced a 'black legend' in the course of the 4th/10th century. Ismaili Shiʿism was depicted as the arch-heresy of Islam, carefully designed by some non-ʿAlid impostors to destroy Islam from within. By the 5th/11th century, this fiction, with its extensive details and seven stages of initiation, had been circulated widely and was accepted as an accurate and reliable description of Ismaili motives, beliefs and practices, leading to further anti-Ismaili polemics and theological accusations.[3] Under the initial leadership of Hasan-i Sabbah (d. 518/1124), the struggle of the Persian Ismailis against the ardently Sunni Saljuq Turks, the new overlords of the Abbasids, called forth another vigorous Sunni reaction against the Ismailis. The new literary campaign, accompanied by military expeditions, was initiated by al-Ghazali (d. 505/1111), the most eminent contemporary Sunni theologian and jurist. He was commissioned by the Abbasid caliph al-Mustazhir (r. 487–512/1094–1118) to compose a major treatise in refutation of the Batinis – another designation meaning 'esotericists', coined for the Ismailis by their detractors who accused them of dispensing with the *zahir*, or the commandments and prohibitions of the sacred law of Islam (*shariʿa*), because they claimed to have found access to the *batin*, or the inner meaning of the Islamic message as interpreted by the Ismaili imam. In this widely circulated book, commonly known as *al-Mustazhiri*, al-Ghazali imaginatively fabricated his own detailed version of an Ismaili system of initiation in stages that would ultimately lead to atheism and unbelief.[4] In the event, a multitude of myths and misinformation about the Ismailis were put into circulation, generation after generation, within Muslim society. And these fictions, in time, were accepted as reliable facts.

Other Shiʿi communities, especially the Twelvers, attracted less polemical attention, mainly because of their quietist policies, but they too were nevertheless treated as deviators from the 'right path' in the heresiographical literature and other works of the Sunni authors. The Zaydis, who by the end of the 3rd/9th century had established two territorial states, in northern Persia and in Yaman, did attract some marginal attention, though mainly on a regional basis. Theologically, the Zaydis had adopted certain stances less antagonistic to the Sunni positions despite pursuing activist policies. In medieval times, the Zaydis also indulged in polemical disputations and political confrontations with their Ismaili neighbours in both Persia and Yaman.[5] The Ismailis, however, remained the main targets of Sunni polemical attacks and theological refutations.

Medieval European perceptions

Medieval Europeans' knowledge and perceptions of Shiʿi Islam as a religion and of its internal divisions were even more deficient and fictitious, as their overall knowledge of Islam was extremely limited; to make matters worse, this limited knowledge was founded more in 'imaginative ignorance' than in any accurate sources of information to which Europeans could have obtained access if they had so desired. The earliest Western impressions and perceptions of Islam, which were retained for several centuries, were almost exclusively rooted in religious polemics, as the medieval Europeans intended to uphold the theological claims of Christianity and to disclaim those of the Muslims. Consequently, they soon entered into theological polemics and consciously fabricated gross misrepresentations of Islam and its history. As the Muslim armies embarked on their wars of conquest outside the Arabian peninsula, extending the boundaries of the nascent Islamic state to both the east and the west, the seeds of prolonged antagonism between the Christian and Muslim worlds were planted; and Islam, the 'other' world, began to be perceived as a problem by Western Christendom, a problem which in time acquired important religious and intellectual dimensions, in addition to its original political and military aspects. Indeed, Islam, which had aroused so much fear and apprehension in medieval Christian Europe, was to become a lasting trauma for Europe. And this basically negative perception of Islam was retained for almost a thousand years, well into the 17th century when the Ottoman Turks, who had rekindled the past aspirations and glories of the Muslims in their own flourishing empire, still represented a serious military threat to the peace and stability of Christendom and European lands.

For almost four centuries after its advent, Europeans effectively chose to ignore Islam, as both a military and an intellectual phenomenon, also denying its status as a new monotheistic religion in the Abrahamic tradition. In the event, European perceptions of Islam were essentially rooted in fear and ignorance, resulting in a highly distorted and utterly absurd image of Islam in Western minds. It is important to note that this image was generally retained throughout the Middle Ages and beyond, even though Europeans had gradually found access to information about Islam from different sources, especially after their participation in the Crusader movement, launched towards the end of the 11th century.

An investigation into the nature of the complex Christian–Muslim encounters of medieval times, and the various stages in the development of the Europeans' perception of Islam, is beyond the scope of this chapter.[6] Here we shall cover only selective features of the topic. During the first four centuries of contact between Christendom and Islam, lasting until around the end of the 11th century when the Crusading movement began, knowledge about Islam was extremely limited in Europe, as were its scattered sources; furthermore, these sources were mainly of a polemical genre, including the polemical works written by St John of Damascus (d. ca. 750) and those of the Byzantine theologians, as well as the occasional reports of the Mozarabs, the Christians living in Spain under Muslim domination. In the course of these early centuries of Christian–Muslim relations, representing effectively what has come to be known as the 'age of ignorance', Europeans viewed Islam as one of their major enemies, which they attempted to understand in the light of the Bible. Thus, the origins of the Muslims, or the Saracens as they were incorrectly designated in medieval Europe, were sought in the text of the Old Testament. Several Christian theologians living in Spain, such as Eulogius (d. 859), bishop of Toledo, even portrayed Islam as a sinister conspiracy against Christianity; for them, Muhammad was the Antichrist and the advent of Islam heralded the imminent apocalypse.

By the final decades of the 11th century, Europeans had also begun to respond militarily to the challenge of Islam by means of the Christian Reconquista in Muslim Spain, which culminated in the conquest of Toledo in 1085, and the Crusading movement for fighting the enemies of Christendom in the Holy Land. A new era in Christian–Muslim encounters thus commenced with numerous Crusades to the Near East, where the European Crusaders were to acquire permanent bases for some two centuries. The Christian pilgrim-soldiers of the First Crusade (1096–1099) seized Jerusalem, their primary destination, in 1099. The swift victory of the First Crusade, however, was in no small measure due to political decline and disunity in the Muslim camp. In the immediate aftermath of their triumph over the Muslims, the Frankish leaders of the First Crusade established four small states in the conquered territories of the Near East, a region which became known to them as the Outremer or the 'land beyond the sea'.

The events of the Crusades and their four Frankish states in Outremer, especially those relating to the Latin kingdom of Jerusalem, which enjoyed supremacy among the Frankish territories by virtue of possessing the Holy Places of Christendom, were recorded by numerous contemporary occidental chroniclers. Some of these, such as William of Tyre (d. ca. 1184), actually lived in the Latin East, and they provided important primary sources for the Crusaders' knowledge of contemporary Muslims. William of Tyre, the greatest of the Crusader historians who knew Arabic and lived and worked in the Near East for a long period, does not provide any important information on Islam as a religion, as this was clearly not one of his main concerns. In line with the tradition established by his predecessors, the main objective of William, who was elected as archbishop of Tyre in 1175, was to show that the Crusade was a holy war against the Saracen infidels, and that its victories were divine deeds done through the Franks.

The Crusaders themselves were not interested in gathering accurate information about the Muslims and their religious doctrines. This lack of interest becomes all the more obvious when it is recalled that both the Crusaders and some of their most eminent historians, such as William of Tyre and James of Vitry (d. 1240), bishop of Acre, lived for long periods in close proximity to the Muslims, with whom they had extensive military, diplomatic, social and commercial contacts. In fact, the Frankish rulers and the Crusader settlers in the Near East were sustained by an Arabic-speaking indigenous community, comprised mainly of Sunni and Shiʿi Muslims. In sum, direct contact between the Franks and Muslims in Crusader times did not lead to improved Western perceptions of Islam, either in the Latin East or in Europe, since the Crusaders continued to remain ignorant of almost every aspect of Islam as a religion and civilisation.

Nonetheless, as a result of the Crusading movement, Europeans did become more aware of the presence of Islam. Thus, Islam and the Prophet Muhammad became more familiar in Europe from the early decades of the 12th century, while the knowledge held by Europeans on these matters was still based essentially on their imagination. In the words of R. W. Southern (1912–2001), the authors of this new perception had luxuriated in the ignorance of triumphant imagination.[7] Based on oral testimony and misinformation, and stimulated by the fireside tales of the returning Crusaders, this picture of Islam was fabricated at a time of great imaginative development in Europe, which was then also witnessing the appearance of a host of popular European tales such as the romances of Charlemagne. It is, therefore, not surprising that legends about Islam circulated so readily, purporting to be reliable descriptions of Muslims and their teachings, until at least the middle of the 13th century. According to these legends, which soon acquired a literary life of their own, the Saracens (Muslims) were idolators worshipping a false trinity, and Mahomet (Muhammad) was a magician; he was even depicted as a dissident cardinal of the Roman Church who had rebelled and fled to Arabia where he had founded a church of his own.

Meanwhile, some scattered and exceptional attempts were made by a few individuals in Europe to study Islam in a more serious manner, supplementing travesties with observation and textual evidence, though their basic aim still remained refutation and condemnation. This new spirit of enquiry, which led to the earliest factual observations about Islam as a religion, appeared mainly in Spain. There was also Peter the Venerable, abbot of the Benedictine monastery of Cluny in France from 1122 until his death in 1156. He was convinced that instead of defeating them militarily, Muslims could more practically be won over through missionary activity. Consequently, he was concerned to collect information about Islam, especially on its weaknesses, so that the false tenets of this religion could be exposed. With these aims in mind, Peter conceived a grandiose scheme involving the translation of a number of Islamic texts, including the Qur'an, from Arabic into Latin while he was on a journey to Spain in 1142. He entrusted this task to a team of translators in Toledo, which had then recently become a centre for the translation of Arabic scientific works into Latin. The results of this ambitious project, a dozen Latin texts known as the Culniac Corpus or the Toledo Collection, represented the first scholarly sources for studying Islam in medieval Europe. However, the Culniac Corpus, too, failed to have any immediate or lasting impact on Europeans' perceptions. The serious study of Islam on a wider scale did not present itself as a desideratum to Christian Europeans who were then, in the second half of the 12th century, still aspiring to defeat the Muslims through their Crusades. Consequently, legends about Islam continued to circulate widely in both Europe and the Outremer, and the fictions were treated as accurate accounts.

By the end of the 13th century, the Crusading movement had finally run its course, after some two centuries of pilgrimage and 'holy war'; and the historical reality of Islam was now about to receive some recognition from medieval Europeans and Christendom at large. Certain scholars, espousing a Christian point of view, now talked more seriously of replacing the Crusading movement with missionary activities among the Muslims, endeavours that would require more systematic investigations of Islamic tenets and languages. Raymond of Lull (d. 1315), for instance, in 1276 founded a school of Arabic in Majorca for future Christian missionaries; it was also due to his ideas that the Council of Vienna in 1311 recommended that chairs of oriental languages be established at five European universities. But these efforts, too, had few lasting results, while the ensuing missionary attempts had all proved ineffective. Indeed, during the 14th century and later medieval times, the impulse to study and understand Islam once again disappeared almost completely in Europe. By contrast, the colourful tales of Marco Polo (d. 1324) provided a new impetus to European fantasies about Islam and the Middle East. By the end of the 15th century, the standard European perception of Islam, sanctioned by the Roman Church, still represented a polemical and highly distorted image rooted in ignorance and fantasy. Accordingly, Islam was still basically perceived as a false religion of violence, and Muhammad was regarded as the Antichrist.[8]

If the medieval Europeans remained shockingly ignorant about the most basic aspects of the Islamic message, they doubtless knew (and cared to know) even less about its internal divisions, including especially the Sunni–Shiʿi division, and the intricacies of interpretation with regard to the Islamic communities and their tenets. Indeed, there is no evidence suggesting that even the most learned of the Crusader historians, who spent decades in the Near East where they had extensive contact with the local Muslims, made any efforts to gather information on the Muslim communities of the region. Oddly, some of these occidental historians, such as William of Tyre and James of Vitry, were also theologians who served as bishops and archbishops in the Crusader states of the Outremer, and, as such, aimed at converting members of the local Muslim communities. Perceiving Islam as a false religion or even as a Christian heresy, the Crusaders and their historians were not interested in acquiring first-hand knowledge about it; their purpose of refutation and condemnation would be more readily served by fabricating the required evidence in addition to believing in the false reports that were then in circulation.

It was under such circumstances that Europeans remained almost completely ignorant of Shiʿi Islam and its differences with Sunni Islam, even though from the opening years of the 12th century the Crusaders had come into contact with various Shiʿi communities in the Near East, starting with the Nizari Ismailis of Syria and the Fatimids of Egypt. The Crusaders had obviously also failed to realise that the Syrian Nizaris, made famous by them in Europe as the Assassins, and the Fatimids then belonged to rival factions of Ismaili Shiʿism, which itself represented a major branch of Shiʿi Islam; nor were they aware that the Twelver Shiʿi communities, then present in Syria and other regions of the Near East, constituted another major branch of Shiʿi Islam. Needless to add, the religious Shiʿi identity of the Nusayris, now called ʿAlawis, was not recognised either by the Crusaders who had several castles in the vicinity of Nusayri settlements in Syria.

Nevertheless, as a result of their contact with various Shiʿi communities, the Crusaders did somehow become aware, though in an utterly confused manner, of certain differences that separated the Shiʿis from the rest of the Muslim community. For instance, William of Tyre, the earliest Crusader historian who has something to say on the subject, around 1180 summed up his knowledge of Shiʿi Islam by merely stating that, according to the Shiʿa themselves, God had intended to entrust the message of Islam to ʿAli (Hali), the only true prophet, but the angel Gabriel erred (or was misled) and handed the message to Muhammad (Mehemeth).[9] James of Vitry, another supposedly well-informed historian of the Crusades, does show some awareness of the theological differences between Sunnis and Shiʿis, but he too misunderstands these differences and states that the followers of ʿAli observed a law different from that instituted by Muhammad who, according to James, was also slandered by ʿAli and his supporters.[10] It was only after the adoption of Twelver Shiʿism as the state religion of Safawid Persia in 907/1501 that Europeans travelling to that land began to collect more reliable information on Shiʿi Islam.

In sum, in Crusader times and following centuries, Europeans remained almost completely ignorant of Shiʿism and the internal divisions of Islam in general, including the tenets of various Shiʿi communities with whom the Crusaders had extensive interactions. Given the situation, it is all the more astonishing that the Crusader circles should claim to have acquired knowledge of the secret teachings and practices of the Syrian Nizari Ismailis, evidently the earliest Shiʿi Muslims encountered by them. The Nizaris and the Crusaders sporadically fought over various strongholds in central Syria. But it was particularly in the second half of the 12th century, when Rashid al-Din Sinan had succeeded to the leadership of the Syrian Nizaris, that occidental travellers, diplomatic emissaries and chroniclers of the Crusades began to write about the followers of a mysterious 'Old Man of the Mountain', who were designated by them in different European languages by variant forms of the term 'Assassin'. The term Assassin was evidently based on a variant of the Arabic word *hashishi* (plural, *hashishiyya* or *hashishin*), applied to the Nizaris pejoratively by other Muslims in the sense of the 'people of lax morality', and the designation was picked up locally in the Levant by the Crusaders and their European observers. At the same time, the Crusader circles and their occidental chroniclers, as noted, had remained completely ignorant of Islam and its tenets, including those held by the Ismailis and other Shiʿi Muslims. It was under such circumstances that Frankish circles themselves began to fabricate and circulate, both in the Latin Orient and in Europe, a number of tales about the secret practices of the Nizari Ismailis.

The Crusaders were particularly impressed by the highly exaggerated reports and rumours of the Nizari assassinations and the daring behaviour of their *fidaʾis*, the young devotees who carried out targeted missions in public places and often lost their own lives in the process. This explains why these fictions revolved around the recruitment and training of the *fidaʾis*: fictions that were meant to provide satisfactory explanations for behaviour that would otherwise seem irrational or strange to the medieval Western mind. These so-called Assassin legends consisted of a number of separate but interconnected tales, including the 'training legend', the 'paradise legend', the 'hashish legend' and the 'death-leap legend'. The legends developed gradually in stages and finally culminated in a synthesised version popularised by Marco Polo.[11] The Venetian traveller also added his own contribution to this imaginary field of knowledge in the form of a 'secret garden of paradise', where bodily pleasures were supposedly procured for the would-be *fidaʾis*, as part of their training and indoctrination, by their mischievous leader, the 'Old Man'.

By the early decades of the 14th century, the Assassin legends had acquired wide currency and were accepted as reliable descriptions of secret Nizari practices, reminiscent of the manner in which the earlier anti-Ismaili 'black legend' of Muslim polemicists had been treated as an accurate explanation of Ismaili motives, beliefs and practices. It is important to note that the Assassin legends do not appear in any contemporary Islamic texts, in which the Nizaris are referred to by the derogatory term *hashishi* (plural, *hashishiyya*).[12] The textual sources of the Nizari Ismailis, explaining their actual teachings and practices, were not made accessible to Europeans until the later decades of the 19th century. But, meanwhile, the Nizaris had been continuously portrayed in medieval and even later European sources as a sinister order of drugged assassins bent on senseless murder and mayhem.

As noted, with the establishment of Twelver Shiʿism as the state religion of Safawid Persia in 907/1501, the ground was laid for better availability of information on Shiʿi Islam to Westerners who visited that country. In the wake of growing diplomatic, commercial and cultural contacts between the Safawids and European powers, numerous Westerners travelled to Persia, and some of them, like Sir John Chardin (1643–1712),[13] stayed there for long periods. Amongst such European visitors, many wrote eyewitness accounts of the Safawid court and Persia's religious rituals and public practices. However, little notice was taken in Europe of the travelogues of these diplomats, merchants and missionaries, which could have been used in academia as valuable source materials on aspects of Shiʿi Islam as observed by their authors. European scholars, trained in theology and philological studies, had not yet found access to Islamic texts that would lead to a breakthrough in their study of Islam free from the assumptions of anti-Islamic polemics of earlier generations. Indeed, the beginnings of systematic studies of Islamic theology and history in Europe may be traced to the late 16th century, when regular teaching of Arabic commenced at the Collège de France in Paris. And it was only after the establishment of chairs in Arabic at Leiden in 1613 and at Cambridge and Oxford in the 1630s that serious studies of Islamic sources really took off in Europe.

Meanwhile, Arabic texts were increasingly becoming known in Europe, as contacts developed with the Ottoman empire. However, it was not until the beginning of the 18th century, the age of Enlightenment (with its emphasis on the use of human reason to attain understanding of all subjects), that scientific approaches towards the study of Islam eventually began, though gradually, to displace the narrow and strictly polemical frame of mind within which all the medieval European investigations of Islam had hitherto been conducted.[14] The disappearance of the general tendency to prefer fictitious and polemical accounts to objective knowledge based on authentic textual evidence, together with an increased availability of rich collections of Islamic manuscripts in the Bibliothèque Royale, Paris, and other libraries in Europe, finally prepared the ground for the academic study of Islam within the broader field of orientalism in early modern times.

By the dawn of the 19th century, European orientalists were at last ready to investigate Islam as a religion in a scholarly and structured manner, with the goal of understanding rather than condemning it.

Orientalist perspectives

Scientific orientalism, based on the study of textual evidence, effectively began in Europe with the establishment in 1795 of the École des Langues Orientales Vivantes in Paris. Baron A. I. Silvestre de Sacy (1758–1838), the most distinguished orientalist of his time, became the first Professor of Arabic in that newly founded institution and was also appointed in 1806 to the new chair in Persian at the Collège de France. With an ever-increasing number of students and a wide circle of disciples, de Sacy acquired the unique distinction of being the teacher of many prominent orientalists of the first half of the 19th century. At the same time, oriental studies had received an important boost from the Napoleonic expeditions of 1798–1799 to Egypt and Syria. In the aftermath of these developments, there were significant increases in the number of orientalists in Europe, particularly in France and Germany, as well as chairs in oriental languages at European universities. The enhanced scholarly interest in orientalism also found expression in the publication of specialised periodicals, starting in 1809 with the *Fundgruben des Orients*, and in the foundation of learned societies.

European scholars now started to produce their studies of Islam on the basis of the Arabic texts, then available mainly in manuscript form, and the Islamic tradition itself. However, the bulk of the original texts then available in Europe had been written by Sunni authors and reflected their particular perspectives, since few Shiʿi texts found their way to European libraries during the 19th century. Consequently, the orientalists studied Islam according to the Sunni perspectives of their manuscript sources and, borrowing classifications from their own Christian contexts, they too treated the Sunni interpretation of Islam as 'orthodoxy', in contrast to Shiʿism which was taken to represent a 'heterodoxy', or at its extreme a 'heresy'. The Sunni-centric approach to the study of Islam, even when undertaken on a scientific basis, has continued to hold prominence to various degrees in Western scholarship in the field, as reflected in the entries of the first edition of the *Encyclopaedia of Islam*, published in English, French and German during 1913–1938, resulting from the collaboration of the most eminent orientalists of the time. The revised edition of this encyclopaedia, published during 1954–2004, did not fare much better even though numerous Shiʿi texts had become available in the interim period. Only the perspectives guiding the third edition of this standard work of reference, in the course of publication since 2007, promise to ameliorate the situation. The more recent *Encyclopaedia Iranica* and *Encyclopaedia Islamica*, too, are noted for their more balanced treatment of Shiʿi Islam and non-Arab Muslims.

It is noteworthy, however, that the Ismailis were singled out as the main Shiʿi community for scholarly attention by the 19th-century orientalists, even though they still did not have Ismaili manuscripts at their disposal. The new wave of orientalist interests in the Ismailis had been rekindled indirectly by the anti-Ismaili accounts of the Sunni sources which seemed to complement the Assassin legends of the European sources – legends that had never lost their fascination. All this explains why a number of eminent orientalists, starting with de Sacy, who had now correctly identified the Ismailis as a branch of Shiʿi Islam, concerned themselves with the Ismailis of Persia and Syria, as well as the Fatimids of Egypt.

De Sacy investigated the early Ismailis in connection with his lifelong interest in the Druze religion.[15] He also succeeded in finally solving the mystery of the name Assassin. In a *Memoir*, originally composed in 1809, he showed the connection of the variant forms of this name, such as *assassini* and *assissini*, to the Arabic word *hashish*, arguing that they were derived from the alternative Arabic form *hashishi* (plural, *hashishiyya*) and citing Abu Shama's application of these terms to medieval Nizari Ismailis of Syria.[16] By drawing on the generally hostile Sunni sources and the fanciful accounts of the Crusaders, however, de Sacy too was obliged unwittingly to endorse, at least partially, the anti-Ismaili 'black legend' of the Sunni polemicists and the Assassin legends of the Crusader circles.

De Sacy's work set the stage for the investigations of the Ismailis undertaken by later orientalists. The most widely read among such orientalist studies of the Ismailis was a book on the Nizari Ismailis of the Alamut period written by Joseph von Hammer-Purgstall (1774–1856), an Austrian diplomat-orientalist. In his book, originally published in

German in 1818, von Hammer-Purgstall fully accepted the Assassin legends as well as all the defamations heaped on the Ismailis by their Sunni detractors.[17] This book achieved great success in Europe; it was soon translated into French and English and continued to be treated as the standard history of the Nizari Ismailis. It should be recalled that von Hammer, who used the various chronicles of the Crusades in addition to Islamic manuscripts held in the Imperial Library, Vienna, as well as those in his own private collection, did not have access to a single Ismaili source of any period.[18] With few exceptions, European scholarship on the Ismailis made little further progress until the 1930s, as tales and anti-Ismaili polemics of the earlier generations continued to determine the basic perspectives within which European orientalists collected references to, and investigated, this Shiʿi community. Some Ismaili manuscripts had, meanwhile, been recovered from Syria, Yaman and Central Asia. And a handful of mainly French and Russian orientalists had started working with this material, while access to Ismaili texts on any substantial scale had continued to be still rather limited.[19]

Modern scholarship on Shiʿi Islam

Until around the middle of the 20th century, systematic progress in Islamic studies had not led to any significant improvement in the scholarly investigation of Shiʿi Islam and its various branches, as genuine Shiʿi textual materials of any kind still remained relatively inaccessible to Western scholars who were essentially obliged to continue to rely on Sunni sources. In the entire course of the 19th century, only sporadic attempts were made to obtain Shiʿi manuscripts for libraries and private collections in Europe; and the publication of Shiʿi texts, including those of the Twelvers, was for all practical purposes the exception to the preoccupation of contemporary orientalists. Indeed, Shiʿism was not selected as a major field of interest for orientalism. Nonetheless, there were a few significant departures. In the context of the paucity of Shiʿi texts in the West, the pioneering contributions of several scholars, in particular Julius Wellhausen (1844–1918) and Ignaz Goldziher (1850–1921), cannot be overemphasised.[20] While the eminent German scholar Wellhausen disentangled the complex events of the formative period of Islam and Shiʿism,[21] the renowned

Hungarian orientalist Goldziher investigated numerous Shiʿi doctrines, also refuting the contemporary Western myths attributing the rise of Shiʿi Islam to the anti-Arab sentiments of the Persians.[22] However, Goldziher, too, was basically influenced by the anti-Shiʿi biases of his largely Sunni sources. Somewhat later, Rudolf Strothmann (1877–1960) made pioneering contributions to Zaydi and Ismaili studies on the basis of original sources, in addition to pursuing his interest in Twelver Shiʿism.[23] And the first attempt at a history of Twelver Shiʿism was made by Dwight M. Donaldson (1884–1976), a Christian missionary working in Persia.[24] His book, published in 1933, remained the standard work on Twelver Shiʿism for several decades.

Subsequently, a selective group of scholars sought to devote more serious attention to the study of Shiʿi Islam in its different branches. Led by the French orientalist Louis Massignon (1883–1962), these scholars investigated Shiʿism with particular reference to its spiritual, esoteric and mystic dimensions, and as manifested in its Twelver and Ismaili traditions. Meanwhile, new research possibilities had been opened up by the cumulative effects of studying numerous Shiʿi texts, mainly of the Twelver Imami tradition, which had appeared in both lithograph and print forms, in Persia, Iraq, Lebanon and India. Massignon, in fact, pioneered the modern study of Shiʿi Islam in the West, also launching the careers of several scholars of the next generation, notably Paul Kraus (1904–1944) and Henry Corbin (1903–1978).

The contributions of Corbin, who served as Massignon's successor at the École Pratique des Hautes Études, Paris, are invaluable in understanding Shiʿi thought in general and its theosophical and metaphysical aspects as developed in Persia in particular. Corbin's works, also reflecting the benefit of his close collaboration with several leading traditional Twelver Shiʿi religious scholars of Persia, undoubtedly represent the most important single source in any European language on many intellectual aspects of Shiʿism. The bulk of Corbin's writings, including his editions of numerous Twelver and Ismaili texts, appeared in his own Bibliothèque Iranienne series, published simultaneously in Tehran and Paris from 1949.[25]

In spite of these advances, the first international colloquium devoted entirely to Twelver Shiʿism did not take place until 1968.[26] The occasion was celebrated forty years later by a collection of essays on Imami Shiʿism published in honour of Etan Kohlberg.[27] By the

1960s, a number of Islamicists and religious scholars belonging to the Twelver community had taken the initiative of elaborating the doctrines of their branch of Shiʿism on a more systematic, yet traditional, basis. These religious scholars, such as ʿAllama Sayyid Muhammad Husayn Tabataba'i (1903–1981),[28] also held teaching sessions at the religious seminaries of Persia, notably those in Qumm, Isfahan and Mashhad. These institutions have continued to train impressive numbers of Twelver Shiʿi traditional scholars in Persia. It should, however, be added that serious dialogues between the traditional Shiʿi scholars and their Western counterparts have still not really taken place on any meaningful scale, while a number of academics adhering to one of the Shiʿi communities, such as Seyyed Hossein Nasr, have made contributions to the study of Shiʿism. All in all, Shiʿi studies have been extremely marginalised in the Muslim countries outside of Iran and Iraq with their vibrant religious seminaries and Shiʿi theological traditions as well as massive collections of Shiʿi manuscripts. In Iran itself, Islamic studies predominantly imply Shiʿi, and more specifically Twelver Shiʿi, studies, with full consideration of the fields of theology, philosophy and jurisprudence as well as the Shiʿi contributions to Qur'anic and *hadith* studies.

A new interest in the study of Shiʿi Islam in Iran, and to some extent globally, was kindled by the Islamic Revolution of 1979. The Islamic Revolution proved to be a turning point not only in the socio-political fabric of Iran but also in the popularity of the Iranian form of Twelver Shiʿism and its theological basis under the leadership of a politically powerful class of clerics. As a result, attention has been increasingly devoted to a series of new research topics such as relations between Shiʿi Islam and the authority-power structure of the state. At the same time, the study of Shiʿi Islam, with special reference to its Twelver form, increased significantly in Iran in the aftermath of the establishment of an Islamic republic under the supreme leadership of Ayatullah R. Khumayni (1902–1989) and his advocation of the doctrine of '*vilayat-i faqih*' or the 'guardianship of the jurist (*faqih*)'. Consequently, a great number of primary sources, including the classical texts of the Twelver Imami Shiʿi tradition as well as Twelver works on history, theology and jurisprudence, are continuously edited and published under the auspices of Iran's religious seminaries. Institutional attempts towards the study of Shiʿi Islam have also taken place in

Iran. In this respect, in addition to the massive projects sponsored by the religious seminaries of the country, particular mention should be made of two academic organisations responsible for producing extensive multi-volume Islamic encyclopaedias in Persian with substantial entries on Shiʿi personalities, doctrines and events.[29] In sum, contemporary Iranian scholars and institutions are making major contributions to the field of modern Shiʿi studies.

In the West, meanwhile, a select group of scholars belonging to a new generation, such as E. Kohlberg, H. Algar, N. Calder (1950–1998), M. A. Amir-Moezzi, A. Newman, S. Amir Arjomand and R. Gleave, have been producing some highly influential works on various aspects of Twelver Shiʿism. However, it has still taken half a century for Donaldson's book to be superseded by M. Momen's more scholarly and comprehensive work on the subject.[30] It should also be mentioned that few scholars, in the West or in Muslim countries, have concerned themselves with all branches of Shiʿi Islam. In more recent times, only W. Madelung has made original contributions to the study of the Twelver, Ismaili and Zaydi branches, having also written seminal entries on two of them for the second edition of the *Encyclopaedia of Islam*.[31] Josef van Ess, too, has investigated theological aspects of the various Shiʿi traditions in his monumental work on Islamic theology.[32]

Ismaili studies, as a new field of Islamic studies, has had its own trajectory of development in modern times. The field was effectively revolutionised in a relatively short period of time by the recovery and study of genuine Ismaili texts on a large scale – manuscript sources which had been preserved in numerous collections in Yaman, Syria, Persia, Central Asia, Afghanistan and South Asia. This breakthrough actually occurred in the 1930s in India, where significant collections of Ismaili manuscripts have been preserved; and it was brought about mainly through the efforts of Wladimir Ivanow (1886–1970), a Russian orientalist who had by then settled in Bombay.[33] He was, in fact, charged in 1931 by Sultan Muhammad (Mahomed) Shah Aga Khan III (1877–1957), the 48th Nizari Ismaili Imam, to conduct methodical research into the literature and history of the Ismailis.

Modern scholarship in Ismaili studies received additional boosts from the pioneering efforts of three Ismaili Bohra scholars, namely Asaf A. A. Fyzee (1899–1981), Husayn F. al-Hamdani (1901–1962) and Zahid ʿAli (1888–1958), who had received their university education in England and were now producing scholarly studies on the basis of their ancestral collections of manuscripts. Subsequently, parts of these manuscript collections were donated to various academic institutions and, thus, were made available to scholars at large. These Bohra scholars also collaborated with Ivanow who, meanwhile, had found access to the literary heritage of the Nizari Ismailis. As a result, Ivanow compiled the first detailed catalogue of Ismaili works, citing some 700 separate titles which attested to the hitherto unknown richness and diversity of Ismaili literary and intellectual traditions.[34] The publication of this catalogue in 1933 provided for the first time a scientific framework for further research in the field, heralding an entirely new era in Ismaili studies.

Ismaili scholarship received another major impetus through the establishment in 1946 of the Ismaili Society in Bombay under the patronage of Aga Khan III. Ivanow played a crucial role in the creation of the Ismaili Society, whose publications mainly comprised his own monographs as well as editions and translations of Nizari Ismaili texts.[35] Ivanow also acquired a large number of Arabic and Persian manuscripts for the library of the Ismaili Society, and made them available to many scholars, such as Henry Corbin, who were then entering this new field of Islamic studies. Numerous Ismaili texts now began to be critically edited, preparing the ground for further progress in Ismaili studies.

By 1963, when Ivanow published an expanded edition of his Ismaili catalogue, many more sources had become known, and advances in Ismaili studies had been truly astonishing.[36] The subsequent progress in the recovery and publication of Ismaili texts, as well as scholarly studies, is well reflected in two later catalogues produced by I. K. Poonawala and the present author.[37] Meanwhile, these developments had enabled Marshall G. S. Hodgson (1922–1968) to compose the first scholarly history of the Nizari Ismailis of the Alamut period which finally replaced von Hammer-Purgstall's 19th-century polemical work.[38] At the same time, a new generation of scholars, notably B. Lewis, S. M. Stern (1920–1969), W. Madelung and A. Hamdani, produced original studies, especially on the early Ismailis and their relations with the dissident Qarmatis.

Scholarship in Ismaili studies has proceeded at a rapid rate during the last few decades through the efforts of yet another generation of scholars, including I. K. Poonawala, H. Halm, P. E. Walker and M. Brett; by the 1990s the present writer was able to produce surveys of Ismaili history.[39] Several other scholars, such as Ali S. Asani, Azim Nanji and Aziz Esmail, have concerned themselves with the Satpanthi tradition of the Nizari Khojas of South Asia as reflected in the *ginan* devotional literature. However, regional and anthropological studies of Shiʿi Islam, in general, remain underdeveloped. Be that as it may, Ismaili scholarship promises to continue at an ever greater pace as new Ismaili texts are regularly recovered from Badakhshan (now divided between Tajikistan and Afghanistan) and other regions, and the Ismailis themselves are becoming more interested in studying their own heritage. In this context, the work of The Institute of Ismaili Studies, established in 1977 in London by Prince Karim Aga Khan IV, the 49th and present Imam of the Nizari Ismailis, represents a significant undertaking. This institution is now making its own contributions to the field through a variety of research and publications programmes, as well as making its Ismaili resources available to scholars worldwide. The Institute's library contains the largest collection of Ismaili manuscripts in the West. In addition to the collections previously held by the Ismaili Society and augmented by ongoing acquisitions, the Institute now holds the Zahid ʿAli Collection and part of the Hamdani Collection of Ismaili manuscripts.[40] The largest single collection of *ginan*s, written mainly in the Khojki script, is also to be found in the Institute's library. At present, the Ismaili Bohras of India, who have extensive collections of Ismaili manuscripts in their libraries at Surat and Bombay, do not make these resources available to scholars, nor do they themselves embark on editing and publishing these Ismaili texts, as they are generally not permitted by their leadership to do so.

Until more recent times, Nusayri (ʿAlawi), and to a much lesser extent Zaydi, studies had remained relatively underdeveloped areas of Shiʿi studies in terms of the scholarship both from within these communities as well as from the West. However, much progress has now been made in Zaydi studies. It is known that large collections of manuscripts on Zaydi theology and jurisprudence are held in various locations in Yaman, where the community is exclusively concentrated. And in recent decades, much Zaydi scholarship has taken place in Yaman. In the West, too, a number of scholars have specifically concerned themselves with studying Zaydi history and thought. After the pioneering efforts of R. Strothmann, and to a lesser extent E. Griffini (1878–1925) and C. van Arendonk (1881–1946), only W. Madelung has made substantial contributions to this field of Shiʿi studies. Indeed, Madelung may be considered as the founder of modern Zaydi studies in the West. Amongst other modern scholars who have written on the Zaydis, mention may be made of B. Abrahamov and M. S. Khan.[41]

Scholarship on the Nusayris, now called ʿAlawis, has been even more complicated, as scholars generally could not agree on the origin of this Shiʿi community, commonly characterised as belonging to the *ghulat* or extremist Shiʿi groups. In medieval times, the Nusayris had prolonged confrontations with their Ismaili neighbours in Syria and, in the event, they lost part of their literary heritage which could not have been substantial to begin with. By the late 19th century, Nusayri manuscripts of Syrian provenance began to appear in European libraries. However, only a few of these texts have been studied and published so far. René Dussaud (1868–1958) was the first European scholar to publish a monograph on the Nusayri religion on the basis of some Nusayri texts then available at the Bibliothèque Nationale in Paris.[42] This was followed by more pioneering studies on the Nusayris by R. Strothmann, and L. Massignon who regarded both the Nusayris and the Ismailis as the heirs of the Khattabis, the most renowned group amongst the early Shiʿi *ghulat*. More recently, Heinz Halm has studied the Nusayris within the broader *ghulat* milieus,[43] while new inroads into this neglected field are now under way through the study and publication of more Nusayri texts.[44] As a result, Dussaud's pioneering history of the community, published in 1900, was finally superseded by a comprehensive work in 2010.[45]

All in all, Shiʿi studies have come a long way since the Crusader and earlier times, when Muslims were generally perceived fancifully and polemically by European observers who knew next to nothing about (Shiʿi) Islam and its own internal divisions. The accessibility of Shiʿi texts has led to drastic revisions in the mindset and perceptions of Western scholars, who until recent times regarded Shiʿism very marginally as the 'heterodoxical' interpretation of Islam. As noted above, the progress of scholarship on the major branches of Shiʿi Islam has advanced along different paths and at varying paces. This book draws on the results of modern scholarship on Shiʿi Islam and attempts to present these findings in an unbiased and coherent fashion.

2

The Origins and Early History of Shiʿi Islam

Muhammad, the Messenger of God (*rasul Allah*), laid the foundations of a new religion which was portrayed as the seal of the great revealed religions of the Abrahamic tradition. He succeeded in founding a religious community (*umma*) of considerable power and prestige. It was during basically a single decade, stretching from the time of Muhammad's emigration (*hijra*) from Mecca to Medina in the September of 622 (marking the initiation of the Islamic era) until his death after a brief illness in 11/632, that most of the desert-dwelling bedouin tribes of the Arabian peninsula pledged their allegiance to the Prophet. The death of the Prophet Muhammad, however, confronted the nascent Islamic community with its first major crisis.

Origins of Shiʿism

The origins of Islam's main divisions into Sunni and Shiʿi may, indeed, be broadly traced to the crisis of succession to the Prophet Muhammad. The successor to Muhammad could not be another prophet or *nabi*, as it had already been made known through divine revelation that Muhammad was the 'seal of the prophets' (*khatam al-anbiya'*). Apart from delivering and interpreting the message of Islam, the Prophet Muhammad had also acted as the leader of the Islamic community. A successor was, therefore, necessary in order to ensure the continued unity of the Islamic community. According to the Sunni view, the Prophet had left neither formal instruction nor a testament regarding his succession. Amidst much ensuing debate, Abu Bakr, one of the earliest converts to Islam and a trusted Companion of the Prophet, was elected by a group of leading Muslim notables as the successor. Abu Bakr's election was effectuated on the suggestion of 'Umar b. al-Khattab, who had emigrated with the Prophet from Mecca to Medina, and by the acclamation of other leading Companions, who now accorded Abu Bakr their oath of allegiance (*bayʿa*). Abu Bakr took the title of *khalifat rasul Allah* or 'successor to the Messenger of God', a title which was soon simplified to *khalifa* (whence the word 'caliph' in Western languages). By electing the first successor to the Prophet, Muslims had also founded the distinctive Islamic institution of the caliphate (*khilafa*).

The precise nature of the authority of Abu Bakr and his immediate successors remains rather obscure. But it is now becoming increasingly evident that from its very inception the historical caliphate embodied both the religious and political aspects of the leadership of the community.[1] This unique arrangement was to be expected from the very nature of Islam's teachings and the limited experience of governance of the early Islamic community under the leadership of the Prophet himself. The early Muslims did not recognise any distinction between religion and state, or between religious and secular authorities, distinctions so familiar to modern-day Westerners. Indeed, a strictly theocratic conception of an order, in which Islam is not merely a religion but a complete system ordained by God for the socio-political as well as the moral and spiritual governance of humankind, had been an integral part of the Prophet Muhammad's message and established practice (*sunna*). At the time, it may be recalled, myriad groups had begun to formulate different conceptions of religio-political authority and the caliph's moral responsibility towards the community.

Abu Bakr (r. 11–13/632–634) and his next two successors, ʿUmar (r. 13–23/634–644) and ʿUthman (r. 23–35/644–656), belonging to the influential Meccan tribe of Quraysh, were among the earliest converts to Islam and Companions of the Prophet (*sahaba*). ʿUthman was generally also considered to belong to the Prophet's close kin. He was a grandson of Muhammad's aunt, Umm Hakim bt. ʿAbd al-Muttalib, and also married to two of the Prophet's daughters, Ruqayya and Umm Kulthum. However, only the fourth caliph, ʿAli b. Abi Talib (r. 35–40/656–661), who occupies a unique position in the annals of Shiʿi Islam, belonged to the Prophet's own clan of Banu Hashim within the Quraysh. ʿAli was also very closely related to the Prophet, being his cousin and son-in-law bound in matrimony to the Prophet's daughter Fatima. These first four caliphs are generally known as *al-khulafaʾ al-rashidun* or the 'Rightly

Guided Caliphs'. Thus, after the Prophet's death the early caliphate was established on the basis of a privileged position for the Quraysh as a whole, while the Prophet's family (*ahl al-bayt*) were deprived of the spiritual status they had enjoyed in his lifetime and were also prevented from receiving their share of the *khums*, the fifth of the war booty reserved for the Prophet, and other property incomes. The Banu Hashim, defined broadly until the end of the Umayyad period in 132/750 as covering all branches descending from the Prophet's great-grandfather Hashim b. ʿAbd Manaf, protested in vain against the loss of their privileged status.

In the meantime, immediately after the death of the Prophet, there had appeared openly in Medina a small group believing that ʿAli was better qualified than any other Muslim, including Abu Bakr, to succeed the Prophet. This minority group, originally comprised of some of ʿAli's friends and supporters, expanded in time and in ʿAli's brief caliphate became generally designated as the *shiʿat ʿAli*, or the 'Party of ʿAli', and then simply as the Shiʿa. As noted, ʿAli eventually succeeded to the leadership of the Muslims as the fourth caliph, instead of fulfilling the aspiration of the Shiʿa in becoming the immediate successor to the Prophet. ʿAli himself was firmly convinced of the legitimacy of his own claim to Muhammad's succession, based on his close kinship and association with him, his intimate knowledge of Islam as well as his early merits in the cause of Islam. Indeed, ʿAli made it plain in his speeches and letters that he considered the Prophet's family or the *ahl al-bayt* to be entitled to the leadership of the Muslims as long as there remained a single one of them who recited the Qur'an, knew the *sunna* and adhered to the religion of the truth.[2] In this context, ʿAli himself can be regarded as the first teacher of the Shiʿa. And from early on, ʿAli did have a circle of supporters who believed he was better qualified than any other Companion to succeed the Prophet. Before long, ʿAli's opponents spoke of *din ʿAli* or 'ʿAli's religion' in reference to his supporters, a notion actually resented by ʿAli who insisted that he represented the religion of Muhammad.[3] In any event, matters are further complicated as, after a delay of about six months, ʿAli himself finally recognised Abu Bakr's caliphate, a lapse of time coinciding with Fatima's death. It should also be mentioned in passing that Fatima had been involved in a rather complicated inheritance dispute with Abu Bakr over an estate held by the Prophet.

There is a more specific Shiʿi view on the origins of Shiʿi Islam. It is the fundamental belief of the Shiʿa of all branches that the Prophet himself had designated ʿAli as his successor, a designation or *nass* instituted through divine command and revealed by the Prophet at Ghadir Khumm on 18 Dhu'l-Hijja 10/16 March 632, shortly before his death and while returning from his Farewell Pilgrimage. As reported in both Shiʿi and Sunni *hadith* collections, on that occasion the Prophet, wanting to make an important declaration to the pilgrims who accompanied him, took ʿAli by the hand and uttered the famous sentence: *man kuntu mawlahu fa-ʿAli mawlahu* (He of whom I am the patron, ʿAli is also his patron).[4] This *hadith*, interpreted differently by Shiʿi and Sunni Muslims, was in fact proclaimed publicly in Kufa by ʿAli himself during his caliphate, to back up ʿAli's own claims to have been the Prophet's *wasi* or legatee and as such his rightful successor. The Shiʿa have also interpreted certain Qur'anic verses in support of ʿAli's designation. However, many members of the community of the faithful had turned away from ʿAli, ignoring the Prophet's *nass*.

The Shiʿa also held a particular conception of religious authority that set them apart from other Muslims. They believed that Islam contained inner truths that could not be understood directly through human reason. They had, thus, recognised the need for a religiously authoritative guide, or *imam* as the Shiʿa have traditionally preferred to call their spiritual leader. In addition to being the guardian of the Islamic revelation and leader of the community, as perceived by the majority of the Muslims, the succession to the Prophet was thus seen by the Shiʿa as a key spiritual function connected with the elucidation and interpretation of the Islamic message. And for the Shiʿa the Prophet's family, or the *ahl al-bayt*, provided the sole authoritative channel for elucidating the teachings of Islam. According to this view, the possibility of the Shiʿi interpretation of Islam existed within the very message of Islam, and this possibility was actualised in Shiʿism.[5] These ideas eventually found their full elaboration in the central Shiʿi doctrine of the imamate. But it may safely be stated that the earliest Shiʿi ideas centred broadly on a particular notion of religious authority connected with the Prophet's own religious knowledge or *ʿilm*. Moreover, it may be added that the partisans of ʿAli, by contrast to other Muslims, seem to have been more inclined in their thinking towards the hereditary attributes of individuals. The idea that certain special qualities were hereditary was, of course, in line also with the pre-Islamic Arab notion that outstanding human attributes were transmitted through tribal stock. It was, therefore, natural for ʿAli's religiously learned followers, including the Kufan-based Qurʾan reciters (*qurraʾ*), who had special respect for the Prophet's family, to believe that some of Muhammad's special attributes, notably his religious knowledge or *ʿilm*, would be inherited by the members of his clan of Banu Hashim, and his immediate family. And in this context, ʿAli as the leader of the Banu Hashim now clearly stood out in terms of representing the *ahl al-bayt*.

The case of the Shiʿa was ignored by the rest of the community, however, and their protestations proved futile. Nevertheless, the Shiʿa persisted in holding that all spiritual matters should be referred to ʿAli, who in their opinion was then the sole person possessing religious authority. The Shiʿi point of view on the origins of Shiʿism contains distinctive doctrinal elements that admittedly cannot be attributed in their entirety to the early Shiʿis, especially the original partisans of ʿAli. The fact remains that very little is known with historical certainty about the earliest Shiʿi ideas and tendencies which developed gradually and found their full expression in the doctrine of the imamate, formulated by the middle of the 2nd/8th century.

The early Shiʿa

Pro-ʿAli sentiments and broad Shiʿi tendencies persisted in ʿAli's lifetime. But after their initial defeat, the Shiʿa lost much of their enthusiasm. Shiʿism remained in a practically dormant state during the caliphates of both Abu Bakr and ʿUmar, when ʿAli himself maintained a passive and secluded attitude. During this early period in Islamic history (11–23/632–644), ʿAli's behaviour is best illustrated by his lack of participation in the ongoing wars of conquest and his exclusion from the affairs of the community. This was in stark contrast to his earlier active role in the community, and his appearance in the forefront of almost all the battles fought in the Prophet's time. The first two caliphs, in fact, attempted to exclude ʿAli from any position of importance in the community. Nevertheless, he was appointed to the six-member council of the Companions that was to select ʿUmar's successor.

The situation of ʿAli and his partisans changed during the caliphate of ʿUthman b. ʿAffan (r. 23–35/644–656), a period of strife in the community which also saw a revival of Shiʿi aspirations. Soon there erupted mounting grievances against ʿUthman and his economic and social policies, including those related to favouring his own clan of Banu Umayya. As the provincial opposition to ʿUthman, centred especially in the garrison towns of Kufa and Basra in southern Iraq, gained momentum during the later years of his caliphate, the Kufan *qurra'* and other partisans of ʿAli now found it opportune to revive their suppressed aspirations. The Shiʿa, also drawing general support from the Banu Hashim whose interests had been ignored by the Umayyads, joined the discontented provincial groups and called for ʿUthman's removal. ʿAli succeeded to the caliphate in the turbulent circumstances following ʿUthman's murder in Medina in 35/656 at the hand of a group of provincial mutineers.[6]

In the aftermath of ʿUthman's murder, the Islamic community became greatly divided over the question of his guilt that had led to a widespread rebellion against him. From the start of his own rule, ʿAli was confronted with difficulties which soon escalated into the first civil war or *fitna* in Islam, lasting throughout his short-lived caliphate. Indeed, ʿAli never succeeded in enforcing his caliphal authority throughout the Islamic state, especially in the territory of ʿUthman's relative, Muʿawiya b. Abi Sufyan, who had governed Syria with an iron hand for almost twenty years.

As a member of the influential Banu Umayya clan of the Quraysh, and as ʿUthman's kinsman, Muʿawiya found the call for avenging ʿUthman's murder a suitable pretext for transferring the caliphate to the Umayyads. Thus, Muʿawiya, at the head of a pro-ʿUthman party, launched a campaign against the new caliph to whom he refused to give his allegiance. ʿAli was trapped in an unenviable situation. The actual murderers of ʿUthman had fled Medina, while many of the *qurra'* surrounding ʿAli were equally implicated. As ʿAli was either unable or unwilling to punish those directly responsible, Muʿawiya rose in open revolt and challenged the very legitimacy of his caliphate. Meanwhile, ʿAli had entered Kufa to mobilise support for the anticipated confrontation with Muʿawiya. The garrison town of Kufa on the Euphrates, the scene of many events in the early history of Shiʿism, served as ʿAli's temporary capital during his brief caliphate. ʿAli reorganised the Kufan tribal groups and restored a number of leaders of the early Kufan *qurra'*, men like Malik al-Ashtar, to positions of authority. These men, with similarly situated Kufans who had been eclipsed by the tribal aristocracy (*ashraf al-qaba'il*) under ʿUthman, along with their followers, provided the backbone of ʿAli's forces; in fact, they became the new leaders of the Shiʿa.[7] It was under such circumstances that the forces of ʿAli and Muʿawiya met at Siffin on the upper Euphrates in the spring of 37/657. A long battle ensued, perhaps the most controversial in the history of early Islam. The events of the battle of Siffin, the Syrian arbitration proposal and ʿAli's acceptance of it, and the resulting arbitration verdict issued about a year later, have all been critically examined by a number of modern scholars, as have the intervening circumstances leading to the secession of a group of dissidents from ʿAli's army, the seceders being later designated as the Khawarij. These events irrevocably undermined ʿAli's political position and he was obliged to retreat to Kufa. ʿAli was murdered in Kufa by a Khariji in 40/661.

The Islamic community emerged from its first civil war split into factions that were to confront one another throughout subsequent times. The main factions had already begun to take shape during the final years of ʿUthman's rule, but they crystallised more explicitly into opposing parties during the first civil war. Henceforth, these parties acquired denominations which, in an eclectic sense, revealed their personal loyalties as well as their regional attachments. The supporters of ʿAli came to be called the *ahl al-ʿIraq* (People of Iraq) as well as the *shiʿat ʿAli* (Party of ʿAli), while their adversaries were designated the *shiʿat ʿUthman* (Party of ʿUthman) or more commonly the ʿUthmaniyya. The latter party, after the battle of Siffin, constituted mainly the *ahl al-Sham* (People of Syria), also referred to as the *shiʿat Muʿawiya* (Party of Muʿawiya). The partisans of ʿAli, the Shiʿa proper, now also referred to themselves by terms with more precise religious connotations such as the *shiʿat ahl al-bayt* or its equivalent the *shiʿat al Muhammad* (Party of the Prophet's Household). As noted, ʿAli's opponents, led by Muʿawiya and the Umayyads, now spoke of *din ʿAli* or the 'religion of ʿAli', a notion evidently resented by ʿAli. Starting with the battle of Siffin, a third faction, the Khawarij, appeared in the community. The Khawarij, seriously opposed to both ʿAli and Muʿawiya and their parties, managed to organise a rapidly spreading movement that many times in the later history of Islam challenged any form of legitimacy and dynastic privilege. The Khawarij adhered to strict Islamic egalitarianism, maintaining that any meritorious Muslim of any ethnic or tribal origin could be chosen through popular election as the legitimate leader or imam of the community.[8] They, thus, aimed to establish a form of society in which authority and leadership would not be based on tribal or hereditary considerations.

The early Shiʿa survived ʿAli's murder and numerous subsequent tragic events. After ʿAli, his partisans in Kufa remained convinced that only a member of the Prophet's family could legitimately succeed him; they now recognised ʿAli's eldest son al-Hasan as his successor to the caliphate. Under obscure circumstances, al-Hasan abdicated a few months later in favour of Muʿawiya, whose power had become unchallengeable. Muʿawiya was speedily recognised as the new caliph, and he was to found the first dynasty in Islam, the Umayyads, who stayed in power for nearly a century. Meanwhile, following his peace treaty with Muʿawiya, which allowed for the safety of life and property for the *shiʿat ʿAli*, al-Hasan retired to Medina and abstained from any political activity. However, the Shiʿa continued to regard him as their imam after ʿAli, while the ʿAlids considered him as the head of their family.

On al-Hasan b. ʿAli's death in 49/669 (or perhaps a year later), the Kufan Shiʿa again revived their aspirations for restoring the caliphate to the Prophet's family and invited al-Hasan's younger full-brother al-Husayn, their new imam, to rise against the oppressive rule of the Umayyads and restore the legitimate rule of the *ahl al-bayt*. Meanwhile, Muʿawiya had ordered his governor of Kufa to curse ʿAli from the pulpits in the Friday prayers. Al-Husayn declined to act as long as Muʿawiya reigned, in observance of his brother's treaty with him. In the aftermath of Muʿawiya's death and the succession of his son Yazid in 60/680, the leaders of the Kufan Shiʿa once again wrote to al-Husayn and offered him their support against the Umayyads. Having declined to pledge allegiance to Yazid, al-Husayn finally responded to this summons and set out for Kufa. On 10 Muharram 61/10 October 680, al-Husayn and his small band of relatives and companions were ruthlessly massacred at Karbala, near Kufa, where they were intercepted by an Umayyad army. Only women and some children were spared; ʿAli b. al-Husayn, who received the honorific title Zayn al-ʿAbidin (Ornament of the Pious) and was later counted as the fourth imam of the Imami Shiʿis, was one of the few male survivors.

The martyrdom of al-Husayn, the Prophet's grandson, together with numerous other members of the *ahl al-bayt*, infused a new religious fervour in the Shiʿa and contributed significantly to the consolidation of Shiʿi ethos and identity. Henceforth, the call for repentance and martyrdom became integral aspects of Shiʿi spirituality. It also led to the formation of radical trends among the Shiʿa; the earlier Kufan Shiʿa had remained relatively moderate in their outlook regarding the historical caliphate. Abu Mikhnaf (d. 157/774) is the earliest Muslim historian to record al-Husayn's martyrdom and the subsequent Shiʿi risings of the Umayyad times; his detailed accounts have been partially preserved in later sources, notably al-Tabari (d. 310/923).[9] Later, the Shiʿa began to commemorate the martyrdom of Imam al-Husayn b. ʿAli annually on the tenth of Muharram (*ʿAshura'*) with special ceremonies and the so-called passion plays (*taʿziya*).[10]

In the immediate aftermath of the events of Karbala, the old partisans of ʿAli and many other Kufans who had invited al-Husayn and then failed to come to his aid were moved by a sense of repentance. Led by Sulayman b. Surad al-Khuzaʿi, they organised the movement of the Penitents (Tawwabun), calling for self-sacrifice and revenge for the Prophet's grandson. On the death of the caliph Yazid in 64/683, and the ensuing unsettled conditions of the second civil war in Islam, some 4,000 Penitents visited Karbala to weep and repent on al-Husayn's grave before joining battle with an Umayyad army. By the end of the three-day battle in 65/684 the majority of the Penitents had been killed. The movement of the Tawwabun marks the end of what may be regarded as the Arab and unified phase of early Shiʿism.

During its first half-century, Shiʿism remained unified and maintained an almost exclusively Arab composition with a limited appeal to non-Arab Muslims or the so-called *mawali*. These features changed with the next important event in the early history of Shiʿism, the movement of al-Mukhtar b. Abi ʿUbayd al-Thaqafi. As the old leaders of the Shiʿa were disappearing, new ones had emerged in Kufa. Al-Mukhtar, who now sought the leadership of the Kufan Shiʿa, was one such capable leader. He launched his own Shiʿi campaign with a general call to avenge al-Husayn's murder. Winning the support of the majority of the Kufan Shiʿa, al-Mukhtar claimed to be acting on behalf of ʿAli's then only surviving son, Muhammad b. al-Hanafiyya who had been closely associated with ʿAli during his reign. Muhammad b. al-Hanafiyya was ʿAli's son by Khawla, a woman of the Banu Hanifa; he was half-brother to al-Hasan and al-Husayn, ʿAli's sons by the Prophet's daughter Fatima. Ibn al-Hanafiyya, who declined to assume the active leadership of the movement and remained in Medina, was proclaimed by al-Mukhtar as the imam and Mahdi or 'the divinely guided one', the messianic saviour imam and the restorer of true Islam who would establish justice on earth and deliver the oppressed from tyranny.

The concept of the Mahdi proved to be a very important doctrinal innovation and acquired a particular appeal for the *mawali*, the non-Arab converts to Islam who, under the Umayyads, were treated as second-class Muslims. The *mawali* (singular, *mawla*) represented a substantial intermediate class between the Arab Muslims and the non-Muslim subjects of the Islamic state. In the wake of the Islamic conquests, a need had arisen for a term to designate the new converts from amongst the Persian, Aramaean, Berber and other non-Arab natives of the conquered territories. For this purpose, the old term *mawla*, which was originally used in Arab society in reference to certain types of kinship as well as a relationship by covenant (particularly between individuals and tribes), was adopted. In its new sense, *mawla* meant a Muslim of non-Arab origin attached as a client to an Arab tribe, because, on embracing Islam, non-Arabs were expected to become affiliated as clients to Arab tribes. According to this type of clientage, a special relationship would be established between the protected client and his protector. The *mawali* represented different cultures and religious traditions. In Iraq, they comprised mainly Aramaeans, though also included Persians and other non-Arabs representing the older strata of the province's population.

In line with the spread of Islam, the total number of the *mawali* increased very rapidly. In fact, within a few decades they had come to outnumber the Arab Muslims. As Muslims, the *mawali* expected the same rights and privileges as their Arab co-religionists. After all, the Prophet himself had declared the equality of all believers before God, despite their differences stemming from descent, race and tribal affiliation. However, the Islamic teaching of equality was not conceded by the Arab ruling class under the Umayyads, although in earlier times, when the *mawali* were still a minority group, the precepts of Islam had been observed more closely. At any rate, under the Umayyads the *mawali* had come to represent the socially and racially inferior class, a second-class citizen compared with Arab Muslims. The *mawali* were, however, set apart from the non-Muslim subjects of the Islamic state who were accorded an even more inferior status. These so-called 'people of protection', *ahl al-dhimma* or simply *dhimmi*s, were the followers of certain recognised religions, notably Judaism, Christianity and, later, Zoroastrianism. They received the protection (*dhimma*) of the Islamic state in return for the payment of a distinguishing tribute called *jizya*. A *dhimmi*, who was also subject to certain social restrictions, would acquire *mawla* status by converting to Islam and becoming duly attached to an Arab tribe. However, the Arabs discriminated in various ways, especially economically, against the *mawali*. Above all, the taxes paid by the new converts were often similar to those required of the non-Muslim subjects. This constituted perhaps the single major cause of the *mawali*'s discontent, since many of them had converted precisely in order to be less heavily taxed.

As a large and underprivileged social class, concentrated in urban milieus, and aspiring for the establishment of an order based on the egalitarian precepts of Islam, the *mawali* provided a major recruiting ground for any movement opposed to the exclusively Arab hegemony of the Umayyads. And they became particularly drawn to al-Mukhtar's movement and Shiʿism, calling themselves the *shiʿat al-mahdi*, 'Party of the Mahdi'. Al-Mukhtar readily won control of Kufa in an open revolt in 66/685. The Shiʿa now took revenge for Imam al-Husayn, killing those responsible for the massacre at Karbala.

However, al-Mukhtar's success was short-lived, as he was opposed by a coalition comprised of the Kufan tribal chiefs, who were particularly against his conciliatory policies towards the *mawali*, the Umayyads and eventually the anti-caliphate Zubayrids, who had also rebelled against the Umayyads and were then in control of southern Iraq. In 67/687, al-Mukhtar was defeated and killed together with thousands of his *mawali* supporters.[11] The movement founded by al-Mukhtar survived his demise and spread in southern Iraq and elsewhere. The followers of al-Mukhtar, recognising Ibn al-Hanafiyya as their imam and Mahdi until his death in 81/700, were initially called the Mukhtariyya. But they were soon more commonly referred to as the Kaysaniyya, after the chief of al-Mukhtar's bodyguards Abu ʿAmra Kaysan.

The sixty-odd years intervening between the revolt of al-Mukhtar and the Abbasid revolution mark the second phase in the early history of Shiʿism. During this period different Shiʿi groups, consisting of both Arabs and *mawali*, came to coexist, each one having its own line of imams and propounding its own doctrines. Furthermore, the Shiʿi imams now hailed not only from the major branches of the extended ʿAlid family, namely the Hanafids (descendants of Muhammad b. al-Hanafiyya), the Husaynids (descendants of al-Husayn b. ʿAli) and, later, the Hasanids (descendants of al-Hasan b. ʿAli), but also from other branches of the Prophet's clan of Banu Hashim. This is because the Prophet's family or the *ahl al-bayt*, whose sanctity was supreme for the Shiʿa, was then still broadly defined in its old Arabian tribal sense. It therefore covered the various branches of the Banu Hashim, including the ʿAlids (both the Fatimids, covering Husaynids and Hasanids, and the non-Fatimids, covering the descendants of ʿAli by Khawla), as well as the descendants of the Prophet's two paternal uncles, namely, the Talibids, descendants of Abu Talib through his sons ʿAli and Jaʿfar al-Tayyar (d. 8/629), and the Abbasids, descendants of al-ʿAbbas (d. ca. 32/653).[12] In sum, the Fatimid and non-Fatimid ʿAlids as well as many non-ʿAlid Hashimids, belonging to the Banu Hashim, apparently all qualified as belonging to the *ahl al-bayt*. It was after the Abbasid revolution that the Shiʿa came to define the *ahl al-bayt* more restrictively to include only the Fatimid ʿAlids, covering both the Husaynids and the Hasanids, while the majority of the non-Zaydi Shiʿis had come to acknowledge chiefly the Husaynid ʿAlids.

In this fluid and often confusing setting, Shiʿism developed in terms of two main branches or factions, the Kaysaniyya and the Imamiyya, each with its own internal divisions; later, a further ʿAlid movement led to the foundation of another major Shiʿi community, the Zaydiyya. There were also those Shiʿi *ghulat* (singular, *ghali*), individual theorists with small groups of followers, who existed in the midst or on the fringes of the major Shiʿi communities. For information on these early groups and their various subdivisions, we must rely mainly on the heresiographical literature of the Muslims produced by later generations with different perspectives. The heresiographical works were supposedly written to explain the internal divisions of Islam. However, the heresiographers all had one major aim: to uphold the legitimacy of the particular community to which they belonged, while condemning and refuting other communities as deviators from the 'right path'. Furthermore, Muslim heresiographers often exaggerated the number of communities or sects, for which the term *firqa* (plural, *firaq*) was loosely used without particular regard to the size or importance of the defined entity. This particular feature was first noticed by Ignaz Goldziher who linked it to a certain *hadith*, or Prophetic tradition, holding that Muslims will be divided into 73 sects, of which 72 are erring and only one is saved (*al-firqa al-najiya*) and destined for Paradise. This tradition itself had evidently come into existence as a result of a misunderstanding of a somewhat similar *hadith* which is included in the major *hadith* compendia.[13]

At any rate, despite their shortcomings and misrepresentations, heresiographies continue to provide an important category of primary source for the study of diversity in early Islam and Shiʿism. Of particular importance in this context are the heresiographies of al-Ashʿari (d. 324/935), al-Baghdadi (d. 429/1037) and Ibn Hazm (d. 456/1064), who were devout Sunnis; and al-Shahrastani (d. 548/1153), the famous Ashʿari theologian who was greatly influenced by Ismaili ideas if not himself a crypto-Ismaili. There are also those earliest Imami Shiʿi heresiographers al-Nawbakhti (d. between 300 and 310/912 and 922) and al-Qummi (d. 301/913–914), who were much better informed than their Sunni counterparts, including their contemporary al-Ashʿari, on the internal divisions of Shiʿism during its formative period.

The Kaysaniyya

In the second phase of its early history, as noted, Shiʿism evolved in terms of two main branches, the Kaysaniyya and the Imamiyya. A radical branch, in terms of both doctrine and policy, evolved out of al-Mukhtar's movement and accounted for the majority of the Shiʿa until shortly after the Abbasid revolution. This branch, breaking away from the religiously moderate attitudes of the early Kufan Shiʿa, was generally designated as the Kaysaniyya by the heresiographers who were responsible for coining the names of numerous early Muslim communities. The Kaysaniyya, as described in the heresiographical works, comprising a number of interrelated groups recognising various Hanafid ʿAlids and other Hashimids as their imams after Muhammad b. al-Hanafiyya, drew mainly on the support of the *mawali* in southern Iraq, Persia and elsewhere, though there were also many Arabs among them. Heirs to a variety of pre-Islamic traditions, the *mawali* played a crucial role in transforming Shiʿism from an Arab party of limited size and doctrinal basis to a dynamic movement. The Kaysanis in due course elaborated some of the doctrines that came to distinguish the radical wing of early Shiʿism, which was also characterised by messianic aspirations.

The Kaysani Shiʿis were left without leadership for some time after al-Mukhtar, while Muhammad b. al-Hanafiyya was not actively involved in the movement. On Ibn al-Hanafiyya's death in 81/700, the Kaysaniyya split into at least three groups commonly designated as sects (*firaq*) by the heresiographers, who use the term indiscriminately for an independent group, a subgroup, a school of thought or even a minor doctrinal position. One group denied Ibn al-Hanafiyya's death and awaited his reappearance as the Mahdi to fill the earth with justice since it had formerly been filled with injustice and oppression. A second group, while affirming Ibn al-Hanafiyya's death, maintained that he and his partisans would return to life in time to establish justice on earth. In these Kaysani beliefs, circulated mainly among the *mawali*, we have the earliest Shiʿi statements of the eschatological doctrines of *ghayba*, the absence or occultation of an imam whose life has been miraculously prolonged and who is due to reappear as the Mahdi; and *rajʿa*, the return of a messianic personality from the dead, or from occultation, sometime before the Day of Resurrection (*qiyama*). The closely related concept of the Mahdi had now acquired a more specific eschatological meaning as the messianic deliverer in Islam, with the implication that no further imams would succeed the Mahdi during his occultation. As the term Mahdi does not occur in the Qur'an, the origin of this eschatological idea has been the subject of varying explanations, including pre-Islamic Iranian and Judaeo-Christian sources. Be that as it may, the idea of a future deliverer who would appear before the end of time soon became a doctrinal feature for most Muslim groups,including the early Ismaili and the Ithnaʿashari, or Twelver, Shiʿis.

The majority of the Kaysaniyya, however, recognised Ibn al-Hanafiyya's son Abu Hashim as their new imam. Abu Hashim took an active part in organising a secret revolutionary Shiʿi movement, and his partisans, the Hashimiyya, accounted for the core of the contemporary Shiʿa. It is also known that from their base in Kufa, the Hashimiyya recruited adherents in other regions, especially among the *mawali* of Khurasan. On Abu Hashim's death in 98/716, the Hashimiyya split into several groups. The majority recognised the Abbasid Muhammad b. ʿAli b. ʿAbd Allah b. al-ʿAbbas, the great-grandson of the Prophet's uncle, as their imam after Abu Hashim. They held that Abu Hashim had personally appointed his Abbasid relative as his successor to the imamate. This party continued to be known as the Hashimiyya and, later, also as the ʿAbbasiyya. The authenticity of Abu Hashim's testament in favour of the Abbasids has been questioned throughout the centuries. The fact remains, however, that with this transference of the imamate the Abbasids did inherit the party and the propaganda organisation of the Hashimiyya that would serve as the main instrument of the Abbasid movement, which succeeded in overthrowing the Umayyads.

The Kaysani groups elaborated some of the doctrines that came to distinguish the radical wing of early Shiʿism. For instance, they condemned the first three caliphs before ʿAli as usurpers and also held that the majority of the Prophet's Companions as well as the community had gone astray by accepting their illegitimate rule. They considered ʿAli b. Abi Talib and his three sons, al-Hasan, al-Husayn and Muhammad, as their four original imams, successors to the Prophet, who had been divinely appointed and were also endowed with supernatural attributes. Certain aspects of the intellectual heritage of the Kaysaniyya, especially their ideas on the imamate and eschatology, were later adopted and further elaborated in the teachings of the main Shiʿi communities of the early Abbasid times, including the Imami Ithnaʿasharis and the Ismailis. On the other hand, those teachings of the early radical Shiʿis that implied any compromise in the unity of God were disciplined in the Imami branch of Shiʿism, but, subsequently, such notions were retrieved by the Nusayris and the Druzes, who split off from the Ismailis, amongst other religious communities.

The *ghulat*

Many of the Kaysani doctrines were propounded by the so-called *ghaliya* or *ghulat*, 'exaggerators'. The *ghulat* were accused by the more moderate Shiʿis of exaggeration (*ghuluww*) in religious matters and in respect to their imams. It also seems that the criteria of exaggeration changed over time.[14] However, practically all the early radical Shiʿis and their free religious speculations, which were considered as innovation (*bidʿa*) by the Imami (Twelver) Shiʿis of the end of the 3rd/9th century and thereafter, qualified for this general term of disapproval. Thus, the earlier eschatological doctrines of *ghayba*, *rajʿa* and Mahdism, which had become commonly accepted Shiʿi views, no longer represented exaggeration. In this increasingly partisan context, the Sunni Muslims and their heresiographers adopted harsher positions on the Shiʿi *ghulat*, often treating them as unbelievers (*kafir*). The heresiographers usually trace the origins of the Shiʿi *ghulat* to a certain ʿAbd Allah b. Sabaʾ, who denied ʿAli's death and is alleged to have preached his divinity.

In addition to attributing superhuman qualities to their imams, the early Shiʿi *ghulat* speculated freely on a range of wider issues and they were responsible for many doctrinal innovations (*bidʿa*).[15] They speculated on the nature of God, often with strong tendencies towards anthropomorphism (*tashbih*) inspired by certain Qurʾanic passages. Several of the *ghulat*, notably al-Mughira b. Saʿid (d. 119/737) and Abu Mansur al-ʿIjli (d. 124/742), are known particularly for their descriptions of God in terms of human features. More commonly, many of the *ghulat* maintained that God in His essence (*dhat*) is the divine spirit or light, which may be manifested in diverse forms and creatures; and they also believed in the incarnation (*hulul*) of the divine essence in the human body, especially in the imams. In addition, they allowed for *badaʾ* or change in God's will, a doctrine first expounded by al-Mukhtar to justify his failed prophecies.

The *ghulat* were equally interested in speculating about different types of divine inspiration, often in the context of defining the imam's attributes. Consequently, they revived the notion of prophecy (*nubuwwa*) and conceived of the possibility that God may continue to speak to man through other intermediaries and messengers after the Prophet Muhammad. Therefore they often ascribed a prophetic authority to their imams, though one secondary to that of Muhammad and without expecting a new divine revelation that would replace the message of Islam. Indeed, the imam above all others was the focus of many of these speculations. While some believed in the *hulul* of the divine essence in his person, others attributed superhuman qualifications to him. More frequently, if not attributing a prophetic authority to the imam, the *ghulat* believed that he received at least some form of divine guidance and protection. As a result, the imam was thought to be endowed with certain divinely bestowed attributes, such as sinlessness and infallibility (*ʿisma*).

These notions provided perspectives for speculating about the soul, death and the afterlife. Many of the *ghulat* thought of the soul in terms of the doctrine of metempsychosis or transmigration of souls (*tanasukh*), involving the passing of the individual soul (*nafs* or *ruh*) from one body to another, presupposing the belief in the independent existence of the soul from the body. Some further maintained that this process of transmigration of souls would take place in cycles, perhaps indefinitely, with each cycle (*dawr*) consisting of a specific number of thousands of years. In a similar manner, some of the *ghulat* held a cyclical view of the religious history of humankind, with different prophets initiating new cycles. The *ghulat* also conceived of the spirit of one imam transmigrating into the body of his successor. This belief provided an important justification for legitimising a candidate's imamate.

By emphasising the idea of transmigration and immortality of the soul, the *ghulat* also put forward a spiritual interpretation of Resurrection (*qiyama*) and denied corporeal resurrection of the dead at the end of time. For similar reasons, they denied the existence of Paradise, Hell and the Day of Judgement in their conventional sense. Instead, many believed in a purely spiritual resurrection in this world, whereby reward and punishment would fall on the soul. According to their beliefs, one's soul would be reincarnated into the bodies of pious persons, or lower and subhuman creatures on the basis of one's goodness and wickedness. The main criterion for determining the piety or sinfulness of a person was essentially related to his recognition or ignorance of the rightful imam of the time. With this emphasis on the acknowledgement of the rightful Shiʿi imam of the time as the most important religious obligation of the true believer (*muʾmin*), the role of the then developing sacred law of Islam (*shariʿa*) apparently became less important for the Kaysani Shiʿis and their *ghulat*.

Consequently, they were often accused of advocating *ibaha* or antinomianism, allegedly dispensing with the commandments and prohibitions of the law. However, these and similar charges may well reflect the inferences and hostilities of the heresiographers.

It should be noted that practically no Shiʿi group of this formative period in Islam remained completely devoid of some *ghulat* thinkers, although the Kaysaniyya attracted the greatest number. Initially many of the *ghulat* leaders were Arabs and it is possible that some of their ideas had pre-Islamic Arab origins; the expectation that a dead hero might return to life is one such probable instance. A few of their notions may even be traced to Islamic teachings. However, the *ghulat* soon arose also from amongst the *mawali* who then comprised the majority of the radical Shiʿis. The non-Arab *ghulat*, along with the *mawali* in general, brought with them a multitude of ideas from their varied backgrounds.

The speculations on the soul and the nature of its reward and punishment probably originated from Manichaeism which, in turn, might have derived them from earlier sources. Be that as it may, the spiritual independence of the early *ghulat* and their daring speculations contributed significantly to giving Shiʿism its distinctive religious basis and identity. And much of the heritage of the early radical Shiʿis, especially the *ghulat* amongst them, was in due course absorbed into the main Shiʿi communities. In particular, their ideas on the imamate and on eschatology were adopted and elaborated by the Twelver and Ismaili Shiʿis. By condemning the caliphs before ʿAli and the Umayyads as usurpers of the rights of ʿAli and the ʿAlids, amongst other Hashimids, and aiming to restore the caliphate to the *ahl al-bayt*, the radical Shiʿis also pursued an active, anti-establishment, policy. And as the Umayyad regime began to show signs of disintegration, several Kaysani groups, led by their *ghulat* theorists, such as Bayan b. Samʿan, al-Mughira and Abu Mansur al-ʿIjli, engaged in rebellious activities against the Umayyads and their governors in Iraq, especially in and around Kufa.[16] As these Kaysani revolts were poorly organised and their centres were too close to the seats of the Umayyads in Damascus, they all proved abortive. By the middle of the 3rd/9th century, with the gradual formation of the various Shiʿi communities, the term *ghulat* began to lose its earlier significance. Indeed, the heresiographers use the term *ghulat* rather sparingly in reference to individuals or groups appearing after the imamate of Jaʿfar al-Sadiq (d. 148/765).

The early Imamiyya

It was during this formative period of Shiʿi Islam that there had appeared another major branch or faction of Shiʿism, later designated as the Imamiyya, the common heritage of the Twelvers and the Ismailis. The Imami Shiʿis recognised a particular line of the Husaynid ʿAlid imams. The early Imamiyya, who like other Shiʿis of the Umayyad period were centred in Kufa, adopted a quiescent policy in the political field while doctrinally they subscribed to some of the radical views of the Kaysaniyya, such as the condemnation of the caliphs before ʿAli. The Imamiyya traced the imamate through al-Husayn b. ʿAli's sole surviving son, ʿAli b. al-Husayn Zayn al-ʿAbidin, the progenitor of the Husaynid line of the ʿAlid imams. After the events of Karbala, he retired to Medina, the permanent home of the ʿAlids, and adopted a quiescent attitude towards the Umayyads, and later towards al-Mukhtar's movement. Indeed, he kept aloof from all political activity, a stance which was later justified doctrinally by his successors to the imamate of the Imami Shiʿis. However, after the death of his uncle Muhammad b. al-Hanafiyya, Zayn al-ʿAbidin as the eldest Husaynid ʿAlid began to enjoy an influential position within the ʿAlid family. In addition, due to his renowned piety, he had gradually come to be held in great esteem in the pious circles of Medina. But since he refrained from any form of political activity and dedicated his time mainly to devotional deeds and prayer (whence his additional title al-Sajjad), he did not acquire any significant or growing following. By the closing years of his life, however, Zayn al-ʿAbidin had gathered an entourage consisting of relatives and pious Arabs.

In sum, during Zayn al-ʿAbidin's lifetime, the moderate Imami branch of Shiʿism was eclipsed by the radical branch, represented mainly by the Hashimiyya. It was after Zayn al-ʿAbidin's death around 95/714 that the Imamiyya began to gain some importance under his son and successor Muhammad b. ʿAli, known as al-Baqir, who engaged in active Shiʿi teachings. Considering himself the sole legitimate ʿAlid authority and acquiring followers who regarded him as such,[17] Muhammad al-Baqir maintained his father's quiescent attitude towards the Umayyads but engaged in religious and legal teachings that were further elaborated by his son and successor Imam Jaʿfar al-Sadiq and which formed the basis of Imami Shiʿism. Indeed, the Imami Shiʿi community, with its distinctive identity in terms of doctrine and ritual, crystallised around the teachings of these two imams.[18]

Imam Muhammad al-Baqir concentrated on teaching and expounding the rudiments of the ideas that were to become the legitimistic principles of the Imami branch of Shiʿi Islam. Above all, he seems to have concerned himself with the religious rank and spiritual authority of the imams who possessed what was considered to be a divinely inspired knowledge. He taught that the world was in permanent need of such an imam. He is also credited with introducing the principle of *taqiyya*, the precautionary dissimulation of one's true religious belief and practice that was to protect the imam and his followers under adverse circumstances. This principle was later adopted by the Twelver and Ismaili Shiʿis, while it did not find any particular prominence in Zaydi teaching.

It may be recalled that al-Baqir's imamate also coincided with the initial stages in the development of Islamic jurisprudence (*fiqh*). However, it was in the final decades of the second Islamic century that the old Arabian concept of *sunna*, the normative custom or the established practice of the community, which had reasserted itself under Islam, came to be explicitly identified by pious Muslims with the *sunna* of the Prophet. This identification, in turn, necessitated the collection of those *hadith*s or traditions which claimed to be the authentic reports on the sayings and actions of the Prophet, handed down orally through an uninterrupted chain of trustworthy authorities. The activity of collecting and studying *hadith*, which had initially arisen mainly in opposition to the extensive use of human reasoning by the Islamic judges (*qadi*s), and for citing the authority of the Prophet to determine proper legal practices, soon became another major field of Islamic learning, complementing the science of Islamic jurisprudence. In this formative period of Islamic religious sciences, Imam al-Baqir has been mentioned as a reporter of *hadith*, particularly of those supporting the Shiʿi cause and derived from his great-grandfather ʿAli. However, Imam al-Baqir also interpreted the law mostly on his own authority, with little recourse to earlier authorities. It is worth noting that in Shiʿism, *hadith* is reported on the authority of the imams and it includes the sayings of the imams themselves in addition to the Prophetic traditions.

Imam al-Baqir's legal and ritual teaching comprised many of the features that were later regarded as distinctive aspects of Imami Shiʿi law, such as the expression *hayy ʿala khayr al-ʿamal* in the call to prayer (*adhan*), the prohibition of the wiping of the soles of one's footwear (*mash ʿala'l-khuffayn*) in the ritual ablution and the permission of *mutʿa* or temporary marriage,[19] which was not upheld by the Ismaili and Zaydi laws. It should be added here that the teaching of ʿAbd Allah b. al-ʿAbbas b. ʿAbd al-Muttalib (d. 68/687), the paternal cousin of the Prophet and ʿAli, had significant impact on early Imami Shiʿi religious and legal doctrine.[20] Imam al-Baqir adopted the views of ʿAbd Allah b. al-ʿAbbas on a number of disputed questions, including *mutʿa*. In permitting *mutʿa*, for instance, ʿAbd Allah b. al-ʿAbbas maintained that it had been practised in the time of the Prophet and during the caliphate of Abu Bakr and the early part of the caliphate of ʿUmar, who later prohibited it.

In spite of many difficulties, Imam Muhammad al-Baqir succeeded in the course of his imamate of some twenty years in expanding his following and acquiring an esteemed position amongst the Shiʿa in Kufa, while he was widely respected as a traditionist amongst Sunni scholars as well. He also acquired a number of adherents from amongst the famous traditionists and jurists of Kufa, such as Zurara b. Aʿyan (d. 150/767). The renowned poet al-Kumayt b. Zayd al-Asadi (d. 126/743) was another follower of Imam al-Baqir.

Imam al-Baqir was also the first imam of the Husaynid ʿAlid line to attract a few *ghulat* theorists to his following. It may be added here in passing that al-Baqir occupies a central position in the enigmatic book entitled *Umm al-kitab*, preserved by the Nizari Ismailis of Central Asia. This book, written in archaic Persian, contains the discourses of Imam al-Baqir in response to questions raised by Jabir al-Juʿfi (d. 128/745) and other disciples. Modern scholarship has shown that the *Umm al-kitab* was evidently composed in the middle of the 2nd/8th century within a Kufan group of the *ghulat* known as the Mukhammisa or Pentadists, who existed on the fringe of the Imamiyya and believed in a divine pentad comprised of Muhammad, ʿAli, Fatima, al-Hasan and al-Husayn.[21]

The names of the notable adherents of al-Baqir and other imams of the Husaynid ʿAlid line are recorded in the earliest biographical compendium of Shiʿi personalities compiled by the Imami traditionist al-Kashshi, who flourished in the first half of the 4th/10th century.[22] Later works, belonging to the same category of the *kutub al-rijal*, or bio-bibliographical books, composed by other prominent Twelver Shiʿi scholars, such as al-Najashi (d. 450/1058) and Shaykh al-Tusi (d.

460/1067), also contain valuable information on the Imami Shiʿis.[23] Having established a distinctive identity for Imami Shiʿism, Imam Abu Jaʿfar Muhammad b. ʿAli al-Baqir died around 114/732, one century after the death of the Prophet.

On Imam al-Baqir's death, his Imami Shiʿi following split into several groups.[24] One group, the Baqiriyya, awaited his reappearance as the Mahdi, while another group switched their allegiance to the Hasanid ʿAlid movement launched in the name of Muhammad b. ʿAbd Allah, known as al-Nafs al-Zakiyya (the Pure Soul), great-grandson of al-Hasan b. ʿAli b. Abi Talib, who had been groomed by his father for the role of the Mahdi. However, the majority of Imam al-Baqir's partisans now recognised his eldest son Abu ʿAbd Allah Jaʿfar, later called al-Sadiq (the Trustworthy), as their new imam designated as such by the *nass* of his father. The Imamiyya expanded significantly and became a major religious community during the long and eventful imamate of Jaʿfar al-Sadiq, the foremost scholar and teacher amongst the Husaynid ʿAlids. Imam al-Sadiq's rise to eminence, however, occurred rather gradually during the turbulent period when the Abbasids finally succeeded in uprooting the Umayyads. During the first twenty years of his imamate, lasting until shortly after the accession of the Abbasids in 132/750, the Imamiyya were still overshadowed by the Kaysaniyya, including especially the revolutionary Hashimiyya-ʿAbbasiyya who were then conducting an anti-Umayyad campaign, and other radical Shiʿi movements. It was only during the final decade of his imamate that Jaʿfar al-Sadiq acquired a unique prominence.

In the earlier years of Imam al-Sadiq's imamate, the movement of his uncle Zayd b. ʿAli Zayn al-ʿAbidin, al-Baqir's half-brother, was launched with some success, leading to the formation of the Zaydiyya faction of Shiʿi Islam. Zayd visited Kufa in 122/739 and was surrounded by the local Shiʿis who urged him to lead an uprising against the Umayyads, the first Shiʿi attempt of its kind since al-Mukhtar's revolt and the second one led by an ʿAlid after Karbala. Zayd's revolt failed. Zayd and many of his followers were killed in 122/740, not only because the Kufans had once again proved unreliable but also because Yusuf b. ʿUmar al-Thaqafi, the Umayyad governor of Iraq, had discovered the rebellious plot in time.[25] Despite this, Zayd's movement was continued by his son Yahya, who concentrated his activities in the region of Khurasan where many Kufan

Shiʿis had been exiled by the governors of Iraq. The Zaydi Shiʿis were subsequently led by others recognised as their imams.

Few details are available on the ideas propagated by Zayd and his original followers. According to some later unreliable reports, Zayd was an associate of Wasil b. ʿAta' (d. 131/748), a reputed founder of the theological school of the Muʿtazila. However, modern scholarship has shown that the doctrinal positions of the early Shiʿis and the Muʿtazilis were rather incompatible during the 2nd/8th century. It was only in the later part of the 3rd/9th century that both Zaydi and Imami Shiʿism were influenced by Muʿtazilism.[26] We shall consider Zayd's teachings and the subsequent history of the Zaydiyya in a later chapter; here it suffices to state that Zayd's recognition of the rule of the first two caliphs, even though he acknowledged ʿAli's right to succeed the Prophet, a position repellent to both Kaysani and Imami Shiʿis, won him the general sympathy of many non-Shiʿi Muslims. The combination of Zayd's militant policy and his otherwise conservative teaching also appealed to many Shiʿis who supported the Zaydi movement that evolved out of his revolt.

Meanwhile, the disintegration of Umayyad rule accelerated on Hisham b. ʿAbd al-Malik's death in 125/743. The caliphate of Hisham's successor al-Walid II was brought to a speedy end in 126/744 by a *coup d'état* engineered by the Syrian army in collaboration with members of the Umayyad family. This event marked the imminent end of what J. Wellhausen called the 'Arab Kingdom'. Subsequently, dynastic rivalries led to a chaotic civil war. During the brief caliphate of Ibrahim b. al-Walid I, who was acknowledged only in southern Syria, general conditions deteriorated rapidly into complete chaos. By 127/744, when Marwan II marched to Damascus, deposed Ibrahim and proclaimed himself the new caliph, revolts were raging in various parts of the Umayyad state.

Under these circumstances, the Shiʿis of Kufa and elsewhere were encouraged to make bolder efforts towards seizing the caliphate from the Umayyads. In 125/743, the leading representatives of the Banu Hashim met in a secret gathering at al-Abwa', near Medina, to discuss the choice of a Hashimid candidate to succeed the Umayyads. The leading Hasanid, ʿAbd Allah al-Mahd b. al-Hasan al-Muthanna b. al-Hasan b. ʿAli, succeeded in persuading all the participants to pledge their oath of allegiance to his son Muhammad b. ʿAbd Allah al-Nafs al-Zakiyya and to recognise him as the most suitable Hashimid candidate for the caliphate. Amongst those who complied were even the leading Abbasids. Only Jaʿfar al-Sadiq, the most respected Husaynid ʿAlid, is reported to have withheld his approval. Jaʿfar al-Sadiq was clearly not prepared to accept the claims of his Hasanid cousin or any other ʿAlid since he regarded himself as the rightful imam of the time. After this family reunion, al-Nafs al-Zakiyya and his brother Ibrahim embarked on a vigorous campaign, which also received the support of many Zaydis and several *ghulat* groups. However, the Hasanid movement of al-Nafs al-Zakiyya lacked organisation and was easily overtaken and then crushed by the Abbasids in 145/762–763.

Meanwhile, the Abbasids had learned important lessons from the numerous abortive Shiʿi revolts against the Umayyads. Consequently, they paid particular attention to developing the organisation of their own movement, establishing secret headquarters in Kufa but concentrating their revolutionary activities in the remote eastern province of Khurasan. The Abbasid *daʿwa*, or propaganda activity, was cleverly preached anonymously in the name of *al-rida min al Muhammad*, an enigmatic phrase which spoke of an unidentified person belonging to the Prophet's family.[27] Apart from reflecting a precautionary tactic, this slogan aimed to maximise support from the Shiʿis of different groups who commonly upheld the leadership of the *ahl al-bayt*.

The Abbasid *daʿwa* in Khurasan was initially organised in the form of small clandestine groups. Nevertheless, many of the Abbasid *daʿis* who disseminated their revolutionary message were discovered and executed by the Umayyad agents. Consequently, it soon became necessary to create a more formal structure. A supreme council of 12 chiefs, called the *nuqabaʾ*, was set up in Marw, Khurasan, to direct the activities of a large number of newly appointed *daʿis*, a model of *daʿwa* organisation later adopted by the Ismailis. These changes proved successful, especially when ʿAmmar b. Yazid, better known as Khidash (d. 118/736), was sent to Khurasan to head the new *daʿwa* organisation.

Contact between the partisans in Khurasan and the imam of the Hashimiyya-ʿAbbasiyya, who resided secretly in Humayma, Palestine, but remained nameless, was maintained through the leader of the Kufan branch. From around 127/744, the Abbasid *daʿwa* in Khurasan was led by Abu Muslim al-Khurasani, a celebrated personality with an obscure background.[28] Abu Muslim's success was rapid, and by 129/747 he had unfurled the 'black banners' that were to become the emblem of the Abbasids, signifying the open phase of their revolt. Abu Muslim's revolutionary army, the Khurasaniyya, composed of both Persian *mawali* and Arabs, expanded significantly in a short period. It was, indeed, in Abu Muslim's army that complete integration of Arab and non-Arab Muslims was attained for the first time since al-Mukhtar's earlier attempts. After seizing all of Khurasan, the Khurasani army started its advance westward, defeating Umayyad armies along the way. By 132/749, Abu Muslim's Khurasaniyya army had entered Kufa.

The time had finally come for disclosing the name of *al-rida* from the *ahl al-bayt*, who would be acceptable as the new caliph. In the event, the Khurasaniyya chose Abu'l-ʿAbbas al-Saffah, the brother of the previous Abbasid imam, Ibrahim b. Muhammad, who had recently been killed in Umayyad captivity. He and other members of the Abbasid family had a little earlier moved from Humayma to Kufa, where they had remained in hiding. On 12 Rabiʿ II 132/28 November 749, Abu'l-ʿAbbas was proclaimed as the first Abbasid caliph in the mosque of Kufa. Shortly afterwards, in 132/750, the Khurasaniyya achieved their final victory against the Umayyad forces in Iraq. The Abbasids installed their own dynasty to the caliphate and ruled over diverse portions of the Islamic lands with varying authority for five centuries, until they were overthrown in 656/1258 by the Mongols. From 145/762, the new city of Baghdad served as the Abbasid capital.

The Abbasid revolution marked a turning point in the history of early Islam, representing not only a dynastic change but also initiating many socio-political and economic alterations in the established order. Under the early Abbasids, the hegemony of the Arab aristocracy and the distinction between the Arab Muslims and the *mawali* disappeared rapidly. Now a new multiracial ruling class, with Islam as its unifying feature, emerged to replace the Arab ruling class of the Umayyad times. With the emancipation of the *mawali* and the new alignment of classes on non-racial grounds, some of the most pressing demands of the radical Shiʿis and others opposed to the social order established under the Umayyads were satisfied. As a result, revolutionary or radical Shiʿism henceforth ceased to be identified with the aspirations of the *mawali*, who had at last acquired equal status with Arab Muslims and were soon to disappear as a distinct and oppressed social class.

The Abbasid victory, however, proved a source of utter disillusionment for the Shiʿa who had expected an ʿAlid, rather than an Abbasid, from the *ahl al-bayt* to succeed to the caliphate. The animosity between the Abbasids and the ʿAlids accentuated when, soon after their accession, the Abbasids began to persecute many of their former Shiʿi supporters and the ʿAlids. The Shiʿi disappointment was further aggravated when the Abbasids renounced their own Shiʿi past and became the spiritual spokesmen of Sunni Islam. The Abbasids' breach with their Shiʿi roots and their efforts to legitimise their own independent rights to the caliphate were finally completed by the third caliph of the dynasty, Muhammad al-Mahdi (r. 158–169/775–785). The Abbasids now claimed the caliphate by right of inheritance, arguing that al-ʿAbbas, the Prophet's uncle, was more closely related to him than his cousin ʿAli. This, of course, implied the repudiation of the analogous claims of the ʿAlids.

With these developments, those remaining Kaysani Shiʿis who had not been absorbed into the Abbasid movement now sought to align themselves with alternative movements. In Khurasan and other eastern regions, many of these alienated radical Shiʿis attached themselves to various syncretic groups generically termed the Khurramiyya or Khurramdiniyya, espousing a variety of anti-Abbasid and anti-Arab ideas.[29] In Iraq, however, they rallied to the side of Imam Jaʿfar al-Sadiq or Muhammad al-Nafs al-Zakiyya, then the main ʿAlid claimants to the imamate of the Shiʿa. In other words, the majority of the Shiʿa were now obliged to follow one or other of these two Fatimid imams. It was from this time that stress was also laid increasingly on direct descent from the Prophet through Fatima and ʿAli, and thus Fatimid ʿAlid ancestry acquired its special significance for the Shiʿis. Doubtless, the messianic claims and militant attitude of al-Nafs al-Zakiyya, who had been prepared for the role of Mahdi and refused to render homage to the Abbasids, subsequently launching his rebellion against them, held greater attraction for at least some of the more activist Shiʿis. But with the demise of the Hasanid movement of al-Nafs al-Zakiyya in 145/762–3, the Husaynid ʿAlid Imam al-Sadiq emerged as the main rallying point for Shiʿis of diverse backgrounds, other than the Zaydi Shiʿis who followed their own imams. It was under such circumstances that al-Sadiq's imamate acquired its special prominence.

Meanwhile, Jaʿfar al-Sadiq had gradually acquired a widespread reputation as a religious scholar. He was a reporter of *hadith*, and was later cited as such in the chain of authorities (*isnad*) accepted by Sunni Muslims as well. He also taught *fiqh*, or jurisprudence, and has been credited with founding, after the work of his father, the Imami Shiʿi school of religious law (*madhhab*), named Jaʿfari after him. Imam al-Sadiq was accepted as a teaching authority not only by his Shiʿi partisans but by a wider circle that included many of the piety-minded Muslims of Medina and Kufa, where the majority of the Imamiyya were located. Over time, al-Sadiq had surrounded himself with a noteworthy group of scholars comprising some of the most eminent jurist-traditionists and theologians of the time, such as Hisham b. al-Hakam (d. 179/795), the foremost representative of Imami scholastic theology (*kalam*).[30] Indeed, the Imami Shiʿis now came to possess a distinctive body of ritual as well as theological and legal doctrines.

Imam al-Sadiq, too, attracted a few *ghulat* thinkers to his circle of associates, but kept the speculations of the more extremist elements of his following within tolerable bounds by imposing a certain doctrinal discipline. As a result, while his imamate was invigorated by the ideas of various thinkers in his entourage, such ideas were kept in check. This also contributed to the wider Shiʿi recognition of the Husaynid line of imams. The foremost radical theorist in al-Sadiq's following was Abu'l-Khattab al-Asadi, the most renowned of all the early Shiʿi *ghulat*.[31] Abu'l-Khattab propagated extremist ideas about the imam in addition to other exaggerated views. Abu'l-Khattab acquired many followers of his own, the Khattabiyya, and adopted a revolutionary policy in conflict with Imam al-Sadiq's quiescent stance. The early Khattabis preached the divinity of the imams, on the basis of the divine light inherited by them, in addition to their preoccupation with esotericism, cyclicism, hierarchism and symbolic or allegorical exegesis (*ta'wil*) of the Qurʾan. In time, the views and policies of this outspoken and zealous disciple of al-Sadiq became intolerable to the imam, who publicly denounced and refuted Abu'l-Khattab. Soon afterwards, in 138/755, Abu'l-Khattab and a group of his supporters, who had gathered in the mosque of Kufa for rebellious purposes, were attacked and killed by the forces of the city's Abbasid governor.

Table 2.1 The Hashimids and Early Shiʿi Imams

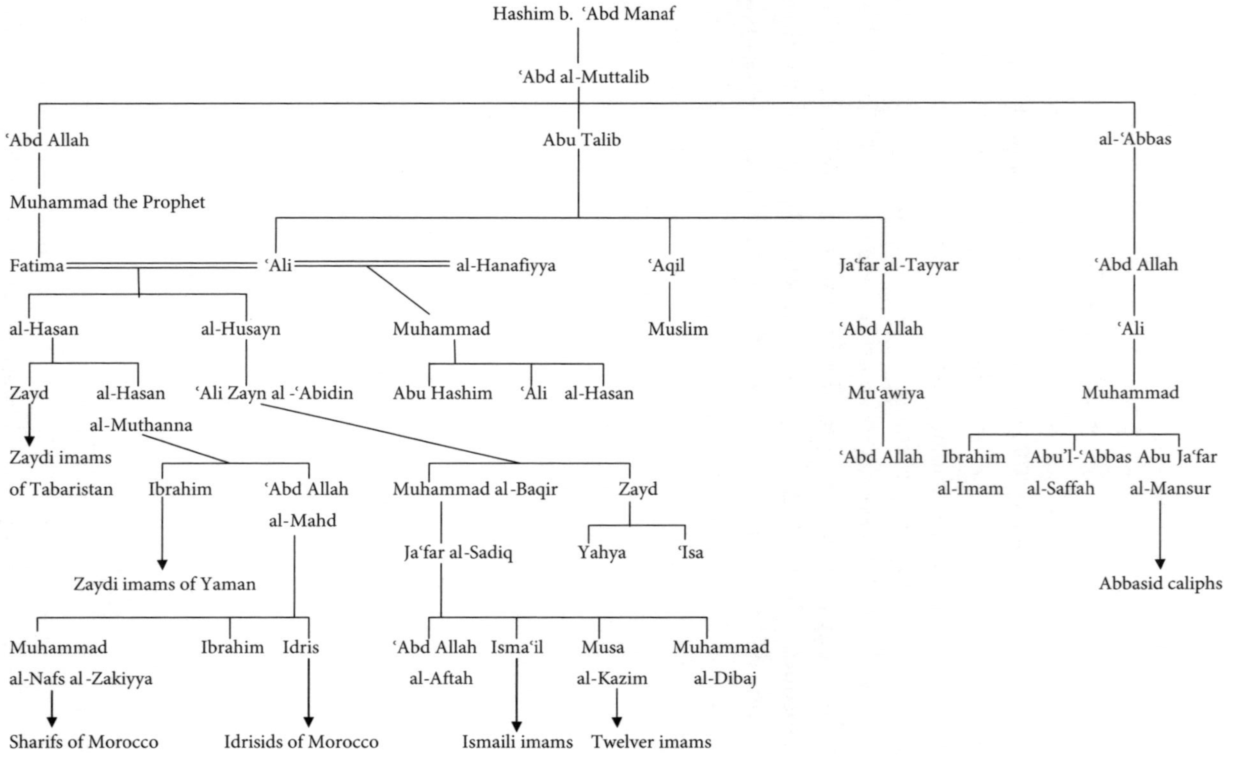

The Imami Shiʿi doctrine of the imamate

As a result of the intellectual activities of Imam al-Sadiq and his circle of learned associates, and building on the teachings of Imam al-Baqir, the basic conception of the Imami Shiʿi doctrine of the imamate was now elaborated.[32] This central Shiʿi doctrine, essentially retained by the later Imami Ithnaʿasharis and the Ismailis, was based on certain principles. These principles were emphasised by Imam al-Sadiq in response to the challenges of the time and, as such, they proved effective in strengthening his imamate.

The first principle was that of imamate by *nass*, defined as a prerogative bestowed by God upon a chosen member of the *ahl al-bayt*, who, before his death and with divine guidance, transfers the imamate to his successor by an explicit designation or *nass*. On the authority of the *nass*, the imamate remained located in a specific individual, whether or not he claimed the caliphate. Thus, Imam al-Sadiq maintained that there was always in existence an imam, designated by the *nass* of the previous imam, who possessed all the authority of the sole legitimate imam of the time, whether or not he was ruling over the community. Furthermore, the antecedence of Imam al-Sadiq's own *nass* was traced back to ʿAli, who had been appointed as the Prophet's *wasi* or legatee and successor. This first *nass*, initiated by the Prophet under divine command, had remained in the Husaynid ʿAlid line of imams until it had reached Jaʿfar al-Sadiq. On the basis of the principle of *nass*, it was no longer necessary for an imam to rebel against the unjust ruler and the established regime in order to assert his claim to caliphal power. The institutions of imamate and caliphate were thus separated from one another. In other words, the imam was not required to seize the caliphal authority if circumstances did not permit it. This explains why Imam al-Sadiq did not participate in any of the ʿAlid risings of his time, instead maintaining political quietism. It also explains why the Husaynids were largely spared the persecutions that the Abbasid caliph al-Mansur (r. 136–158/754–775) meted out to the Hasanid ʿAlids.

The second fundamental principle embodied in the doctrine of the imamate, and closely related to the *nass* principle, was that of an imamate based on *ʿilm*, or special religious knowledge. In the light of this *ʿilm*, divinely inspired and transmitted through the *nass* of the preceding imam, the rightful imam of the time became the sole authorised source of the knowledge on how to guide Muslims along the right path. Consequently, the imam could perform the all-important function of providing spiritual guidance for his adherents and explain the inner meaning of the Qur'an and the religious injunctions, even when not occupied with the caliphal function of ruling over the community. Imam al-Sadiq's followers, too, attributed to him a uniquely authoritative *ʿilm*, necessary to guide the true believers. And as in the case of the *nass*, Imam al-Sadiq's *ʿilm* was traced back through the Husaynid ʿAlid line of imams to ʿAli, who had acquired it from the Prophet.

Furthermore, the teaching authority of the imam was strengthened by the doctrine of their immunity from sin and error (*ʿisma*). In line with his passivity and prudence, Imam al-Sadiq also refined the principle of *taqiyya*, precautionary dissimulation, and made it an absolute article of faith.[33] Doubtless, it must have been dangerous for the imams and their partisans to openly propagate their beliefs, and to publicly announce that certain individuals, other than the ruling caliphs, were the divinely appointed spiritual leaders of the Muslims. The observance of *taqiyya* conveniently protected the Imami Shiʿis from persecution, and served in the preservation of their religious identity under adverse circumstances, at least under pressing conditions and for short periods. By placing emphasis on an imamate based on *nass* and *ʿilm*, and recommending the practice of *taqiyya*, Imam al-Sadiq had elaborated a completely new interpretation of the functions and attributes of the imam. At the same time, by underlining the hereditary and divinely inspired aspects of the imam's attributes, Imam al-Sadiq had now restricted the sanctity of the *ahl al-bayt* to the ʿAlids, and especially his own Husaynid line of imams amongst them, to the exclusion of the Abbasids and all other non-ʿAlid Hashimids.

The basic conception of the Imami Shiʿi doctrine of the imamate, expressed in numerous *hadith*s reported mainly from Jaʿfar al-Sadiq, is preserved in the earliest corpus of Imami Shiʿi *hadith*s, compiled by Abu Jaʿfar Muhammad al-Kulayni (d. 329/940), and retained by the Ismailis in their foremost legal compendium, produced by al-Qadi al-Nuʿman (d. 363/974).[34] This doctrine was founded on belief in the permanent need of mankind for a divinely guided, sinless and infallible (*maʿsum*) imam who, after the Prophet Muhammad, would act as the authoritative teacher and guide of men in all their spiritual affairs. Although the imam, who could practise *taqiyya* when necessary, would be entitled to temporal leadership as much as to religious authority, his mandate would not depend on his actual rule or any attempt at gaining it. The doctrine further taught that the Prophet himself had designated ʿAli b. Abi Talib as his legatee (*wasi*) and successor, by an explicit designation (*nass*) under divine command and that the majority of the Companions ignored the Prophet's designation. After ʿAli, the imamate would be transmitted from father to son by the rule of the *nass*, amongst the descendants of ʿAli and Fatima; and after al-Husayn b. ʿAli, it would continue in the Husaynid line until the end of time. This ʿAlid imam, the sole legitimate imam at any time, is deemed to be in possession of special knowledge or *ʿilm*, and to have perfect understanding of the outward, or exoteric (*zahir*), and inward, or esoteric (*batin*), aspects and meanings of the Qurʾan and the message of Islam. Indeed, the world could not exist for a moment without such an imam who would be the proof of God (*hujjat Allah*) on earth. Even if only two men were left on the face of the earth, one of them would be the imam. And there could only be a single imam at any given time, though there might be a silent one (*samit*), his successor, beside him. The imam's existence in the terrestrial world was viewed as so essential that his recognition and obedience to him were made the absolute duty of every believer (*muʾmin*). Hence, the famous *hadith* reported from Imam al-Sadiq that 'whosoever dies without having acknowledged the true imam of his time dies as an unbeliever (*kafir*)'.[35]

In sum, the Imams al-Baqir and al-Sadiq, through their teachings, endowed the Imami Shiʿi community with a distinctive religious identity, which proved invaluable in preventing the assimilation of this Shiʿi community into the Sunni synthesis of Islam that was simultaneously being worked out by other Muslim groups. Furthermore, by abstaining from any anti-regime activities, while the rebellious campaigns of numerous other Shiʿi groups were proving abortive, the imams saved their community from destruction by the Umayyad and Abbasid rulers and their governors in Iraq. That Imami Shiʿism survived numerous hardships (and, indeed, the Abbasid revolution) was due, in no small measure, to the foresight and teachings of its spiritual leadership.

Having established a solid doctrinal basis for Imami Shiʿism, Abu ʿAbd Allah Jaʿfar b. Muhammad al-Sadiq, the last of the imams recognised by both the Twelvers and the Ismailis, and counted as the sixth one for the former and the fifth for the latter, died in 148/765. He was buried in the Baqiʿ cemetery in Medina, next to his father and grandfather, whose tombs were destroyed by the Wahhabi regime of Saudi Arabia in modern times. The dispute over Imam al-Sadiq's succession caused historic divisions in Imami Shiʿism, leading to the eventual formation of independent Ithnaʿashari (Twelver) and Ismaili communities. In subsequent chapters we shall consider the ensuing histories of these two Shiʿi communities, as well as that of the Zaydis, who appeared in this formative period of Shiʿi Islam, while the Nusayris (ʿAlawis) evolved later out of the Imami community.

3

The Ithnaʿasharis or Twelvers

The Twelvers or Ithnaʿasharis, who would become the predominant Shiʿi community believing in a line of twelve (Arabic, *ithnaʿashar*) imams, evolved out of the earlier Imami Shiʿism as it had been consolidated by Imam Jaʿfar al-Sadiq. The Imami doctrine of the imamate, emphasising the necessity of the earthly presence of an imam at all times, had equipped the Imami Shiʿis of the 2nd/8th century with their central teaching. Subsequently, the Imami Shiʿis themselves gradually split into various groups, as enumerated in the heresiographical literature – especially in the earliest Imami works written by al-Hasan b. Musa al-Nawbakhti (d. after 300/912) and Saʿd b. ʿAbd Allah al-Qummi (d. 301/913–914).[1]

However, it was not until the middle of the 4th/10th century that one of the then developing Imami Shiʿi groups acquired the distinctive designation of Twelver, evidently first used in heresiographical works. By then, the twelfth and final imam of this group had already remained in occultation (*ghayba*) for several decades since the year 260/874. The particular Imami Shiʿis who had become known as Twelvers were then characterised by their upholding of the doctrine of the twelve imams, starting with ʿAli b. Abi Talib and ending with Muhammad b. al-Hasan, acknowledged as the eschatological Mahdi who was in hiding and whose reappearance (*rajʿa*) was awaited by the members of his Shiʿi community. Thus, it took more than a century after the death of Imam al-Sadiq for the doctrine of the twelve imams to be crystallised and, strictly speaking, one cannot use the term 'Twelvers' in reference to any Imami Shiʿi group prior to the time of the twelfth imam. With this caveat in mind, we will use the terms 'Imami' and 'Twelver' interchangeably. During this rather confusing period in the formative phase of Shiʿism, Imami Shiʿism evolved in terms of a multitude of groups and short-lived sects, some of which evolved into Twelver and Ismaili communities, while the Zaydi Shiʿis followed their own separate, historical path.

The later Twelver imams and the hidden Mahdi

The formative phase of Twelver Shiʿism coincided partially with the period of their twelve imams when the believers received direct spiritual guidance from these imams, who lived in Medina or in various localities in Iraq. We have already briefly covered the careers of the first six ʿAlids recognised as imams by the Twelvers, namely from ʿAli until Jaʿfar al-Sadiq. In this section we shall present a brief survey of the next stage in the early history of this community, covering the second sextet of the imams who in due course were acknowledged as such by the Twelver Shiʿis.

On Imam Jaʿfar al-Sadiq's death in 148/765, his succession was disputed and simultaneously claimed by three of his sons, ʿAbd Allah al-Aftah, Musa al-Kazim and Muhammad al-Dibaj. As we shall see in the next chapter, there were also those Imami Shiʿis, constituting the earliest Ismailis, who recognised the imamate of al-Sadiq's second son Ismaʿil, the deceased imam's original heir-designate, or the latter's son Muhammad b. Ismaʿil. At any rate, the unified Imami Shiʿis of al-Sadiq's time now split into six competing groups.[2]

One small group denied al-Sadiq's death and awaited his return as the Mahdi. These partisans were called the Nawusiyya, named after their leader, a certain ʿAbd Allah b. al-Nawus. Another small group recognised Muhammad b. Jaʿfar, known as al-Dibaj, the younger full-brother of Musa b. Jaʿfar, and they became known as the Shumaytiyya (or Sumaytiyya), after their leader, Yahya b. Abi'l-Shumayt (al-Sumayt). In 200/815–816, Muhammad al-Dibaj revolted unsuccessfully against the Abbasid caliph al-Maʾmun (r. 198–218/813–833), and he died soon afterwards in 203/818. Another two groups, as we shall see, recognised Ismaʿil b. Jaʿfar as their Mahdi or alternatively traced their imamate to Ismaʿil's son Muhammad. However, a majority of al-Sadiq's Imami partisans now recognised his eldest son ʿAbd Allah al-Aftah, the full-brother of Ismaʿil, as their new imam after al-Sadiq. His adherents, known as the Aftahiyya or Fathiyya, cited a *hadith* from Imam al-Sadiq to the effect that the imamate must be transmitted through the eldest son of the previous imam. At any rate, when ʿAbd Allah died about seventy days after his father, in 149/766, without leaving a son, many of his followers went over to his younger half-brother Musa, later called al-Kazim, who already had an Imami following of his own. The Imami Shiʿis who continued to recognise ʿAbd Allah as the rightful imam before Musa constituted an important Imami sect in Kufa, where the majority of the Imami Shiʿis were then concentrated, until the late 4th/10th century.

Musa al-Kazim, later counted as the seventh imam of the Twelvers who excluded ʿAbd Allah al-Aftah from the list of their imams, soon received the allegiance of the majority of the Imami Shiʿis, including the most renowned scholars in al-Sadiq's entourage, such as Hisham b. al-Hakam and Mu'min al-Taq, who had supported Musa from the beginning. Imam Musa al-Kazim strengthened and further developed the rudimentary organisation of his Imami group, by appointing agents (*wukala*; singular, *wakil*) to supervise his followers in various localities. These agents also regularly collected the *khums* and other donations made to the imam. In line with the tradition established by his predecessors, Musa refrained from all political activity and was even more quiescent than his father. He was, in fact, one of the two ʿAlids who reportedly refused to support al-Husayn b. ʿAli, known as Sahib Fakhkh. This Hasanid ʿAlid, a great-nephew of ʿAbd Allah al-Mahd (al-Nafs al-Zakiyya's father), revolted in the Hijaz in 169/786 against the Abbasids during the short caliphate of al-Hadi, and was killed at Fakhkh, near Mecca, together with many other ʿAlids.[3] Nevertheless, Musa was not spared the persecutions by the Abbasids. In 179/795, he was arrested in Medina and banished to Basra and then Baghdad on the order of the fifth Abbasid caliph, Harun al-Rashid (r. 170–193/786–809), who had retained the anti-ʿAlid policies of his predecessors. Imam Musa al-Kazim died in 183/799 in a Baghdad prison, perhaps due to poisoning, as the Twelvers claim in the case of most of their imams. He was buried in the cemetery of the Quraysh in a northern district of Baghdad. Subsequently, the shrines of Musa al-Kazim and his grandson (acknowledged as the ninth Twelver imam) became a pilgrimage site in Baghdad, known as Kazimayn (the two Kazims).

On Musa al-Kazim's death his Imami Shiʿi following split into several sects. One large group denied his death and held that he would return as the Mahdi, perhaps attributing special significance to his being their seventh imam. They became known as the Waqifiyya, 'those who stop', because they ended the line of their imams with him. The Waqifiyya, therefore, did not recognise his son ʿAli b. Musa, later called al-Rida, as their imam, though some of the Waqifi Imamis considered him and his descendants as the lieutenants (*khulafa*ʾ) of the hidden Mahdi during his absence. Many of the Kufan Shiʿi transmitters of *hadith* in the 3rd/9th century belonged to the Waqifiyya; and several Waqifis, mostly Kufan, wrote works in defence of the occultation (*ghayba*) of their seventh imam, as later Imamis did in the case of their own twelfth imam.

However, another significant group of Musa al-Kazim's followers now acknowledged his son ʿAli as their next imam, later counted as the eighth imam of the Twelvers.[4] They claimed that ʿAli had, in fact, received the *nass* from his father to succeed him to their imamate. ʿAli kept aloof from a number of ʿAlid and Zaydi revolts, including those launched by his own brothers. These revolts erupted in the Abbasid lands after Harun al-Rashid's death in 193/809, which also led to civil war and dynastic rivalries between the deceased Abbasid caliph's two sons and heirs, al-Amin and al-Maʾmun, who initially ruled over different parts of the empire. These were the circumstances under which the caliph al-Maʾmun, departing from the established anti-Shiʿi policies of his predecessors, wrote to ʿAli b. Musa in 201/816 inviting the imam to go from Medina to his capital at Marw (now in Turkmenistan) in Khurasan. Al-Maʾmun had now effectively decided to attempt a major reconciliation between the ʿAlid and the Abbasid branches of the Prophet's clan of Banu Hashim by appointing ʿAli b. Musa as his heir-apparent, also bestowing on him the title of al-Rida. This title had been used previously in Shiʿi rebellions (including especially that organised by the Abbasids themselves) in reference to a descendant of the Prophet upon whose designation as caliph the Muslim community would agree. After some initial resistance, ʿAli set out for Khurasan, accepted the offer and joined al-Maʾmun's entourage as his heir-apparent.[5] In the event, the black banners of the Abbasids were replaced, at least for a couple of years, by green ones, signifying the Abbasid–ʿAlid reconciliation. This decision aroused strong opposition from the Abbasid family.

By 202/817, relations between al-Maʾmun and ʿAli al-Rida were further strengthened by marriage between the Shiʿi imam and one of the Abbasid caliph's daughters, as well as another marriage arranged between Imam al-Rida's son and future successor Muhammad, who was then only six years old and had remained behind in Medina, and another one of al-Ma'mun's daughters. Soon afterwards, in 203/818, as al-Ma'mun had set off for Baghdad taking ʿAli al-Rida with him, the imam died suddenly at Tus. The Shiʿa have claimed that there was a strong probability that the imam may have actually been poisoned at the instigation of al-Ma'mun, who then tried to reverse his policy in order to please the Abbasid opposition in Baghdad. Be that as it may, al-Ma'mun buried ʿAli b. Musa al-Rida next to the grave of his own father, Harun al-Rashid. A new city, called Mashhad (martyr's place), developed around Imam al-Rida's burial place, representing the most important Shiʿi shrine in Persia. Twelver Imami Shiʿis flock to this shrine, the only one of the Twelver imams in the country, for *ziyara* or pilgrimage with its prescribed ritual, as in the case of the shrines of other imams and their close relatives. The shrine of Imam al-Rida's sister, Fatima al-Maʿsuma, who had travelled to Persia to see her brother and died on the way, is located in Qumm, an important centre of Shiʿi activity and learning from the 2nd/8th century.

On Imam al-Rida's death his Imami followers subdivided into a number of sects. One group recognised his only son, Muhammad b. ʿAli, known by the titles al-Jawad and al-Taqi, who was then seven years of age, as their imam.[6] The succession to the imamate of a minor led to considerable controversy and debate among the followers of al-Rida, especially regarding the knowledge (*ʿilm*) expected of the imam. A group of these Imamis, in fact, now recognised the late imam's brother Ahmad b. Musa as their new imam, while others joined the Waqifiyya or even attached themselves to the Zaydi movements then spreading across Iraq. However, Muhammad al-Jawad, counted as the ninth imam of the Twelvers, retained the allegiance of an Imami group who held that even a minor imam would possess the requisite knowledge through divine inspiration. The marriage ceremony of Muhammad al-Jawad to al-Ma'mun's daughter, which had been arranged earlier, actually took place in 215/830 in Baghdad, to where he had been summoned from Medina. Subsequently, the imam, who was treated lavishly by al-Ma'mun, returned to his estate near Medina. In 220/835, the Abbasid caliph al-Muʿtasim (r.

218–227/833–842), al-Ma'mun's brother and successor, summoned the imam to Baghdad again. Muhammad al-Jawad died in the same year in the Abbasid capital; he was twenty-five years of age. He was buried next to his grandfather Musa al-Kazim on the west bank of the Tigris. Muhammad al-Jawad had two sons, ʿAli and Musa.

The majority of Muhammad al-Jawad's Imami followers then acknowledged the imamate of his son ʿAli b. Muhammad, who would carry the epithets al-Hadi and al-Naqi. Born in 212/828, ʿAli al-Hadi, counted as the tenth imam of the Twelver Shiʿis, was also a minor when he succeeded his father in 220/835. On his accession to the Abbasid caliphate in 232/847, al-Mutawakkil launched his anti-ʿAlid as well as anti-Muʿtazili policies. In 233/848, he brought ʿAli al-Hadi with his entire entourage from Medina to Samarra', the new Abbasid capital, situated to the north of Baghdad where the Turkish guards were also based. Samarra' served as the Abbasid capital from 221/836 to 279/892. ʿAli al-Hadi spent the rest of his life in Samarra' under the watchful eyes of the Abbasid agents. Nevertheless, the imam managed to remain in contact with his followers, also consolidating the organisation of his Imami communities in Iraq, Persia and elsewhere through his various representatives who collected the *khums* and other religious dues for him.

By the time of this imam, the financial administration of the Imami community had developed into an organised institution. In line with his anti-Shiʿi policies, al-Mutawakkil also ordered the destruction of the mausoleum of Imam al-Husayn at Karbala so as to put an end to Shiʿi pilgrimages to the site. However, ʿAli al-Hadi does not seem to have been poisoned on the order of al-Mutawakkil, as reported in some, but not all, Imami sources. Imam al-Hadi died in 254/868 at Samarra', where he and his son and successor al-Hasan al-ʿAskari are buried in the twin shrines known as the ʿAskariyayn (the two ʿAskaris), since these imams had been obliged to live in the caliph's army camp (*ʿaskar*) in Samarra'. Imam ʿAli al-Hadi was survived by two sons, al-Hasan and Jaʿfar.[7]

On ʿAli al-Hadi's death, the majority of his partisans acknowledged his son al-Hasan as their next imam. According to Imami tradition, he had been designated to succeed to the imamate by his father a month before the latter's death in 254/868. Born around 232/846, al-Hasan had accompanied his father to Samarra' in 233/848, and spent the rest of his life there. Counted as the eleventh Twelver imam, al-Hasan al-ʿAskari, whose epithet reflected the fact that he lived in the military district of Samarraʾ, spent his brief imamate of some six years under the close surveillance of the Abbasids. Imam al-Hasan al-ʿAskari fell ill on 1 Rabiʿ I 260/25 December 873, and died a week later on 8 Rabiʿ I 260/1 January 874; he was twenty-eight years old. His estate passed to his brother Jaʿfar, who had earlier unsuccessfully claimed the imamate for himself.[8]

Upon the death of al-Hasan al-ʿAskari, his Imami partisans, who by then constituted a large and expanding community in several regions, faced a serious crisis of succession as the deceased imam had left no manifest heir. In Shiʿi tradition this phase of their history is referred to as a period of confusion (*hayra*) lasting several decades before it was resolved doctrinally. In the event, the Imami Shiʿis split into more than a dozen groups, of which only one (the Imamiyya proper) was to survive as the Twelver Shiʿis.[9] Amongst the main groups that now emerged were those who denied Imam al-ʿAskari's death and held that he had gone into occultation (*ghayba*) and would return as the Mahdi, as the world could never remain without an imam. Others acknowledged the deceased imam's brother, Jaʿfar b. ʿAli, as their new imam on the bases of a variety of arguments.

However, a main group, later designated as the Ithnaʿashariyya or Twelvers, soon came to hold that a son named Muhammad had been born to Imam al-ʿAskari in 255/869, five years before his death. They further held that the child, who had received his father's designation as his successor, had been kept hidden from the beginning, though his existence had been divulged to a few trusted associates of the imam. It was explained that the imam had hidden his future successor out of fear of Abbasid persecution. Indeed, the Abbasids had continued to persecute the Shiʿis under al-Mutawakkil's son and successor al-Muʿtamid (r. 256–279/870–892). According to this Imami tradition, Muhammad succeeded his father to the imamate in due course in 260/874, while remaining in occultation as before. It seems that, initially, at least some of these Imamis expected Muhammad to reappear and take charge of the communal affairs, also holding that the imamate would then continue through his progeny. However, before long, the Imamis identified their hidden imam with the eschatological Mahdi and its equivalent the *qaʾim* (the 'riser'), and ended their line of imams with him, as the Mahdi could not be succeeded by another imam.

With the end of the historical imamate for the Imamis, and numerous competing arguments and sectarian rivalries regarding the rightful imam after al-Hasan al-ʿAskari, the Imami Shiʿis experienced a most difficult and confusing period for several decades. It was during this period, before the line of the twelve imams and the doctrine of occultation (*ghayba*) were crystallised, that numerous Imamis joined alternative Shiʿi movements in Iraq, Yaman and Persia – especially the revolutionary movement of the Ismailis (Qarmatis), which was then spreading in southern Iraq and adjacent regions.

In the course of the difficult decades following the death of Imam al-Hasan al-ʿAskari in 260/874, a group of influential leaders and agents, well placed in the central administration of the Imamis, looked after the affairs of their community. Filling the leadership gap created by the absence of a manifest imam, they also collected the religious dues through the established network of regional agents. There were evidently a number of such leaders, called variously the emissary (*safir*), deputy (*na'ib*), agent (*wakil*) or gate (*bab*), who were believed to have also acted as intermediaries between the hidden imam and his community. Later, in the 4th/10th century, the number of these intermediaries was fixed at four, with each one having designated his successor reportedly on the instructions of the hidden imam. The first of these chief representatives of the hidden imam was Abu ʿAmr ʿUthman b. Saʿid al-ʿAmri, who had been a close associate of Imam al-ʿAskari and had administered the funerary rites for him. He reportedly passed on the petitions of the believers addressed to the hidden imam and, in response, made available in his own handwriting the imam's periodical letters and decrees.[10]

ʿUthman al-ʿAmri did not survive Imam al-ʿAskari for long; after him, his son Abu Jaʿfar Muhammad b. ʿUthman al-ʿAmri became the second chief representative of the hidden imam, taking care of the affairs of the Imami community for more than forty years until his own death in 305/917. Meanwhile, in 279/892, the Abbasid caliph al-Muʿtadid had abandoned Samarra' and moved the Abbasid court back to Baghdad after almost sixty years. Soon afterwards, the seat of the Imami secretariat, too, was transferred from Samarra', where the later imams had lived, to Baghdad. There, the Imami leadership could now count on the support and protection of a number of influential Imami families who were politically powerful in the service of the Abbasids, especially during the caliphates of al-Muqtadir (r. 295–320/908–932) and al-Radi (r. 322–329/934–940). It was during this period that the Imami members of the Ibn al-Furat family intermittently controlled the Abbasid caliphal administration as viziers or other officials. And the influential Banu Nawbakht family played significant roles, both intellectually and practically, within the perplexed Imami community. For instance, the Imami ʿAli b. Muhammad al-Furat held the office of vizier three times under the caliph al-Muqtadir, while in 325/937 al-Husayn b. ʿAli al-Nawbakhti served as vizier to the caliph al-Radi. Thus, the Imamis and their leadership hierarchy were able to count on the support of influential patrons in Baghdad, even within the inner circles of the Abbasid court.

Nawbakht, the ancestor of the extended Persian family of Banu Nawbakht, had been the court astrologer of the second Abbasid caliph, al-Mansur. In the 4th/10th century, several Nawbakhtis served as state secretaries (*kuttab*) in the central administration of the Abbasids in Baghdad. The Nawbakhtis played a key role in the political legitimisation of Imami Shiʿism as well. At the beginning of the 4th/10th century, the Banu Nawbakht also seem to have been closely linked to the policies of Ibn al-Furat, the Imami vizier to the Abbasids. Abu Sahl Ismaʿil b. ʿAli al-Nawbakhti (d. 311/923), head of the Banu Nawbakht and a prominent official, was in fact the leader of the Imami community of Baghdad. He played a significant part in making the occultation (*ghayba*) of the imam an integral feature of the doctrine of the imamate, arguing that the imam's occultation does not obviate the divine guidance of mankind. It may be added here that Abu Sahl Ismaʿil al-Nawbakhti and his nephew al-Hasan b. Musa al-Nawbakhti, the author of the famous Imami heresiography, were accomplished theologians, and were, in fact, the founders of the first school of thought amalgamating selectively Muʿtazili theology with Imami doctrine.[11]

The Nawbakhtis had close relations with the hidden imam's second chief representative, Muhammad b. ʿUthman al-ʿAmri, whose authority was endorsed by them. And when Muhammad b. ʿUthman died in 305/917, a Nawbakhti, namely Abu'l-Qasim al-Husayn b. Ruh al-Nawbakhti (d. 326/938), succeeded him as the head of the community's central administration; he was later counted as the third representative.

He was, in fact, now considered as the sole intermediary, *safir* or *wakil*, of the hidden imam, and once again communications with the hidden imam were resumed after a lapse of some twenty-five years. The Nawbakhti circles of Baghdad may indeed have been responsible for shaping and formalising the doctrine that allowed for the representation of the hidden imam by a single person. According to this Imami tradition, which has been maintained down to present times, the hidden imam communicated with his following for a period through four intermediaries who succeeded one another without interruption from the time of the imam's occultation.

The fortunes of the Imamis in Baghdad were somewhat reversed with the downfall and execution of the Shiʿi vizier Ibn al-Furat in 312/924. Having lost his patron, the third Imami intermediary, Ibn Ruh al-Nawbakhti, spent a considerable time in prison. Later, he appointed a certain Abu'l-Husayn ʿAli b. Muhammad al-Samarri as his successor; he would be the fourth and the last intermediary (*safir*), holding office for only three years. A few days before his death in 329/941, al-Samarri reportedly produced a decree from the hidden imam announcing that his complete (*tamma*) occultation had now commenced. With this declaration, the institution of the *sifara*, or representation of the hidden imam through intermediaries, also came to an end. Al-Samarri is thus regarded by the Imami Shiʿis as the last person who corresponded with their hidden imam. The period of some sixty-seven years from the death of Imam al-ʿAskari in 260/874 until the death of the hidden imam's fourth chief emissary in 329/941 was later designated as the 'lesser occultation'. By then, the hidden imam was clearly considered as the Mahdi or *qaʾim*, the seal of the imamate for the Imami Shiʿis who had now also fixed the number of their imams at twelve.

Table 3.1 Imams of the Twelver Shiʿis

1. ʿAli b. Abi Talib (d. 40/661)
2. al-Hasan b. ʿAli (d. 49/669)
3. al-Husayn b. ʿAli (d. 61/680)
4. ʿAli b. al-Husayn Zayn al-ʿAbidin (d. ca. 95/714)
5. Muhammad b. ʿAli al-Baqir (d. ca. 114/732)
6. Jaʿfar b. Muhammad al-Sadiq (d. 148/765)
7. Musa b. Jaʿfar al-Kazim (d. 183/799)

8. ʿAli b. Musa al-Rida (d. 203/818)
9. Muhammad b. ʿAli al-Jawad, al-Taqi (d. 220/835)
10. ʿAli b. Muhammad al-Hadi, al-Naqi (d. 254/868)
11. al-Hasan b. ʿAli al-ʿAskari (d. 260/874)
12. Muhammad b. al-Hasan al-Mahdi (in occultation)

In sum, according to the Twelver Shiʿi tradition, the occultation of Muhammad b. al-Hasan al-Mahdi fell into two phases. During the initial 'lesser occultation' (*al-ghayba al-sughra*), covering the years 260–329/874–941, the Imam-Mahdi remained in regular communication with his community through four successive chief representatives, who intermediated between him and his followers. But in the 'greater occultation' (*al-ghayba al-kubra*), initiated in 329/941 and still continuing, the hidden Imam-Mahdi has chosen not to have any representative while living on earth and participating in worldly experience. The Imam-Mahdi enjoys a miraculously prolonged life, as explained in a multitude of Twelver theological treatises. And his titles include the 'lord of the age' (*sahib al-zaman*), the 'expected imam' (*al-imam al-muntazar*) and the 'remnant of God' (*baqiyyat Allah*), amongst others.

Since the 4th/10th century, Twelver Shiʿi scholars have written extensively on the eschatological doctrines of occultation (*ghayba*) of their twelfth, hidden Imam-Mahdi and the conditions that would need to prevail before his return (*rajʿa*) or manifestation (*zuhur*). And, according to Shiʿi beliefs, the Imam-Mahdi is expected to reappear in glory before the final Day of Judgement (*qiyama*), to rule the world with justice. By the first half of the 4th/10th century, when the line of the twelve imams had been clearly identified, those Imami Shiʿis believing in that series of imams, with the twelfth one acknowledged as the Mahdi, became designated as the Ithnaʿashariyya or Twelvers, and as such they were distinguished from all earlier or contemporary Imami groups.

From the occultation of the twelfth imam to the Mongol invasions

In the first period of their religious history, stretching from its origins to the occultation of the twelfth imam, the Imami Shiʿis benefited from the direct spiritual guidance and teachings of their imams. It was during the second period of their history, from around 260/874 until the Mongol age, that Twelver scholars (*ʿulama*) emerged as influential guardians and transmitters of the teachings of their imams, compiling collections of Imami *hadith* and formulating Imami law. Initially, however, the doctrines of the twelve imams and the *ghayba* of the twelfth imam had to be formalised and regularised. Indeed, the belief that the twelfth imam had gone into occultation and that he would return as the Mahdi gradually prevailed during the 4th/10th century, overshadowing all earlier Imami teachings including, especially, the doctrines of the earlier Waqifiyya. Through these developments, the very doctrine of the twelve imams, too, came to be crystallised. These doctrinal stances found their earliest statements in the heresiographical literature of the Imami authors al-Nawbakhti and al-Qummi who, in a fundamental sense, treat all Imami sects, other than the one evolving into Twelver Shiʿism, as deviations from the 'orthodox' line of the Husaynid ʿAlid imams acknowledged by their own community.

It should be noted that the 4th/10th century witnessed the rise to power of the Buyids, or Buwayhids, in Persia and Iraq, as overlords of the Abbasids. The Buyids hailed from the mountainous region of Daylam in northern Persia, where they served as commanders in the armies of various local rulers. Daylam remained a stronghold of Zaydi and Ismaili Shiʿism for several centuries. The Buyids themselves originally adhered to the Zaydi branch of Shiʿi Islam. However, after establishing their own dynasty, they supported Muʿtazilism and Shiʿism without strong allegiance to any specific branch, though they may have become more inclined towards the Twelver branch. Under Buyid rule, in 352/963 the Twelvers were able to commemorate for the first time the martyrdom of Imam al-Husayn at Karbala. The Buyids paid particular attention to reconstructing or repairing the shrines of the Twelver imams in Iraq, also endowing them with donations. The social prestige of the extended ʿAlid families, who were now treated as aristocracy (*ashraf*), was clearly enhanced under the Buyids; and in large towns, especially Baghdad, the ʿAlids had their own doyen, known as *naqib*, who enjoyed much social and political influence in the locality. However, the Shiʿi Buyids retained the Abbasid caliphs who continued to function as spiritual spokesmen of Sunni Islam. Be that as it may, under the Buyids, Shiʿi scholars, including especially Twelver scholars who lived in Iraq and Persia, enjoyed an unprecedented degree of freedom. They could write and express their views without fear of persecution and the necessity of observing *taqiyya*.

The earliest comprehensive collections of the sayings and teachings of the Twelver imams, which were first transmitted in Kufa and elsewhere, were in fact compiled according to the subject matters of these traditions in Qumm, in Persia. By the end of the 2nd/8th century, Qumm, like Kufa, was already a stronghold of Imami Shiʿism, while in Kufa the Shiʿa were divided into many rival factions, including especially the Zaydis. By contrast, in Qumm the Shiʿi Muslims were united in their allegiance to the Imami line of imams that evolved into the Twelver series of imams. And by the 3rd/9th century, Qumm had served for more than a century as a chief centre for Imami Shiʿi learning. It was thus in Qumm that the traditions of the Imami imams were first collected and catalogued systematically. The earliest and the most authoritative of the compendia of the Imami *hadith*, still in use today, was the *al-Kafi fi ʿilm al-din* (The One who is Competent in Religious Science), compiled by Muhammad b. Yaʿqub al-Kulayni (d. 329/940). Al-Kulayni was born in Kulayn, between Rayy and Qumm, and it was in the latter city that he heard most of the *hadith*s from various Imami transmitters. Al-Kulayni's book, in eight volumes, also came to be recognised as the first of the four canonical collections of *hadith*, known as *al-kutub al-arbaʿa*, which deal with Imami theology and jurisprudence. All these, and subsequent works, have been written in Arabic, the language of scholarship amongst Muslims, though an increasing number of Twelver Imami authors hailed from various towns in Persia.

The most accomplished Imami author of the 4th/10th century also hailed from Qumm. He was Ibn Babawayh, also known as al-Shaykh al-Saduq (d. 381/991), who travelled extensively to collect traditions, *hadith* or *akhbar* (singular, *khabar*). Indeed, the traditionist school of Qumm, which rejected all forms of *kalam* theology based on extensive use of reason (*ʿaql*) and instead relied on the traditions of the Prophet and the imams, reached its peak in the works of Ibn Babawayh. He produced the second major compilation of Imami *hadith*, entitled *Man la yahduruhu'l-faqih* (He who has no Jurist in his Proximity). After al-Kulayni's *al-Kafi*, this is considered the second of the 'four books' of the Imami *hadith* collections. Ibn Babawayh was strongly opposed to the Muʿtazila and their *kalam* theology; and he elaborated his own Imami doctrine on the basis of *hadith*, with a minimum use of reasoning.[12] Ibn Babawayh spent the last decade of his life in Rayy, the Buyid capital, as the guest of the local Buyid ruler Rukn al-Dawla (r. 366–387/977–997). He also produced seminal works on the doctrine of the twelve imams, and on the *ghayba* of the hidden twelfth imam.

Meanwhile, in the course of the 4th/10th century, the traditionist school of Qumm began to be overshadowed by the rise of a rival school, the school of Imami theology (*kalam*) of Baghdad, which adhered to the rationalist theology of the Muʿtazila and also produced the principles of Imami jurisprudence (*usul al-fiqh*).[13] In contrast to the school of Qumm's emphasis on *hadith*, the Imami school of Baghdad rejected unqualified adherence to traditions and assigned a fundamental role to reason (*ʿaql*) in theology and jurisprudence. It may be recalled here that, earlier, several members of the influential Imami family of the Banu Nawbakht in Baghdad, such as Abu Sahl Ismaʿil, had already pioneered the amalgamation of Muʿtazili theology with Imami doctrine.

The first leader of the 'rationalist' Imami school of Baghdad was Muhammad b. Muhammad al-Harithi, better known as al-Shaykh al-Mufid (d. 413/1022), who criticised the creed of Ibn Babawayh, his own teacher. In particular, he criticised Ibn Babawayh's emphasis on *hadith* and his rejection of reasoning. In contrast, al-Mufid argued for the methodology of *kalam*, religious disputation or reasoned argumentation; a methodology developed by the Muʿtazili theological school in Basra and Baghdad. Thus, al-Mufid considered himself as a *mutakallim*, an exponent of *kalam*. In addition to this methodology, al-Mufid adopted a number of doctrines from the Muʿtazila, espousing their acceptance of human free will and their denial of predestination, and also rejecting anthropomorphism (*tashbih*). On the other hand, the adherents of the Baghdad school rejected those Muʿtazili doctrines that were in conflict with the basic Imami doctrine of the imamate. Thus, refuting the Muʿtazili dogma of the unconditional punishment of the Muslim sinner, they allowed for the intercession (*shafaʿa*) of the imams for the sinners of their community to save them from punishment, also condemning the adversaries of the imams as infidels and maintaining that the imamate too, like prophecy, was a rational necessity.

Shaykh al-Mufid was succeeded as chief authority of the Baghdad school and head of the Imami community by his student Sharif al-Murtada ʿAlam al-Huda (d. 436/1044). Sharif al-Murtada and his younger brother Sharif al-Radi (d. 406/1015) were Musawi Sayyids, descendants of Imam Musa al-Kazim. After their father, Abu Ahmad al-Tahir al-Musawi, Sharif al-Radi and Sharif al-Murtada held the office of *naqib* successively in Buyid Baghdad. The two brothers were also highly esteemed at the Abbasid court. Sharif al-Radi is responsible for having compiled the *Nahj al-balagha* (The Way of Eloquence), an anthology of letters and sermons attributed to Imam ʿAli b. Abi Talib which, after the Qur'an and Prophetic traditions, is regarded by Twelver Shiʿis as their most venerated sacred book. Other Shiʿi communities also hold this book in high esteem.

Sharif al-Murtada had also studied with several Muʿtazili scholars, including Qadi ʿAbd al-Jabbar (d. 415/1024) of Rayy, and he went further than al-Mufid in his support of *kalam* theology. He insisted, like the Muʿtazila, that the basic truths of religion could be established by reason (*ʿaql*) alone. Even transmitted *hadith*s were to be subjected to the test of reason rather than being accepted uncritically. He rejected totally the validity of the *akhbar al-ahad*, traditions based on a single transmitter, as a source for the law. Sharif al-Murtada attempted to found the law mainly on the principle of consensus (*ijmaʿ*) of the Imami community, including the opinions of the imams. However, al-Murtada's legal doctrines found few later supporters, while his theological views, based on the more radical Basran school of Muʿtazilism as compared with the Baghdad Muʿtazilism expounded by al-Mufid, prevailed until the Mongol conquests of the 7th/13th century. It should be noted, however, that the independent legal judgements, or *ijtihad*, of scholars that were to become an increasingly important practice in later Twelver Shiʿism, had not yet become prevalent in Imami circles of this period.

Muhammad b. al-Hasan al-Tusi, known as Shaykh al-Ta'ifa (d. 460/1067), was another prominent member of the Baghdad school. Born in 385/995 in Tus, Khurasan, in 408/1017 he went to Baghdad where he studied with both al-Mufid and Sharif al-Murtada. Al-Tusi's two main works, *al-Istibsar*, on considering the disputed traditions, and *Tahdhib al-ahkam*, on the appeal of decisions, are counted among the 'four books' of the Twelvers' *hadith* collections. In these and other works, al-Tusi concerned himself with separating reliable from false traditions which could then serve as the basis of the law; indeed, he became the most authoritative early systematiser of what was to become the Twelver law. Through his scholarship, Shaykh al-Tusi also partially rehabilitated the traditionist Imami school of Qumm and its reliance on *hadith* or *akhbar*. He argued that although many of the traditions of the Imami traditionists were of the *ahad*, or singly transmitted, category and therefore not acceptable on rational grounds, they were nevertheless to be sanctioned for having been universally used by the Imami community in the presence of the imams themselves. Consequently, the *hadith*s reported from the imams, while not serving as ultimate authority as held by the school of Qumm, were to be used as primary source material in Shiʿi law.

It was also during the Buyid period that the earliest Imami bio-bibliographical works, listing trustworthy authorities and transmitters of *hadith*, were compiled by al-Tusi himself as well as others such as al-Najashi (d. 450/1058). Meanwhile, the Imami authors, including al-Tusi, still found it necessary to defend the doctrine of the *ghayba* of the twelfth imam in dedicated treatises; they also considered the nature of the relationship between the Imami faithful and the unjust rulers and states, since all rulers before the advent of the Mahdi were theoretically deemed unjust. In particular, the Imami scholars considered which of the prerogatives of the hidden twelfth imam should be observed in the community in his absence.[14]

The school of Qumm itself disintegrated in the 5th/11th century, and its traditionist focus remained somewhat dormant in Twelver Shiʿi thought until it was restated vigorously by Muhammad Amin b. Muhammad al-Astarabadi (d. 1033/1624), the founder of the so-called Akhbari school in the 11th/17th century. In the meantime, the main centre of Twelver Shiʿi scholarship in Iraq had effectively moved from Baghdad to Najaf, where the shrine of Imam ʿAli b. Abi Talib was located, when Shaykh al-Taʾifa Muhammad b. al-Hasan al-Tusi had settled there in 448/1056 after being subjected to persecution in the Abbasid capital. At the same time, Sharif al-Murtada's basic approach to *kalam* theology, holding that reason alone was the sole source of the fundamentals of religion, had become widely accepted in Twelver circles. The same approach was, indeed, adopted without significant revisions more than two centuries later by the then chief exponent of Twelver Imami *kalam*, namely, Nasir al-Din al-Tusi.

Meanwhile, the Saljuq Turks had succeeded in laying the foundations of a powerful new empire in central Islamic lands. As a family of chieftains, the Saljuqs had led the Oghuz (Arabic, Ghuzz) Turks westwards from Khwarazm and Transoxania in Central Asia. The Saljuq leader Tughril I defeated the Ghaznawids, another Turkish dynasty ruling over the Iranian lands, and proclaimed himself sultan at Nishapur in 429/1038. Soon, Tughril conquered the greater part of Persia and then crossed into Iraq. The Saljuqs regarded themselves as the new champions of Sunni Islam, which gave them a suitable pretext for wanting to liberate the Abbasids from the tutelage of the Shiʿi Buyids, and also to rid the Muslim world of the Shiʿi Fatimids. At any rate, Tughril entered Baghdad in 447/1055 and deposed al-Malik al-Rahim Khusraw Firuz, the last member of the Buyid dynasty of Iraq. The Abbasid caliph al-Qa'im (r. 422–467/1031–1075) confirmed Tughril's title of sultan. The Sunni Saljuq sultan had now replaced the Shiʿi Buyid king as the overlord of the Abbasids. Despite their stated aims, however, the Saljuqs did not succeed in defeating the Fatimids, nor did they manage to dislodge the Nizari Ismailis of Persia from their mountain strongholds. But the ardently Sunni Saljuqs did make life very difficult for various Shiʿi communities existing throughout their empire which soon stretched from Central Asia to Syria and Anatolia. Already in Tughril's time, his vizier al-Kunduri had all the Shiʿis cursed regularly from the pulpits throughout the Iranian lands. But later the Saljuqs targeted their hostility more towards the Ismaili rather than Twelver Shiʿis.

Twelver Shiʿi communities had, meanwhile, appeared in many parts of the Iranian lands, not only in Qumm and Rayy, but also in different towns of Khurasan, such as Nishapur and Tus, and in Balkh and Samarqand in Transoxania and in central Persia, including Kashan, Isfahan, Sawa, Qazwin and Hamadan, as well as in Khuzistan in south-western Persia. Minority Twelver communities also existed in the coastal region of northern Persia, particularly in Tabaristan (modern-day Mazandaran) and Gurgan. Most towns of any size had their own local ʿAlid spokesperson who controlled the ʿAlid genealogies of the area as well as the donations of pious Shiʿis to shrines of the sayyids and descendants of the imams. The tombs of these sayyids were widely scattered in Persia demonstrating that Twelver Shiʿism was well established throughout much of the Iranian world before the Mongol invasions. However, Twelver communities predominated only in a few minor towns with the exception of Qumm; and, generally, they constituted a small minority next to their Sunni neighbours.

Outside Persia, too, Shiʿism received a serious blow when the Saljuqs, adhering to the Hanafi school of Sunni jurisprudence, succeeded the Shiʿi Buyids. But the situation of the Shiʿa improved when the Mongols established their rule over south-western Asia. By then, a number of local dynasties in Iraq and Syria adhered to Twelver Shiʿism, or had Shiʿi sympathies, and patronised the efforts of their *ʿulama*. Amongst such Twelver dynasties, mention may be made of the Hamdanids and ʿUqaylids of Iraq, the Hamdanids and Mirdasids of Syria with their capital at Aleppo, and the Banu ʿAmmar of Tripoli. It should be noted that with the collapse of the Qarmati state of Bahrayn in 470/1078, a number of Twelver communities also began to gain influence in eastern Arabia as well as other localities around the Persian Gulf. Foremost among these local Twelver dynasties, however, were the Mazyadids who had their capital at Hilla on the banks of the Euphrates. Indeed, from 495/1101 Hilla was established as an important centre of Shiʿi activity, and later it even superseded Qumm and Baghdad as the main stronghold of Twelver Imami scholarship.

From Nasir al-Din al-Tusi to the advent of the Safawids

By the end of the 6th/12th century, important political changes had taken place in Persia and the eastern lands of Islam. The Saljuq sultanate had been distintegrating after Sultan Sanjar's death in 552/1157, when a host of more or less independent Turkish amirs had found it possible to rule over various principalities. At the same time, a new power with great political ambitions, based in Khwarazm in Central Asia, had appeared on the political scene of the East. The hereditary rulers of Khwarazm, who had acted as vassals of the Saljuqs, adopted the old title of the kings of the region, calling themselves the Khwarazmshahs. Soon the Khwarazmshahs filled the vacancy created by the demise of the Saljuqs, and they came to have an impressive empire of their own, stretching from the borders of India to Anatolia.

By 616/1219, however, Chingiz Khan, the mighty ruler of the new Mongol empire, was already leading his armies into the lands of Islam. Early in 618/1221, Chingiz Khan crossed the Oxus and seized Balkh. He then sent his youngest son Toluy to complete the conquest of Khurasan, a task accomplished with unprecedented thoroughness.

The Mongols totally destroyed Marw and Nishapur, massacring the populations of both cities. The Khwarazmian empire, too, did not escape the Mongol debacle that was soon to end Abbasid rule as well. In 618/1221, the Mongol hordes of Chingiz Khan decisively defeated Sultan Jalal al-Din, the last of the Khwarazmshahs, who was subsequently murdered in 628/1231. The death of Chingiz Khan in 624/1227 had brought only a brief respite. The Mongols made new efforts, under Chingiz's son and first successor Ögedei, to conquer all of Persia, a task completed in the reign of the Great Khan Möngke. By 656/1258, when Möngke's brother Hülegü entered Baghdad and murdered the last Abbasid caliph al-Mustaʿsim, after having destroyed the Nizari Ismaili state of Persia, the Mongols had indeed completed their conquest of south-western Asia.

It was during this eventful period in Islamic history that Nasir al-Din al-Tusi, one of the most eminent Shiʿi scholars of all time, lived and benefited from the patronage of the Nizari Shiʿis before attaching himself to the court of the Mongol Ilkhanid rulers of Persia and Iraq, a dynasty (654–754/1256–1353) founded by Hülegü himself. Al-Tusi played significant roles in the political events of his time, under both the Ismailis and the Mongols. The chief contemporary exponent of the Twelver Imami *kalam*, Nasir al-Din al-Tusi may be considered to have initiated the next phase of the intellectual history of Twelver Shiʿism. Al-Tusi, and his disciple al-Hasan b. Yusuf Ibn al-Mutahhar al-Hilli, in fact, represented the last school of original thought in Twelver theology. Subsequently, Twelver Shiʿi scholars produced mainly works of the genre of commentary (*sharh*) on, or restatements of, the earlier treatises and teachings.

Khwaja Nasir al-Din Muhammad b. Muhammad al-Tusi was born in 597/1201 into a Twelver Shiʿi family in Tus. In his youth, around 624/1227, he entered the service of Nasir al-Din ʿAbd al-Rahim b. Abi Mansur (d. 655/1257), the Nizari Ismaili *muhtasham*, or leader, in Quhistan, in south-eastern Khurasan. During his long stay in Nizari fortress communities of Quhistan, al-Tusi developed a close friendship with his patron, the *muhtasham* Nasir al-Din, who was a learned man himself. Later, al-Tusi went to the fortress of Alamut in northern Persia and enjoyed directly the munificence of the Nizari imams there until the destruction of the Nizari Ismaili state in 654/1256. Subsequently, al-Tusi became a trusted adviser to Hülegü and accompanied him to Baghdad to witness the demise of the Abbasid caliphate. The Mongol conqueror built a great observatory for al-Tusi at Maragha in Adharbayjan and made him responsible for the management of religious endowments. He also served Abaqa (r. 663–681/1265–1282), Hülegü's son and successor, whilst engaged in his philosophical, scientific and theological enquiries. Having contributed to many fields of learning, al-Tusi died in 672/1274 in Baghdad.

Nasir al-Din al-Tusi's religious affiliation has been the subject of much controversy and speculation. The medieval Twelver *ʿulama*, who considered al-Tusi as one of their co-religionists, persistently denied that he ever embraced Ismaili Shiʿism. Later Twelver writers, including his modern Persian biographers, hold that al-Tusi, observing *taqiyya* as an Imami Shiʿi, was obliged to compose the Ismaili works attributed to him, for fear of his life during his stay at the Nizari strongholds. The facts remain, however, that al-Tusi was born and trained initially as a Twelver Shiʿi, but later spent some three decades in the Ismaili fortress communities of Persia, a most prolific period in his life during which he evidently converted to Ismailism as vividly recounted in his spiritual autobiography,[15] the authenticity of which cannot be doubted. Whilst amongst the Ismailis, al-Tusi wrote his major works on ethics, the *Akhlaq-i Nasiri* with an Ismaili preamble and the *Akhlaq-i muhtashami*, both dedicated to his friend and patron, the *muhtasham* Nasir al-Din, as well as other philosophical treatises such as his commentary on *al-Isharat wa'l-tanbihat* of Ibn Sina (d. 428/1037), known in Europe as Avicenna. After the destruction of the Nizari state by the Mongols, al-Tusi joined the entourage of Hülegü and partook of Mongol patronage.[16] It was at that time that he reverted back to Twelver Shiʿism and produced major works on the Imami theological principles, notably the *Qawaʿid al-ʿaqaʾid* and the *Tajrid al-ʿaqaʾid*, as well as a treatise on the imamate.[17] Indeed, al-Tusi's *Tajrid al-ʿaqaʾid* became the most widely used *kalam* text in Persia and the eastern lands, and received numerous commentaries by Shiʿi and Sunni authors.

Nasir al-Din al-Tusi was also the first Twelver scholar to have been at once a theologian and a philosopher, having been particularly influenced by Ibn Sina's philosophy. While in the service of the Mongols, he wrote a treatise defending Ibn Sina's philosophy against the criticisms of Abu'l-Fath Muhammad al-Shahrastani (d. 548/1153), the

Ashʿari theologian and the author of the well-known heresiography who may have been a crypto-Ismaili.[18] At any rate, al-Tusi incorporated Avicennan and other philosophical concepts into Shiʿi theology, a tradition of philosophical theology fully elaborated later in Persia under the Safawids. In this third period of the development of Twelver Shiʿism, the influence of Khwaja Nasir al-Din al-Tusi in both theology and philosophy was certainly a key factor, while close relations were also developing between Twelver theology and the Sufism of Ibn al-ʿArabi (d. 638/1240).

Like Khwaja Nasir al-Din al-Tusi, his student Ibn al-Mutahhar al-Hilli (d. 726/1325) gained eminence at the court of the Mongol Ilkhanid rulers of Persia. It was under his influence that Öljeitü (r. 703–716/1304–1316), known in Islamic sources as Muhammad Khudabanda, converted to Twelver Shiʿism in 709/1310 and minted coins with the names of the twelve imams. Ibn al-Mutahhar al-Hilli, called ʿAllama, or the 'most learned one', and his uncle Jaʿfar b. al-Hasan al-Hilli (d. 676/1277), known as the Muhaqqiq al-Hilli or al-Muhaqqiq al-Awwal, were two major scholars from Hilla, which superseded Qumm and Baghdad as the stronghold of Twelver Shiʿi learning in the aftermath of the Mongol conquests. These scholars had a significant impact on the direction of Imami law that was to prevail widely. In particular, ʿAllama al-Hilli, a prolific writer and author of numerous legal treatises, had lasting influence on the development and foundations of Twelver jurisprudence. Having argued against the unreliability of *hadith*, and following in the tradition of the Baghdad school, he reorganised jurisprudence so as to make reason (*ʿaql*) its central focus, as well as introducing new principles of legal methodology adapted from Sunni practice. After the work of his uncle, ʿAllama al-Hilli provided a theoretical foundation for *ijtihad*, the principle of legal ruling by the jurist through reasoning (*ʿaql*). He held that the jurist could arrive at valid judgements in religious law using reason and the principles of jurisprudence (*usul al-fiqh*).

In his *Mabadiʾ al-wusul*, ʿAllama al-Hilli expounds the principles of *ijtihad*, exercised by *mujtahid*s who, he argues, are fallible in comparison to infallible imams.[19] The *mujtahid* can, therefore, revise his decision. *Ijtihad*, being fallible, also allowed for *ikhtilaf*, or differences of opinions, among *mujtahid*s. Infallible authority is the prerogative only of the hidden twelfth imam, in whose absence any ruling by a qualified *mujtahid* is nevertheless binding. Al-Hilli's acceptance of *ijtihad* represents a crucial step towards the enhancement of the juristic authority of the *ʿulama* in Twelver Shiʿism in the absence of a manifest imam. However, the *mujtahid* requires special skills and knowledge, including the prevailing consensus (*ijmaʿ*) of the scholars, so that his decisions are not in conflict with it. These ideas provided the basis for the practices of the later Twelver jurists, or *fuqahaʾ*. Within the same juristic context, one can see the antecedents of the concept of *taqlid*, or emulation, namely authorisation by those who are not qualified to use *ijtihad*, accounting for the majority of the community. These emulators, the *muqallid*s, seek the opinions of *mujtahid*s and are obliged to abide by their judgements. These theoretical foundations were to achieve their full practical and political applications in the Islamic Republic of Iran. *Ijtihad* also gained importance within the Zaydi Shiʿi communities, earlier than its adoption by the Twelvers, but it was rejected by the Ismailis. It may be added here that after the 3rd/9th century, the rationalism of *kalam* had been superseded by the *hadith* orientation of the Sunni legal schools of jurisprudence. The non-Muʿtazili works on the principles of jurisprudence mostly allow *ijtihad*, while a major difference between the later Twelver Shiʿi doctrine of *ijtihad* and the Sunni doctrine is that the Twelver Shiʿi *muqallid*s are not allowed to follow the *ijtihad* of the jurists who are no longer alive or of their books.

Meanwhile, since the 7th/13th century Shiʿi tendencies had been spreading, especially in Persia and Central Asia, creating a more favourable milieu in many predominantly Sunni regions for the activities of the Shiʿis (both Twelvers and Ismailis) as well as a number of extremist movements with Shiʿi inclinations. In this connection, particular reference should be made to the Hurufi movement founded by the Shiʿi Sufi Fadl Allah Astarabadi (d. 796/1394), whose doctrines were later adopted by the Bektashi dervishes of Anatolia, and the Nuqtawis who split off from the Hurufiyya under the initial leadership of Mahmud-i Pasikhani (d. 831/1427). Early on, Hurufism spread to Anatolia due to the missionary efforts of ʿAli al-Aʿla (d. 822/1419), one of Fadl Allah's original disciples and the author of several Hurufi works. In fact Anatolia soon became the main stronghold of Hurufism, and the Hurufi doctrines were adopted there by several Sufi orders, especially the Bektashiyya. Subsequently, the Hurufis disappeared in Persia, but their doctrines have continued to be upheld by the Bektashi dervishes of Turkey, who have also preserved the early literature of the group. The Nuqtawiyya, also called Pasikhaniyya, movement became very popular in Persia, and by the time of the early Safawids, it had numerous followers in the Caspian region and in the cities of Qazwin, Kashan, Isfahan and Shiraz in Persia. The Nuqtawis disbanded completely in Persia after the Safawid persecutions, while many of them sought refuge in India. In contrast to Hurufism, which emphasised the secret of the letters of the alphabet (*huruf*), Mahmud-i Pasikhani elaborated a system based on points (singular, *nuqta*).[20] There were also the Twelver-related Mushaʿshaʿ of Khuzistan founded by Ibn Falah (d. ca. 866/1461) who claimed Mahdism. The Mushaʿshaʿ ruled over parts of Iraq, and under their persecutionary policies Hilla lost its prominence as a centre of Twelver learning to Jabal ʿAmil in Lebanon. These movements normally entertained chiliastic or Mahdist aspirations for the deliverance of the oppressed and underprivileged groups.

Instead of propagating any particular form of Shiʿism, however, a new syncretic type of popular Shiʿism was now arising in post-Mongol Central Asia, Persia and Anatolia, which culminated in early Safawid Shiʿism. Marshall Hodgson designated this as '*tariqah* Shiʿism', as it was transmitted mainly through a number of Sufi orders then being formed.[21] The Sufi orders (*tariqa*s) in question remained outwardly Sunni, following one of the Sunni *madhhab*s, while being particularly devoted to ʿAli b. Abi Talib and the *ahl al-bayt*. ʿAli was in fact included in the spiritual chains (*silsila*s) of the masters of these Sunni Sufis. Among the Sufi orders that played a leading role in spreading this type of popular Shiʿism mention should be made of the Nurbakhshiyya and the Niʿmat Allahiyya *tariqa*s. Both orders, as well as the more effective Safawiyya, eventually became fully Shiʿi. In this atmosphere of religious eclecticism, ʿAlid loyalism became more widespread, and Shiʿi elements began to be superficially imposed on Sunni Islam. By the 9th/15th century, the general outlook of predominantly Sunni Persia and elsewhere was increasingly moulded by this type of Sufi-diffused Shiʿi–Sunni syncreticism.[22] Claude Cahen (1909–1991) has referred to this curious process as the 'Shiʿitisation of Sunnism', as opposed to the conscious propagation of Shiʿism of any particular form.[23]

It was under such circumstances that close relations developed between Twelver Shiʿism and Sufism, and, as we shall see, also between Nizari Ismailism and Sufism in Persia. Nasir al-Din al-Tusi himself had already composed a treatise entitled *Awsaf al-ashraf* on the mystical path or *tariqa*. However, the most important Twelver Shiʿi mystic of the 8th/14th century, who developed his own rapport between Twelver Shiʿism and Sufism, was Sayyid Haydar Amuli, the eminent theologian, theosopher and gnostic (*ʿarif*) who died not long after 787/1385.[24] He hailed from the town of Amul in the Caspian region of Tabaristan and served there for sometime as vizier to the local Bawandids, but later emigrated to Baghdad and studied under ʿAllama al-Hilli's son. Influenced by the Sufi teachings of Ibn al-ʿArabi, Sayyid Haydar combined the latter's mystical ideas with his own Shiʿi thought into an original synthesis in his *Jamiʿ al-asrar* and other works. More than anyone else before him, Sayyid Haydar Amuli emphasised the common grounds of Shiʿism and Sufism and prepared the way for the doctrines held by many of the Persian Sufi orders.

According to Haydar Amuli, a Muslim who combines *shariʿa* with *haqiqa* and *tariqa*, the spiritual path followed by the Sufis, is not merely a believer but a believer put to the test (*al-muʾmin al-mumtahan*). Such a Muslim, at once a Sufi and a true Shiʿi, would preserve the balance between the *zahir* and the *batin*, equally avoiding the literalist interpretations of Islam undertaken by jurists (*fuqahaʾ*) as well as the antinomian tendencies of the radical groups such as the Shiʿi *ghulat*.[25] Haydar Amuli's work of integrating Sufism into Twelver Shiʿi thought was continued by others, notably the Twelver scholar Muhammad b. ʿAli al-Ahsaʾi (d. after 904/1499) known as Ibn Abi Jumhur, who hailed from al-Ahsaʾ in Bahrayn and later taught in Najaf and Mashhad. Thus, in his *Kitab al-mujli*, anticipating the contribution of the so-called school of Isfahan, Ibn Abi Jumhur al-Ahsaʾi offers a synthesis of Twelver Imami *kalam*, Avicennan philosophy, the illuminationist (*ishraqi*) thought of al-Suhrawardi (d. 587/1191) and the Sufism of Ibn al-ʿArabi's school.

During this time, Ilkhanid rule, which had been extended to all of Persia, had effectively ended with Abu Saʿid (r. 717–736/1317–1335), the last great member of this Mongol dynasty. Subsequently, until the advent of the Safawids, Persia became increasingly fragmented, with the exception of certain periods during the reign of Timur (d. 807/1405), who reunited the Iranian lands, and that of his son Shahrukh (r. 807–850/1405–1447). During this turbulent period in the history of Persia, in the absence of any strong central authority, different regions were held by local dynasties, including the minor Ilkhanids, the later Timurids, the Jalayirids, and the Qara Qoyunlu and Aq Qoyunlu dynasties, based on federations of Turkoman tribes. The political fragmentation of Persia had doubtless provided more favourable conditions for the activities of various religio-political movements, most of which were essentially Shiʿi or influenced by Shiʿi ideas. The same political atmosphere had been conducive to the rising tide of Shiʿi tendencies and ʿAlid loyalism diffused through Sufi orders in post-Mongol Persia.

From the Safawids to early modern times

A fourth phase may be identified in the historical development of Twelver Shiʿism, from the establishment of the Shiʿi dynasty of the Safawids in Persia in 907/1501 to around 1215/1800. Post-Mongol Persia, as noted, was politically fragmented, while Shiʿi sentiments and ʿAlid loyalism had continued to spread, especially through a number of Sufi orders. Amongst the Sufi orders that played a leading role in spreading Shiʿism in predominantly Sunni Persia, the most direct part was played by the Safawiyya *tariqa*, founded by Shaykh Safi al-Din (d. 735/1334), a Sunni of the Shafiʿi *madhhab*. It was only after the establishment of the Safawid state that the dynasty claimed an ʿAlid genealogy, tracing Shaykh Safi's ancestry to the seventh Twelver imam, Musa al-Kazim.[26] The Safawi order, centred in Ardabil, spread rapidly throughout Adharbayjan, eastern Anatolia and other regions, acquiring strong influence over several Turkoman tribes. With Shaykh Safi's fourth successor, Junayd (d. 864/1460), the order was transformed into a militant revolutionary movement. Shaykh Junayd was also the first Safawi master to display Shiʿi sentiments combined with extremist religious notions of the type held by the earlier Shiʿi *ghulat*. This type of Shiʿi extremism, characterised by chiliastic expectations and even deification of the order's masters, had little in common with the established theological doctrines of Twelver Shiʿism, other than the veneration of the twelve imams.

Shaykh Junayd's policies and political ambitions were maintained by his son and successor Haydar, who lost his life in one of his own military expeditions in 893/1488. Shaykh Haydar was responsible for instructing his Sufi-soldier followers to adopt the scarlet headgear of twelve gores (triangular pieces of cloth) commemorating the twelve imams, for which they became designated as the Qizilbash, a Turkish term meaning 'red-head'. Haydar's son and successor, Sultan ʿAli, also fell in battle, in 898/1493. By that time, the Safawi order enjoyed a strong military organisation, supported by a multitude of local adherents and powerful Turkoman tribes, who constituted the backbone of the Qizilbash soldiery.

The extremist characteristics of the Shiʿism of the Qizilbash Turkomans, who had very little understanding of the Shiʿism of any particular branch, were more clearly manifested when Ismaʿil, Sultan ʿAli's youthful brother, became the master of the Safawi order. Ismaʿil presented himself to his Qizilbash Turkoman followers as the representative of the hidden imam, or even of the awaited Mahdi himself, also claiming divinity. Ismaʿil's extant poetry is permeated with such ideas.[27] With the help of his Qizilbash forces, Ismaʿil speedily seized Adharbayjan from the Aq Qoyunlu dynasty and entered their capital, Tabriz, in the summer of 907/1501. He now proclaimed himself *shah* or king and at the same time declared Twelver Shiʿism the official religion of his newly founded Safawid state, inaugurating a new era for Shiʿi Islam and the activities of Shiʿi scholars. Shah Ismaʿil brought all of Persia under his control during the ensuing decade and his dynasty, under which Persia became a 'national' state for the first time since the Arab conquests, ruled effectively until 1135/1722.

The Safawids originally adhered to an extremist, eclectic type of Shiʿism which was gradually disciplined and brought into conformity with the 'mainstream' Twelver Shiʿism. In order to justify their legitimacy in a predominantly Sunni environment, Shah Ismaʿil (r. 907–930/1501–1524) and his immediate successors claimed variously to represent the hidden Mahdi, in addition to fabricating an ʿAlid genealogy for their dynasty, tracing their ancestry to Imam Musa al-Kazim. Shiʿism was imposed over Persia and the subjects of the Safawid realm, in fact, rather gradually. From early on, the Safawids also strove to eliminate any major religio-political challenge to their supremacy. As a result, under Shah Ismaʿil and his son and successor Shah Tahmasp I (r. 930–984/1524–1576), who was deified by the Qizilbash, the Safawids adopted a religious policy for the elimination of all millenarian and extremist movements, for the persecution of Sufi orders and popular dervish groups and for the suppression of Sunnism, while actively propagating Twelver Shiʿism, or what in due course would widely correspond to 'mainstream' Twelver Shiʿism. The repressive policies of the Safawids were directed even against the Qizilbash Turkomans who had brought their dynasty into power.

As Persia still did not have an established class of Twelver religious scholars, however, the Safawids were obliged for quite some time to invite theologians and jurists from the Arab centres of Twelver scholarship, notably Najaf, Bahrayn and Jabal ʿAmil in southern Lebanon, to instruct their subjects. It should be noted that Shiʿism had permeated Jabal ʿAmil since the early Islamic centuries. Foremost among these Arab Twelver *ʿulama* was Shaykh ʿAli al-Karaki al-ʿAmili (d. 940/1534), known as the Muhaqqiq al-Thani, who hailed from the Biqaʿ valley in Jabal ʿAmil. He adhered to the Hilla school of Imami *kalam* theology with its recognition of *ijtihad* and *taqlid*, which prevailed in southern Lebanon and were subsequently propagated in Persia.

Shaykh al-Karaki was recognised by Shah Tahmasp I as the 'seal of the *mujtahids*' (*khatam al-mujtahidin*), and even as the 'deputy of the imam' (*na'ib al-imam*), with full authority to oversee the promulgation of Twelver Shiʿism in his realm. Indeed, al-Karaki himself elaborated the notion of the 'general deputyship' of the imam during his occultation. Under this notion, the Twelver jurists could consider themselves empowered by the hidden imam and thus could transfer some of the functions of the imam to themselves, such as holding the Friday congregational prayer. Shaykh al-Karaki also ruled emphatically against the permissibility of following a dead *mujtahid*, as practised in Sunni Islam. With these developments, Imami hierocracy was firmly established during the *ghayba* of the hidden twelfth imam. Al-Karaki also defended the early Safawid practice of cursing the early caliphs Abu Bakr and ʿUmar. Most of al-Karaki's religious views were upheld by later Twelver scholars, and some of al-Karaki's commentaries on earlier legal texts became popular books for religious instruction. Sunni anti-Safawid polemicists targeted al-Karaki particularly among Twelver scholars, accusing him of being a Druze or having fabricated a new religion.[28]

Meanwhile, the important office of *sadr*, responsible for the management of religious endowments and coordination of the propagation of

Shiʿi Islam throughout the Safawid realm, was created. The first holder of this office was Qadi Shams al-Din Lahiji. In time, major cities of the Safawid state, such as Isfahan, Tabriz and Mashhad, also came to possess a chief religious authority known as the *shaykh al-Islam*, as well as prayer leaders (singular, *pishnamaz*), in their mosques. At the same time, the Safawids encouraged the systematic training of a class of Imami legal scholars (*fuqahaʾ*), who would disseminate the established doctrines of Twelver Shiʿism and check the extremist ideas still circulating in the Safawid realm, including the Safawids' own brand of millenarian Shiʿism.

By the time of Shah ʿAbbas I (r. 995–1038/1587–1629), the greatest member of the dynasty, who established his flourishing capital at Isfahan in 1006/1598, the Safawids' claims to any divine authority or to representing the Mahdi during his *ghayba* were rapidly fading, while the Qizilbash had lost their influence and the Sufi orders had disappeared almost completely in Persia. The few surviving Sufi orders dwindled to local significance, while the Niʿmat Allahiyya transferred their activities to India; the words *sufi* and *mulhid*, or heretic, had by then become synonymous. On the other hand, Twelver Shiʿi rituals and practices, such as regular visiting (*ziyara*) of the shrines of the imams and their relatives in the *ʿatabat*, namely Najaf, Karbala and other shrine cities of Iraq, as well as in Mashhad and Qumm in Persia, had gained wide currency. Shah ʿAbbas I's long rule represented the golden age of the Safawid dynasty when sciences and learning as well as artistic activities were flourishing under their patronage. The training of the Twelver scholars was now further facilitated through the foundation of several religious colleges (*madrasa*s) in Isfahan, where a growing number of eminent Imami *ʿulama*, such as Mulla ʿAbd Allah al-Shushtari (d. 1021/1612), held teaching sessions. Indeed, by the closing decades of the 11th/17th century, an influential class of Twelver religious scholars had appeared in the Safawid state.

The Safawid period witnessed a renaissance of Islamic sciences and Shiʿi scholarship. Foremost among the intellectual achievements of the period are the original contributions of a number of Twelver Shiʿi scholars belonging to the so-called 'school of Isfahan', studied extensively in modern times by H. Corbin and S. H. Nasr.[29] These Shiʿi scholars, who were at once theologians and philosophers, integrated in an original fashion a number of philosophical, theological and gnostic traditions within a Shiʿi perspective in a metaphysical synthesis known as *al-hikma al-ilahiyya* (Persian, *hikmat-i ilahi*), divine wisdom or theosophy. The founder of the 'school of Isfahan' was Sayyid Mir Muhammad Baqir Astarabadi (d. 1040/1630), better known as Mir Damad because his father was the son-in-law (Persian, *damad*) of the influential Shaykh al-Karaki. A Twelver theologian, philosopher and poet, Mir Damad was also the *shaykh al-Islam* of Isfahan, the Safawid capital. He produced his own complex metaphysical system of thought, drawing on peripatetic (*mashaʾi*) philosophy reflecting an amalgamation of Aristotelian and Neoplatonic philosophies with Islamic tenets as worked out by al-Farabi and Ibn Sina (known as Avicenna in medieval Europe); the illuminationist or *ishraqi* tradition of Shihab al-Din Yahya al-Suhrawardi; and the gnostic-mystical teachings of Ibn al-ʿArabi. And all these traditions were now harmonised by Mir Damad with Twelver Shiʿi doctrines.

The most important representative of the 'school of Isfahan' and the leading theosopher of the Safawid period was, however, Mir Damad's principal student Sadr al-Din Muhammad Shirazi (d. 1050/1640), better known as Mulla Sadra. Like his teacher, Mulla Sadra was influenced by the teachings of Ibn Sina, al-Suhrawardi and Ibn al-ʿArabi as well as being deeply grounded in the study of the Qurʾan, *hadith* and Twelver Imami tenets. Mulla Sadra also studied with Shaykh Bahaʾ al-Din al-ʿAmili (d. 1030/1621), known as Shaykh Bahaʾi, a polymath and another key early figure in the 'school of Isfahan' of theosophical Shiʿism.

Mulla Sadra produced his own synthesis of four major schools of Islamic thought, namely, *kalam* theology, peripatetic philosophy, the illuminationist philosophy of al-Suhrawardi and gnostic traditions (*ʿirfan*) – particularly the Sufism of Ibn al-ʿArabi. He reformulated aspects of these traditions within an esoteric Shiʿi frame and called the resulting synthesis *al-hikma al-mutaʿaliya*, transcendent wisdom or theosophy. In this syncretic system, expounded in his *al-Asfar al-arbaʿa* (The Four Journeys), Mulla Sadra attempted to harmonise three paths available to man in his quest for the truth, namely, divine revelation (*wahy*), rational demonstration (*ʿaql*) and mystical unveiling (*kashf*). Similary to the intellectual tradition of 'philosophical Ismailism' elaborated by the Ismaili *daʿis* of the Iranian lands during the Fatimid period, the members of the 'school of Isfahan', too, developed an original intellectual perspective in philosophical Shiʿism.

Mulla Sadra trained eminent students in Shiraz, Isfahan and Qumm, such as ʿAbd al-Razzaq Lahiji (d. 1072/1661) and Mulla Muhsin Fayd Kashani (d. 1091/1680). Subsequently, these and others, as well as their own generation of students, in both Persia and India passed down the traditions of the 'school of Isfahan', in which theology per se no longer occupied a predominant position in relation to other intellectual traditions. Meanwhile, by the end of the 11th/17th century, the theosophers adhering to the 'school of Isfahan' had been subjected to persecution instigated by the Twelver jurists who had acquired increasing influence in the Safawid court. Qadi Saʿid al-Qummi (d. 1103/1691), for instance, was imprisoned for a while at Alamut, the former seat of the Nizari Ismaili state, which had survived as a prison under the Safawids.

The Twelver *ʿulama*, especially the jurists (*fuqaha'*) amongst them, played an increasingly powerful religio-political role in the affairs of the Safawid state. This trend reached its climax under the later Safawids, whose own authority was in rapid decline, with Muhammad Baqir al-Majlisi (d. 1111/1699), who held the highest clerical offices and consolidated the influence of the Twelver hierocracy. As the *shaykh al-Islam* of Isfahan, al-Majlisi led the coronation ceremonies of the last Safawid monarch Shah Sultan Husayn I (r. 1105–1135/1694–1722), and was allowed to initiate a campaign of persecution against Sufis and philosophers, including the contemporary members of the 'school of Isfahan' – a desideratum sought by many Twelver jurists. In particular, the Sufis and popular dervish orders were severely persecuted. The excessive influence of the *ʿulama* over the last Safawid ruler, in fact, won him the epithet of 'Mulla Husayn'. Al-Majlisi also compiled the most comprehensive corpus of Imami *hadith*s, the *Bihar al-anwar* (Seas of Lights). In 1124/1712, Shah Sultan Husayn created the office of *mulla-bashi*, supreme leader of the Twelver hierocracy, and entrusted it to Mulla Muhammad Baqir Khatunabadi.[30]

However, the Shiʿi *ʿulama*, who had continued to disagree amongst themselves on certain theological and juristic issues, now became more sharply divided into two opposing camps, generally designated as Usuli and Akhbari, reflecting their positions on the role of reason versus traditions (*hadith* or *akhbar*) in religious matters. As noted, from early on, opposing traditionist and rationalist currents had existed within Twelver Shiʿism, as expressed by the schools of Qumm and Baghdad. The traditionist Akhbari school of Qumm, supported by the *hadith* collections of al-Kulayni and Ibn Babawayh, lost its early prominence to the rationalist Usuli school of Baghdad, which was put on a firm basis during the Buyid period by its three key figures, namely, Shaykh al-Mufid, Sharif al-Murtada and Shaykh al-Ta'ifa al-Tusi; they adopted Mu'tazili theological principles in their fundamentals of jurisprudence (*usul al-fiqh*). The Usulis, thus, permitted speculative reasoning in the principles (*usul*) of theology and law, as compared with the Akhbaris who relied primarily on the traditions (*akhbar*) of the imams. Later, the Usuli faction adopted the principles of *ijtihad* and *taqlid* as systematised by the Hilla school. However, by the early 11th/17th century, Mulla Muhammad Amin al-Astarabadi (d. 1033/1624) had articulated the Akhbari position afresh in his *al-Fawa'id al-madaniyya*, and effectively became the founder of the revived Akhbari school that sought to re-establish Shi'i jurisprudence on the basis of traditions (*akhbar*) rather than the rationalistic principles (*usul*) of jurisprudence used in *ijtihad* and *taqlid*. Al-Astarabadi criticised what he regarded as the innovations of the three Imami scholars of the Buyid age mentioned above, and attacked even more vehemently 'Allama al-Hilli and the principles of jurisprudence used in *ijtihad*. Indeed, al-Astarabadi attacked the very idea of *ijtihad* and branded the Usuli *mujtahids* as enemies of religion. His basic argument against the Usulis was that the *akhbar* of the imams take precedence over the apparent, literal meaning of the Qur'an, the Prophetic traditions and reason, because the imams are the divinely appointed interpreters of these sources.[31]

The Akhbari school flourished in Persia and the shrine cities of Iraq for almost two centuries, until the second half of the 12th/18th century. The Akhbari teachings of al-Astarabadi were adopted by many eminent Twelver scholars such as Muhammad Taqi al-Majlisi (d. 1070/1660) and Mulla Muhsin Fayd Kashani (d. 1091/1680), who were both representatives of gnostic Shi'ism with interests in Sufism and philosophy. The influential Lebanese al-Hurr al-'Amili (d. 1104/1693), who collected a vast compendium of 'reliable' *akhbar* attributed to the imams and which are not found in the 'four books' of Imami *hadith*, was another upholder of Akhbari traditionalism. With al-Hurr al-'Amili, the Akhbari school also gained popularity among the Arab Shi'i *'ulama*, especially in Bahrayn. The Akhbari doctrine and al-Astarabadi's criticism of the Usuli *mujtahids* were variously retained and propagated by other Twelver scholars in Persia, Iraq, Lebanon and Bahrayn, such as ʿAbd Allah al-Samahiji al-Bahrani (d. 1135/1723) and Yusuf b. Ahmad al-Bahrani (d. 1186/1773).

Meanwhile, Persia had gone through an interregnum marked by several decades of political instability and dynastic changes with a variety of implications for Shiʿism.[32] The Sunni Afghans invaded Persia in 1135/1722 effectively ending Safawid rule, though minor Safawids held on to certain regions for a while longer. On the demise of the Safawids, Iranian Shiʿism lost the protection of the dynasty that had accorded it unchallenged supremacy in the state. In the chaotic circumstances that ensued from these events, Nadir Shah eventually succeeded in establishing his own Afsharid dynasty with their capital at Mashhad. Under Nadir Shah (r. 1148–1160/1736–1747), Twelver Shiʿism received a more serious setback since he adhered to Sunni Islam and at best was willing to recognise Twelver Shiʿism, or its Jaʿfari school of jurisprudence, only as a *madhhab* equal to the four Sunni schools of jurisprudence. After Nadir Shah, Persia was ruled mainly by the short-lived Zand dynasty (1164–1209/1751–1794) founded by Karim Khan Zand, who once again accorded Twelver Shiʿism high esteem in his realm. The Zands were, in turn, uprooted by the Qajars, belonging to a Turkoman tribe that was destined to rule over Persia until 1344/1925. Qajar rule was firmly established by Agha Muhammad Khan (r. 1193–1212/1779–1797), who adhered to Twelver Shiʿism. By that time, the Twelver *ʿulama* had become rather independent of any dynastic or state support and could often seek refuge in the *ʿatabat*, the shrine cities of Iraq, then under the control of the Sunni Ottomans, who generally left these sanctuaries unharmed. It was under such turbulent and unstable political circumstances that the Akhbari school of Twelver jurisprudence enjoyed a final brief revival in Persia, Iraq and certain other Arab lands.

In the second half of the 12th/18th century, when Twelver Shiʿism had become quite widespread in Persia, the Usuli doctrine found a new champion in Muhammad Baqir al-Bihbahani (d. 1208/1793), an Isfahani who remained in Karbala after completing his religious studies. In his *al-Ijtihad wa'l-akhbar* and other works, al-Bihbahani defended *ijtihad* and restated the Usuli doctrine. He successfully led the fight against the Akhbaris in Iraq and Persia, denouncing them even as 'infidels'. In a sense, al-Bihbahani may be considered as the reviver of the Usuli school which was to predominate henceforth in Twelver Shiʿism. Thereafter, the Akhbaris rapidly lost their position, with a minor exception in Persia, to the Usulis who now emerged as the prevailing school of jurisprudence in Twelver Shiʿism. This led to an unprecedented strengthening in the authority of the Twelver *ʿulama* under the Qajar monarchs of Persia and in modern times, also placing *ijtihad* and *taqlid* at the very centre of Twelver juristic structure. The Akhbari position was revived only for a brief time under the second Qajar monarch, Fath ʿAli Shah (r. 1212–1250/1797–1834), by Mirza Muhammad Amin al-Akhbari, the last prominent representative of the Akhbari school who was eventually exiled to Iraq and was murdered there by an Usuli mob in 1233/1818. At present, the only known minority Akhbari Twelver communities are situated in Basra and the adjacent areas in the south-western Iranian province of Khuzistan, as well as in Bahrayn.

From around 1215/1800 to the present

It was during a fifth and final phase, coinciding with the modern period, that the Usuli school, advocating *ijtihad* and *taqlid*, finally acquired widespread dominance in Persia and Iraq; and Twelver Shiʿism, especially in terms of its jurisprudence, acquired its current form. The victory of the Usuli *ʿulama* was accompanied by the development of the religious scholars into a hierarchical class of *mujtahids* in Qajar Persia during the 19th century. A group of qualified scholars selected on the basis of their knowledge of the principles of jurisprudence (*usul al-fiqh*) were now widely permitted to practise *ijtihad*, reaching binding decisions. At the same time, ordinary Twelvers were to follow such a qualified *mujtahid* designated as *marjaʿ-i taqlid* (Arabic, *marjaʿ al-taqlid*), the 'source of emulation' or the 'supreme exemplar'. The triumph of the Usuli school thus divided the Twelver Shiʿi community into *muqallid*, persons obliged to practise *taqlid*, and *mujtahid*, those qualified to practise *ijtihad*. Under the circumstances, the choice of a *mujtahid* or a *marjaʿ-i taqlid* as the source of guidance depended mainly upon the observation of a superior degree of learning and piety. On the death of a *marjaʿ-i taqlid*, it became necessary to choose a new one, as only the decisions of a living *mujtahid* satisfy the requirements of *taqlid* and are binding. As a result, the institutions of *taqlid* and *marjaʿiyyat* are continuously renewed.

In principle, every *mujtahid* could be a *marjaʿ-i taqlid*, but in practice only one or very few at any time have been recognised as such. The Qajar monarchs, unlike the Safawids, did not claim any ʿAlid ancestry, nor could they claim to represent the hidden imam, a role that now devolved upon the collectivity of the legal scholars, with monarchs themselves being mere *muqallid*s. In this sense, the authority of the Qajar monarchs was subservient to that of the *ʿulama*, and this brought about persistent tensions between the Qajar monarchy and the *ʿulama* which ultimately led to the participation of a group of *ʿulama* in the prolonged Constitutional Revolution of 1906–1911 that resulted in a consultative assembly (*Majlis*) and curtailed the despotic authority of the king.[33] There were, however, also those *mujtahid*s like Shaykh Fadl Allah Nuri (d. 1909) who were opposed to a constitutional monarchy in which the *shariʿa* did not hold a central position.

Shaykh Murtada Ansari (d. 1281/1864), author of an important legal work entitled *Faraʾid al-usul*, was the first person to attain the position of the highest or sole *marjaʿ-i taqlid* for almost the entire Twelver community, not only in Persia and Iraq but also in other Arab lands and India.[34] Living in Persia and then Iraq, Ansari attained significant authority and political influence. The *ʿatabat* continued to hold an important place throughout the Qajar period and thereafter; it was in these shrine cities of Iraq, especially Najaf, where Twelver pilgrims gathered regularly, that Twelver scholars were trained or often resided for long periods. It was also from these religious centres in Iraq that opposition to Qajar autocracy was organised. After Ansari's death, no other *mujtahid* was able to enjoy the position of being the sole *marjaʿ* until Mirza Hasan Shirazi (d. 1312/1895), who exercised the full political power of his office by successfully forbidding in a *fatwa*, or formal legal opinion, issued in 1308/1891 the use of tobacco in Persia after the establishment of a British tobacco monopoly in the country during the long reign of Nasir al-Din Shah Qajar (r. 1264–1313/1848–1896), who awarded numerous lucrative concessions to the British.[35]

Meanwhile, the *ʿulama* had gradually appropriated for themselves various prerogatives of the hidden imam. These included the collection of the *khums* and other religious taxes during the *ghayba*. In the

Qajar period, the *khums* was regularly collected and distributed by the assistants of every *marja'-i taqlid* from his *muqallids*. In addition, these religious dignitaries enjoyed substantial revenues from religious endowments (*waqf*; plural, *awqaf*), enabling the *'ulama* to live independently of the state treasury. Other prerogatives of the hidden imam appropriated by the Twelver hierocracy were leading the Friday prayer, reciting the sermon (*khutba*) and the imposition of corporal punishments (*hudud*) as specified in the Qur'an. Finally, the *mujtahids* had now appropriated the right to declare holy war (*jihad*) against unbelievers. It was under such religious pressures that Fath 'Ali Shah Qajar declared war on Russia on two occasions, with disastrous results in terms of losing vast territories in the Transcaucasus to Russia. As the authority of the *'ulama* steadily increased they also began to use excommunication, or the charge of unbelief (*takfir*), which deprived a person of his Islamic status,[36] reducing him to a non-believer (*kafir*).

During this time, an important school of esoteric theology had appeared within Twelver Shi'ism in Persia and Iraq. The eponymous founder of this school, known as Shaykhiyya, was Shaykh Ahmad Ahsa'i (d. 1241/1826), one of the leading Twelver *'ulama* of the early Qajar period. After spending his early life in his native Bahrayn, Shaykh Ahmad settled in Iraq before moving in 1221/1806 to Persia where he was to spend most of the rest of his life. From his youth, Shaykh Ahmad began to experience a series of compelling dreams and visions of the twelve imams, allowing him to claim a privileged understanding of the Qur'an and the *hadith*. Emphasising the esoteric aspects of Shi'ism, Shaykh Ahmad Ahsa'i also elaborated a spiritual rather than a physical interpretation of the Prophet Muhammad's ascension (*mi'raj*) and of the Resurrection (*qiyama*). Originally, Shaykhi doctrine represented a synthesis between theosophical and gnostic Shi'ism of the 'school of Isfahan' and the waning Akhbari tendencies, with special attention to intuitive knowledge as well as cosmological, crypto-Ismaili and cabalistic doctrines. However, in time, Shaykhism achieved a certain doctrinal compromise with the Usuli school of Twelver Shi'ism, though never showing any distinct concern with legalistic matters.

The early popularity of Shaykh Ahmad Ahsa'i resulted in the bitter envy and opposition of some *'ulama* of Qazwin and elsewhere, leading to the formal declaration of *takfir* against him. Under these adverse circumstances, Shaykh Ahmad spent his final years mainly in Karbala. He was succeeded as the leader of the Shaykhiyya by a young Persian disciple, Sayyid Kazim Rashti (d. 1259/1844), who remained in Karbala. After his death, several individuals claimed the leadership of the Shaykhiyya. But Hajj Muhammad Karim Khan Kirmani (d. 1288/1871), a member of the Qajar family, found widest acceptance. Henceforth, the leadership of the Shaykhis, centred in the Kirman province of Persia, remained amongst the descendants of Hajj Muhammad Karim Khan in the Ibrahimi family of Kirman, who are generally addressed by the Shaykhis as Sarkar Aqa. The Shaykhis have produced a voluminous literature which remains mainly in manuscript form.[37]

The Twelver Shiʿi context of Qajar Persia also witnessed the rise of Babism and its twin successors, Azalism and Bahaism. In 1260/1844, exactly 1,000 lunar years after the occultation of the twelfth imam, Sayyid ʿAli Muhammad Shirazi, a former student of the Shaykhi leader Sayyid Kazim Rashti in Karbala, predicted the imminent reappearance of the hidden twelfth imam and declared himself in Shiraz to be his 'gate' (*bab*), that is, the intermediary between the hidden imam and his community. However, he soon changed the nature of his claim and it was suggested that he was the twelfth imam or the Mahdi himself. Still later, Sayyid ʿAli Muhammad, now generally known as the Bab, abrogated the Islamic *shariʿa* and proclaimed himself the recipient of a new scriptural revelation and divine law. These claims met with strong opposition from the Twelver *ʿulama* and several disputations occurred between them and the Bab, who was banished to Adharbayjan in 1263/1847. By then, he had acquired a growing number of followers who had commenced armed rebellions against the Qajar establishment in different parts of Persia. However, soon afterwards, the Bab was executed in Tabriz in 1266/1850 on the order of the grand vizier, Mirza Taqi Khan Amir Kabir (d. 1268/1852).

The messianic Babi movement inspired by the Bab's teachings did not disappear on his demise. Already in 1268/1852 there was an assassination attempt by several Babis on Nasir al-Din Shah Qajar in revenge for the Bab's execution. This led to a widespread persecution of the Babis and their leading figures in Persia. Although a large number of the leading individuals who embraced Babism were originally Shaykhis, it would be erroneous to consider Shaykhism as the forerunner of Babism. Be that as it may, a certain Mirza Yayha Nuri, commonly known as

Subh-i Azal, now took charge of the leadership of the Babis from Baghdad. But in 1280/1863, his half-brother, Mirza Husayn Nuri, with the title of Baha' Allah, claimed in Baghdad to be the Bab's true successor. The dispute over the Bab's succession split the Babis into the Azalis, followers of Subh-i Azal (d. 1330/1912) who adhered to the Bab's original teachings, and the Bahais, followers of Baha' Allah (d. 1310/1892) who espoused a new religion and considered himself as the manifestation of the divine (*mazhar-i ilahi*). Meanwhile, the Ottoman authorities in Iraq had exiled these two brothers to Cyprus and ʿAkka in Palestine, respectively, while their followers remained mainly in Persia. Most of the Babis eventually joined the Bahai faction, while Azali Babism stagnated and ultimately became an insignificant and highly secretive group.[38] Subsequently, Bahaism received new converts in Persia from Jewish and Zoroastrian communities there. As an independent religion, Bahaism clearly cannot be considered as belonging to Shiʿism or any other Islamic tradition. Under Baha' Allah's successors, Bahaism with its intricate global organisation spread to all the continents of the world.

By the final decades of the Qajar period, the Shiʿi clergy had evidently evolved into an important social class in Persia with much influence and active participation in the country's public affairs. The political activities of the *ʿulama* had attained their peak in their involvement in the Persian Constitutional Revolution, which resulted, in the first decade of the 20th century, in a system of constitutional monarchy with an elected parliament (*Majlis*) and a constitution (*qanun-i asasi*), unprecedented achievements in the Middle East. When the first parliament convened in Tehran in 1906, around 20 per cent of its members were actually comprised of the *ʿulama*. Persia's then leading *mujtahid*s, Sayyid ʿAbd Allah Bihbahani, assassinated in 1910, and Sayyid Muhammad Tabataba'i, who were the earliest of their rank to have been designated by the title of Ayatullah ('sign of God'), as well as a number of *ʿulama* residing in Iraq, contributed to the success of the Constitutional Revolution that ended the absolutism of the Persian monarchy.[39] However, the fortunes of the Shiʿi clergy were soon reversed drastically before resurging again more powerfully in the final decades of the 20th century in Persia.

A new phase in the modern history of Persia, more commonly designated as Iran in the West since 1936, and in the country's clergy–state relations, was initiated by the rise to power of Rida (Reza) Shah, founder of the Pahlavi dynasty (1925–1979).[40] Originally an officer in the Cossack Brigade of Persia organised by the Russians, Rida Khan, as he was originally known, participated in the British-backed *coup* of 1921 that signalled the demise of the Qajars. A charismatic soldier who emulated Mustafa Kemal Atatürk (1881–1936), the founding father of the Turkish republic, as his role model in secularism and modernisation, Rida Khan consolidated his position rapidly after brief stints as Minister of War and Prime Minister. By 1925, he was ready to depose the last Qajar monarch, Ahmad Shah (r. 1909–1925), and declare a republic in Persia. However, due to the staunch opposition of the leading *'ulama* against the idea of republicanism, which in their view would have led to the type of secular statism adopted by Atatürk in Turkey, Rida Khan vied for the monarchical alternative and declared himself king (Shah) in 1925, following the parliamentary deposition of the Qajar dynasty.

Subsequently, as Rida Shah restored law and order to various regions of Persia and moved to modernise the country, he began his systematic assault on the hitherto privileged position of the *'ulama* in Persian society, through adopting a range of policies that directly or indirectly removed their vital sources of revenue and curtailed their socio-political influences.[41] In particular, he passed a series of laws, based on European models, that would exclude the *'ulama* from the country's judiciary and educational systems, fields previously mainly under the control of the clergy. The promulgations of civil and criminal codes in the late 1920s, for instance, resulted in the abandonment of the *shari'a* courts in favour of secular ones controlled by the Ministry of Justice created in 1927; and, from 1936, after the establishment of Tehran University, only lawyers with recognised academic degrees could act as judges in the country's judiciary system. At the same time, secular education at all levels was introduced and religious *maktab*s (primary schools) and *madrasa*s of various types soon disappeared or stagnated.

Another serious affront to the clergy was the official prohibition of public religious ceremonies, including those commemorating the martyrdom of Imam al-Husayn at Karbala. As a further affront to the clergy, in 1936 women were forbidden to appear in public wearing the traditional Persian veil (*chadur*). Around the same time, government was given discretionary powers to intervene in the administration of the religious endowments (*awqaf*), while also taking over from the clergy all their public notary functions, with all that these measures implied in terms of cutting the revenues accruing to the religious establishment. Furthermore, Rida Shah's dictatorial regime did not grant any privileged exemptions to the members of the clergy, such as Sayyid Hasan Mudarris (d. 1937), who, like members of any other social class, could be exiled, imprisoned or killed. However, there is no evidence suggesting that Rida Shah intended to uproot the *ʿulama,* on the model of Atatürk in Turkey.

The *ʿulama,* including those acknowledged as *marjaʿ-i taqlid*, on the whole adopted a quiescent attitude towards Rida Shah's anticlerical policies and various infringements on their position. The main development of this period in the camp of the *ʿulama* was the revival and expansion of the principal religious teaching institution (*hawza-yi ʿilmiyya*) in Qumm through the efforts of Shaykh ʿAbd al-Karim Ha'iri Yazdi, the only Persian *mujtahid* then recognised as a *marjaʿ*, besides two other authorities in Najaf, Sayyid Abu'l-Hasan Musawi Isfahani (d. 1946) and Mirza Muhammad Husayn Na'ini (d. 1936). Initially, Ha'iri taught in the city of Arak, near Qumm, where he had acquired a substantial group of disciples and students, including the young Ruhullah Khumayni, the future leader of the Islamic Revolution. In the early 1920s, Ha'iri moved to Qumm and taught there until his death in 1937. It was mainly due to Ha'iri's efforts that Qumm rapidly became an alternative to Najaf and Karbala as a centre of Shiʿi teaching and learning. Ha'iri did not become involved in politics, similarly to his student and the future sole *marjaʿ* Ayatullah Burujirdi, but he did train students who later became activist religious leaders. In fact the seminary (*hawza*) in Qumm, effectively founded by Ha'iri, was to become in due course a bastion of Islamic militancy under the leadership of Ayatullah Khumayni. The era of repression for the *ʿulama,* who had been completely marginalised in society, ended in 1941 when Rida Shah was forced to abdicate by the Allies during the Second World War in favour of his son Muhammad Rida Shah.

A detailed account of the history of the Shiʿi clergy in Iran under the second Pahlavi monarch is beyond the scope of this chapter. We shall, however, cover certain developments that eventually led to the establishment of an Islamic republic in Iran. During the first decade of Muhammad Rida (Mohammad Reza) Shah's rule (1941–1979), when political parties and the media could once again operate freely, the clergy also began to regain, at least partially, some of their traditional privileges. By 1947, Ayatullah Husayn Tabataba'i Burujirdi, a highly learned religious scholar, had emerged as the sole *marjaʿ-i taqlid* of the Twelver Shiʿis of the world, a distinction he retained until his death in 1962.[42] The seminary (*hawza*) in Qumm flourished under the leadership of Burujirdi, who also made various attempts to promote Shiʿi–Sunni rapprochement. However, Ayatullah Burujirdi, too, refrained from any political activity. Indeed, in 1949 he convened a conference of *ʿulama* in Qumm that sought to prevent the Shiʿi clergy from engaging in any anti-regime political activity in Iran. Meanwhile, a number of Islamic organisations with radical religio-political platforms had appeared in Iran. One such group, under the initial spiritual leadership of Ayatullah Sayyid Abu'l-Qasim Kashani (d. 1962), who played an active part on the political stage, was the Fida'iyan-i Islam ('the Devotees of Islam') founded in 1945, representing perhaps the first group of its kind in 20th-century Iran with the goal of establishing an Islamic state and a radical strategy for achieving it. While Ayatullah Burujirdi expressed his dissatisfaction with the activities of the Fida'iyan-i Islam in Qumm, the young Ruhullah Khumayni had early association with the group.[43]

After the death of Ayatullah Burujirdi, once again several eminent *mujtahid*s were acknowledged simultaneously by their *muqallid*s as their *marjaʿ*, with none enjoying general supremacy over the others. Before long, Ayatullah Sayyid Ruhullah Musawi Khumayni would also be recognised as one such *marjaʿ* among this select group of *mujtahids*.[44] A brilliant scholar, a charismatic leader and an excellent strategist, Khumayni had followed his teacher Shaykh ʿAbd al-Karim Ha'iri to Qumm in 1922 when he was twenty years of age. In his studies at the newly revived seminary at Qumm, Khumayni excelled in Shiʿi gnosis (*ʿirfan*) and philosophy in addition to jurisprudence. However, from early on he was particularly inclined towards political activity. Already in 1944, he had expressed some of his radical ideas in his *Kashf al-asrar*, a tract written in defence of the Shiʿi hierarchy against certain anti-clerical attacks and which also contained a criticism of Rida Shah's policies as well as rudiments of his future doctrine of *vilayat-i faqih* ('the guardianship of the jurist').

Khumayni's overt campaign against the Pahlavi regime took off in 1963. By then, a strand of clerical opposition to the regime in Iran had become clearly solidified under the leadership of Khumayni, who in his classes and lectures at the Faydiya Madrasa in Qumm publicly criticised the Shah and aspects of his reform package designated as the White Revolution. In the aftermath of the clashes between the security forces and the religious students (*tullab*) in Qumm and the bloody suppression of Khumayni's broader urban supporters in Tehran, Khumayni was arrested and then in 1964 exiled to Turkey and then Najaf, where he remained until 1978. It was after the violent suppression of the demonstrations in 1963 that Khumayni was recognised as a *marjaʿ-i taqlid*.

Khumayni maintained his political activities and covert contacts with various religious groups within Iran during his years of exile in Iraq. It was also at Najaf that he delivered a series of lectures in 1970 on the subject of Islamic government. These innovative lectures were, in due course, published in Beirut, Najaf and Qumm under the title of *Hukumat-i Islami* (Islamic Government) with *vilayat-i faqih* as the subtitle.[45] This doctrine, holding that the *ʿulama/fuqahaʾ* were effectively heirs to the political authority of the twelve imams, was to serve as the cornerstone of the future constitution of the Islamic Republic of Iran.

Ayatullah Khumayni argued that the right to rule devolves from the imams to the jurists, during the occultation (*ghayba*) of the twelfth imam, because they are best qualified to know the divine revelation and the *shariʿa*; and this right would devolve to a single jurist (*faqih*) if he succeeds to establish a government. Otherwise, it is the duty of the jurists (*fuqahaʾ*) collectively to establish an Islamic government. The doctrine of *vilayat-i faqih* (Arabic, *wilayat al-faqih*), thus, refuted the very legitimacy of the Pahlavi regime while rationalising the rise of the *ʿulama/fuqahaʾ* to the highest positions of political authority. At the same time, Ayatullah Khumayni criticised the traditional Twelver clergy for their narrow interpretation of the principle of *ijtihad* and their preoccupation with the devotional acts of Shiʿi jurisprudence.

It was on such a doctrinal basis, initially not widely publicised, that Ayatullah Khumayni organised and led a revolutionary movement of an unprecedented nature and scope. Using a popular strategy, he capitalised on every blunder of the Pahlavi regime while welcoming collaboration with any political group or party – factors that contributed immeasurably to the ultimate success of his broadly based Islamic movement.[46] Ayatullah Khumayni returned triumphantly to Tehran in

February 1979, shortly after the departure of Muhammad Rida Shah (d. 1980), and completed the first stage of the Islamic Revolution that soon abolished the Pahlavi monarchy and established an Islamic republic in Iran. Henceforth, Khumayni was no longer referred to as Ayatullah or Grand Ayatullah (*Ayatullah al-Uzma*), like other *marja*ʿs, but as Imam; he was now recognised as the leader (*rahbar*) of the Islamic Revolution and the *vali-yi faqih* (Arabic, *wali al-faqih*), the 'guardian jurist' of the Islamic state he had created in Iran, unique ranks that accorded Khumayni clear supremacy over that of the 'supreme exemplar'. In modern times, different titles have been applied to the Twelver *ʿulama* in the religious hierarchy. A *mujtahid* on becoming a *marjaʿ-i taqlid* has normally carried the title of Ayatullah and, more recently, Ayatullah al-Uzma or Grand Ayatullah. Lower ranking *mujtahid*s are also designated as Ayatullah, while aspiring *mujtahid*s are more commonly designated as Hujjat al-Islam or 'proof of Islam'.

The historical evolution in the authority/power paradigm of the Twelver *ʿulama* from the first articulation of the principle of *ijtihad* had thus reached its extreme and ultimate conclusion in the establishment of a theocratic Islamic state with its leader as the *vali-yi faqih*, conceived as the full representative of the hidden imam (*naʾib al-imam*). In such a state, the Twelver *ʿulama* in general, and their leader(s) in particular, would acquire a unique position of religious authority with unlimited political power. On Imam Khumayni's death in 1989, Sayyid ʿAli Khamanaʾi, not a senior *mujtahid* at the time but highly active in the Islamic Republic, succeeded to the position of leader (*rahbar*) and *vali-yi faqih*, but with less spiritual authority than his predecessor. At the same time, other *mujtahid*s now more readily gained prominence as *marjaʿ-i taqlid*; they included several Grand Ayatullahs such as Marʿashi (d. 1991), al-Khuʾi (d. 1992), Gulpayagani (d. 1993), Araki (d. 1994) and al-Sistani, amongst others.

As already noted, Twelver Shiʿi communities also flourished, under different political fortunes and subject to various oppressive policies by Sunni rulers, in several parts of the Arab world.[47] In Iraq, the cradle of Shiʿism, the Shiʿis and their leaders traditionally had close links to the Shiʿi establishment in Persia. The shrine cities of Iraq, notably Najaf and Karbala, served until the middle of the 20th century as the undisputed centres of Shiʿi learning. However, these centres had developed dependencies on external sources of funds, provided not only by the continuous influx of pilgrims but also by governments and wealthy individuals in Persia and India. At the same time, the influence of the Iraqi *ʿulama* was persistently undermined by the Sunni regimes ruling over Iraq, beginning with the Ottomans who controlled the region until the end of the First World War.

Since the 1920s, under monarchy or republican regimes, the Shiʿi *ʿulama* of Iraq have been treated even less favourably by the country's rulers. As a result, the Twelver *ʿulama* never emerged as a politically influential class in Iraq. Under the existing adverse circumstances, many eventually settled in Iran, also attracted there by the reputation of Qumm's seminary (*hawza*) which rapidly surpassed Najaf as the chief centre of Shiʿi learning. From 1962 until his death in 1970, Ayatullah Sayyid Muhsin al-Hakim was the undisputed *marjaʿ-i taqlid* in Najaf. Subsequently, various members of the Hakim family rose to positions of Shiʿi leadership in Iraq, while Ayatullah Muhammad Baqir al-Sadr taught at Najaf and enjoyed much esteem amongst the Iraqi Twelver community. Nevertheless, he was executed in 1980 on the order of Saddam Hussain, who generally pursued severe anti-Shiʿi policies. In more recent times, Grand Ayatullah Abu'l-Qasim al-Khu'i (d. 1992) and his successor at Najaf, Ayatullah ʿAli al-Sistani, have been acknowledged as *marjaʿ* by the Twelvers of both Iraq and Iran. At present, at least 60 per cent of Iraq's total population of some 31 million are believed to be of the Twelver Shiʿi persuasion, concentrated in Basra and other southern districts as well as in Baghdad.

In Lebanon, the Twelver Shiʿis are mainly concentrated in the rural districts of Jabal ʿAmil in the south, where they account for some 80 per cent of the region's population. Another important Twelver community is located in the Biqaʿ valley in eastern Lebanon. Since Safawid times, relations between the Twelvers of Jabal ʿAmil and Persia have remained generally close. In modern times, Sayyid ʿAbd al-Husayn Sharaf al-Din, who had studied at Najaf and Cairo, operated as the spiritual leader of the Lebanese Shiʿis for some time until his death in 1957. In 1959, Musa al-Sadr, son of an Iranian *mujtahid* whose ancestors hailed from Jabal ʿAmil, came to Lebanon and became the spiritual leader of the Twelvers there. Imam Musa al-Sadr, as he came to be generally known, worked tirelessly for improving the living conditions of the impoverished Lebanese Shiʿis who had lagged behind the country's other religious communities. In 1975, he founded a militant

Shiʿi organisation, later designated as Amal, an acronym for Afwaj al-Muqawama al-Lubnaniyya (The Lebanese Resistance Brigades), which later received help from the Islamic Republic of Iran. Musa al-Sadr vanished mysteriously in 1978 while on a visit to Libya.

At present, the leadership of the Lebanese Twelver Shiʿis is in the hands of a small group of influential individuals. Also of particular importance in this context is the Shiʿi organisation known as the Hizbullah (Party of God), founded in the mid-1980s under the spiritual leadership of Shaykh Muhammad Husayn Fadl Allah (d. 2010), who later became closely allied with the Islamic regime in Iran. Hizbullah has played a crucial role, both as a political party and as a radical Islamic movement, in the modern history of Lebanon. Hizbullah's ideological platform includes a commitment to Shiʿi Islam as well as support for the doctrine of *wilayat al-faqih* as expounded by Imam Khumayni. However, individual members are free to choose their source of emulation (*marjaʿ al-taqlid*) in religious matters. Since 1992, Sayyid Hasan Nasr Allah has been the political leader of Hizbullah. Though a religious scholar, he does not rank highly enough to be a *marjaʿ*; Hasan Nasr Allah himself remains a follower of Imam Khumayni's successor in Iran, Ayatullah Khamanaʾi. The Twelver Shiʿis of Lebanon now probably account for one half of the country's total Muslim population of some 6.4 million, which itself accounts for more than 60 per cent of Lebanon's mixed Muslim–Christian population.

In Bahrayn, as noted, Shiʿi communities and traditions of learning have deep roots. Although constituting the majority of Bahrayn's total population of around one million, the Twelvers have been regularly and openly repressed by the country's Sunni tribal leaders, including especially the ruling al-Khalifa family. The Twelver Shiʿis of Saudi Arabia live predominantly in the eastern al-Hasa (al-Ahsaʾ) province, where the medieval Qarmatis had established their own dissident Shiʿi state. The Twelvers probably account for one half of that Saudi province's population. Since the early decades of the 20th century when the Wahhabis under Malik Ibn Saʿud (d. 1953) reoccupied Arabia, after the departure of the Ottomans, the local Shiʿis have frequently been regarded with hostility and disdain under the Wahhabi-dominated order of Saudi Arabia, which was formally established in 1932.

In the 1920s, the Wahhabis also destroyed the highly revered tombs of the Shiʿi imams at the Baqiʿ cemetery in Medina.

The discovery of oil in the Saudi province of al-Hasa in 1938 did not result in any significant improvements in the lives of its large Shiʿi community. The significant religious minority Twelvers and other Shiʿi communities of Saudi Arabia, accounting for about 10 per cent of the country's total population of 25.5 million, have been intermittently persecuted by the Saudi regime under the influence of its extremist Wahhabi-Salafi fundamentalist ideology, which essentially does not recognise or tolerate any type of pluralism within Islam. Indeed, Sufis and Shiʿis have been singled out as theological deviants deserving of *takfir*, or excommunication, with its violent implications in the Saudi kingdom. Smaller Twelver communities are located in other parts of the Arabian Peninsula, especially on the southern shores of the Persian Gulf, notably in Kuwait, Qatar and the United Arab Emirates.

In India, Twelver Shiʿism had already spread in the region of the Deccan under the Bahmanids (r. 748–934/1347–1528), who had founded the first Islamic state in the Indian subcontinent.[48] But it was after the disintegration of the Bahmanid kingdom that Twelver *mujtahid*s became particularly active in the five independent states succeeding the Bahmanids in the Deccan, namely the ʿImad-Shahis of Berar, the Barid-Shahis of Bidar, the ʿAdil-Shahis of Bijapur, the Nizam-Shahis of Ahmadnagar and the Qutb-Shahis of Golconda. The Twelver *mujtahid*s who operated in India were often of Persian origins; and they, as well as most of the Muslim rulers of the Deccan, were generally under the influence of the Safawids of Persia. The ʿAdil-Shahis (r. 895–1097/1490–1686) were, in fact, the first Muslim dynasty in India to adopt Twelver Shiʿism in 908/1503 as their state religion.

In 928/1522, Shah Tahir al-Husayni (d. ca. 956/1549), a learned scholar and the most famous imam of the Muhammad-Shahi Nizari Ismailis who had escaped persecution at the instigation of the Twelver *ʿulama* of Persia, arrived in Ahmadnagar. Shah Tahir had for long dissimulated, for *taqiyya* purposes, as a Twelver Shiʿi scholar, cleverly concealing his important Ismaili connection. At any rate, in Ahmadnagar, Shah Tahir soon became a trusted adviser to Burhan I Nizam Shah (r. 915–961/1509–1554) and succeeded in converting him from Sunnism to the Ithnaʿashari form of Shiʿi Islam. Soon afterwards, in

944/1537, Burhan I Nizam Shah proclaimed Twelver Shiʿism as the official religion of his realm, to the absolute delight of the Safawids. Henceforth, an increasing number of Twelver *ʿulama* gathered in the Nizam-Shahi state and enjoyed the patronage of its rulers. It should be noted, however, that Shah Tahir may have actually propagated his own syncretic form of Nizari Ismailism in the guise of Twelver Shiʿism,[49] which was more acceptable to the Muslim rulers of India who were then interested in cultivating close cultural, religious and political relations with the Twelver Shiʿi Safawids of Persia.

Sultan Quli (r. 901–950/1496–1543), the founder of the Qutb-Shahi dynasty, too, adopted Twelver Shiʿism as the religion of his realm. Even after these Deccan sultanates were absorbed into the Sunni Mughal empire, Twelver Shiʿi minorities survived in many parts of India, especially in Hyderabad. However, the Twelvers and their *ʿulama* encountered intermittent persecution even under the religiously tolerant Mughals. For instance, Nur Allah al-Shushtari, another eminent Persian Twelver theologian and jurist who had emigrated to India and enjoyed some popularity at the Mughal court, was executed in 1019/1610 at the instigation of the Sunni *ʿulama* and on Emperor Jahangir's order.

Twelver Shiʿism also spread to northern India and was adopted as the state religion in the kingdom of Awadh (Oudh) with its capital at Lucknow (now in Uttar Pradesh); this kingdom (1134–1272/1722–1856) served as the main stronghold of Twelver Shiʿism in South Asia. Towards the end of the 12th/18th century, Sayyid Dildar ʿAli Nasirabadi (d. 1235/1820), an Indian *mujtahid* who had studied with Muhammad Baqir al-Bihbahani in Karbala, became the founder of the Twelver Usuli school of Lucknow where numerous Ithnaʿashari scholars were trained. Indeed, under the Nawwabs of Awadh, Lucknow became the stronghold of Shiʿism in India with a hierarchy of Twelver clerics. The Nawwab Asaf al-Dawla (r. 1189–1212/1775–1797), and his successors, also endowed the Shiʿi shrines of Iraq, in addition to undertaking renovation and construction projects there. Lucknow still possesses the main Twelver institutions of learning in India. In the Punjab, before the partition of India in 1947, the Twelver Shiʿis were perhaps the largest religious community after the Sikhs, but the Punjabi Twelvers are now located mainly in Pakistan, in the region of Lahore. There are significant numbers of Twelvers also in Karachi, where numerous Shiʿis from Awadh settled after the partition. In India, the Twelvers account for 10–35 per cent of the country's total Muslim population of around 178 million, whereas in Pakistan they make up about 10 per cent of that country's total population of 180 million.

During the 19th century, Twelver Shiʿism reached Zanzibar and the East African mainland from both India and Persia. In each case, the Shiʿi influx was encouraged by a combination of commercial and tolerant religious policies of Sultan Sayyid Saʿid (r. 1220–1273/1806–1856), of the Ibadi Al Bu Saʿid dynasty of ʿUman and Zanzibar. Waves of Shiʿi Khojas, engaged in trade, emigrated mainly from Gujarat and Bombay in western India to the island of Ẓanzibar, and then to the growing urban centres of the East African coastline, notably Mombasa, Tanga and Dar es Salaam. The number of Asian Khoja settlers in East Africa increased substantially after 1256/1840 when Sultan Saʿid transferred his capital from Muscat to Zanzibar. While the majority of the Shiʿi Khojas arriving from India were Nizari Ismailis, there were also Ithnaʿasharis amongst them. The Twelver Khojas had for the most part seceded from the main Ismaili body of the Khoja community in India over certain disputes with the leadership of their community.[50] The disputes also related to the distinct identity of the Khojas, some of whom now rejected their Ismaili origins and embraced Twelver Shiʿism.

In East Africa the Twelver Khojas, who initially lacked any formal organisation of their own and retained certain ideas from their Hindu past, mixed freely with their Ismaili neighbours. In due course, the Ithnaʿashari Khojas contacted certain Shiʿi *ʿulama* of Persia and Iraq requesting help for their religious education. In particular, they petitioned Shaykh Zayn al-ʿAbidin Mazandarani (d. 1309/1892), who resided at Karbala and was then regarded by the Indian Twelvers as their *marjaʿ al-taqlid*. A certain Sayyid ʿAbd al-Husayn Marʿashi, who arrived in East Africa in 1302/1885, was the first of such religious teachers dispatched from Persia, Iraq and Lucknow. Meanwhile, Persian Twelver groups, too, had settled in Zanzibar and the coastland of East Africa. The Persian settlers who came mainly from the southern Persian province of Fars, with its capital at Shiraz, had already developed commercial ties with ʿUman and Zanzibar. In more recent times, the Twelver Khojas of Africa, situated chiefly in Tanzania, Kenya and Uganda, united their various small communities (*jamaʿats*) into an African Federation of Khoja Ithna-Ashari Jamats, a transnational organisation responsible for leading its constituencies and caring for their religious and cultural needs in the African context. In the 1970s, due to the anti-Asian policies of the Ugandan and other East African governments, many Twelver Khojas, together with Ismaili Khojas and Bohras, emigrated from East Africa to various countries of the West.

4

The Ismailis

Representing the second largest Shiʿi community, the Ismailis have had their own complex history. In medieval times, the Ismailis established states of their own on separate occasions, and for relatively long periods played crucial parts in the history of the Muslim world. During the second century of their history, the Ismailis founded the first Shiʿi caliphate under the Fatimid caliph-imams. At the same time, they made important contributions to Islamic thought and culture during the Fatimid phase of their history. Later, after a schism that split Ismaili Shiʿism into its two major Nizari and Mustaʿlian branches, the leaders of the Nizari branch succeeded in founding a cohesive state in scattered territories stretching from eastern Persia to Syria. The Nizari Ismaili state, comprised of numerous mountain strongholds and towns, collapsed under the onslaught of the all-conquering Mongols in 654/1256. Thereafter, the Ismailis, belonging to the Nizari and Tayyibi Mustaʿlian factions, survived in many lands as minority Shiʿi communities.

The Nizaris have continuously benefited from the guidance of their hereditary line of imams, who have acquired international fame since the middle of the 19th century under the title of Aga Khan. On the other hand, the Tayyibis, who have split into several groups, have been led by lines of *daʿis* while their imams have remained in concealment since 524/1130. There were also the radical Qarmatis, who split off from the Ismailis and founded their own state in eastern Arabia and engaged in hostilities with both the Shiʿi Fatimids as well as the Sunni Abbasids. By the end of the 5th/11th century, however, the Qarmatis had disappeared from the historical stage.

As noted, much progress has taken place in modern times in the study of the Ismailis and their teachings. On the basis of the findings of modern scholarship, Ismaili history and thought may be conveniently studied in terms of a number of distinct phases; such a categorisation is also adopted in this chapter.[1]

The early Ismailis

The history of the Ismailis as an independent Shiʿi community may be traced to the dispute over the succession to Imam Jaʿfar al-Sadiq, who died in 148/765. According to the majority of the available sources, Imam al-Sadiq had originally designated his second son Ismaʿil, the eponym of the Ismaʿiliyya, as his successor to the imamate by the rule of the *nass*. There can be no doubt about the authenticity of this designation, which forms the basis of the claims of the Ismailis. According to the Ismaili religious tradition, Ismaʿil succeeded his father in due course. However, as related in the majority of the sources, Ismaʿil died before his father, and this raised questions in the minds of some of al-Sadiq's Imami Shiʿi followers, who did not understand how a divinely guided imam could be fallible regarding so crucial a matter as his *nass*. A group of these Shiʿis had evidently already left Imam al-Sadiq's following during his lifetime.[2] It is not absolutely certain whether Imam al-Sadiq designated another son after Ismaʿil, although the later Twelver Shiʿis claimed such a *nass* for Musa b. Jaʿfar, the younger half-brother of Ismaʿil, producing several *hadith*s to this effect.[3] At any rate, Ismaʿil was not present in Medina or Kufa at the time of Imam al-Sadiq's death, when three other sons (ʿAbd Allah, Muhammad and Musa) simultaneously claimed his succession. As noted previously, this confusing succession dispute split the Imami Shiʿis into several groups, two of which may be identified with the earliest Ismailis. These Kufan-based splinter groups had actually come into being earlier, as pro-Ismaʿil or proto-Ismaili factions of the Imamiyya, but they seceded from the rest of the Imami Shiʿis only after al-Sadiq's death in 148/765.

One group, denying the death of Ismaʿil during his father's lifetime, maintained that he was the true imam after al-Sadiq, and they also held that he remained alive and would eventually return as the Mahdi. These Imami Shiʿis further believed that Imam al-Sadiq had announced Ismaʿil's death merely as a ruse to protect him from the persecution of the Abbasids who were angered by his political activities. The Imami heresiographers al-Nawbakhti and al-Qummi call the members of this group, who recognised Isma'il as their Imam-Mahdi, the 'pure Ismailis' (*al-Isma'iliyya al-khalisa*), while some later heresiographers such as al-Shahrastani designate this group as *al-Isma'iliyya al-waqifa*, or those Ismailis who stopped their line of imams with Isma'il.[4]

There was a second group of pro-Isma'il Shi'is who, affirming Isma'il's death during the lifetime of his father, now recognised his son Muhammad b. Isma'il as their imam. They held that Imam al-Sadiq had personally designated him as the rightful successor to Isma'il, after the latter's death. The Imami heresiographers call this group the Mubarakiyya, evidently named after Isma'il's epithet al-Mubarak ('the blessed one').[5] The Mubarakiyya held that the imamate could not be transferred from brother to brother after the case of Imams al-Hasan and al-Husayn b. 'Ali; and this is why they could not accept the claims of any of Isma'il's brothers. At any rate, it is clear that the Mubarakiyya had come into existence in Isma'il's lifetime and they were originally his supporters; it was only after al-Sadiq's death that the majority of Isma'il's supporters rallied to the side of Muhammad b. Isma'il and recognised him as their new imam. At the same time, Isma'il himself had to be elevated retrospectively to the imamate. It may safely be assumed that Mubarakiyya was one of the original names of the nascent Isma'iliyya.

Few biographical details are available on Isma'il, who is counted as the sixth in the series of the Ismaili imams. Abu Muhammad Isma'il b. Ja'far (al-Mubarak) and his full-brother 'Abd Allah al-Aftah were the eldest sons of Imam al-Sadiq by his first wife Fatima, a granddaughter of Imam al-Hasan b. 'Ali. Isma'il evidently had contacts with the activist Shi'is in his father's following, including al-Mufaddal b. 'Umar al-Ju'fi.[6] Isma'il, who was reportedly involved in certain anti-Abbasid plots, may also have collaborated with Abu'l-Khattab al-Asadi, another activist Shi'i originally in the entourage of al-Sadiq.

As in the case of Isma'il, little is known about Muhammad b. Isma'il, the seventh imam of the Isma'iliyya. The relevant information contained in Ismaili sources has been collected by the *da'i* Idris 'Imad al-Din, who provides the most detailed biographical account of him.[7] Muhammad was the eldest son of Isma'il and the eldest grandson of Imam al-Sadiq. Born around 120/738, he was twenty-six years old at the time of al-Sadiq's death. Muhammad became the eldest member of al-Sadiq's family on the death of his uncle ʿAbd Allah al-Aftah in 149/766; he was older than his uncle Musa by about eight years. Soon after the recognition of Musa al-Kazim's imamate by the majority of al-Sadiq's followers, however, Muhammad b. Ismaʿil left Medina for the East and went into hiding to avoid Abbasid persecution, initiating the *dawr al-satr*, or 'period of concealment', in early Ismaili history which was to last until the establishment of the Fatimid caliphate. Henceforth, Muhammad b. Ismaʿil acquired the epithet al-Maktum ('the hidden one'), in addition to al-Maymun ('the fortunate one'). Nonetheless, he maintained his contacts with his Mubarakiyya following, who, like most other radical Shiʿi groups of the time, were centred in Kufa. Muhammad seems to have spent the later part of his life in Khuzistan, in south-western Persia, where he had some Shiʿi partisans. He died not long after 179/795, during the caliphate of the celebrated Harun al-Rashid (r. 170–193/786–809).

On the death of Muhammad b. Ismaʿil, the Mubarakiyya themselves split into two groups. One small and obscure group apparently traced the imamate in the progeny of the deceased imam. However, the bulk of the Mubarakiyya refused to accept Muhammad b. Ismaʿil's death. For these earliest Ismailis, identified by the Imami heresiographers as the immediate predecessors of the Qarmatis, Muhammad b. Ismaʿil was regarded as their seventh and last imam, who was expected to reappear soon as the Mahdi or *qaʾim* (riser) – terms which were basically synonymous in their early usage by the Ismailis and other Shiʿis.[8] This also explains why the Ismaʿiliyya later acquired the additional denomination of the Sabʿiyya, or the Seveners. Thus, by the time of Muhammad b. Ismaʿil's death, the earliest Ismailis were comprised of three distinct groups. Nothing is known with certainty regarding the subsequent history of these groups, and their interrelations, until shortly after the middle of the 3rd/9th century, when a unified Ismaili movement emerged openly in various regions.

Drawing on a variety of primary sources, including the Ismaili literature of the Fatimid period, the heresiographical works of the Imami scholars al-Nawbakhti and al-Qummi and even the anti-Ismaili tracts of Sunni polemicists, modern scholarship has to a large extent succeeded in clarifying the circumstances leading to the emergence of the Ismaili movement in the 3rd/9th century. It is certain that for almost a century after Muhammad b. Ismaʿil, a group of leaders worked secretly for the creation of a unified and expanded revolutionary movement against the Abbasids. These leaders, in all probability the imams of that obscure group that issued from the Mubarakiyya who maintained continuity in the imamate in the progeny of Muhammad b. Isma'il, did not openly claim the imamate for three generations. 'Abd Allah, the first of these secret leaders, had in fact organised his campaign around the central doctrine of the majority of the earliest Ismailis, namely, acknowledging Muhammad b. Isma'il as the awaited Mahdi. As explained later by the Ismaili imams, this was a *taqiyya* tactic to safeguard the early leaders of the movement against Abbasid persecution.

The existence of such a group of early Ismaili leaders is, indeed, confirmed by both the official view of the later Fatimid Ismailis regarding the pre-Fatimid phase of their history, and the hostile Sunni accounts of the same period. On the basis of this evidence it is clear that the leaders in question were members of the same family who succeeded one another on a hereditary basis. Ismaili tradition recognises three generations of leaders between Muhammad b. Isma'il and 'Abd Allah al-Mahdi, founder of the Fatimid state and the last of the concealed leaders during the *dawr al-satr* in early Ismaili history. The first of these leaders, 'Abd Allah, hailed originally from Khuzistan where his father Muhammad b. Isma'il had spent his final years. Subsequently, 'Abd Allah settled in Salamiyya, in central Syria, disguising himself as a Hashimid merchant. Henceforth, Salamiyya served as the secret and central headquarters of the early Ismaili movement. The Ismailis now referred to their movement simply as *al-da'wa*, the mission, or *al-da'wa al-hadiya*, the rightly guiding mission, in addition to using expressions such as *da'wat al-haqq*, summons to the truth.

The sustained efforts of 'Abd Allah, designated in later Ismaili sources as al-Akbar (the Elder), and his successors began to bear fruit by the early 260s/870s, when numerous *da'is* appeared in southern Iraq and other regions. In 261/874, soon after the death of the eleventh imam of the Twelver Shi'is, Hamdan Qarmat was converted to Ismailism in the Sawad of Kufa. Hamdan and his chief assistant 'Abdan organised the *da'wa* in southern Iraq and adjacent regions. A learned theologian, 'Abdan later trained numerous *da'is*, including the Persian Abu Sa'id al-Hasan b. Bahram al-Jannabi, the future founder of the Qarmati state of Bahrayn. The Ismailis of southern Iraq became generally known as the Qaramita (singular, Qarmati), after their first local leader. Later, the same term was applied pejoratively to other Ismaili communities not organised by Hamdan Qarmat. At the time, there was a single Ismaili movement centrally directed from Salamiyya in the name of Muhammad b. Isma'il as the awaited Mahdi.

Centred on the expectation of the imminent emergence of the Mahdi who would establish the rule of justice in the world, the Ismaili *da'wa* of the 3rd/9th century had a great deal of messianic appeal for underprivileged groups of diverse social backgrounds. Among such groups mention may be made of the landless peasantry and bedouin tribesmen whose interests were set apart from those of the prospering urban classes. Indeed, the Ismaili *da'wa* now appeared as a movement of social and religious protest against the Abbasids and their order, including especially the privileged urban classes and the centralised administration of their state. The Ismaili *da'is* also capitalised on regional grievances. It was on the basis of such a well-designed strategy that the religio-political message of the early Ismaili *da'wa* spread in different regions and among different social strata. However, the *da'is* were initially more successful in rural milieus, removed from the administrative centres of the Abbasid caliphate. The early Ismaili *da'wa* also achieved particular success among those Imami Shi'is of Iraq and elsewhere who had hitherto acknowledged Musa al-Kazim and certain members of his descendants as their imams. These Imamis shared a theological heritage with the Ismailis, while many amongst them had become disillusioned with the quietist policies of their own imams and leaders. It was particularly in the confusing circumstances following the death of the eleventh imam of the Twelver Shi'is, al-Hasan al-'Askari, in 260/874 that large numbers of Imami Shi'is responded to the summons of the Ismaili *da'wa*.

Meanwhile, the Ismaili *da'wa* spread to other regions. In Fars and other parts of southern Persia, 'Abdan's brother al-Ma'mun and Abu Sa'id al-Jannabi operated as *da'is*. Abu Sa'id was later sent to eastern Arabia, then known as Bahrayn, where he campaigned successfully among the bedouin tribesmen and the local Persian community. The *da'wa* in Yaman was initiated by Ibn Hawshab (d. 302/914), later known as Mansur al-Yaman (the Conqueror of Yaman), where he arrived in 268/881 accompanied by his chief collaborator 'Ali b. al-Fadl.[9] Both of these *da'is* themselves, like many early *da'is*, had been converted from Imami (Twelver) Shiʿism. By 293/905, almost all of Yaman had been brought under the control of the Ismaili *daʿis*. However, the Ismailis were later obliged to abandon the greater part of their conquests under pressure from the local Zaydi imams who had established a state in northern Yaman in 284/897. Yaman also served as an important base for the extension of the *daʿwa* to adjoining areas as well as to remote lands, such as Sind and North Africa. Indeed by 280/893, on Ibn al-Hawshab's instructions, the *daʿi* Abu ʿAbd Allah al-Shiʿi (d. 298/911) was already active among the Kutama Berbers of the Lesser Kabylia mountains in the Maghrib (in present-day Algeria). Abu ʿAbd Allah, too, had originally belonged to the Imami community of Kufa.

It was in the same decade of the 260s/870s that the Ismaili *daʿwa* was initiated in the Jibal, the west-central and north-western parts of Persia, where the *daʿis* adopted a new conversion policy, targeting the elite and the educated ruling classes. The fifth *daʿi* of the Jibal, Abu Hatim al-Razi (d. 322/934), spread the *daʿwa* to various parts of Daylam in northern Persia, where he converted several *amirs*. After its initial success in the Jibal, the same policy was later adopted by the *daʿis* of Khurasan and Transoxania in Central Asia, where the *daʿi* Muhammad b. Ahmad al-Nasafi converted the Samanid *amir* Nasr II (r. 301–331/914–943) as well as many of his courtiers. The *daʿi* al-Nasafi, who was executed in Bukhara soon afterwards in 332/943, has also been credited with introducing a form of Neoplatonic philosophy into Ismaili thought – a tradition further developed by the *daʿis* of the Iranian lands starting with al-Nasafi's student and successor Abu Yaʿqub al-Sijistani. The most detailed account of this phase of the early *daʿwa* is related by Nizam al-Mulk (d. 485/1092), the learned Saljuq vizier and a staunch enemy of the Ismailis.[10]

By the early 280s/890s, a unified and expanding Ismaili movement had replaced the earlier Kufan-based splinter groups. This single Ismaili movement was centrally directed from Salamiyya by leaders who made every effort to conceal their true identity. The central leaders of the *daʿwa* were, however, in contact with the *daʿis* of different regions, propagating a revolutionary messianic message in the name of the hidden Imam-Mahdi Muhammad b. Ismaʿil, whose advent was eagerly anticipated. In 286/899, soon after ʿAbd Allah al-Mahdi, the future Fatimid caliph, had succeeded to the central leadership of the *daʿwa* in Salamiyya, Ismailism was rent by a major schism.[11] ʿAbd Allah now felt secure enough to claim the imamate openly for himself and his predecessors, the same individuals who had organised and led the early Ismaili *daʿwa*. Later, in a letter sent to the Ismaili community in Yaman,[12] he attempted to reconcile his doctrinal declaration with the actual course of events in early Ismaili history. He explained that as a form of *taqiyya*, the central leaders of the *daʿwa* had adopted different pseudonyms, also assuming the rank of *hujja*, proof or full representative, of the absent Muhammad b. Ismaʿil. ʿAbd Allah further explained that the earlier propagation of the Mahdism of Muhammad b. Ismaʿil was itself another dissimulating measure, and that the Mahdi was in reality a collective code name for every true imam in the progeny of Jaʿfar al-Sadiq.

ʿAbd Allah al-Mahdi's reform split the then unified Ismaili movement into two rival branches. One faction remained loyal to the central leadership and acknowledged continuity in the Ismaili imamate, recognising ʿAbd Allah al-Mahdi and his ʿAlid ancestors as their imams, which in due course became the official Fatimid Ismaili doctrine. These Ismailis allowed for three hidden imams between Muhammad b. Ismaʿil and ʿAbd Allah al-Mahdi. This loyalist faction included mainly the majority of the Ismailis of Yaman and those communities in Egypt, North Africa and Sind founded by *daʿis* sent from Yaman. On the other hand, a dissident faction, originally led by Hamdan Qarmat (d. 321/933) and ʿAbdan (d. 286/899), rejected the reform and maintained their belief in the Mahdism of Muhammad b. Ismaʿil. Henceforth, the term Qarmati came to be applied more specifically to the dissident Ismailis who did not acknowledge ʿAbd Allah al-Mahdi, as well as his predecessors and successors in the Fatimid dynasty, as their imams. The dissident Qarmati faction comprised the communities in Iraq, Bahrayn and most of those situated in the Iranian lands. The Qarmatis, who lacked central leadership, quickly acquired their most important stronghold in Bahrayn, where a Qarmati state had been founded in the same eventful year 286/899 by Abu Saʿid al-Jannabi. Not long after these events, ʿAbd Allah left Salamiyya, in 289/902, and embarked on a historic journey which ended several years later in North Africa where he founded the Fatimid caliphate.

The early Ismailis established the basic framework of a system of religious thought which was further developed or modified in the

Fatimid period, while the Qarmatis followed a separate doctrinal course. Central to the Ismaili system of thought was a fundamental distinction between the exoteric (*zahir*) and the esoteric (*batin*) aspects of the Qur'an, and the sacred scriptures in general, as well as the commandments and prohibitions of religion. They further held that the *zahir*, or the religious laws enunciated by prophets, underwent periodical changes, while the *batin*, containing the spiritual truths (*haqa'iq*), remained immutable and eternal. These truths, representing the message common to Judaism, Christianity and Islam, were explained through the methodology of *ta'wil*, or esoteric interpretation, which often relied on the mystical significance of letters and numbers.

In every age, however, the esoteric truths would be accessible only to the elite (*khawass*) of humankind, as distinct from the ordinary people (*'awamm*), who were only capable of perceiving the apparent, literal meaning of the revelations. Thus, in the era of Islam, the eternal truths of religion could be explained only to those believers who had been properly initiated into the Ismaili *da'wa* and as such recognised the teaching authority of the Prophet Muhammad, and after him, that of his *wasi* 'Ali b. Abi Talib and the rightful 'Alid imams who succeeded him. These authorities were the sole possessors of *ta'wil* in the era of Islam. The centrality of *ta'wil* for the Ismailis is attested by the fact that a good portion of the literature produced by them during the early and Fatimid periods of their history is comprised of this genre, seeking justification for Ismaili doctrines in Qur'anic verses.[13] Although similar processes of exegeses or hermeneutics existed in earlier Judaeo-Christian as well as Gnostic traditions, the immediate antecedents of Ismaili *ta'wil*, also known as *batini ta'wil*, may be traced to the Shi'i milieus of the 2nd/8th century in Iraq.

Initiation into Ismailism, known as *balagh*, took place after the novice had taken an oath of allegiance, known as *'ahd* or *mithaq*. The initiates were bound by their oath to keep secret the *batin*, imparted to them by a hierarchy (*hudud*) of *da'is* and teachers authorised by the imam. The *batin* was thus not only hidden but also secret, and its exclusive knowledge had to be kept away from the uninitiated common people, the non-Ismailis who were not capable of understanding it. Initiation into the Ismaili community was gradual. Valuable details on this process may be found in the *Kitab al-'alim*, one of a handful of extant early texts attributed to Ibn Hawshab Mansur al-Yaman's son Jaʿfar.[14] But there is no evidence of any system of fixed seven stages of initiation, as claimed in the anti-Ismaili sources.

The eternal, esoteric truths or *haqaʾiq* formed a gnostic system of thought for the early Ismailis, representing their distinct world-view. The two main components of this system were a cyclical history of revelations or prophetic eras and a mythical cosmological doctrine. The Ismaili cyclical conception, applied to Judaeo-Christian as well as several other pre-Islamic religions, was developed in terms of eras of different prophets recognised in the Qurʾan. This view was also combined with their doctrine of the imamate which had essentially been inherited from the earlier Imamiyya. Accordingly, they held that the sacred history of humankind proceeded through seven prophetic eras (*dawr*s) of various durations, each inaugurated by a speaker-prophet or enunciator (*natiq*) of a divinely revealed message which in its exoteric (*zahir*) aspect contained a religious law (*shariʿa*). The *natiq*s of the first six eras were Adam, Noah, Abraham, Moses, Jesus and Muhammad. Each *natiq* was succeeded by a spiritual legatee (*wasi*), also called the silent one (*samit*), and later the foundation (*asas*), who explained to the elite the esoteric truths (*haqaʾiq*) contained in the *batin* dimension of that era's message. Each *wasi* was, in turn, succeeded by seven imams, who guarded and interpreted the true meaning of the sacred scriptures and laws in their *zahir* and *batin* aspects. The seventh imam of every era would rise in rank to become the *natiq* of the following era, abrogating the *shariʿa* of the previous era and enunciating a new one in its place.[15]

As the seventh imam of the era of Islam, Muhammad b. Ismaʿil was initially expected to return as the Mahdi as well as the *natiq* of the seventh eschatological era when, instead of promulgating a new law, however, he would fully divulge the esoteric truths of all the preceding revelations. In the final, millenarian age, the *haqaʾiq* would be completely freed from all their veils; and there would no longer be any distinction between the *zahir* and the *batin* in that age of pure spirituality before the physical world is consummated. This original cyclical view of hierohistory was somewhat modified after ʿAbd Allah al-Mahdi's doctrinal reform, which allowed for more than just one heptad of imams in the era of Islam. Recognising continuity in the imamate, the advent of the seventh era now lost its earlier messianic appeal for the loyal Fatimid Ismailis, for whom the final eschatological age was postponed indefinitely into the future. On the other hand, the Qarmatis of Bahrayn and elsewhere continued to consider Muhammad b. Isma'il as their Mahdi, who, on his reappearance as the seventh *natiq*, was expected to initiate the final age; and the Qarmatis made specific predications for his advent.

The cosmological doctrine of the early Ismailis represented a gnostic cosmological myth.[16] In this system, it was explained how God's creative activity brought forth letters and words; and how with the resulting names there appeared simultaneously the very things they symbolised. The early cosmology, which was espoused by the entire Ismaili (Qarmati) movement until it was superseded in the 4th/10th century by a Neoplatonised cosmology, also had a soteriological purpose. It aimed at showing that man's salvation depended on his acquisition of a specific type of knowledge imparted by God's messengers (*natiq*s) and their legitimate successors in every era of sacred history.

The Fatimid phase in Ismaili history

The Fatimid period represents the 'golden age' of Ismaili Shi'ism, when the Ismailis possessed a state of their own and Ismaili scholarship and literature attained their summit.[17] The foundation of the Fatimid caliphate in 297/909 in Ifriqiya, North Africa (modern-day Tunisia and eastern Algeria), indeed marked the crowning success of the early Ismailis. The religio-political *da'wa* of the Isma'iliyya had finally led to the establishment of a state or *dawla* headed by the Ismaili imam, 'Abd Allah al-Mahdi (r. 297–322/909–934). The ground for Fatimid rule had been prepared meticulously by the *da'i* Abu 'Abd Allah al-Shi'i, who had been active amongst the region's Kutama Berbers. He converted the larger part of the Kutama tribal federation and transformed them into a disciplined army. With the help of his Kutama army, Abu 'Abd Allah speedily achieved his conquest of Ifriqiya, which was then ruled by the Aghlabids on behalf of the Abbasids. Meanwhile, after a long and eventful journey out of Salamiyya, 'Abd Allah al-Mahdi had settled in the remote town of Sijilmasa (in today's south-eastern Morocco). In 296/909, Abu 'Abd Allah handed over the reins of power to al-Mahdi in Sijilmasa. With these events, the period of concealment in early Ismaili history came to an end.

On 20 Rabiʿ II 297/4 January 910, al-Mahdi made his triumphant entry into Qayrawan, the capital of Ifriqiya, and was proclaimed as caliph there. The new dynasty came to be known as Fatimid (Fatimiyya), derived from the name of the Prophet's daughter Fatima, to whom al-Mahdi and his successors traced their Husaynid ʿAlid ancestry. In line with their universal claims, the Fatimid caliph-imams did not abandon their *daʿwa* activities on assuming power, since they aimed to extend their rule over the entire Muslim community. However, the first four Fatimid caliph-imams, ruling from Ifriqiya, encountered numerous difficulties while consolidating their power with the help of the Kutama Berbers, who provided the backbone of the Fatimid armies. Specifically, the early Fatimids confronted the hostility of the Khariji Berbers and the Sunni Arab inhabitants of Qayrawan and other cities of Ifriqiya led by their Maliki jurists. This was in addition to their rivalries and conflicts with the Umayyads of Spain, the Abbasids and the Byzantines. Under these circumstances, the Ismaili *daʿwa* remained rather inactive during the North African phase of the Fatimid caliphate.

Table 4.1 Fatimid Caliph-Imams (297–567/909–1171)

1. al-Mahdi (297–322/909–934)
2. al-Qaʾim (322–334/934–946)
3. al-Mansur (334–341/946–953)
4. al-Muʿizz (341–365/953–975)
5. al-ʿAziz (365–386/975–996)
6. al-Hakim (386–411/996–1021)
7. al-Zahir (411–427/1021–1036)
8. al-Mustansir (427–487/1036–1094)
9. al-Mustaʿli (487–495/1094–1101)
10. al-Amir (495–524/1101–1130)
11. al-Hafiz
    as regent (524–526/1130–1132)
    as caliph (526–544/1132–1149)
12. al-Zafir (544–549/1149–1154)
13. al-Faʾiz (549–555/1154–1160)
14. al-ʿAdid (555–567/1160–1171)

Fatimid rule was established firmly only under the fourth member of the dynasty, al-Muʿizz, who succeeded in transforming the Fatimid caliphate from a regional state into a great empire. He was also the first Fatimid caliph-imam to concern himself distinctly with the propagation of the Ismaili *daʿwa* outside the Fatimid dominions, especially after the transference of the seat of the Fatimid state in 362/973 to Egypt, where he founded Cairo as his new capital city. The *daʿwa* policy of al-Muʿizz was based on a number of religio-political considerations. In particular, he was apprehensive of the success of the Qarmati *daʿwa* activities in the eastern regions, which not only undermined the efforts of the Fatimid Ismaili *daʿis* operating in the same lands, notably Iraq, Persia, Transoxania and Sind, but also aroused the general anti-Ismaili sentiments of the Sunni Muslims who did not distinguish the Ismailis from the dissident Qarmatis, who had acquired a reputation for extremism and lawlessness. The policies of al-Muʿizz soon bore fruit as the Ismaili *daʿwa* and Fatimid cause began to be significantly reinvigorated outside the Fatimid state. Most notably, Abu Yaʿqub al-Sijistani (d. after 361/971), the *daʿi* of Khurasan and Transoxania who had earlier belonged to the dissident Qarmati faction, transferred his allegiance to the Fatimids. Consequently, the majority of al-Sijistani's followers in eastern Persia and Central Asia now acknowledged the Fatimid caliphs as their Ismaili imams. Ismaili Shiʿism also acquired a permanent stronghold in Multan, Sind, where an Ismaili principality was established for a few decades.

Information on the structure and functioning of the *daʿwa* was among the most closely guarded secrets of the Ismailis. The religio-political messages of the Ismaili *daʿwa* were disseminated by networks of *daʿis* within the Fatimid dominions as well as in other regions designated as the *jazaʾir* (singular, *jazira*, 'island'). The regions falling outside Fatimid jurisdiction were divided into twelve 'islands' for the purpose of propagating the *daʿwa*. Each *jazira* was placed under the charge of a high-ranking *daʿi* referred to as *hujja*; and every *hujja* had a number of *daʿis* of different ranks working under him. The *daʿis*, in turn, had their own assistants, designated as *maʾdhun*. The ordinary Ismaili initiates, the *mustajib*s or respondents, did not occupy a rank in the *daʿwa* hierarchy (*hudud*). Organised in a strictly hierarchical manner, the Fatimid *daʿwa* was under the overall supervision of the imam of the time and the *daʿi al-duʿat* (chief *daʿi*), also known as the *bab* (gate), who acted as its executive head. The *daʿwa* organisation developed over time and reached its culmination under al-Mustansir (r. 427–487/1036–1094), the eighth member of the Fatimid dynasty. It was, however, in non-Fatimid regions, the *jazaʾir*, especially Yaman, Persia and Central Asia, that the Fatimid *daʿwa* achieved its lasting success.[18]

The Ismailis held learning in high esteem and elaborated distinctive traditions and institutions of learning under the Fatimids. The Fatimid *daʿwa* was particularly concerned with educating the Ismaili converts in esoteric doctrine, known as *hikma*, or 'wisdom'. As a result, a variety of lectures or 'teaching sessions', generally designated as *majalis* (singular, *majlis*), were organised over time for different Ismaili audiences, including women. The private lectures on Ismaili esoteric doctrine, known as the *majalis al-hikma*, or 'sessions of wisdom', were reserved exclusively for the Ismaili initiates who had already taken the oath of allegiance (*ʿahd*) and secrecy. These lectures, delivered by the *daʿi al-duʿat* at the Fatimid palace in Cairo, were approved beforehand by the imam. Only the imam was the source of the *hikma*, and the *daʿi al-duʿat*, called *bab* in Ismaili sources, was the imam's mouthpiece through whom the Ismailis received their esoteric knowledge. Many of these *majalis* were in due course collected and committed to writing, such as al-Qadi al-Nuʿman's *Taʾwil al-daʿaʾim*. This Fatimid tradition of learning culminated in the *Majalis al-Muʾayyadiyya* of al-Muʾayyad fiʾl-Din al-Shirazi (d. 470/1078), who was the chief *daʿi* in Cairo for some twenty years. Another of the main institutions of learning founded by the Fatimids was the Dar al-ʿIlm, the House of Knowledge. Established in 395/1005 by al-Hakim, this institution taught a variety of religious and non-religious subjects and it was also equipped with a major library. Many *daʿi*s received at least part of their training at the Dar al-ʿIlm, sometimes also called Dar al-Hikma.[19] The Ismaili *daʿwa* took particular care in the selection and training of the *daʿi*s, who had to operate under diverse, and often hostile, conditions.[20] As a result, many of the Fatimid *daʿi*s became eminent scholars in theology, philosophy and jurisprudence, among other fields of knowledge, as well as in the application of the methodology of *taʾwil*.

It was during the Fatimid phase that the Ismaili *daʿi*s, who were at the same time the learned scholars and authors in their community, produced what were to be regarded as the classical texts of Ismaili literature, dealing with a multitude of exoteric and esoteric subjects as well as *ta'wil* which became the hallmark of Ismaili thought.[21] The *da'is* of this period developed distinctive intellectual traditions. In particular, the Ismaili (Qarmati) *da'is* of the Iranian lands set out, in the course of the 4th/10th century, to harmonise Ismaili *kalam* theology with Neoplatonism and other philosophical traditions, into complex metaphysical systems of thought. This led to the development of a unique intellectual tradition of 'philosophical theology' within Ismailism. The earliest proponents of this tradition were the *da'is* Muhammad b. Ahmad al-Nasafi, Abu Hatim al-Razi and Abu Ya'qub al-Sijistani, who wrote numerous treatises in Arabic.

These Iranian *da'is*, who were also involved in a long-drawn-out theological debate, wrote for the elite and the educated classes of society, aiming to attract them intellectually. This may explain why they expressed their theology, always revolving around the central Imami Shi'i doctrine of the imamate, in terms of the then most intellectually fashionable themes and terminologies, without compromising the essence of their religious message. In their metaphysical systems, the earlier gnostic cosmology was replaced by a Neoplatonised Ismaili cosmology. The Iranian *da'is* also expounded a doctrine of spiritual salvation as part of their metaphysical system. In their soteriology, the ultimate goal of salvation is the human soul's progression towards its Creator in quest of a spiritual reward in an eternal afterlife. This, of course, would depend on guidance provided by the authorised sources of wisdom in every era of religious history.[22] Nasir-i Khusraw (d. after 462/1070), the chief *da'i* (or *hujja*) of Khurasan who spread the *da'wa* in Badakhshan, was the last major member of this Iranian school of philosophical Ismailism.[23]

The Fatimid caliph-imam al-Mu'izz permitted the assimilation of the Neoplatonised cosmology, developed originally by al-Nasafi and other Qarmati *da'is* of the Iranian lands, into the teachings of the Fatimid Ismaili *da'wa*. The Neoplatonised Ismaili cosmology went through further transformation at the hands of Hamid al-Din al-Kirmani (d. ca. 411/1020), the most learned theologian-philosopher of the Fatimid period. Drawing on a variety of philosophical traditions, al-Kirmani expounded his own metaphysical system in his *Rahat al-'aql* (The Tranquillity of the Intellect). In his cosmology, al-Kirmani replaced the Neoplatonic dyad of universal intellect (*ʿaql*) and universal soul (*nafs*) in the spiritual world, adopted by his Ismaili predecessors, by a system of ten separate intellects in partial adaptation of al-Farabi's Aristotelian school of philosophy. Indeed, al-Kirmani's thought represents an unparalleled syncretic tradition within the Iranian school of philosophical Ismailism.[24] Al-Kirmani also acted as an arbiter in the theological debate that had earlier taken place among the Iranian *daʿi*s. In his *Kitab al-riyad*, he reviewed the debate from the perspective of the Fatimid *daʿwa* and in particular upheld certain views of Abu Hatim al-Razi against those of al-Nasafi by affirming the indispensability of both the *zahir* and the *batin*, the letter of the law and its inner meaning.

Similarly, Neoplatonic philosophy influenced the cosmology expounded by the Ismaili-affiliated Ikhwan al-Safa', the 'Brethren of Purity', an anonymous group of authors in Basra, who produced an encyclopaedic work of fifty-two epistles, known as the *Rasa'il Ikhwan al-Safa'*, on a variety of sciences during the early 4th/10th century. Like the Iranian *daʿi*s, the Ikhwan aimed to harmonise religion and philosophy, but they do not seem to have had any impact on Ismaili thought of the Fatimid period. Later, the *Rasa'il* were introduced into the literature of the Tayyibi Mustaʿlian *daʿwa* in Yaman, as was al-Kirmani's cosmology.

The Sunni polemicists always accused the Ismailis of ignoring the *shariʿa*, supposedly because they had found access to its hidden meaning; hence, they were commonly designated as the Batiniyya. However, from early on the Fatimids concerned themselves increasingly with legal matters. The process of codifying Ismaili law had already started in ʿAbd Allah al-Mahdi's reign when the precepts of Imami Shiʿi law were put into practice. At the time, there still did not exist a distinctly Ismaili *madhhab* or school of jurisprudence.

The promulgation of an Ismaili *madhhab* resulted mainly from the efforts of al-Qadi Abu Hanifa al-Nuʿman b. Muhammad (d. 363/974), the foremost Ismaili jurist who was officially commissioned to prepare legal compendia. He codified Ismaili law by systematically collecting the firmly established *hadith*s transmitted from the *ahl al-bayt*, drawing on existing collections. Al-Qadi al-Nuʿman's efforts culminated in the *Daʿa'im al-Islam* (The Pillars of Islam), which was scrutinised closely by al-Muʿizz and endorsed as the official code of the Fatimid state. Ismaili law, explained on a weekly basis in public sessions in the mosques of Fatimid Cairo, accorded special importance to the Shiʿi doctrine of the imamate. The authority of the infallible ʿAlid imam and his teachings became the third principal source of Ismaili law, after the Qur'an and the *sunna* of the Prophet.[25] In comparison with the Twelver and the Zaydi Shiʿi *madhhab*s, the legal literature of the Ismailis is extremely meagre. The Ismaili system of law is almost exclusively the work of al-Qadi al-Nuʿman, since few other Ismaili jurists, either during or after the Fatimid period, concerned themselves with producing legal compendia. Indeed, after al-Nuʿman there has been no significant development in Ismaili law. The *Daʿaʾim al-Islam* has continued to be used by Tayyibi Ismailis as their principal authority in legal matters, while the Nizari Ismailis have been guided in their legal affairs by their 'imam of the time'.

The Fatimid caliph-imam al-Hakim's reign witnessed the opening phase of what was to become known as the Druze religion.[26] A number of *daʿi*s who had come to Cairo from Persia and Central Asia, notably al-Akhram (d. 408/1018), Hamza and al-Darazi, now began to propagate certain extremist ideas regarding al-Hakim and his imamate. Drawing on the traditions of the Shiʿi *ghulat* and eschatological expectations of the early Ismailis, these *daʿi*s effectively founded a new religious movement, proclaiming the end of the era of Islam and the abrogation of its *shariʿa*. By 408/1017 (the opening year of the Druze calendar), Hamza and al-Darazi were also publicly declaring al-Hakim's divinity. It was after al-Darazi that the adherents of this new movement later became known as Daraziyya or Duruz; hence their general designation as Druzes.

The Fatimid *daʿwa* organisation in Cairo launched a campaign against the new doctrine. As part of this campaign, the *daʿi* al-Kirmani was invited to Cairo to officially refute the new doctrine from a theological perspective. He composed a number of treatises, such as *Mabasim al-bisharat* and *al-Risala al-waʿiza*, reiterating the Ismaili Shiʿi doctrine of the imamate and rejecting the idea of al-Hakim's divinity. He also argued that the era of Islam and the validity of its *shariʿa* would continue under al-Hakim's countless successors until the end of time. In fact the doctrine of the imamate provided an essential subject matter for numerous treatises written by Ismaili authors of different periods.[27] Al-Kirmani's writings were to some extent successful in preventing the spread of extremist Druze ideas within the inner circles of the *daʿwa* organisation. Nonetheless, the Druze movement acquired momentum and popular appeal; and when al-Hakim disappeared mysteriously during one of his nocturnal outings in 411/1021, the Druze leaders interpreted this as a voluntary act initiating al-Hakim's *ghayba* or occultation. In the same year, Hamza went into hiding and he was succeeded as the leader of the movement by Baha' al-Din al-Muqtana. With the subsequent persecution of the Druzes in Fatimid Egypt, the movement found its greatest success in Syria where a number of Druze *daʿis* had been active.

The Druzes eventually developed their body of theological doctrine and sacred scriptures. In particular, the extant letters and other writings of Hamza and al-Muqtana have been collected into a canon, arranged in six books and designated as the *Rasa'il al-hikma* (The Epistles of Wisdom), which has survived as the sacred scripture of the Druzes.[28] A highly closed and secretive community who observe *taqiyya* very strictly, the Druzes who call themselves the Muwahhidun (Unitarians) possess complex doctrines of Neoplatonic cosmology, eschatology and metempsychosis (*tanasukh*). Considering al-Hakim as the last *maqam* or locus of the Creator, the Druzes await his reappearance (*rajʿa*) together with Hamza, who is recognised as an imam. Druze teachings effectively represent a new religion falling outside of Ismaili Shiʿism. Under the Ottomans, the Druzes of Syria and Lebanon were ruled by their own *amir*s, especially those belonging to the Maʿnid and Shihabid dynasties.

Meanwhile, the Qarmatis had survived in Bahrayn and in scattered communities across Iraq, Yaman, Persia and Central Asia. All the Qarmatis were still awaiting the reappearance of Muhammad b. Ismaʿil as the Mahdi and final *natiq*, though some Qarmati leaders now intermittently claimed Mahdism for themselves. After Abu Saʿid al-Jannabi (d. 301/913), several of his sons rose to leadership of the Qarmati state of Bahrayn, where communal and egalitarian principles played an important role. Under his youngest son, Abu Tahir Sulayman (r. 311–332/923–944), the Qarmatis became infamous for their regular anti-Abbasid raids into Iraq and their pillaging of the Meccan pilgrim caravans. Abu Tahir's ravages culminated in his attack on Mecca during the pilgrimage season in 317/930, when the Qarmatis committed numerous desecrating acts and dislodged the Black Stone (*al-hajar al-aswad*) from the corner of the Ka'ba and carried it to al-Ahsa', their capital in Bahrayn. This sacrilegious act, presumably committed in preparation for the coming of the Mahdi, shocked the Muslim world and led to Sunni scholars' condemnation of the entire Ismaili movement as an organised conspiracy to destroy Islam. They also alleged that Abu Tahir had secretly received his instructions from 'Abd Allah al-Mahdi, who was then reigning in North Africa as the first Fatimid caliph-imam.

Modern scholarship has shown, however, that the Qarmatis of Bahrayn were at the time, like other Qarmatis, predicting the imminent appearance of the Mahdi and did not acknowledge the first Fatimid caliph, or any of his successors, as their imams.[29] In fact, on the basis of certain astrological calculations, the Qarmatis had been predicting the advent of the Mahdi for the year 316/928, an event that, according to contemporary Qarmati doctrine, would end the era of Islam and its law and initiate the final (lawless) era of history. This explains why Abu Tahir sacked Mecca and then recognised the expected Mahdi in a young Persian, to whom he briefly handed over power in 319/931 with disastrous consequences. The obscure episode of the 'Persian Mahdi' seriously demoralised the Qarmatis. Subsequently, the Qarmatis of Bahrayn reverted to their former beliefs, and their leaders once again claimed to be acting on the orders of the hidden Mahdi. The Qarmatis eventually returned the Black Stone in 339/950, for a large ransom paid by the Abbasids and not, as alleged by anti-Ismaili sources, at the instigation of the Fatimid caliph.

In Persia, Qarmatism had spread widely after 286/899. The *da'is* of the Jibal did not generally recognise 'Abd Allah al-Mahdi's imamate, and awaited the return of Muhammad b. Isma'il as the Mahdi. Abu Hatim al-Razi, the fifth *da'i* of the Jibal, prophesied the Mahdi's advent for the year 316/928; as his predictions did not materialise he encountered the hostility of his co-religionists and sought refuge in Adharbayjan, where he died in 322/934. Later, some rulers of Adharbayjan and Daylam, belonging to the Musafirid (or Sallarid) dynasty, adhered to Qarmatism and recognised Muhammad b. Isma'il as the Mahdi. In Khurasan and Transoxania, too, dissident Qarmatism persisted for some time after the establishment of the Fatimid state. The *da'i* al-Nasafi affirmed the Mahdism of Muhammad b. Isma'il in his major treatise, *Kitab al-mahsul* (Book of the Yield), which acquired a prominent status within Qarmati circles in different regions. By the time the Qarmati state of Bahrayn was finally uprooted in 470/1077 by the local tribal chieftains, other Qarmati communities in Persia, Iraq and elsewhere had either disintegrated or switched their allegiance to the Ismaili *daʿwa* of the Fatimids. There was now, once again, only one unified Ismaili *daʿwa* under the supreme leadership of the Fatimid caliph-imam.

In the meantime, the Ismaili *daʿwa* activities, especially outside of the Fatimid dominions, reached their peak in the long reign of al-Mustansir, even after the Sunni Saljuqs replaced the Shiʿi Buyids as overlords of the Abbasids in 447/1055. The Fatimid *daʿis* won many converts in Iraq, Persia and Central Asia as well as in Yaman where the Sulayhids ruled as vassals of the Fatimids from 439/1047 until 532/1138. The Sulayhids also played an active part in the renewed Fatimid efforts to spread the *daʿwa* on the Indian subcontinent. The Ismaili *daʿwa* had continued successfully in many parts of the Iranian world. By the early 460s/1070s, the Persian Ismailis in the Saljuq dominions were under the overall leadership of ʿAbd al-Malik b. ʿAttash, who had his secret headquarters in Isfahan, the main Saljuq capital. In Badakhshan and other eastern parts of the Iranian world, too, the *daʿwa* had continued to spread after the downfall of the Samanids in 395/1005. One of the most eminent *daʿis* of al-Mustansir's time was Nasir-i Khusraw, who played a key role in propagating the *daʿwa* in Central Asia as the *hujja* of Khurasan, while maintaining his contacts with the chief *daʿi* al-Muʾayyad fi'l-Din al-Shirazi and the *daʿwa* headquarters in Cairo.[30] The *daʿi* al-Mu'ayyad himself was another learned Persian *daʿi* who, after an earlier successful career at the Buyid court in Fars, settled in Cairo and served as chief *daʿi* there for twenty years.

On al-Mustansir's death in 487/1094, the unified Ismaili *daʿwa* split into two rival factions, as his son and original heir-designate Nizar (d. 488/1095) was deprived of his succession rights by the all-powerful Fatimid vizier al-Afdal, who installed Nizar's younger half-brother to the Fatimid throne with the title of al-Mustaʿli bi'llah (r. 487–495/1094–1101). The imamate of al-Mustaʿli was recognised by the Ismaili communities of Egypt, Yaman and western India. These Ismailis, who depended on the Fatimid regime, later traced the imamate in the progeny of al-Mustaʿli. On the other hand, the Ismailis of Persia, who were then already under the leadership of Hasan-i Sabbah, supported the succession rights of Nizar and his descendants. The two factions were later designated as the Mustaʿliyya and the Nizariyya.

During its final decades, the Fatimid caliphate declined rapidly. The Mustaʿlian Ismailis themselves split into Hafizi and Tayyibi branches on the assassination of al-Mustaʿli's son and successor al-Amir in 524/1130. Al-Amir's successor to the Fatimid throne, al-Hafiz, and the later Fatimid caliphs were recognised as imams by the *daʿwa* headquarters in Cairo and the Mustaʿlian Ismailis of Egypt and Syria and by part of the community in Yaman. These Mustaʿlian Ismailis, now designated as the Hafiziyya, did not survive the downfall of the Fatimid dynasty for long. The Mustaʿlian community of Sulayhid Yaman, however, recognised the imamate of al-Amir's infant son al-Tayyib and became known as the Tayyibiyya.[31]

The Ayyubid Salah al-Din (Saladin of the Crusader sources), who had acted as the last Fatimid vizier, ended Fatimid rule in Muharram 567/September 1171 when he had the *khutba* read in Cairo in the name of the reigning Abbasid caliph. A few days later, al-ʿAdid, the fourteenth and final Fatimid caliph, died after a brief illness. The Fatimid *dawla* had thus ended after 262 years. On the collapse of the Fatimid state, Egypt's new Sunni Ayyubid masters began to persecute the Ismailis, also suppressing the Hafizi Ismaili *daʿwa* organisation and all the Fatimid institutions. Henceforth, Mustaʿlian Ismailism survived only in its Tayyibi form.

The Tayyibi Ismailis: The Yamani and Indian phases

The Tayyibi Ismailis rejected the claims of al-Hafiz and the later Fatimid caliphs to the imamate. Tayyibi Ismailism found its permanent stronghold in Yaman, where it received the initial support and protection of the Sulayhid dynasty. Indeed, the effective ruler of Sulayhid Yaman, Queen Arwa, who also carried the epithet of Hurra, became leader of the Tayyibi *daʿwa* in Yaman and severed her ties with Cairo and the Fatimid regime. Nothing is known about the fate of al-Tayyib, who was probably murdered secretly on the order of the Fatimid caliph al-Hafiz. According to Yamani Tayyibi tradition, however, al-Amir himself had placed his infant son in the custody of a group of trusted *daʿis* who, in due course, managed to hide him, and made it possible for the Tayyibi imamate to continue through his progeny. The Tayyibi

Mustaʿlian Ismailis are, indeed, of the opinion that their imamate has been handed down among al-Tayyib's descendants to the present time, with all these imams remaining in concealment.

The Tayyibis divide their history into succeeding eras of concealment (*satr*) and manifestation (*kashf* or *zuhur*), during which the imams are concealed or manifest. The first era of *satr*, coinciding with the pre-Fatimid period in Ismaili history, ended with the appearance of ʿAbd Allah al-Mahdi. This was followed by an era of *zuhur* which continued in the Fatimid period until the concealment of the twenty-first Tayyibi imam, al-Tayyib, soon after al-Amir's death in 524/1130. Al-Tayyib's concealment, it is held by the Tayyibis, initiated another era of *satr*, during which the Tayyibi imams have all remained hidden (*mastur*) from the eyes of their followers; and the current *satr* will continue until the appearance of an imam from al-Tayyib's progeny. The current period of *satr* in Tayyibi Ismailism has, in turn, been divided into a Yamani phase, extending from 526/1132 to around 997/1589, when the Tayyibis were split into Da'udi and Sulaymani factions, and an Indian phase, essentially covering the history of the Da'udi Tayyibi *daʿwa* and community during the last four centuries. There were initially no doctrinal differences between the two Tayyibi communities (and later a third, ʿAlawi, community), which in the absence of their imams followed separate lines of *daʿi*s.

The history of the Yamani phase of Tayyibi Ismailism is a history of the activities of the various *daʿi*s who led the community, and their relations with the Zaydi and other local dynasties of medieval Yaman. The Tayyibi *daʿwa*, as noted, survived the downfall of the Fatimids because from early on it had developed independently of the Fatimid regime. It received its initial support from the Sulayhid Queen al-Sayyida Arwa (d. 532/1138), who had been looking after the affairs of the Ismaili *daʿwa* in Yaman with the help of the *daʿi* Lamak b. Malik al-Hammadi (d. ca. 491/1098) and then of his son Yahya (d. 520/1126). It was soon after 526/1132 that the Sulayhid queen completely broke relations with Cairo and declared Yahya's successor, al-Dhu'ayb b. Musa al-Wadiʿi, as *al-daʿi al-mutlaq*, or *daʿi* with absolute authority, to lead the Tayyibi Mustaʿlian *daʿwa* on behalf of the hidden imam, al-Tayyib. This marked the foundation of the independent Tayyibi *daʿwa*, henceforth called *al-daʿwa al-Tayyibiyya*. Having already broken off relations with the Fatimid regime, she now also made the new Tayyibi *daʿwa* independent of the Sulayhid regime, a measure that ensured the survival of Tayyibi Ismailism under the leadership of a *daʿi mutlaq*. Al-Dhu'ayb's successors have retained this title to the present day.

On al-Dhu'ayb's death in 546/1151, Ibrahim b. al-Husayn al-Hamidi (d. 557/1162), belonging to the influential Hamdan tribe of Yaman, succeeded to the headship of the Tayyibi *daʿwa* as the second *daʿi mutlaq*. The third *daʿi* produced, in his *Tuhfat al-qulub*, the earliest history of the Tayyibi *daʿwa* in Yaman.[32] Subsequently, the leadership of the *daʿwa* passed into the hands of the members of the Banu al-Walid al-Anf clan of the Quraysh and remained in that family, with minor interruptions, until 946/1539. The Tayyibi *daʿwa* spread successfully in the Haraz region of Yaman, winning an increasing number of converts in western India as well. It is also worth noting that the Tayyibis preserved a good portion of the Ismaili literature of the Fatimid period.

In the doctrinal domain, the Tayyibis maintained the Fatimid Ismaili traditions, and, in like manner, they emphasised the equal importance of the *zahir* and *batin* aspects of religion. They also retained the established interest of the Ismailis in cyclical history and cosmology, which served as the basis of their gnostic, esoteric *haqa'iq* system of religious thought with its distinctive eschatological and salvational themes. This system was, in fact, founded largely by the *daʿi* Ibrahim al-Hamidi who drew extensively on al-Kirmani's *Rahat al-ʿaql* and synthesised its cosmological doctrine of ten separate intellects with gnostic mythical elements. The Tayyibi modification of al-Kirmani's system, first expounded in al-Hamidi's *Kanz al-walad*, in effect represents the fourth and final stage in the development of cosmology in Ismaili thought. Based on astronomical and astrological speculations, the Yamani Tayyibis also introduced certain innovations into the previous cyclical conception of religious history, expressed in terms of the seven prophetic eras. The Tayyibi *haqa'iq*, explained in many sources, such as al-Hamidi's *Kanz al-walad* and the *Kitab al-dhakhira fi'l-haqiqa* of the *daʿi* ʿAli b. Muhammad b. al-Walid (d. 612/1215), found their fullest description in Idris ʿImad al-Din's *Zahr al-maʿani*, an extensive compendium of esoteric doctrines. Subsequently, the Tayyibis made few further doctrinal contributions, instead copying the earlier texts. Idris (d. 872/1468), the nineteenth *daʿi* of the Tayyibis, was also a major Ismaili historian; his historical works include the *ʿUyun al-akhbar*, a comprehensive seven-volume history of the Ismaili *daʿwa* from its beginnings until the opening phase of the Tayyibi *daʿwa*. From the outset, the Tayyibis used al-Qadi al-Nuʿman's *Daʿaʾim al-Islam* as their most authoritative legal compendium.

The Tayyibi *daʿwa* organisation drew on Fatimid antecedents with certain modifications and simplifications dictated by the changed realities of Yaman. As in the case of the imams, every *daʿi mutlaq* appointed his successor by the rule of the *nass*; and the position has normally been handed down on a hereditary basis. The Tayyibi *daʿi*s in Yaman were among the most educated members of their community; many became outstanding religious scholars and produced the bulk of the classical Tayyibi literature related to the *haqaʾiq*.[33] The *daʿi mutlaq* was assisted in the affairs of the *daʿwa* by several subordinate *daʿi*s designated as *maʾdhun* and *mukasir*. The Tayyibi *daʿwa* generally retained, on a much reduced scale, the traditions of the Fatimid *daʿwa* in terms of initiation, secrecy and education of the initiates.

Meanwhile, the Yamani *daʿi*s had maintained close relations with the Tayyibi community of western India. There, the Ismaili converts, mostly of Hindu descent, were known as Bohras, a name believed to have been derived from the Gujarati term *vohorvu* meaning 'to trade', since the *daʿwa* originally spread among the trading community of Gujarat. The head of the Tayyibi *daʿwa* in India, known locally as the *wali*, was regularly appointed by the *daʿi mutlaq* residing in Yaman. As the Tayyibis of Gujarat were not harassed by the region's Hindu rulers, the community was able to expand significantly until the Muslim conquest of Gujarat in 697/1298. Subsequently, the Ismaili Bohras were scrutinised by the region's Muslim governors; their situation deteriorated under the independent Sunni sultanate of Gujarat. With the establishment of Mughal rule in 980/1572, however, the Bohras began to enjoy a certain degree of religious freedom in India and they were no longer obliged to convert to Sunni Islam.

On the death of the twenty-sixth *daʿi mutlaq*, Daʾud b. ʿAjabshah, in 997/1589 or two years later, dispute over his succession led to the Daʾudi–Sulaymani schism in the Tayyibi *daʿwa* and community, reflecting Indian–Yamani rivalries. By then, the Tayyibi Bohras in India, who greatly outnumbered their Yamani co-religionists, desired to attain their independence from Yaman. As a result, they acknowledged Daʾud Burhan al-Din (d. 1021/1612) as their next *daʿi* and became known as Daʾudis. On the other hand, a minority of Tayyibis, who accounted for almost the entire community in Yaman, now recognised Sulayman b. Hasan (d. 1005/1597) as their own new, twenty-seventh, *daʿi*; they became known as Sulaymanis. Henceforth, the Da'udi and Sulaymani Tayyibis followed separate lines of *daʿi*s. The Da'udi *daʿi*s continued to reside in India, while the headquarters of the Sulaymani *daʿwa* remained in Yaman. The Sulaymanis represent a small minority within the Tayyibi community. Subsequently, the Da'udi Bohras were further subdivided in India because of periodic challenges to the authority of their *daʿi mutlaq*. In one such instance, in 1034/1624, ʿAli b. Ibrahim (d. 1046/1637) founded the ʿAlawi splinter group who established their own separate line of *daʿi*s, starting with ʿAli b. Ibrahim himself as their twenty-ninth *daʿi*. At present, the ʿAlawi Bohras are a very small community centred at Baroda (Vadodara) in Gujarat.

Meanwhile, the main Da'udi community continued to grow and prosper, free from persecution by the Mughal emperors and their governors in Gujarat. In 1200/1785, the headquarters of the Da'udi *daʿwa* was transferred to Surat, where the forty-third *daʿi*, ʿAbd ʿAli Sayf al-Din (1213–1232/1798–1817), founded a seminary known as Sayfi Dars (also Jamiʿa Sayfiyya) for the education of Da'udi scholars and functionaries. Since 1232/1817, the office of the *daʿi mutlaq* of the Da'udi Tayyibi Bohras has remained among the descendants of Shaykh Jiwanji Awrangabadi, while the community has continued to experience intermittent strife and crisis rooted in opposition to the *daʿi*'s authority and policies. The present *daʿi mutlaq* of the Da'udi *daʿwa*, Sayyidna Muhammad Burhan al-Din, succeeded his father Sayyidna Tahir Sayf al-Din (1333–1385/1915–1965) as the fifty-second in the series. The total Da'udi population of the world is currently estimated at around one million, located mainly in India. Since the 1920s, Bombay (Mumbai), with its largest single concentration of Bohras, has served as the administrative seat of the Da'udi *daʿi mutlaq*. Outside India, the largest Da'udi community is situated in Karachi. The Tayyibi Bohras were also among the first Asian communities to settle in East Africa.[34]

Unlike the Da'udis, the Sulaymani Tayyibis of Yaman have not experienced succession disputes and schisms. Since the time of their thirtieth *daʿi mutlaq*, Ibrahim b. Muhammad b. al-Fahd al-Makrami (1088–1094/1677–1683), Sulaymani leadership has remained hereditary, with few exceptions, in the same Makrami family. The Sulaymani *daʿi*s established their headquarters in Badr, Najran, in north-eastern Yaman. They ruled independently over Najran with the military support of the local Banu Yam. In the 20th century, the political prominence of the Sulaymani *daʿi*s, checked earlier by the Zaydis and Ottomans, was further curtailed by the rising power of the Saʿudi family. Najran, the seat of the Sulaymani Makrami *daʿi*s, was in fact annexed to Saudi Arabia in 1934, and the present, fifty-first, *daʿi mutlaq* of the Sulaymanis, Sayyidna ʿAbd Allah b. Muhammad al-Makrami, who succeeded to office in 2005, lives in Saudi Arabia under official surveillance. Indeed, since the 1990s, the Sulaymanis of Najran have been severely persecuted by the Saudi government. At present the Sulaymani Tayyibi Ismailis, in Yaman and Saudi Arabia, number around 300,000.

The Sulaymani Bohra community in South Asia has remained very small. By contrast to the Daʾudis, the Sulaymanis of India have developed closer affinities to other Muslims in terms of language, dress and behaviour. There are certain differences between the traditions of the Arabic-speaking Yamani Sulaymanis and the Daʾudi Bohras who use a form of the Gujarati language. The Bohras have also incorporated many Hindu customs in their marriage and other ceremonies.[35] Nor are the Sulaymanis under the strict central control of their *daʿi*.

The Nizari Ismailis: The Alamut phase

The Nizari Ismailis have had their own complex history and separate doctrinal development. The circumstances of the early Nizaris of the Alamut period were radically different from those faced by the Ismailis of the Fatimid state and the Tayyibis of Yaman. From early on, the Nizaris, who had broken away from the Fatimid regime, were preoccupied with a revolutionary campaign and their survival in an extremely hostile environment. Accordingly, they produced military commanders rather than highly trained *daʿi*s and scholars addressing different intellectual issues. Furthermore, adopting Persian as the religious language of the community, the early Nizaris, who were concentrated in Persia and adjacent Persian-speaking eastern lands, did not have ready access to the Ismaili literature produced in Arabic during the Fatimid period, although the Syrian Nizaris who spoke Arabic did preserve some of the earlier Arabic texts. Under such circumstances, the Persian Nizaris did not produce a substantial literature.[36] And the majority of their writings, including the collections in the famous library at the fortress of Alamut, were either destroyed in the Mongol invasions or else perished soon afterwards.

The Nizari Ismailis of the Alamut period did, nevertheless, maintain a sophisticated intellectual outlook and a literary tradition, propounding their teachings in response to changing circumstances. They maintained a historiographical tradition, compiling chronicles in Persian recording the events of their state according to the reigns of the successive lords of Alamut, who initially were *daʿis* before the Nizari imams themselves took charge of the affairs of their community, *daʿwa* and state.[37] All these chronicles, kept at Alamut and other strongholds, perished during the period of Mongol Ilkhanid rule over Persia. However, some were seen and used extensively by three Persian historians of the Ilkhanid period, namely ʿAta-Malik Juwayni (d. 681/1283), Rashid al-Din Fadl Allah (d. 718/1318) and Abu'l-Qasim ʿAbd Allah Kashani (d. ca. 738/1337). The Ismaili accounts by these authorities remain our main primary sources for the history of the Nizari *daʿwa* and state in Persia during the Alamut period.[38] After the pioneering efforts of W. Ivanow, modern scholarship has done much to correct the distorted image of the early Nizaris, who were made famous in medieval Europe as the Assassins.[39]

Table 4.2 Nizari Ismaili Rulers at Alamut (483–654/1090–1256)

As *daʿis* and *hujjas*:

1. Hasan-i Sabbah (483–518/1090–1124)
2. Kiya Buzurg-Umid (518–532/1124–1138)
3. Muhammad b. Buzurg-Umid (532–557/1138–1162)

As imams:

4. Hasan II *ʿala dhikrihi'l-salam* (557–561/1162–1166)
5. Nur al-Din Muhammad (561–607/1166–1210)
6. Jalal al-Din Hasan (607–618/1210–1221)
7. ʿAla' al-Din Muhammad (618–653/1221–1255)
8. Rukn al-Din Khurshah (653–654/1255–1256)

By the time of the Nizari–Mustaʿli schism of 487/1094, Hasan-i Sabbah, who preached the Ismaili *daʿwa* within the Saljuq dominions, had already emerged as the undisputed leader of the Persian Ismailis. His seizure in 483/1090 of the fortress of Alamut, in northern Persia, had in fact signalled the initiation of the Persian Ismailis' open revolt against the Saljuqs, as well as the foundation of what would become the Nizari Ismaili state. This state, centred at Alamut, with territories scattered in different parts of Persia and Syria, lasted some 166 years until it was destroyed by the Mongols in 654/1256.

Hasan-i Sabbah, who was born into a Twelver Shiʿi family in Qumm and converted to Ismailism in his youth, had a complex set of religio-political motives for his revolt. As an Ismaili Shiʿi, he could not tolerate the anti-Shiʿi policies of the Saljuqs, who, as the new champions of Sunni Islam, aimed to uproot the Fatimids. Hasan's revolt was also an expression of Persian 'national' sentiments, the alien rule of the Saljuq Turks being greatly detested by Persians of different social classes. This may explain why he substituted Persian for Arabic as the religious language of the Persian Ismailis, accounting also for the popular appeal of his movement.[40] It was under such circumstances that during the Fatimid caliph-imam al-Mustansir's succession dispute, Hasan, who had already drifted away from the Fatimid regime, supported Nizar's cause and severed his relations completely with the *daʿwa* headquarters in Cairo which had lent its support to al-Mustaʿli. By this decision, Hasan also founded the independent Nizari Ismaili *daʿwa* on behalf of the Nizari imams who then remained inaccessible.

Hasan-i Sabbah did not divulge the name of Nizar's successor to the imamate after Nizar's execution in Cairo in 488/1095. The early Nizaris were thus left without an accessible imam in another *dawr al-satr*; and, as in the pre-Fatimid period of concealment, the hidden imam was represented in the community by a *hujja*, his chief representative. Hasan and his next two successors as heads of the Nizari *daʿwa* and state were, indeed, recognised as *hujja*s. It seems that already in Hasan-i Sabbah's time many Nizaris believed that a son or grandson of Nizar had been brought secretly from Egypt to Persia, and he became the progenitor of the line of the Nizari imams who later emerged at Alamut.

The revolt of the Persian Ismailis soon acquired a distinctive pattern and method of struggle, suited to the decentralised power structure of the Saljuq sultanate and their much superior military power. Hasan-i Sabbah devised a strategy to overwhelm the Saljuqs locality by locality, *amir* by *amir*, from a multitude of impregnable mountain strongholds. He acquired numerous fortresses in Rudbar, the centre of Nizari power in northern Persia, as well as castles and towns in Quhistan, in south-eastern Khurasan, the second most important territory of the Nizari state in Persia. Later, the Nizaris acquired fortresses in Qumis and other regions of Persia, while Hasan extended his activities to Syria by sending *da'is* there from Alamut. In Syria, however, it took the Nizaris several decades before they succeeded in acquiring a network of castles, collectively referred to as the *qila' al-da'wa*, in the Jabal Bahra' (present-day Jabal Ansariyya). These castles included Qadmus, Kahf and Masyaf, which often served as the headquarters of the chief *da'i* of the Syrian Nizaris.[41]

Although he was a capable strategist and organiser, Hasan-i Sabbah did not succeed in uprooting the Saljuqs; yet neither did the Saljuqs manage to dislodge the Nizaris from their mountain strongholds, despite their prolonged military campaigns.[42] By the final years of Hasan-i Sabbah (d. 518/1124), Ismaili–Saljuq relations had entered a new phase of stalemate, which lasted even under the Saljuqs' successors in Persia. Hasan-i Sabbah was also a learned theologian and is credited with restating in a more rigorous form the old Shi'i doctrine of *ta'lim*, or authoritative teaching by the 'imam of the time'. He expounded this doctrine in a theological treatise entitled *al-Fusul al-arba'a* (The Four Chapters). This treatise, originally written in Persian, has been preserved only in fragments, in Arabic,[43] by al-Shahrastani, with shorter Persian quotations by Juwayni, Rashid al-Din and Kashani. Emphasising the autonomous teaching authority of each imam in his own time, the doctrine of *ta'lim* became central to the Nizari Ismailis who, henceforth, were designated as the Ta'limiyya, the propounders of *ta'lim*. The intellectual challenge posed to the Sunnis by the doctrine of *ta'lim*, which also refuted the legitimacy of the Abbasid caliph as the spiritual spokesman of all Muslims, called forth a reaction from the Sunni establishment. Many Sunni scholars, led by Abu Hamid Muhammad al-Ghazali (d. 505/1111), refuted this Ismaili doctrine. As a matter of general policy, the Nizaris did not respond to this rejection, but one of the Yamani Tayyibi *da'is* later wrote a detailed refutation of al-Ghazali's major anti-Ismaili treatise, known as *al-Mustazhiri*, named after the Abbasid caliph who had commissioned it.[44]

The Ismaili–Saljuq stalemate essentially continued under Hasan-i Sabbah's next two successors at Alamut, while the Nizaris retained their remarkable unity and sense of mission. Meanwhile, the Nizaris had been eagerly expecting the appearance of their imam, who had remained inaccessible since Nizar's tragic demise. The fourth lord of Alamut, Hasan II, to whom the Nizaris refer with the expression *ʿala dhikrihi'l-salam* (on his mention be peace), declared the *qiyama* or resurrection in 559/1164, initiating a new era in the religious history of the Nizari community. Relying heavily on Ismaili *ta'wil* and earlier traditions, however, Hasan II interpreted the *qiyama*, the long-awaited Last Day, symbolically and spiritually for his community. Accordingly, *qiyama* meant merely the manifestation of unveiled truth (*haqiqa*) in the person of the Nizari imam; and it was a spiritual resurrection only for those who acknowledged the rightful imam of the time and were capable of understanding the truth, the esoteric and immutable essence of Islam. It was in this sense that Paradise was actualised for the Nizaris in this world. They were now to rise to a spiritual level of existence, transcending from *zahir* to *batin*, from *shariʿa* to *haqiqa*, or from the literal interpretation of the law to an apprehension of its spirituality and the eternal truths of religion. On the other hand, the outsiders, the non-Nizaris who were incapable of recognising the truth, were rendered spiritually non-existent and indeed irrelevant.

The imam proclaiming the *qiyama* would be the *qa'im al-qiyama*, 'lord of resurrection', a rank which in the Ismaili hierarchy was always higher than that of an ordinary imam. In due course, Hasan II himself, a descendant of Nizar, was recognised as the imam as well as the *qa'im*. Henceforth, the Nizaris acknowledged the lords of Alamut, beginning with Hasan II, as their imams. Hasan II's son and successor Nur al-Din Muhammad devoted his long reign (561–607/1166–1210) to a systematic elaboration of the *qiyama* in terms of a doctrine. The exaltation of the autonomous teaching authority of the current imam now became the central feature of Nizari Ismaili thought; and the *qiyama* came to imply a complete personal transformation of the Nizaris who were expected to perceive the imam in his true spiritual reality and hence benefit from his indispensable guidance in religious matters.

Nur al-Din Muhammad's son and successor as the sixth lord of Alamut, Jalal al-Din Hasan, who was apprehensive of the isolation of the Nizaris from the larger world of Sunni Islam, attempted his own daring rapprochement with Sunni Muslims. He repudiated the doctrine of the *qiyama* and ordered his community to observe the *shariʿa* in its Sunni form, inviting Sunni jurists to instruct his followers. In 608/1211, the Abbasid caliph al-Nasir acknowledged the Nizari imam's rapprochement and issued a decree to that effect. Henceforth, the rights of Jalal al-Din Hasan to Nizari territories were officially acknowledged by the Abbasids and other Sunni rulers. The Nizari Ismailis themselves evidently viewed Jalal al-Din Hasan's declarations as a restoration of *taqiyya*, which had been lifted in *qiyama* times; observance of *taqiyya* could imply any type of accommodation to the outside world as deemed necessary by the infallible imam of the time. Be that as it may, the Nizari imam had now achieved the much needed peace and security for his community and state.

In the reign of Jalal al-Din Hasan's son and successor, ʿAlaʾ al-Din Muhammad, the Sunni *shariʿa* was gradually relaxed within the community and the Nizari traditions associated with *qiyama* were once again revived, although the Nizaris evidently continued to appear to outsiders in their Sunni guise. Furthermore, the Nizari leadership now made a sustained effort to explain the different doctrinal declarations and religious policies of the lords of Alamut within a coherent theological framework. It is particularly through the Ismaili works written or supervised by the eminent Shiʿi philosopher and theologian, Nasir al-Din al-Tusi (d. 672/1274), who spent some three decades in the Nizari fortress communities and converted to Ismailism, that we have a coherent exposition of Nizari thought of the Alamut period.[45] Indeed, intellectual life flourished in the Persian Nizari community during ʿAlaʾ al-Din Muhammad's reign, when numerous outside scholars, who were then fleeing the first waves of the Mongol invasions, took refuge in Nizari fortress communities and availed themselves of the Nizari libraries at Alamut and other castles as well as their patronage of learning. Nasir al-Din al-Tusi was foremost amongst such scholars who made major contributions to Nizari Ismaili thought during the late Alamut period. The esoteric teachings of the Alamut period brought the Nizaris even closer to the esoteric traditions more commonly associated with Sufism.

The Nizaris of Persia had successfully struggled against too many formidable adversaries and for too long, and they were finally overwhelmed by the all-conquering Mongol armies led by Hülegü. At any rate, the surrender of Alamut to the Mongols in 654/1256 sealed the fate of the Nizari state. Soon afterwards, Rukn al-Din Khurshah, the Nizari imam and the last of the lords of Alamut, was murdered in Mongolia, where he had gone to see the Great Khan himself. The Mongols now massacred large numbers of Nizaris, also destroying their network of fortresses in Persia. In Syria, the Nizaris attained the peak of their power and fame under their most eminent *daʿi* Rashid al-Din Sinan (d. 589/1193), who successfully adopted complex and shifting alliances with the Ayyubids and other Muslim rulers as well as the neighbouring Crusaders.[46] The Syrian Nizaris were spared the Mongol debacle. However, by 671/1273, all the castles of the Syrian Nizaris had fallen into Mamluk hands. The Nizaris of Syria were permitted to remain in their traditional abodes as loyal subjects of the Mamluks and the Ottomans, but much of their literary heritage was lost in prolonged conflicts with the neighbouring Nusayri (ʿAlawi) community.

Later developments in Nizari Ismaili history

The so-called post-Alamut phase in Nizari history covers more than seven centuries, from the fall of Alamut into Mongol hands in 654/1256 to the present. The Nizari communities, scattered from Syria to Persia, Central Asia and South Asia, now espoused a diversity of religious and literary traditions in different languages. Many aspects of Nizari Ismaili history during the earlier centuries of this phase are still not sufficiently understood due to a scarcity of primary sources. Additional research difficulties arise from the widespread practice of *taqiyya* adopted during this phase by the Nizaris of different regions in order to safeguard themselves against rampant persecution. They resorted to Sunni, Sufi, Twelver Shiʿi and even Hindu guises, in addition to guarding secretly their limited literature. It is important to note that the Nizaris of many localities observed *taqiyya* for long periods with lasting detrimental consequences. Although this phenomenon still awaits a more thorough investigation, it is certain that long-term dissimulating practices under any guise would eventually result in irrevocable changes in the religious practices and the very religious identity of the dissimulating group. Such influences might have varied from the total acculturation of the

Nizaris of a particular locality into the dominant religious community or tradition selected originally as a protective shield, to various degrees of interfacing and admixture between the Ismaili and 'other' traditions. Nonetheless, for several earlier centuries of this phase, when the Nizaris of various regions were effectively deprived of any form of central leadership, the Nizari communities continued to develop independently of one another under the local leadership of their *daʿi*s, *pir*s, *shaykh*s, *khalifa*s, etc., who often established their own hereditary dynasties.

Modern scholarship in Ismaili studies distinguishes three periods in the post-Alamut phase of Nizari history: an obscure early period covering the first two centuries; the Anjudan revival in the *daʿwa* and literary activities, and the modern period dating to the middle of the 13th/19th century when the residence of the Nizari imams was transferred from Persia to India and then to Europe.

The Nizari Ismailis of Persia survived the downfall of their state. Many migrated to Afghanistan, Badakhshan and Sind, where Ismaili communities already existed. Other isolated Nizari groups soon disintegrated or were assimilated into the religiously dominant communities of their region. The centralised *daʿwa* organisation had now also disappeared. Meanwhile, a group of Nizari dignitaries had managed to hide Imam Rukn al-Din Khurshah's son, Shams al-Din Muhammad, who succeeded to the imamate in 655/1257. He was taken to Adharbayjan, in north-western Persia, where he and his next few successors to the imamate lived clandestinely. Certain allusions in the versified *Safar-nama* (Travelogue) of the contemporary Nizari poet Nizari Quhistani indicate that he may actually have seen the imam there, in Tabriz, in 679/1280.[47] Imam Shams al-Din died around 710/1310, and an obscure dispute over his succession split the line of the Nizari imams and their following into Qasim-Shahi and Muhammad-Shahi (or Mu'mini) branches. The Muhammad-Shahi imams, who initially had substantial followings in Persia, Syria and Central Asia, transferred their seat to India in the 10th/16th century, and by the end of the 12th/18th century this line had become discontinued. The sole surviving Muhammad-Shahi Nizari group, currently numbering about 15,000, is to be found in Syria where they are known locally as the Jaʿfariyya. Nizari Ismailism has survived mainly through its Qasim-Shahi faction.

It was in the early post-Alamut times that Persian Nizaris also disguised themselves under the cover of Sufism, without establishing formal affiliations with any of the Sufi *tariqa*s then spreading across Persia and Central Asia. This practice soon gained wide currency among the Nizari Ismailis of Central Asia and Sind as well. By the middle of the 9th/15th century, Ismaili–Sufi relations had become well established in the Iranian world. Indeed, a type of coalescence had emerged between Persian Sufism and Nizari Ismailism, two independent esoteric traditions in Islam that shared close affinities and common doctrinal grounds. This explains why the Persian-speaking Nizaris have also regarded several of the great mystic poets of Persia, such as Sanaʾi, ʿAttar and Jalal al-Din Rumi, as their co-religionists. The Nizaris of Persia, Afghanistan and Central Asia have preserved the works of these poets and continue to use them in their religious ceremonies. Soon, the dissimulating Persian Nizaris adopted even more visible aspects of the Sufi orders and way of life. Thus, the imams appeared to outsiders as Sufi masters or *pir*s, while their followers adopted the typically Sufi appellation of disciple or *murid*s.[48] By then, the Nizari imams of the Qasim-Shahi line had emerged in the village of Anjudan, in central Persia, and initiated the so-called Anjudan revival in their *daʿwa* activities.

The Anjudan revival

Starting with Imam Mustansir bi'llah II (d. 885/1480), who carried the Sufi name of Shah Qalandar, the Qasim-Shahi Nizari imams became established secretly at Anjudan, where several of their tombs are still preserved.[49] Taking advantage of the changing religio-political climate of post-Mongol Persia, including the spread of ʿAlid loyalism and Shiʿi tendencies through Sufi orders, the imams successfully began to reorganise and reinvigorate their *daʿwa* activities to win new converts and reassert their authority over various Nizari communities, especially in Central Asia and India. The imams gradually replaced the local hereditary leaders with their own loyal *daʿi*s. The Anjudan period in Nizari history, lasting until the end of the 11th/17th century, also witnessed a revival in the literary activities of the Nizaris. In the context of Nizari–Sufi relations during the Anjudan period, valuable details are preserved in the *Pandiyat-i jawanmardi*, containing the religious admonitions of Imam Mustansir bi'llah II.[50] Other doctrinal works of this period were written by Abu Ishaq-i Quhistani (d. after 904/1498) and Khayrkhwah-i Harati (d. after 960/1553), amongst others. Many Nizari authors of this period now chose verse and Sufi forms of expression to conceal their Ismaili ideas. The Nizaris essentially retained the teachings of the Alamut period, especially as elaborated after the declaration of the *qiyama*.

The advent of the Safawids and their proclamation of Twelver Shiʿism as their state religion in 907/1501 promised even more favourable opportunities for the Nizaris. As noted, however, this optimism was short-lived, as the Safawids and their *fuqaha'* soon suppressed all popular forms of Sufism and those Shiʿi movements that fell outside the confines of Twelver Shiʿism. The Nizaris, too, received their share of persecution. Shah Tahir, the most famous imam of the Muhammad-Shahi line, was obliged to take refuge in India, where he preached a form of Twelver Shiʿism.[51] Indeed, by the time of Shah ʿAbbas I (r. 995–1038/1587–1629), the Persian Nizaris, too, had widely and successfully adopted Twelver Shiʿism, in addition to Sufism, as a second form of disguise. By the end of the Anjudan period, the Qasim-Shahi *daʿwa* had gained the allegiance of the overwhelming majority of the Nizaris. The *daʿwa* had been particularly effective in several regions of the Indian subcontinent.

In South Asia, the Hindu converts originally belonging to the Lohana caste became generally known as Khoja, a word derived from the Persian *khwaja*, an honorary title meaning lord and master corresponding to the Hindu term *thakur* by which the Lohanas were addressed locally. The Nizari Ismaili Khojas developed a religious tradition known as Satpanth or 'true path' (to salvation), as well as a devotional literature, the *ginans*.[52] The term *ginan* (*gnan*) seems to have been derived from the Sanskrit word *jñana* meaning sacred knowledge or wisdom. The *ginans* have attained a very special status within the Nizari Khoja community. Composed in a number of Indic languages and dialects of Sind, Punjab and Gujarat, these hymn-like poems were transmitted orally for several centuries before they were recorded, mainly in the Khojki script developed in Sind within the Khoja community. The authorship of the greatest number of *ginans* is traditionally attributed to a few early *daʿis*, more commonly referred to in India as *pirs*.[53]

The earliest Nizari *pirs*, missionaries or preacher-saints, sent by the imams to India concentrated their efforts in Sind (modern-day Punjab in Pakistan). Pir Shams al-Din is the earliest figure specifically associated in the *ginan* literature with the commencement of the Nizari *daʿwa* in South Asia. By the time of Pir Sadr al-Din, a great-grandson of Pir Shams, the *pir*s in India had established a hereditary dynasty. Pir Sadr al-Din, who died around the beginning of the 9th/15th century, consolidated and organised the *daʿwa* in India. He is also reputed to have built the first *jamaʿat-khana* (literally, community house) in Sind, for the religious and communal affairs of the Khojas. In India, too, the Nizari Khojas developed close relations with Sufism. Multan and Ucch in Sind, in addition to serving as centres of Satpanthi *daʿwa* activities, were the headquarters of the Suhrawardi and Qadiri Sufi orders. Thus the Khojas were able to represent themselves for extended periods as one of the many mystically oriented communities of Sind that existed both among the predominantly Sunni Muslims as well as in Hindu milieus.

The Khojas experienced periodical internal dissensions, while many reverted back to Hinduism or converted to Sunni Islam, the dominant religion of the contemporary Indo-Muslim society.[54] One such group seceding from the main Khoja community in Gujarat, in the 10th/16th century, became known as Imam-Shahis. During the Anjudan revival, the Nizari imams stopped appointing *pir*s while maintaining their contacts with the Khoja community through lesser functionaries known as *wakil*s. The origins and early development of the particular form of Ismaili Shiʿism known as Satpanth, and its religious literature, remain obscure. In particular, it is not clear whether the Satpanthi tradition resulted from the conversion policies of the early *pir*s, or whether it represented a tradition that evolved gradually over several centuries. In any case, Satpanth Ismailism may be taken to represent an indigenous tradition reflecting certain historical, religious, social, cultural and political circumstances prevailing in medieval India. On the evidence of the *ginan*s, it seems that the *pir*s did also attempt cleverly to maximise the appeal of their message to the Hindu audiences of mainly rural and uneducated lower castes. Hence, they turned to Indian vernaculars, rather than the Arabic and Persian used by the educated classes. And for the same reasons, they used Hindu idioms and mythology, interfacing their Ismaili tenets with myths, images and symbols already familiar to the Hindus.

In the meantime, with the fortieth Qasim-Shahi Nizari imam, Shah Nizar (d. 1134/1722), the seat of this branch of the Nizari *daʿwa*, then representing the only branch in Persia, was transferred from Anjudan to the nearby village of Kahak, in the vicinity of Qumm and Mahallat, effectively ending the Anjudan period. By the middle of the 12th/18th century, in the unsettled conditions of Persia, and after the demise of the Safawids and the Afghan invasion, the Nizari imams moved to Shahr-i Babak in the province of Kirman, closer to the pilgrimage route of Khojas who then regularly travelled to Persia to see their imam and deliver the religious dues, the *dassondh*, or tithes, to him. The Khojas were by then acquiring increasing significance in the Nizari community, in terms of both their numbers and financial resources. Meanwhile, the imams were acquiring political prominence in the affairs of the province of Kirman. The forty-fourth imam, Abu'l-Hasan ʿAli, also known as Sayyid Abu'l-Hasan Kahaki, was appointed around 1170/1756 to the governorship of Kirman by Karim Khan Zand, founder of the Zand dynasty of Persia. It was in his time that the Niʿmat Allahi Sufi order was revived in Persia, particularly in Kirman. The Nizari imam had close relations with several leading Niʿmat Allahi Sufis and supported their activities in Kirman.[55] On Imam Abu'l-Hasan's death in 1206/1792, his son Shah Khalil Allah succeeded to the Nizari imamate and eventually settled in Yazd, where he was murdered in 1232/1817.

The modern period

Shah Khalil Allah was succeeded in the imamate by his eldest son Hasan ʿAli Shah, who was later appointed to the governorship of Qumm by Fath ʿAli Shah and also given properties in Mahallat. In addition, the Qajar monarch of Persia gave one of his daughters in marriage to the youthful imam and bestowed upon him the honorific title of Agha Khan (Aga Khan), meaning lord and master – this title has remained hereditary among Hasan ʿAli Shah's successors, the Nizari Ismaili imams of modern times.

Hasan ʿAli Shah, Aga Khan I, the forty-sixth Nizari imam, was appointed to the governorship of Kirman in 1251/1835 by the third Qajar monarch, Muhammad Shah. Subsequently, after some prolonged and controversial confrontations between the imam and the Qajar establishment, Aga Khan I left Persia permanently in 1257/1841. After spending some years in Afghanistan, Sind, Gujarat and Calcutta, Aga Khan I finally settled in Bombay in 1265/1848, marking the commencement of the modern period in Nizari Ismaili history.[56] The Nizari imam now launched a widespread campaign for defining and delineating the distinct religious identity of his Khoja following. The Ismaili Khojas were not always certain about their identity as they had dissimulated for long periods as Sunnis and Twelver Shiʿis, while their Satpanthi tradition had been influenced by Hindu elements. In the event, some dissident Khojas challenged the Aga Khan's authority and questioned their own Ismaili identity. Matters came to a head in 1866 when the dissident Khojas filed a suit in the Bombay High Court, which rendered a judgement in favour of the imam.[57] This judgement legally established the status of the Nizari Khojas as a community of 'Shia Imami Ismailis'. The majority of the Khojas reaffirmed their allegiance to Aga Khan I and acknowledged their Ismaili identity, while minority groups, as noted, seceded and joined the Twelver Shiʿi Khojas.

Table 4.3 Nizari Ismaili Imams of Modern Times

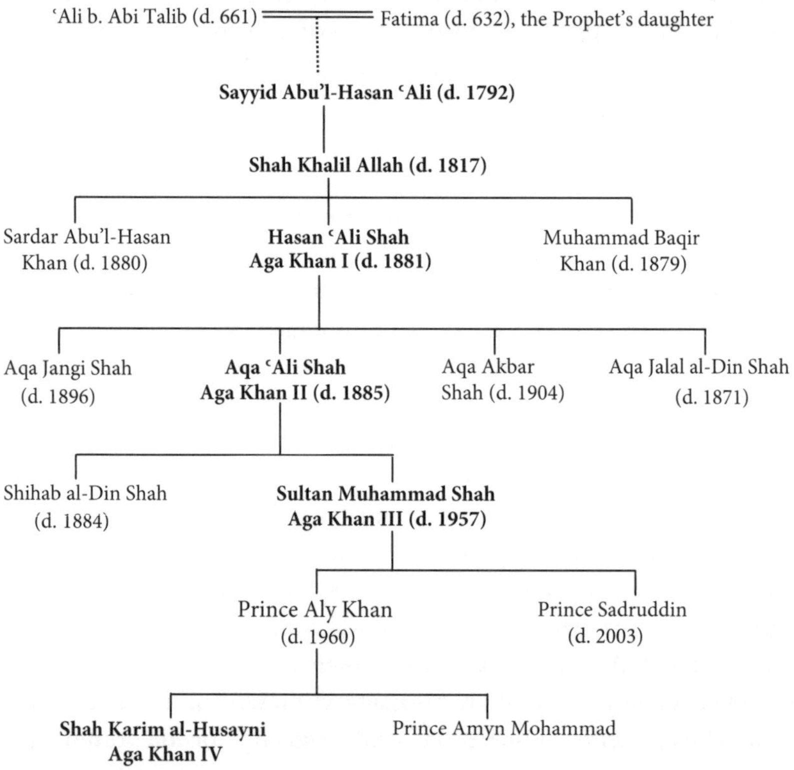

Aga Khan I died in 1298/1881, and was succeeded by his son Aqa ʿAli Shah who led the Nizaris for only four years (1298–1302/1881–1885). The latter's sole surviving son and successor, Sultan Muhammad (Mahomed) Shah, Aga Khan III, led the Nizari Ismailis for seventy-two years, and also became internationally known as a Muslim reformer and statesman. Aga Khan III, too, made systematic efforts to set the identity of his followers apart from that of other religious communities, particularly the Twelver Shiʿis who for long periods had provided dissimulating covers for the Nizari Ismailis of Persia and elsewhere. The Nizari identity was spelled out in numerous constitutions that the imam promulgated for his followers, especially in India, Pakistan and East Africa. Furthermore, he became increasingly engaged with reform policies that would benefit not only his followers but other Muslims as well. Aga Khan III worked vigorously to consolidate and reorganise the Nizari Ismailis into a modern Muslim community with high standards of education, health and social well-being, for both men and women, also developing a network of councils for administering the affairs of his community.[58] The participation of women in communal affairs was a high priority in his reforms. Aga Khan III, who established his residence in Europe, has left an interesting account of his life and public career in his *Memoirs*.[59]

On his death in 1957, Aga Khan III was succeeded by his grandson Karim, known to his followers as Mawlana Hazar Imam Shah Karim al-Husayni. The present Aga Khan, IV, the Harvard-educated Imam of the Nizari Ismailis, the forty-ninth in the series, has substantially expanded the modernisation policies of his predecessor, also developing a multitude of new programmes and institutions of his own for the benefit of his community. At the same time, Aga Khan IV has concerned himself with a variety of social, developmental and cultural issues which are of wider interest to Muslims and the developing countries. Indeed, he has created a complex institutional network, generally referred to as the Aga Khan Development Network (AKDN), which implements numerous projects in a variety of social, economic and cultural domains.[60] The present Imam of the Nizari Ismailis has been particularly concerned with the education of his followers and Muslims in general. In the field of higher education, his major initiatives include The Institute of Ismaili Studies, founded in London in 1977 for the promotion of general Islamic as well as Shiʿi and Ismaili studies, and the Aga Khan

University, set up in Karachi in 1985, with faculties in medicine, nursing and education as well as its Institute for the Study of Muslim Civilisations, based in London. In 2000, he founded the University of Central Asia in Tajikistan, with branches in other Central Asian countries, to address the specific educational needs of the region's mountain-based societies. More recently, he has founded the Global Center for Pluralism in Ottawa, Canada, to promote pluralistic values and practices in culturally diverse societies worldwide.

As a progressive Muslim leader, Aga Khan IV has devoted much of his resources to promoting a better understanding of Islam, not merely as a religion with multiple expressions and interpretations but also as a major world civilisation with its plurality of social, intellectual and cultural traditions. In pursuit of these aims, he has launched a number of innovative programmes for the preservation and regeneration of the cultural heritage of Muslim societies. The apex institution here is the Aga Khan Trust for Culture (AKTC) which was set up in 1988 in Geneva for the promotion of an awareness of the importance of the built environment in both historical and contemporary contexts, and for the pursuit of excellence in architecture. The AKTC's mandate now covers the Aga Khan Award for Architecture, to encourage outstanding architectural achievements in Muslim environments; the Historic Cities Support Programme, to promote the conservation and restoration of buildings and public spaces in historic Muslim cities, such as Cairo, where the Azhar Park has been created; and the Aga Khan Museum, established in Toronto.

Prince Karim Aga Khan IV takes a personal interest in the operations of all his institutions, and supervises their activities from his Secretariat at Aiglemont, outside Paris. By 2007, when the Nizari Ismailis celebrated the fiftieth anniversary of his imamate, Aga Khan IV had accomplished an impressive record of achievement not only as an Ismaili Imam but also as a Muslim leader deeply aware of the demands of modernity. Numbering some 10 million, the Nizari Ismailis have emerged as progressive Shiʿi Muslim minorities in more than twenty-five countries of the world.[61] And in every country of Asia, the Middle East, Africa, Europe and North America where the Nizari Ismailis live as religious minorities and loyal citizens, they generally enjoy exemplary standards of living while retaining their distinctive religious identity.

5

The Zaydis

The Zaydis represent another major Shiʿi Muslim community. The general influence and geographical distribution of the Zaydiyya branch of Shiʿi Islam, named after their fourth imam, Zayd b. ʿAli Zayn al-ʿAbidin (d. 122/740), have been relatively more restricted compared with the Twelver and Ismaili Shiʿis. In fact, after some initial success in Iraq, the Zaydi Shiʿi imamate remained mainly confined to the Caspian region in northern Persia, and then, more importantly, to Yaman, where Zaydis have continued to live to the present. However, Zaydi activities were more widespread in the Islamic lands. Currently, the total Zaydi population of the world, concentrated in northern Yaman, numbers between 5 and 10 million. The Zaydis have always emphasised the significance of religious education, especially as one of the main qualifications of their imams and jurists. Consequently, they have produced an impressive volume of religious literature over the centuries, which remains largely unpublished.[1] Indeed, it is estimated that currently there is in existence, in numerous private collections in Yaman, some 100,000 Zaydi manuscripts, many of which remain unknown to the scholarly world. It is, however, regrettable that in recent decades a Salafi campaign, supported by Saudi Arabia, has increasingly succeeded in obtaining and destroying the literary heritage of the Yamani Zaydis.

The early Zaydis

The Zaydi branch of Shiʿi Islam, as noted previously, developed out of Zayd's abortive revolt.[2] Born in 75/694, Zayd b. ʿAli Zayn al-ʿAbidin was at least some eighteen years younger than his half-brother Imam Muhammad al-Baqir, who became the head of the Husaynid branch of the ʿAlid family after the death of their father, Imam ʿAli b. al-Husayn

Zayn al-ʿAbidin around 95/714. While Muhammad al-Baqir was then acknowledged by the majority of the Imami Shiʿis as their imam, Zayd too acquired a reputation for his religious learning and transmitted *hadith* from his father as well as Imam al-Baqir, amongst others. Subsequently, the Kufan Shiʿa, who had never given up hope of uprooting the Umayyad rule, contacted Zayd and promised him massive support if he were to rise against the Umayyads. Zayd received pledges of support from other localities in Iraq as well. However, when the battle was finally waged in 122/740, typically of the Kufans, only a fraction of the number expected actually responded to Zayd's call to arms. In the event, the revolt was brutally suppressed in Kufa and Zayd was killed, reminiscent of the fate of his grandfather, al-Husayn b. ʿAli b. Abi Talib.[3] It was in the aftermath of this revolt that the Umayyad caliph Hisham commanded all prominent Talibids (covering the descendants of ʿAli and other sons of Abu Talib) to publicly condemn Zayd and dissociate themselves from all anti-Umayyad activities.

Few details are known with certainty regarding the teachings of Zayd and his original supporters, who belonged to the early Kufan Shiʿa and, as such, generally entertained politically militant but religiously moderate views. In connection with this, it may be added that while Zayd was preparing for his uprising, a portion of the Kufan Shiʿa withdrew their promised support for him because of his refusal to condemn unconditionally the early caliphs preceding ʿAli. Designated as the Rafida (the Rejectors), the seceders switched their allegiance to Zayd's nephew, Jaʿfar al-Sadiq, the contemporary imam of the Imami Shiʿis. Later reports considering Zayd as an associate of Wasil b. ʿAtaʾ (d. 131/748), one of the reputed founders of the Muʿtazili theological school, should be regarded as unfounded. As noted earlier, the doctrinal positions of the early Shiʿa and the Muʿtazila were incompatible during this early period; it was in the later part of the 3rd/9th century that Zaydi Shiʿism, like the Imamiyya, was influenced by the teachings of the Muʿtazila.

A Zaydi movement that would eventually crystallise as the Zaydiyya branch of Shiʿism developed out of Zayd's revolt. The movement was initially led by Zayd's eldest son, Yahya, who had participated in his father's revolt. He escaped from Kufa to Khurasan and concentrated his activities in that eastern region remote from the centre of Umayyad administration. Counted as one of the Zaydi imams, Yahya was ʿAlid also on his mother's side as she was one of the daughters of Abu Hashim b. Muhammad b. ʿAli. At any rate, Yahya found some support amongst the local Shiʿis who had been exiled to Khurasan by the governors of Iraq. However, after three years of futile efforts, Yahya was overcome by the troops of Nasr b. Sayyar, the Umayyad governor of Khurasan, and was killed in battle near Juzjan in 125/743.[4] Revenge for the murders of Zayd and his son Yahya became one of the slogans of the Abbasid movement which was then capitalising on Shiʿi aspirations. The Abbasids did, in fact, attract some Zaydis to their own movement, without supporting their particular Shiʿi cause.

Subsequently, the early Zaydis were led by Muhammad b. ʿAbd Allah b. al-Hasan al-Muthanna, known as al-Nafs al-Zakiyya (d. 145/762), Yahya b. Zayd's younger brother ʿIsa b. Zayd (d. 166/783) and then by Ahmad b. ʿIsa b. Zayd (d. 247/861), along with others recognised as their imams. In early Abbasid times, groups of Zaydis participated in a number of failed ʿAlid, mainly Hasanid, revolts in the Hijaz, Iraq and elsewhere. Amongst such revolts supported by the Kufan Zaydis, mention may be made of those of the Hasanid Muhammad al-Nafs al-Zakiyya and his brother Ibrahim against the caliph al-Mansur in Medina and Iraq in 145/762; the Hasanid al-Husayn b. ʿAli Sahib Fakhkh in Medina in 169/786; the Hasanid Yahya b. ʿAbd Allah in Daylam in 176/792; the Hasanid Muhammad b. Ibrahim Tabataba, known as Ibn Tabataba, in Kufa in 199/815; the Husaynid Muhammad b. al-Qasim Sahib al-Taliqan in Khurasan in 219/834; and the Husaynid Yahya b. ʿUmar b. Yahya in Kufa in 250/864. By the middle of the 3rd/9th century, however, the Zaydis confined their rebellious activities to the remote mountainous regions of Daylam, in northern Persia, and to Yaman, removed from the reach of the centres of Abbasid power and administration in Iraq. Before long, the Zaydis actually succeeded in establishing two territorial states in these regions.

Zaydi Shiʿism was initially formed during the 2nd/8th century by the merger of two currents in Kufan Shiʿism; the two doctrinal currents with their Shiʿi adherents were designated in heresiographical literature as the Batriyya and the Jarudiyya, also referred to as the 'weak' and the 'strong' Zaydis, respectively.[5] The two groups disagreed especially with regard to the legitimacy of the rule (imamate) of the caliphs preceding ʿAli, and the significance of the special knowledge attributed to the *ahl al-bayt*. The name Batriyya seems to have been derived from the nickname al-Abtar of a certain Kathir al-Nawwa and referred to the group's denial and 'mutilating' (*batr*) of the legitimate rights of the *ahl al-bayt*. In fact, it seems that the Batriyya were originally a group of moderate Shiʿis who refused to acknowledge Zayd's brother al-Baqir because they were critical of certain aspects of his teaching. Representing the moderate faction of the early Zaydiyya, the Batriyya upheld the caliphates of Abu Bakr and ʿUmar. They held that though ʿAli was the most excellent (*al-afdal*) of Muslims to succeed the Prophet, nevertheless the caliphates of his predecessors who were less excellent (*al-mafdul*) were valid, because ʿAli himself had pledged allegiance to them. In the case of the third caliph ʿUthman (23–35/644–656) the matter was more complicated. The Batri Zaydis either abstained from judgement or repudiated him for the last six years of his caliphate.

In contrast to the Jarudiyya, the Batriyya did not ascribe any particular religious knowledge to the *ahl al-bayt*, or to the ʿAlids, but accepted the knowledge (and *hadith*) transmitted in the Muslim community. They also allowed the use of individual reasoning (*ijtihad* or *ra'y*) in religious matters in order to establish legal precepts. The Batriyya thus belonged to the traditionist school of Kufa in their legal doctrines. The Batriyya were indeed closely affiliated to the Kufan traditionist school, and with the latter's absorption into Sunnism in the 3rd/9th century, the Batri Zaydi tradition also disappeared. Henceforth, the views of the Jarudiyya on the imamate prevailed in Zaydi Shiʿism. However, with regard to the law, the differences between the 'weak' and the 'strong' Zaydi currents persisted; and in Yaman the legal teaching of al-Qasim b. Ibrahim, based on the non-Shiʿi traditionist school of Medina, prevailed. The early Batriyya generally supported Zayd b. ʿAli, as he basically shared their view on the first two caliphs.

The Jarudiyya, named after Abu'l-Jarud Ziyad b. al-Mundhir who was initially a companion of Imam Muhammad al-Baqir, adopted some of the more radical doctrinal views of the Imami Shiʿis as expounded by al-Baqir and others. Thus, they rejected the legitimacy of the caliphate of the caliphs before ʿAli. They held that the Prophet himself had designated ʿAli by the rule of the *nass* as his legatee (*wasi*) and implicitly as his successor, and that the majority of the Companions had gone astray for not supporting ʿAli's legitimate imamate. Consequently, the Jarudiyya rejected the *hadith*s transmitted by these

Companions and the Sunni traditionists as sources of the law, accepting only those handed down by the Fatimid (Hasanid and Husaynid) 'Alids. The Jarudiyya ascribed superior knowledge to the *ahl al-bayt* in religious matters. However, in contrast to the Imamiyya, they did not confine legal teaching authority to their imams only, but accepted in principle the teaching of any member of the *ahl al-bayt* qualified by religious learning.[6]

By the 4th/10th century, the Zaydi doctrine, influenced by Jarudi and Mu'tazili elements, had largely been formulated. The Zaydis were less radical than Imami Shi'is in their condemnation of the early caliphs and the Muslim community at large. Initially, the Zaydis did not confine the legitimate imams to the descendants of 'Ali. Before the demise of the Umayyads, the Kufan Zaydis had supported 'Abd Allah b. Mu'awiya, the great-grandson of Ja'far b. Abi Talib, 'Ali's brother. This Talibid Ja'far, who had his own Shi'i partisans known as the Janahiyya, had led the last unsuccessful anti-Umayyad revolt during 127–130/744–748.[7] As late as the 4th/10th century there still existed a Zaydi group known as the Talibiyya, who recognised all of the descendants of 'Ali's father Abu Talib as suitable for their imamate. By then, however, the majority of the Zaydiyya considered only the Fatimid 'Alids, descendants of al-Hasan and al-Husayn, as legitimate candidates for the imamate. They also held that the first three imams, 'Ali, al-Hasan and al-Husayn, had been imams by designation (*nass*) of the Prophet. But the designation (*nass*) had been unclear and obscure, *khafi* or *ghayr jali*, so that its intended meaning could be discovered only through investigation. After al-Husayn b. 'Ali, the imamate could be claimed by any qualified descendant of al-Hasan and al-Husayn who was prepared to launch an armed uprising (*khuruj*) against the illegitimate rulers and issue a formal summons (*da'wa*) for gaining the allegiance of the people. Religious knowledge, ability to render independent ruling (*ijtihad*) and piety were emphasised as the qualifications of the imam, in addition to his 'Alid ancestry; as a result, many Zaydi imams have been highly educated religious scholars and authors producing theological and legal treatises. Whilst the Zaydis did not generally consider their imams as divinely protected and immune from error and sin (*ma'sum*), they later attributed such immunity (*'isma*) to the first three imams. The list of Zaydi imams has never been completely fixed, though many of them are unanimously accepted. There were, indeed, periods without any Zaydi imam; and, in practice, at times there were more than one imam in existence. Due to high requirements in terms of religious learning, the Zaydis often distinguished ʿAlid pretenders and rulers as summoners (*daʿis*) or as imams with restricted status, designated as *muhtasibun* or *muqtasida*, from fully authoritative imams, known as *sabiqun*.

Be that as it may, the Zaydis elaborated a doctrine of the imamate that clearly set Zaydi Shiʿism apart from Imami Shiʿism and its two branches, the Twelvers and the Ismailis. In line with the points mentioned above, the Zaydis did not recognise a hereditary line of imams, nor did they attach any significance to the principle of the *nass*, central to the Imami doctrine. Initially, as noted, the Zaydis were prepared to accept any member of the *ahl al-bayt* as an imam, but later the imams were restricted to the Fatimid ʿAlids, descendants of al-Hasan and al-Husayn. According to Zaydi doctrine, if an imam wished to be recognised he would have to assert his claims publicly by means of an uprising and sword in hand if necessary, in addition to having the required religious knowledge (*ʿilm*) and other qualifications. The Zaydis were not, therefore, prepared to acknowledge quiescent claimants to the imamate; and, accordingly, they did not recognise Zayd's father, ʿAli b. al-Husayn Zayn al-ʿAbidin, or Zayd's brother, Muhammad al-Baqir, as imams. For the same reasons, in contrast to the Twelvers and the Ismailis, the Zaydis excluded the imamate of minors. They also rejected the eschatological idea of the concealment (*ghayba*) of an Imam-Mahdi and his return (*rajʿa*) in the future, and, in fact, messianic tendencies remained rather weak in Zaydi Shiʿism. Due to their emphasis on active policies, the observance of *taqiyya*, too, was alien to Zaydi teachings. Conversely, they did develop a doctrine of *hijra* in Yaman, holding the obligation to emigrate from a land under the domination of unjust, non-Zaydi, rulers. The Zaydis evidently based this duty on the Qur'anic injunction to the early Muslims to emigrate from the land of the pagans. A number of early Zaydi imams had written treatises on this duty; noteworthy amongst these is the *Kitab al-hijra* by the Zaydi Imam al-Qasim b. Ibrahim al-Rassi, grandfather of the founder of the Zaydi imamate in Yaman. In subsequent centuries, the term *hijra* evolved to refer to any safe locality or abode of emigration where the local Zaydis could live in accordance with their own religious law without experiencing external difficulties.[8]

In theology, the Kufan Zaydiyya, like the early Imamiyya, were predestinarian and strongly opposed to the Qadariyya and the Mu'tazila, though admitting some responsibility of men for their actions. They also rejected the doctrine of the created nature of the Qur'an, but later developed closer relations, similarly to the Imamis, with the Mu'tazili rationalist school of *kalam* theology. By the 4th/10th century, the Zaydi imams and scholars had adopted practically all of the principal Mu'tazili tenets, including the unconditional punishment of the unrepentant sinner – a tenet rejected by the Twelvers and the Ismailis for whom the imam plays a key role as intercessor for his followers. The Zaydis disagreed with the Mu'tazila mainly on the qualifications of the imam and the method of his selection.

In religious law, the Zaydis initially relied on the teachings of Zayd b. 'Ali himself and other early 'Alid authorities such as Muhammad al-Baqir, Ja'far al-Sadiq and Muhammad al-Nafs al-Zakiyya. They also relied on the claimed consensus of the *ahl al-bayt*. By the 3rd/9th century, however, four Zaydi legal schools (*madhhab*s) had emerged on the basis of the teachings of four Zaydi authorities, namely, Ahmad b. 'Isa b. Zayd (d. 247/861), al-Qasim b. Ibrahim al-Rassi (d. 246/860), founder of the school that later prevailed in Yaman as well as among a faction of the Caspian Zaydis, al-Hasan b. Yahya b. al-Husayn b. Zayd and Muhammad b. Mansur al-Muradi (d. ca. 290/903), the foremost contemporary Kufan Zaydi scholar. These schools are described by the Kufan Zaydi Abu 'Abd Allah Muhammad b. 'Ali al-'Alawi (d. 445/1053) in his *Kitab al-jami' al-kafi*, a summary of the legal doctrines of the four authorities then acknowledged by the Zaydiyya.[9]

The Zaydis of the Caspian region in Persia

The coastal regions along the southern shore of the Caspian Sea, in northern Persia, had resisted the penetration of Islam for quite some time. Protected by the Alburz mountain range, many of the inhabitants of these provinces, notably Gilan and Tabaristan, had continued to adhere to Zoroastrianism. Even later, when Islam achieved greater success in the region, numerous local dynasties, such as the Zoroastrian Dabuyid Ispahbads, the Sunni (and later Twelver Shi'i)

Bawandids, the Sunni Ziyarids, and the Shiʿi Justanids, enjoyed various degrees of independence from the caliphal authority. Almost all this entire region was referred to in medieval times as Daylam. This coastal region provided a safe haven for the ʿAlids, referred to in Persian chronicles as *sadat-i ʿAlawi* (ʿAlid Sayyids), and others who rebelled against the central authority of the caliphate. By the early decades of the 3rd/9th century, Tabaristan (today's Mazandaran), the most populous of the Caspian provinces with its capital at Amul, was technically under the jurisdiction of the Tahirids, the hereditary governors of Khurasan on behalf of the Abbasids.

Zaydi Shiʿism was originally disseminated in a limited manner in Daylaman (also known as Rudbar) by the Hasanid ʿAlid Yahya b. ʿAbd Allah, a much younger half-brother of Muhammad al-Nafs al-Zakiyya. Yahya had studied under Imam Jaʿfar al-Sadiq and is credited with having converted a number of Daylamis to Islam. At any rate, Yahya b. ʿAbd Allah arrived in Daylaman in 175/791 and, in the following year, rose in revolt against the Abbasid caliph Harun al-Rashid with some of his Kufan Zaydi supporters. In Daylaman, Yahya was protected by Justan, founder of the Justanid dynasty. Recognised as a Zaydi imam, Yahya was eventually obliged to surrender to the Abbasids; he was killed in a Baghdad prison in 187/803.[10] Yahya's activities paved the way for other ʿAlid claimants to the Zaydi imamate to seek refuge in the Caspian region, and they also helped the spread of Zaydi Shiʿism among the inhabitants of Tabaristan, Gilan and Daylaman. Henceforth Zaydi Shiʿism and ʿAlid rule became closely intertwined in the mountainous provinces of the Caspian region. Medieval histories of various Caspian provinces as well as biographies of the region's Zaydi ʿAlid imams and rulers provide our main sources of information on the history of Zaydi Shiʿism in northern Persia.[11]

Zaydi Shiʿism was more effectively propagated in the Caspian region by some of the local followers of the Zaydi Imam al-Qasim b. Ibrahim al-Rassi (d. 246/860) during his lifetime. Founder of the legal and theological school that became prevalent among the Yamani Zaydis, this Hasanid ʿAlid lived and taught on the Jabal al-Rass near Medina. Al-Qasim b. Ibrahim's theological and legal teachings, which represented a departure from the early Kufan Zaydi doctrines, were only partially in agreement with Muʿtazili tenets. Nevertheless, his doctrines prepared the way for the adoption of Muʿtazili theology by his later Zaydi followers.[12] This Zaydi imam's teachings were now introduced to the Caspian region by his local followers in western Tabaristan, notably in Ruyan, Kalar and Chalus. As a result, Zaydi Shi'ism, based mainly on Imam al-Qasim's teachings, spread from Ruyan westwards to Daylaman and Gilan as well.

The Zaydis of western Tabaristan consolidated their position rather speedily so that by 250/864, when the inhabitants of Ruyan revolted against Tahirid rule, they turned to Zaydi 'Alids for assistance and invited the Hasanid 'Alid al-Hasan b. Zayd, who was living at Rayy, to lead them. Adopting the title of al-Da'i ila'l-Haqq, al-Hasan readily seized control of Tabaristan from its Tahirid governor, Sulayman b. 'Abd Allah, and established the first Zaydi 'Alid state there, with its capital at Amul. Subsequently, al-Hasan b. Zayd was expelled from Tabaristan for brief periods, on three separate occasions, by the Tahirids, the Abbasid commander Muflih and Ya'qub b. al-Layth, founder of the Saffarid dynasty. However, on each occasion he found refuge in the mountains of Daylaman and, with the support of the Daylamis and their Justanid kings, succeeded in re-establishing his rule in Tabaristan, and also extending it to Gurgan (Arabic, Jurjan) in the east. The Justanids ruled from the valley of Rudbar in Daylaman, and one of them is said to have built in 246/860 the fortress of Alamut which was to become the seat of the Nizari Ismaili state of Persia. It was again with al-Hasan's support that a number of his 'Alid relatives temporarily gained control of Rayy, Zanjan, Qazwin and Qumis in Persia. The founder of 'Alid rule in Tabaristan was a learned scholar and is reported to have written books on law and the imamate, which have not survived. In his religious policy, al-Hasan b. Zayd formally supported Shi'i ritual and law as well as Mu'tazili theology. Designated also as *al-da'i al-kabir*, al-Hasan b. Zayd died in Amul in 270/884, having named his brother Muhammad as his successor.[13]

Muhammad b. Zayd, too, bore the title of al-Da'i ila'l-Haqq, in addition to becoming commonly known as *al-da'i al-saghir*. Muhammad followed his brother's religious policy and employed two prominent Mu'tazili theologians, Abu'l-Qasim al-Balkhi and Abu Muslim al-Isfahani, as his secretaries. However, the two 'Alid brothers, al-Hasan and Muhammad b. Zayd, were not generally recognised as full imams by the later Zaydis, as there were some doubts regarding the justice of their rule. The two 'Alids had evidently taken stern measures against the local Sunni *ʿulama* who were not happy with their Shiʿi doctrine. It should be added that al-Hasan b. Zayd's teachings failed to have any influence on the Caspian Zaydi tradition. But Muhammad b. Zayd gained general popularity amongst the Shiʿa for his restoration of the shrines of Imams ʿAli and al-Husayn in Iraq, which had been destroyed on the order of the Abbasid caliph al-Mutawakkil (r. 256–279/870–892). Muhammad b. Zayd was also noted for his generosity towards the ʿAlids residing outside his own dominions.

Muhammad b. Zayd confronted various challenges to his rule of some sixteen years, starting with an ʿAlid brother-in-law who usurped his rule for ten months in Amul before he was overthrown by Muhammad. In 283/896, Muhammad b. Zayd occupied Nishapur briefly and had the *khutba* read there in the name of the ʿAlids, but he was soon expelled by the Saffarid ʿAmr b. al-Layth. In 287/900, Muhammad was defeated and killed near Gurgan in a battle with a Samanid army. His son and heir-apparent Zayd was taken to Bukhara, and Tabaristan came under Samanid rule. Zaydi ʿAlid rule in Tabaristan thus came to an end at least temporarily. For thirteen years after Muhammad b. Zayd's death, Tabaristan was ruled by Samanid *amir*s, who restored Sunni Islam to the region.

Zaydi ʿAlid rule was re-established in Tabaristan in 301/914 by a Husaynid ʿAlid, Abu Muhammad al-Hasan b. ʿAli al-Utrush, known as al-Nasir li'l-Haqq and also as al-Nasir al-Kabir. Originally from Medina, he had joined the entourage of the two ʿAlid brothers in Tabaristan and had participated in the battle in which Muhammad b. Zayd lost his life. Subsequently, al-Utrush lived in Gilan and Daylaman for several years and conducted two unsuccessful campaigns, with the assistance of the Justanid king, Justan III b. Marzuban, to seize Tabaristan from the Samanids. At that time, large numbers in the coastal regions of Daylaman and Gilan had not yet converted to Islam. Al-Utrush now successfully began to spread Islam and Zaydi Shiʿism in these regions, notably amongst the Daylamis north of the Alburz mountains and the Gilis east of the Safidrud. These Daylami and Gili converts accepted him as their imam with the honorific title al-Nasir li'l-Haqq.

In fact, al-Nasir became the founder of the school of Zaydi Shiʿism distinctive to the western Caspian region. A learned scholar with numerous works on theology and law, al-Nasir's legal and ritual teaching, reflecting his own *ijtihad*, differed somewhat from the doctrine of Imam al-Qasim b. Ibrahim al-Rassi, which had been adopted earlier by the Zaydis of Ruyan and western Tabaristan. In terms of theology, his basic tenets were similar to those of al-Qasim b. Ibrahim, but in ritual and law, in particular, he was closer to the early Kufan Zaydi tradition and often to Imami Shiʿi doctrines. Accordingly, al-Nasir adopted the Imami rules concerning divorce and inheritance and the ritual ablution of the feet. On the other hand, all Zaydis, like Ismailis, rejected temporary marriage (*mutʿa*), which was practised by the Twelver Imami Shiʿis.

Henceforth, the Caspian Zaydiyya became divided into two rival schools (*madhhab*s) and communities, designated after their founders as the Nasiriyya, concentrated in eastern Gilan and most of Daylaman, and the Qasimiyya, situated mainly in western Tabaristan and Ruyan. There was much antagonism between the two Caspian Zaydi communities who often supported different imams, *daʿi*s or *amir*s. The rivalries also had wider political implications, further complicated by ethnic differences between the Daylamis and Gilis as well as the close ties existing between the Caspian Qasimiyya and the Zaydis of Yaman. Yahya b. al-Husayn al-Hadi ila'l-Haqq, a grandson of al-Qasim b. Ibrahim who had founded a Zaydi State in Yaman in 284/897, and his successors to the Zaydi imamate there had adopted and further elaborated al-Qasim's doctrine. As a result, the Qasimi Zaydis of the Caspian region generally looked for guidance to the Zaydi imams of Yaman. Prolonged Zaydi sectarian hostilities finally ceased in the Caspian region around the middle of the 4th/10th century when Abu ʿAbd Allah Muhammad al-Mahdi li-Din Allah (d. 360/970), an imam of the Qasimi Zaydis ruling from Hawsam, in Gilan, declared both doctrinal schools as equally valid. This ruling became generally accepted by the Caspian Zaydis who, nevertheless, remained divided in terms of their adherence to the two schools.

In the meantime, in 301/914 al-Nasir al-Utrush had led his army of followers into Tabaristan and this time succeeded in defeating the Samanids there. Thereupon al-Nasir established himself at Amul, initiating the second period of Zaydi ʿAlid rule in Tabaristan. It may be worth remarking here that it was in al-Nasir's armies that the Buyids of Daylam had first risen to prominence; and that the contemporary Samanid *amir*, Nasr II b. Aḥmad, who began his rule in the same year (301/914), was to be converted to the dissident Qarmati form of Ismailism by the *daʿi* al-Nasafi (d. 332/943).

Al-Nasir al-Utrush died in Amul in 304/917 and was buried there. The later Zaydis universally counted him amongst their imams. The Nasiri Zaydis of the Caspian provinces made pilgrimages for several centuries to al-Nasir's shrine at Amul. They also maintained a strong attachment to his Nasirid ʿAlid descendants, all given the honorific title al-Nasir, preferring them to other ʿAlids as candidates for their imamate. It is notable that the contemporary eminent historian Abu Jaʿfar Muhammad al-Tabari (d. 310/923), himself a Sunni and a native of Amul, paid tribute to this learned Zaydi ʿAlid ruler, praising his justice and exemplary life style.[14]

At the time of al-Nasir al-Utrush, numerous ʿAlids, both Hasanids and Husaynids, including many of his own close relatives, lived in the Caspian region. In accordance with the wishes of his Zaydi supporters in Tabaristan, however, al-Nasir had appointed the commander of his army, the Hasanid ʿAlid al-Hasan b. Qasim, as his successor in preference to any of his own sons, including Ahmad and Jaʿfar. Al-Hasan b. Qasim, too, ruled with the title al-Daʿi ila'l-Haqq, and was also known as *al-daʿi al-saghir*. As noted, not all ʿAlid claimants were recognised as full imams by the Zaydis. In particular, in the Caspian provinces where ʿAlids without the full qualifications for the imamate often became rulers, or even two or more ʿAlids simultaneously gained support amongst the local Zaydis, the Zaydis were obliged to allow their legitimate rulers to hold religious ranks below that of an imam. As a result, these Zaydi leaders were generally designated as *daʿi*s and they became commonly known as *al-daʿi al-kabir* or *al-daʿi al-saghir*, while they themselves often adopted titles with this term in it, such as al-Daʿi ila'l-Haqq. There were also those Zaydi ʿAlid rulers who merely ruled as *amir*s without higher religious aspirations.

The reign of the ʿAlid al-Hasan b. Qasim, known as al-Hasan al-Daʿi, turned out to be rather eventful, with many active challenges to his authority, including some posed by the descendants of al-Nasir al-Utrush who intermittently launched risings against him. On one such occasion in 306/919, two of al-Nasir's sons, Ahmad and Jaʿfar, joined forces and expelled al-Hasan from Tabaristan and Gurgan. However, al-Hasan managed to regain his kingdom after only seven months. Subsequently, in 311/923, he was expelled once again from Tabaristan, which now came to be ruled in rapid succession by the Nasirids Ahmad and Jaʿfar and then by their sons. ʿAlid rule was then clearly on the decline in Tabaristan and adjacent provinces, where real power had come to be held by various local Daylami commanders such as Makan b. Kaki and Asfar b. Shirawayh al-Daylami. It was, in fact, Makan who put al-Hasan al-Daʿi back on the throne in Amul in 314/926. Al-Hasan al-Daʿi and Makan now jointly embarked on an ambitious military campaign and temporarily conquered Rayy and other localities in the Jibal. In their absence, however, Asfar, who then governed Gurgan on behalf of the Samanids, invaded Tabaristan. In 316/928, al-Hasan al-Daʿi returned, without Makan, to confront Asfar at Amul. The Zaydi ruler's army was defeated and al-Hasan al-Daʿi was mortally wounded by Mardawij b. Ziyar (d. 323/935), a lieutenant of Asfar who later founded the Ziyarid dynasty of northern Persia. Asfar, himself the master of Tabaristan, Gurgan and adjacent areas for a short period, was pressured by the Samanids to depose the last nominal ʿAlid ruler of Tabaristan, Abu Jaʿfar Muhammad (a grandson of al-Nasir al-Utrush), and send him together with other ʿAlids as captives to Bukhara.

It is interesting to note at this juncture that Abu Hatim al-Razi (d. 322/934), the fifth Ismaili (Qarmati) *daʿi* of the Jibal, was at this time active in Tabaristan, where he participated in local politics and supported Asfar against the Zaydi ʿAlid al-Hasan al-Daʿi. Abu Hatim acquired numerous converts and sympathisers in Tabaristan and other Caspian provinces, including Asfar b. Shirawayh (d. 319/331) and the Justanid ruler of Daylaman, Mahdi b. Khusraw Firuz (d. 316/928) known as Siyahchashm.[15] It was under such circumstances that Zaydi ʿAlid rule was once again effectively brought to an end in Tabaristan in 316/928. Subsequently, due to the strong ʿAlid sentiments of the Daylamis and Gilis, al-Nasir al-Utrush's grandsons continued for a while longer to govern Amul as vassals of the Samanids and Ziyarids. As puppets in the hands of the local Daylami *amir*s, however, these minor ʿAlids did not exert any independent authority over Tabaristan or any other Caspian province. By the time the Buyids established their own hegemony over Tabaristan in 331/943, the Zaydi ʿAlids had completely lost their earlier prominence there. Henceforth, al-Nasir al-Utrush's remoter Nasirid descendants retained only limited local influence and social standing in Amul, while some of them continued to serve as governors under the Buyids and Ziyarids.

After the collapse of the second Zaydi ʿAlid state in Tabaristan under Samanid attacks, other ʿAlid rulers had appeared in the Caspian region, notably in Daylaman and eastern Gilan. The town of Hawsam (modern-day Rudsar) in eastern Gilan, where al-Nasir al-Utrush had been active, now became the centre of scholarship of the Nasiri Zaydis as well as the seat of a local ʿAlid dynasty founded around 320/932 by Abu'l-Fadl Jaʿfar b. Muhammad, grandson of al-Nasir al-Utrush's brother al-Husayn al-Shaʿir. Abu'l-Fadl and most of his successors adopted the regnal title al-Tha'ir fi'llah. All the Zaydi ʿAlid members of this Tha'irid dynasty ruled as *amirs* without claiming the Zaydi imamate of the Nasiriyya Zaydis; they played important roles in the political affairs of Gilan for some three centuries. Abu'l-Fadl al-Tha'ir reigned for three decades until his death in 350/961, and on three occasions he succeeded in occupying Amul only for brief periods. His descendants retained their control over Hawsam with some difficulty as they were frequently challenged by the descendants of al-Nasir al-Utrush, amongst other ʿAlids, as well as by various neighbouring powers such as the Ziyarids and Buyids who had their own expansionary ambitions in the Caspian region.[16] When Hawsam was replaced by Lahijan as the chief town of eastern Gilan in the 6th/12th century, descendants of Abu'l-Fadl al-Tha'ir ruled there as *amirs* at least until the early 7th/13th century.

Meanwhile, in 353/964, Abu ʿAbd Allah Muhammad, a son of al-Hasan b. Qasim al-Daʿi, seized Hawsam from the Tha'irids and ruled there until his death in 360/970. A learned scholar in theology and law, he was the first Caspian ʿAlid after al-Nasir to have gained universal recognition by the later Zaydis as a full imam, with the title al-Mahdi li-Din Allah. He enjoyed wide support amongst both the Nasiriyya and the Qasimiyya and devoted much of his time and learning to alleviating the perennial antagonism then existing between the two Caspian schools of Zaydi Shiʿism. He successfully argued that their teachings were equally valid as they had been based on the *ijtihad* of legitimate imams.

After Imam al-Mahdi, the ʿAlid rivalries between the Tha'irids and the Nasirid descendants of al-Nasir al-Utrush were resumed in Hawsam. The situation was further aggravated when in 380/990 contenders from other ʿAlid branches, too, appeared in the area. Two of these Hasanid ʿAlids gained particular prominence and became generally acknowledged as full imams; they were Abu'l-Husayn Ahmad b. al-Husayn b. Harun al-Mu'ayyad bi'llah (d. 411/1020) of the Buthani family and his brother Abu Talib Yahya al-Natiq bi'l-Haqq (d. ca. 424/1033).[17] Both had studied in Baghdad and then joined the circles of the Buyid vizier Ibn ʿAbbad (d. 385/995) and of the Muʿtazili chief *qadi* of Rayy, ʿAbd al-Jabbar al-Hamadhani (d. 415/1024). In fact, Zaydi religious scholarship in the Caspian provinces reached its climax amongst the Qasimiyya in the contributions of these two imams, who wrote major works in the Qasimi Zaydi tradition; several of their theological and legal works have been preserved by the Qasimi Zaydis of Yaman. Imam al-Mu'ayyad is sometimes even considered as the founder of a new Caspian school of Zaydi law, named Mu'ayyadiyya after him. Be that as it may, in theology these two brothers fully espoused the doctrine of the Basran school of Muʿtazilism as represented by *qadi* ʿAbd al-Jabbar.

The close doctrinal relations between the Zaydiyya and the Muʿtazila of this period are also reflected in the contemporary pro-ʿAlid tendency of the Muʿtazili doctrine of the imamate. Several Muʿtazili scholars of the school of ʿAbd al-Jabbar, including Abu'l-Qasim Ismaʿil al-Busti (d. 420/1029), actually became Zaydis. It was perhaps due to the profound hostility of the Zaydis towards the Ismailis that al-Busti wrote a refutation of the Ismaili doctrines; only a fragment of al-Busti's anti-Ismaili treatise is extant.[18] Imam al-Mu'ayyad himself was one of the Zaydi imams who issued *fatwa*s against the Ismailis (Batiniyya), refuting their esoteric teachings. Subsequently, the Ismaili *daʿi* Hamid al-Din al-Kirmani (d. ca. 411/1020) responded to the Zaydi imam's allegations in a brief polemical treatise of his own, refuting forcefully the Zaydi doctrine of the imamate and their charge that the Batiniyya are outside the fold of Islam.[19]

Imam al-Mu'ayyad bi'llah also wrote a treatise on Sufi devotion entitled *Risalat siyasat al-muridin* which, together with his other works, was brought to Yaman and used in defining the selective attitude of the Zaydiyya towards Sufism.[20] The rationalist and *shariʿa*-oriented Zaydis were generally opposed to Sufism and other esoteric traditions in Islam. In particular, the Zaydis were opposed to those mystical or Sufi practices, such as *samaʿ*, chanting and dancing, which aimed at inducing states of ecstasy. They also rejected the speculative mysticism of Ibn al-ʿArabi's school. However, as explained by Imam al-Mu'ayyad, the Zaydiyya could support certain aspects of early Sufi piety, notably its ascetism. Imam al-Mu'ayyad and other Caspian Qasimi Zaydi imams established themselves at Langa, between Hawsam and Chalus, in Daylaman. Langa remained the seat of the ʿAlids claiming the imamate of the Qasimi Zaydis until the end of the 5th/11th century when the (Nizari) Ismailis began to extend their own authority over Daylaman.

The arrival of the Sunni Saljuq Turks in Tabaristan and other Caspian provinces did not lead to any significant curtailment of Zaydi activities in the region. However, the propagation of the Ismaili Shiʿi *daʿwa* in northern Persia did put severe pressures on the Zaydi communities of Daylaman and Ruyan, while Rayy continued to serve as an important centre of Zaydi learning. Ismailism spread rapidly throughout Daylam soon after Hasan-i Sabbah had cleverly captured Alamut in 483/1090 from its Zaydi ʿAlid commander, a descendant of al-Nasir al-Utrush who had held the fortress on behalf of the Saljuq Sultan Malikshah. The Zaydis, it may be recalled, were traditionally opposed on doctrinal grounds to the Ismaili form of Shiʿi Islam and its advocacy of esoteric, gnostic knowledge, much more than they were to the Sunni Sufis. Indeed, as noted, both Caspian and Yamani Zaydi imams and authorities wrote polemical treatises, or issued *fatwa*s, against the Ismailis. The Caspian Zaydis, similarly to the contemporary Sunni authors who referred to the Syrian Nizari Ismailis with the abusive term *hashishi* (plural, *hashishiyya*), also used these derogatory terms (as well as *malahida* or 'heretics') in reference to the Persian Nizaris.[21]

Be that as it may, our sources relate numerous confrontations between the Nizari Ismailis and the Zaydis of the Caspian region, which drastically checked the power and influence of the Zaydis in the region. As the Persian Nizari Ismailis extended their influence and territories in Daylaman and elsewhere in the 6th/12th century, the Caspian Zaydis became essentially confined to eastern Gilan. The fortunes of the Zaydiyya were further curtailed by constant factional fightings and ʿAlid rivalries. In these circumstances, minor ʿAlids, mainly Nasirid or Tha'irid, continued to rule in parts of eastern Gilan. For instance, in 502/1108 Abu Talib Akhir, a great-grandson of Imam al-Mu'ayyad, claimed the imamate and was acknowledged as such in eastern Gilan as far as Hawsam. He was, however, resisted by the

Zaydis of Lahijan, which was then ruled by the Tha'irid *amir* Sulayman b. Isma'il. Abu Talib reportedly also engaged in warfare with the Nizari Ismailis of Daylaman, temporarily capturing some of their fortresses. Later, in 526/1131, the Nizaris, then led by the second lord of Alamut, Kiya Buzurg-Umid, retaliated by sending an army into Gilan against Abu Hashim 'Alawi, another claimant to the Zaydi imamate who had persistently accused the Ismailis of heresy (*ilhad*) and unbelief (*kufr*). The Zaydi fighters were defeated and Abu Hashim was brought to Alamut, where he held religious disputations with Ismaili scholars before eventually being executed.[22]

On a number of subsequent occasions an imam of the Yamani Zaydis was recognised as imam also by the Caspian Zaydis, such as Imam al-Mansur bi'llah 'Abd Allah b. Hamza (d. 614/1217), who gained recognition in Gilan in 605/1208. The history of the Caspian Zaydis and their 'Alid rulers remains rather obscure for the following century. However, the Zaydi communities of this region survived the Mongol debacle. In his history of the Mongol Ilkhanid Öljeitü's reign (703–716/1304–1316), Abu'l-Qasim Kashani refers to a certain 'Alid descendant of al-Nasir al-Utrush, Sayyid Muhammad Kiya b. Sayyid Haydar Kiya, who was then ruling in Kuchispahan and other districts of eastern Gilan among the Nasiriyya Zaydis.[23] By 769/1367, an 'Alid dynasty descended from Imam al-Mu'ayyad bi'llah al-Buthani still ruled, together with other Sayyids, over Tunukabun and some adjacent areas amongst the Qasimiyya Zaydis there.

'Alid rule and the Zaydi cause in Gilan were significantly revived under the dynasty of the Amir (or Kar) Kiya'i Sayyids, also known as Malati Sayyids, who ruled from 769/1367 until 1000/1592 when Gilan was seized by the Safawids. The founder of the dynasty, Sayyid 'Ali Kiya b. Sayyid Amir Kiya al-Malati, was originally the leader of a Sufi movement of Zaydi 'penitents' (*ta'iban*). Sayyid 'Ali Kiya was recognised as an imam by the Zaydi scholars of Ranikuh and Lahijan, who testified that he possessed all five qualities required for the Zaydi imamate.[24] After the death of his father in 763/1361, Sayyid 'Ali Kiya was well received by Sayyid Qiwam al-Din Mar'ashi, an Imami Shi'i who ruled in Amul in 760/1359 and soon brought all Tabaristan under his authority. In 769/1367, Sayyid Qiwam al-Din provided crucial support to the Zaydi Sayyid 'Ali Kiya who, assisted also by his Zaydi followers, conquered eastern Gilan and became master of the whole of Biyapish to the east of the Safidrud. Subsequently, Sayyid ʿAli Kiya (d. 791/1389), still helped by the Marʿashi Sayyids of Tabaristan, extended his authority over Daylaman, Ashkawar, Kuhdum and as far as Tarum and Qazwin.

It is interesting to note that even in the post-Mongol times, the Zaydis had similar confrontations with the Nizari Ismailis, who had continued to be active, on a more limited scale, in Daylaman. Perennial Zaydi–Ismaili hostilities broke into open warfare when in 779/1377 Sayyid ʿAli Kiya dispatched his troops against the Nizari Ismaili ruler of Daylaman, Kiya Sayf al-Din of the Nizari dynasty of Kushayji *amirs*, with the Zaydis gaining victory. Later, Sayyid ʿAli held Alamut for a while. The Zaydi ʿAlid descendants of Sayyid ʿAli Kiya ruled from Lahijan, on the basis of dynastic succession as the Malati Sayyids, until early Safawid times.[25] In 933/1526, pressured by the Safawids in the reign of Shah Tahmasp I, the contemporary Malati Sayyid, Sultan Ahmad Khan (d. 940/1533), and his Zaydi subjects converted to Twelver Imami Shiʿism. Malati rule, too, was ended by the Safawids in 1000/1592, by which time all Zaydi communities in Iraq and Persia, notably in the Caspian provinces as well as smaller groups in Rayy, Fars and Khurasan, had disappeared. Henceforth, Zaydi Shiʿism was confined to Yaman.

The Zaydis of Yaman

The Zaydi imamate in Yaman was founded in 284/897 by the Hasanid ʿAlid Yahya b. al-Husayn, grandson of al-Qasim b. Ibrahim al-Rassi, who was given the honorific title al-Hadi ila'l-Haqq. Born in 245/859 in Medina, he acquired prominence for his learning. Earlier in his career, Yahya spent a few years (270–275/883–889) in Amul seeking the support of the local Zaydis of Tabaristan who already adhered to the teachings of his grandfather. However, Yahya's efforts in the Caspian region were cut short by Muhammad b. Zayd, the contemporary Zaydi imam there. By 280/893, Yayha al-Hadi had arrived in Saʿda in northern Yaman on his first visit at the invitation of the local feuding tribesmen who were counting on his arbitration efforts.[26]

In 284/897, al-Hadi established himself at Saʿda, which was to become his capital as well as the permanent stronghold of Zaydi Shiʿism in terms of the *daʿwa* activities and scholarship in Yaman. Already known for his learning, al-Hadi was recognised as an imam after issuing his formal call, or *daʿwa*, for support. He then embarked on a number of campaigns to extend his authority over other parts of Yaman, while calling himself *amir al-muʾminin*, Commander of the Faithful. He succeeded in establishing his authority over Najran, but failed to keep Sanʿaʾ in the south for any extended period despite leading several expeditions there. At the time, Sanʿaʾ and other localities in Yaman were also controlled periodically by the Ismailis, especially by the *daʿi* ʿAli b. al-Fadl (d. 303/915), who together with his senior colleague Ibn Hawshab Mansur al-Yaman (d. 302/914) had successfully spread the Ismaili *daʿwa* in Yaman. By 293/905, when ʿAli b. al-Fadl occupied Sanʿaʾ, almost all of Yaman had been brought under the control of these Ismaili *daʿi*s who operated on behalf of the Ismaili imams, though the Ismailis later lost the greater part of their early conquests to the Zaydis.

By 299/911, ʿAli b. al-Fadl himself had initiated a Qarmati movement in Yaman, after renouncing his allegiance to the Fatimids. For several years, during 301–307/913–920, the Zaydis confronted the Qarmatis in extended warfare during the imamate of al-Hadi's son and second successor, Ahmad al-Nasir li-Din Allah,[27] who succeeded his brother Muhammad al-Murtada in 310/922. Indeed, Zaydi–Ismaili adversarial relations persisted throughout the centuries in Yaman, and Imam al-Hadi's rule was periodically challenged even in northern Yaman, the seat of the Zaydis, by various tribal rebellions. Nevertheless, he managed to expand the Zaydi community of Yaman, despite the fact that Shiʿism of any form did not have any deep roots in that region of southern Arabia. In addition to enjoying the backing of his ʿAlid relatives, Imam al-Hadi consistently received support from groups of Caspian Zaydis who migrated from Daylaman to Yaman from 285/898.

Imam al-Hadi's theological doctrine was generally very close to the views of the contemporary Muʿtazili school of Baghdad, then led by Abu'l-Qasim al-Balkhi (d. 319/931). Concerning the imamate, he upheld the radical Shiʿi stance of the earlier Jarudi Zaydis, condemning the early caliphs Abu Bakr and ʿUmar as usurpers of ʿAli's rights. In religious law, al-Hadi's teachings, as expounded in his *Kitab al-ahkam* and *Kitab al-muntakhab*, were based on the doctrine of his grandfather, but in certain points, such as the call to prayer, he adopted more distinctive Shiʿi views. Imam al-Hadi's legal doctrine became authoritative among the Zaydis of Yaman and part of the Caspian Zaydi community; and it was developed more fully by al-Hadi's two sons, Muhammad al-Murtada (d. 310/922) and Ahmad al-Nasir li-Din Allah (d. 322/934), each recognised consecutively as imam in succession to al-Hadi. Imam al-Hadi's legal teachings, collected and further elaborated later, provided the basis for the Hadawiyya legal school named after him, sometimes referred to also as Qasimiyya-Hadawiyya, representing the only authoritative legal *madhhab* among the Zaydis of Yaman. Having firmly established the Zaydi imamate in Yaman, which was to continue right up until 1962, Imam al-Hadi died in 298/911 and was buried in the mosque of Saʿda. The tombs of al-Hadi and his two sons and successors to the Zaydi imamate in Yaman became pilgrimage shrines for the Zaydiyya.

The descendants of Imam al-Hadi, after his two sons, quarrelled incessantly among themselves and failed to be acknowledged as imams amongst the Zaydiyya of Yaman. Finally, the Zaydi imamate of the Rassid line was restored in Yaman in 389/999 by al-Mansur bi'llah al-Qasim b. ʿAli al-ʿIyani (d. 393/1003), a descendant of al-Qasim b. Ibrahim al-Rassi through his son Muhammad, an uncle of Imam al-Hadi.[28] Born in the Hijaz, he gained an early reputation as a religious scholar and was visited in his native land by the Yamani Zaydis who urged him to lead an insurrection. In 383/993, he rose in revolt in the Hijaz but was rapidly defeated by the *amir* of Mecca who brought him to Fatimid Cairo in 384/994. There, he was treated kindly by the Fatimid caliph-imam al-ʿAziz, who permitted the Zaydi rebel to return to the Hijaz. A few years later, in his first invasion of Yaman, al-Mansur occupied Saʿda, but lost that stronghold to Imam al-Hadi's descendants soon after his return to the Hijaz. However, in 389/999 he returned to Yaman permanently and succeeded in establishing control over much of northern Yaman, as well as southwards to Sanʿa'.

In Yaman, Imam al-Mansur resided in the town of ʿIyan, to the south-east of Saʿda, which remained under the influence of al-Hadi's descendants and tribes loyal to them. In fact, al-Mansur's rule was challenged in open rebellions by some of al-Hadi's descendants as well as by his own governor of Sanʿa', forcing him to relinquish his rule. Subsequently, Yusuf b. Yahya b. Ahmad al-Nasir, a great-grandson of Imam al-Hadi, acquired wide support amongst the Zaydiyya. However, al-Mansur was also recognised as a full imam by later Zaydis, who did not accord a similar acknowledgement to Yusuf b. Yahya, who was designated merely as al-Daʿi ila'l-Haqq. Imam al-Mansur generally followed the theological and legal teachings of the Qasimiyya-Hadawiyya school.

After al-Mansur, one of his younger sons, al-Husayn, claimed the imamate in 401/1010 and gained much support among the Yamani tribes of Himyar and Hamdan, temporarily taking possession of Saʿda and Sanʿa'. Adopting the title of al-Mahdi li-Din Allah, he now claimed to be not only the rightful imam but also the promised Shiʿi Mahdi, an unprecedented claim in the Zaydi tradition. In the event, he was obliged to fight the tribes that had turned against him and was killed in battle in 404/1013. However, al-Husayn al-Mahdi's remaining Zaydi followers and his family denied his death, holding that he would return in the near future and bring justice to the earth, as traditionally expected from the Mahdi. It was under such circumstances that his relatives succeeded to leadership in this schismatic Zaydi ʿAlid dynasty, but without claiming the imamate, as the Mahdi could not be followed by any further imams. These Rassid ʿAlids ruled merely as *amir*s awaiting the imminent return of al-Husayn al-Mahdi. In fact, these rulers and their tribal supporters now gave rise to a new messianic Zaydi religious movement in Yaman known as the Husayniyya, also designated as *al-shiʿa al-Husayniyya*.[29]

After al-Husayn al-Mahdi, the Husayniyya Zaydis were first led by his elder brother Jaʿfar b. al-Qasim al-ʿIyani. From his base in ʿIyan, which served as the seat of this ʿAlid family, Jaʿfar made several attempts to seize Sanʿa' with the support of the Himyari and Hamdani tribes. For a while, he even allied himself with a ruling Zaydi imam, Abu'l-Fath al-Nasir al-Daylami, who was killed in battle in 444/1052 by Muhammad b. ʿAli al-Sulayhi.[30] By then, all the Zaydi ʿAlid imams and *amir*s were confronted with their strongest common adversary in the person of this Sulayhid ruler. Muhammad b. ʿAli al-Sulayhi (d. 459/1067) had risen in the mountainous region of Haraz in 439/1047, marking the foundation of the Ismaili Sulayhid dynasty of Yaman who ruled as vassals of the Fatimids until 532/1138. Jaʿfar b. al-Qasim was succeeded as leader of the Husayniyya Zaydis by his sons, *amir* al-Fadil al-Qasim (d. 468/1075) and *amir* Dhu'l-Sharafayn Muhammad (d. 478/1085), and then by the latter's son *amir* ʿUmdat al-Islam Jaʿfar. All these ʿAlid *amir*s became involved in lengthy periods of conflict and truce with the Sulayhids. Based at their fortified stronghold of Shahara, these ʿAlid descendants of Jaʿfar, also known as the Qasimi *sharifs*, provided in fact the main opposition to the Sulayhids, who were also in charge of the Ismaili *daʿwa* in Yaman, and frustrated their expansionary designs in northern Yaman during the 5th/11th century. The Husayniyya Zaydis evidently survived into the 9th/15th century, perhaps under the continued leadership of the Qasimi *sharifs*, though specific details are lacking.

A second splinter Zaydi sect, known as the Mutarrifiyya, appeared in northern Yaman later in the course of the 5th/11th century. Named after its founder Mutarrif b. Shihab al-Shihabi (d. after 459/1067), the Mutarrifiyya represented a pietist, rather than a revolutionary, Zaydi movement.[31] The Mutarrifiyya adhered strictly to the teachings of the early Yamani Zaydi imams and authorities. The Mutarrifi teachings were basically elaborated by Mutarrif, who recognised the doctrines of al-Qasim b. Ibrahim al-Rassi, al-Hadi and certain other early Yamani Zaydi imams, but rejected the teachings of the contemporary Zaydi imams as well as the doctrines of the Caspian Zaydiyya who espoused Basran Muʿtazili doctrines. However, the Mutarrifis interpreted the acceptable Zaydi teachings in an arbitrary manner and developed a theology that deviated significantly from the Muʿtazili theology incorporated widely into Zaydi Shiʿism, which was to be condemned, in due course, by Sunni Muslims.

The pious Mutarrifiyya Zaydis were also inclined towards asceticism, which came to characterise their movement. Imam al-Qasim b. Ibrahim and other early Zaydi authorities had already elaborated the doctrine of *hijra* for the Zaydis, defined as the obligation of the faithful Zaydiyya not only to support the rightful imam, but to emigrate from the land of oppression and injustice (*dar al-zulm*). The Mutarrifiyya now interpreted this doctrine as a permanent obligation to emigrate to 'abodes of emigration', designated as *hijras*, where they gathered to engage in penitence (*tawba*), ritual purification, worship and ascetic practices, and generally to live according to the doctrine of the *ahl al-bayt* as defined for them. The first of these *hijras*, or protected enclaves in tribal territory, was founded by Mutarrif himself in Sanaʿ, south of Sanʿaʾ, in the territory of his own tribe, the Banu Shihab. Later, another *hijra* was established at Wadi Waqash, which remained the centre of the Mutarrifi movement and the seat of its leaders until its destruction in 611/1214 by Imam al-Mansur bi'llah ʿAbd Allah b. Hamza. The Mutarrifiyya founded numerous *hijras* in various districts of northern Yaman, and they served as a prototype of such enclaves used by the later Zaydis of Yaman.

Meanwhile, the Zaydi imamate and fortunes were once again restored in Yaman by al-Mutawakkil ʿala'llah Ahmad b. Sulayman (r. 532–566/1138–1171). He succeeded in establishing his rule in Saʿda and other areas such as Najran, and briefly also over Sanʿa'. Imam al-Mutawakkil Ahmad favoured the unity of the Zaydi communities and therefore recognised the equal legitimacy of the Yamani and Caspian Zaydi imams and their teachings. As a result, certain Yamani imams were now acknowledged by the Caspian Zaydis. He also encouraged the large-scale transfer of the religious literature of the Caspian Zaydis to Yaman. A key role was played in these unifying developments by Shams al-Din Jaʿfar b. Abi Yahya (d. 573/1178). A Zaydi *qadi* and scholar, Jaʿfar hailed from a Yamani Ismaili family and originally he had adhered to Ismaili Shiʿism before converting to Zaydi Shiʿism. Oddly, Jaʿfar was initially also a Mutarrifi Zaydi but later turned against them and became the founder of a Zaydi school that recognised the Zaydi imams of the Caspian provinces as being equal in authority to their counterparts in Yaman. Aiming to restore ideological unity to the divided Zaydi communities, as desired by Imam al-Mutawakkil Ahmad, the school of the *qadi* Jaʿfar, also espousing Muʿtazili theology, remained prevalent in the Zaydi community of Yaman under Imam al-Mansur ʿAbd Allah b. Hamza (r. 593–614/1197–1217). Imam al-Mansur endorsed the doctrines of this Zaydi school in his own numerous works, and also established the dominance of the Muʿtazili theology. By this time, Imam al-Mansur, as well as his predecessor Imam al-Mutawakkil Ahmad and the Zaydi *ʿulama*, had also begun to cite *hadith* from the Sunni canonical collections while continuing to use the Zaydi collections of *hadith*.

In line with his general views and religious policies, Imam al-Mutawakkil Ahmad had severely criticised both the Mutarrifiyya and the Husayniyya for undermining the unity of the Zaydiyya in Yaman. However, it was Imam al-Mansur ʿAbd Allah who openly declared the Mutarrifi Zaydis as heretics and persecuted them severely; he destroyed the Mutarrifi *hijras* and succeeded in almost destroying their sect.

Nevertheless, the Mutarrifiyya, like the Husayniyya, lingered on for a couple of centuries before finally disbanding during the 9th/15th century.

The Zaydi imamate prevailed in Yaman even after the occupation of southern Arabia by the Sunni Ayyubids in 569/1174, though the power of the Zaydi imams was now considerably restricted. Under the changed circumstances, the Zaydis of Yaman were at times obliged to develop better relations with the Sunnis, against their own Zaydi doctrines. For instance, Imam al-Mu'ayyad bi'llah Yahya b. Hamza (r. 729–749/1328–1349), a prolific author, praised Abu Bakr, ʿUmar and ʿUthman as the early Companions of the Prophet and deserving respect equal to ʿAli. As we shall see, in later centuries too, especially as the Zaydi imams extended their rule to the predominantly Sunni lowlands of Yaman, the Zaydis attempted in a more sustained fashion to achieve a certain doctrinal rapport with their Sunni subjects.

On the other hand, the Yamani Zaydis maintained their perennial hostility towards the Sufis, even though some Zaydi imams had now adopted a more tolerant stance.[32] For instance, Imam al-Mu'ayyad Yahya, in elaborating his own teachings, acknowledged the validity of the miracles (*karamat*) of the Sufi *shaykh*s. And in his book on religious ethics entitled *Tasfiyat al-qulub*, which was perhaps modelled on al-Ghazali's *Ihya' ʿulum al-din*, this Zaydi imam quoted extensively from the sayings of the early Sufis, while still attacking the Sufis for their *samaʿ* practices – chanting, singing and dancing accompanied by musical instruments. There were evidently no direct contacts between the Zaydis and Sufis in the highlands of Yaman, stretching from Saʿda to Sanʿa'. Meanwhile, organised Sufi orders had appeared, from the 5th/11th century onwards, in the lowlands of Yaman, in areas such as Tihama and Zabid, where Sunni Islam of the Shafiʿi *madhhab* was prevalent. However, from the 7th/13th century, the Zaydi imams, who were now seeking to extend their authority to the lowlands, came into conflict with the influential Sunni Sufi *shaykh*s of the region. In these circumstances, the Yamani Zaydis were increasingly obliged to reconsider their hostile attitude towards Sufism.

It was in such a context that Imam al-Mu'ayyad Yahya's teachings paved the way for the emergence of an indigenous moderate Zaydi order of Sufism in Yaman in the 8th/14th century. The founder of this Sufi order was Ibrahim b. Ahmad al-Kaynaʿi (d. 793/1391), who was a disciple of Shaykh ʿAli b. ʿAbd Allah b. Abiʾl-Khayr, himself a prominent Zaydi scholar. Fully trained in Zaydi law and theology, al-Kaynaʿi was closely associated with al-Nasir Salah al-Din Muhammad b. ʿAli (r. 773–793/1371–1391), and participated in some of this Zaydi imam's campaigns against the Tayyibi Ismailis who were then allied with the Sunni Rasulids of Yaman and posed a major challenge to Zaydi authority in the highlands. Al-Kaynaʿi founded numerous Sufi communities and *hijras* for devotion throughout northern Yaman.

Al-Kaynaʿi elaborated an ascetic school of Sufism for the Zaydiyya, based on rejecting the Sufi practices that were condemned by the Zaydi imams while upholding the Zaydi imamate. As a result, this Zaydi school of Sufism found favour with the contemporary Imam al-Nasir as well. But the subsequent imams revived the traditional Zaydi opposition to Sufism and widely condemned the Sufis for their 'unorthodox' teachings and practices. In fact, Zaydi–Sufi relations had already deteriorated towards the end of Imam al-Nasir's reign. Later, some imams, such as al-Mutawakkil al-Mutahhar b. Muhammad (r. 840–879/1436–1474), again openly attacked Sufi practices connected to chanting and dancing. However, systematic persecution of Sufis was initiated by Imam al-Mutawakkil Sharaf al-Din Yahya b. Shams al-Din (912–965/1506–1558), who went as far as accusing the Sufis of 'unbelief' (*kufr*).[33] This imam also conducted military campaigns against the Tayyibi Ismailis who had then allied themselves with the invading Ottoman Turks.[34]

Anti-Sufi polemics in Yaman reached a new peak under Imam al-Mansur al-Qasim b. Muhammad (r. 1006–1029/1598–1620), founder of the Qasimi dynasty of Zaydi imams, known as *al-dawla al-Qasimiyya* in Yaman. Imam al-Mansur's own deep hostility towards the Sufis was partly a reaction to the initial support of the Sufis for the Ottoman occupation of Yaman in 945/1538, while the Zaydi imam was engaged in prolonged warfare with the Ottoman Turks for more than two decades. It was, however, al-Mansur's son and successor, al-Muʾayyad Muhammad b. al-Qasim (r. 1029–1054/1620–1644), who finally succeeded in expelling the Ottoman Turks from Yaman in 1045/1636. Imam al-Mansur branded the Sufis, like the Ismailis, as 'Batiniyya' and hence qualified to be considered as 'infidels' and 'heretics'. He composed a number of treatises and poems against the Sufis, claiming that their teachings emanated from the pre-Islamic Iranian religions such as Zoroastrianism and Mazdakism and declaring the shedding of their blood as licit. These false accusations were reminiscent of the earlier polemical attacks against the Ismailis. In fact, al-Mansur also cited the *fatwa*s of certain Zaydi imams of the Caspian region against the Batiniyya (Isma'iliyya), defined as apostates, in order to further legitimise his own anti-Sufi position.[35] As W. Madelung has observed, Imam al-Mansur al-Qasim's deep resentment of Sufism set the pattern for his successors in the Qasimi dynasty of the Zaydi imams who ruled until 1962. One of al-Mansur's several sons who succeeded to the imamate, al-Mutawakkil Isma'il b. al-Qasim (r. 1054–1087/1644–1676), for instance, authorised the burning of Ibn al-'Arabi's *Fusus al-hikam*, a work earlier singled out for condemnation by Imam al-Mansur himself. The persecutions of the Sufis continued until the abolition of the Zaydi imamate in Yaman in the 20th century. Even in its closing years, Imam al-Nasir Ahmad b. Yahya Hamid al-Din (r. 1367–1382/1948–1962), following in the footsteps of his father and predecessor, imprisoned the *shaykh* of the Fasiyya Shadhiliyya Sufi brotherhood and had several of his followers executed.

Meanwhile, after the first Ottoman occupation of Yaman ended in 1045/1636, San'a' had continued to serve as the capital of an independent Zaydi state and imamate for more than two centuries until 1289/1872, when Yaman once again became an Ottoman province (*eyalet*) lasting until the First World War. During this period, marked by rivalries over the succession in the Qasimi dynasty as well as tribal conflicts, the Zaydi imamate itself was transformed into a dynastic rule; Zaydi rulers and imams succeeded one another normally on a dynastic basis, without possessing the required religious knowledge and other qualifications expected of the imams according to the Zaydi tradition. In other words, the imams had effectively become kings or sultans, lacking the charisma and spiritual qualities enjoyed by the earlier imams and as required by Zaydi law. In 1296/1879, a new Zaydi ruler and imam, al-Hadi Sharaf al-Din (r. 1296–1307/1879–1890) fought the Ottoman occupiers of Yaman. Subsequently, Zaydi rule and imamate was handed down amongst the members of the Hamid al-Din family (*bayt*) of the Qasimis, starting with al-Mansur Muhammad b. Yayha Hamid al-Din (r. 1307–1322/1890–1904), until the revolution of 1962. On al-Mansur's death in 1904, his son Yahya succeeded with the title al-Mutawakkil ʿala'llah. Adopting a policy of complete isolation from the outside world, he succeeded in entering Sanʿa' in 1918 and starting his rule over an independent Yaman.[36] However, it was in his reign that the Saʿudis occupied the region of Najran in 1934. On al-Mutawakkil Yahya's assassination in 1948, he was succeeded by his son al-Nasir Ahmad who ruled until his own death in 1962, and then Ahmad's son Muhammad al-Badr ruled for only a week before he was deposed by a group of army officers who declared a republic in Yaman. The Zaydi imamate has not been claimed since Muhammad al-Badr's death in exile, which is a permissible situation according to Zaydi doctrine. Thus, the Zaydi Shiʿis currently remain without an imam of any type, while the very nature of Zaydi Shiʿism has undergone a fundamental transformation.

The 'Sunnisation of Zaydi Shiʿism',[37] which had begun in the 12th/18th century, resulted from two separate but fairly simultaneous developments in Yaman, namely, the transformation of the Zaydi imamate into dynastic rule and the penetration of Zaydism by traditionist Sunni doctrines. The first five Qasimi Zaydi imams, from al-Mansur al-Qasim b. Muhammad to al-Mu'ayyad Muhammad b. Ismaʿil, who reigned from 1006/1598 to 1097/1686, possessed all the qualifications required by Zaydi tradition. They were, indeed, men of the pen and the sword, combining scholarly and military attributes; and they all produced numerous works on theology and law.[38] However, the later Qasimi imams lacked the required qualifications, instead succeeding one another merely on a dynastic basis, with each one appointing his successor. By the 12th/18th century, the Qasimi Zaydi imamate had clearly become a ruling dynasty and, as such, the rulers, who no longer lived up to the standards set by Hadawi Zaydi law in Yaman, were in need of alternative legitimisation by the *ʿulama* of the Zaydi state.

Meanwhile, the Qasimi Zaydi rulers had gained control over the more populous and predominantly Shafiʿi Sunni lowlands of Yaman. The expansion of the Qasimi state into Sunni regions led to unprecedented levels of interaction between the Zaydi and Sunni subjects of the state and their scholars. In this milieu, Zaydi scholars began to study, on a more systematic basis, various Sunni works, especially the Sunni collections of *hadith*, though the influence of Sunnism had already been present to some extent in the Zaydi highlands, as reflected in the teachings of Sayyid Muhammad b. Ibrahim al-Wazir (d. 840/1436). Indeed, Ibn al-Wazir, a member of an ʿAlid family of distinguished scholars, is considered as the founder of a neo-Sunni school within the Zaydi tradition. As the first traditionist scholar among the Zaydiyya, Ibn al-Wazir accepted the Sunni canonical collections of *hadith* as unconditionally authoritative in religion while criticising certain aspects of Zaydi teachings. However, Ibn al-Wazir stated that he had not joined any particular Sunni school.

At the same time as the Zaydis penetrated into the mainly Sunni lower lands, the imams found it increasingly desirable to accommodate the religious views of their Sunni subjects, who formed the majority of the population there. As a result, a type of doctrinal rapprochement emerged between the Zaydi ruling class and their Sunni subjects, which essentially took the form of a movement away from the Zaydi Shiʿism of the Hadawi school towards traditionist Sunnism expounded by the Sunni scholars as well as by members of the neo-Sunni school that had arisen within Zaydism. The latter school, rooted in the teachings of Ibn al-Wazir, reached its peak of influence under Muhammad b. ʿAli al-Shawkani (d. 1250/1834), who served as the *mufti* and the chief judge (*qadi al-qudat*) of Yaman under several imams.[39] This neo-Sunni school was primarily influenced by Sunni traditionalism, the Hanbali Sunni school of jurisprudence and the teachings of Ibn Taymiyya (d. 728/1328).

By the end of the 12th/18th century, the imams widely cultivated the *hadith*-centred scholars of the neo-Sunni tradition and offered them patronage, while the Hadawi Zaydi *ʿulama* were rapidly losing favour in the Zaydi state and becoming marginalised. It was under such circumstances that the Sunni-oriented scholars, who did not subscribe to the Zaydi criteria for succession to the imamate, now lent their support to the Zaydi imams and legitimised their rule. Indeed, al-Shawkani went further and actually criticised the Hadawi Zaydi doctrine of the imamate, whose precepts were no longer observed by the ruling imams of the Qasimi dynasty. In his view, Zaydi theological and legal teachings had no basis in revelation but reflected the unsubstantiated opinions of the Zaydi imams and therefore had to be rejected. And in his capacity as chief judge he even sought to persecute certain Zaydi figures. As stated by

B. Haykel, there had now clearly appeared a symbiotic relationship between the Sunni-oriented scholars of the Zaydi state and its dynastic rulers.[40]

As noted, al-Shawkani was the most influential member of the neo-Sunni school that arose in Zaydi Yaman. As chief judge, he appointed many of his followers and students to official posts throughout Yaman, and they, in turn, helped to spread traditionist Sunni views amongst the scholars of the Zaydi highlands and elsewhere. In terms of his longer-term impact, al-Shawkani thus played a key role in the 'Sunnisation' of the Zaydi imamate and the very Zaydi intellectual milieu of Yaman, which had been crystallised in that region's tribal society over the course of a millennium. As a neo-Sunni, al-Shawkani had followed a trend initiated by Sayyid Ibn al-Wazir and retained by several other scholars, such as Salih b. Mahdi al-Maqbali (d. 1108/1696) and Muhammad b. Isma'il al-Amir (d. 1182/1768), who emerged from within the Zaydiyya tradition of Yaman's highlands.

Al-Shawkani, similarly to Ibn al-Wazir, held that the Sunni canonical collections of *hadith* were unconditionally authoritative; and, in line with the teaching of the Sunni traditionists, he emphasised the literal text and meaning of the Qur'an and the *hadith* collection. By contrast, al-Shawkani rejected Zaydi *kalam* theology, which was substantially influenced by Mu'tazili doctrines as well as the teachings of the earlier Zaydi imams. He advocated that all Muslims should practise *ijtihad* for arriving at independent rulings and opinions, on the basis of the Qur'an and the canonical corpus of *hadith*. He condemned *taqlid*, as he did not recognise the acceptance of another person's opinion. In his book entitled *al-Sayl al-jarrar*, al-Shawkani denounced the *Kitab al-azhar fi fiqh al-a'immat al-athar* of Imam al-Mahdi Ahmad b. Yahya al-Murtada (d. 840/1437), the legal corpus of opinions recognised by the Hadawi Zaydi school, which, according to him, represented opinions not rooted in the revelation. Al-Shawkani also manifested the general Zaydi, as well as traditionist Sunni, aversion towards Sufism. All in all, al-Shawkani's views have been well received in the Sunni world, especially by modern Salafis; his teachings remain influential in Saudi Arabia and within any other Sunni milieu where the Salafis are found.

Despite the spread of neo-Sunni ideology in contemporary Yaman, Hadawi Zaydi law remains the official legal code there, next to Shafi'i

Sunni law. However, official ideology in Yaman favours the neo-Sunni school, while marginalising the Zaydi *ʿulama*. Since 1962, republicans in Yaman have continuously used al-Shawkani's teachings and works to undermine the past doctrines of the Zaydi imamate and Zaydi Shiʿism itself. The modern Yamani state has indeed pursued an anti-Zaydi policy in the guise of Islamic reform, drawing extensively on al-Shawkani's teachings. Yet the response of the Yamani Zaydis to the hostility of Sunni traditionalism towards their heritage has remained rather limited in its nature and scope.[41]

6

The Nusayris or ʿAlawis

The study of the Nusayri branch of Shiʿi Islam has remained relatively marginalised and underdeveloped within Shiʿi studies, although some significant progress has occurred in the field during more recent times. The Nusayris, also called ʿAlawis (Arabic, ʿAlawiyyun) since the early 1920s, did not acquire any political distinction in medieval times while living in their traditional mountain abodes in Syria where they were overshadowed by their Nizari Ismaili neighbours. It is also safe to assume that the Nusayris did not produce a substantial religious literature; much of their meagre literary heritage seems to have perished in the course of their extended confrontations with the Ismailis of Syria, as well as other adversaries, throughout the centuries.

The political fortunes of the Nusayris-ʿAlawis changed drastically, however, with the rise to power in 1970 of General Hafiz al-Asad (1930–2000), who was to rule as the first ʿAlawi president of Syria for some three decades. Under Hafiz and his son and successor Bashar, the ʿAlawis occupied many of the prominent civilian and military posts of the Syrian state. The ʿAlawi minority in Syria, accounting perhaps for just over 10 per cent of the country's total population of some 22 million, have thus acquired a socio-political eminence in Syria's ruling and elite classes that is clearly disproportionate to their relative size. As a result of these developments, there has been renewed interest, after the pioneering efforts of the earlier orientalists, in studying and understanding the complex and syncretic doctrines of the Nusayris-ʿAlawis, who are perhaps the sole surviving inheritors of the theological traditions elaborated by the early Shiʿi *ghulat*.

The Nusayris or ʿAlawis are currently to be found in Syria, their main stronghold, with smaller communities in Lebanon and Turkey, where they should not be confused with the Turkish Alevi groups.[1] In Syria, the heartland of the Nusayris, and their original habitat, is the massive mountain range in the north known as the Jabal Ansariyya. However, the Nusayris represent minorities in the towns, such as Ladhiqiyya, Hims and Hama, surrounding Jabal Ansariyya, today also called Jabal al-ʿAlawiyyin. ʿAlawi minority groups are also found in the regions of Maʿarrat al-Nuʿman, Idlib and Aleppo as well as in Damascus. In Lebanon, the ʿAlawis are concentrated immediately to the south of the Syrian frontier, notably in Akkar. Within Turkey, sizeable ʿAlawi groups exist in Antakya (Antioch), on the coastal plain to the south-west of Iskenderun, as well as in Tarsus and Adana.

Nusayri studies

As was the case with the Nizari Ismailis, the Crusaders and their occidental observers had come into contact with the Syrian Nusayris, in the course of the 6th/12th century, without knowing the identity of these sectarians. The first brief scholarly attention in Europe paid to them appeared in the entry 'Nossairioun' in the pioneering encyclopaedia of orientalism compiled by Barthélemy d'Herbelot (1625–1695), who had never visited the Orient but correctly identified the Nusayris as a Shiʿi sect.[2] Carsten Niebuhr (1733–1815), the Danish traveller to Arabia who passed through Jabal Ansariyya in 1766, was perhaps the first European to meet the Nusayris and acquire some first-hand accurate information about them.[3] In subsequent decades, other European travellers to the region, such as Constantine de Volney (1757–1820) who was in Syria in the 1780s, did not add any new details to Niebuhr's account of the Nusayris, who were often also described in European sources as the Ansaris, after their mountainous homeland.[4] The early accounts are particularly confusing in terms of the origins and the religious doctrines of the Nusayris.

By the opening decades of the 19th century, a few scattered attempts had been made by European diplomats, dragomans, missionaries and travellers, who had come into contact with the Nusayris of Syria, to collect more reliable information on the peculiar religion and customs of these sectarians. Jean Baptiste Rousseau (1780–1831), the French consul-general in Aleppo during 1809–1816 who also had an interest in oriental studies and maintained a close professional relationship with the contemporary doyen of the orientalists, A. I. Silvestre de Sacy (1758–1838), was perhaps the first European of his time to draw serious and widespread attention to the existence of the Nusayris as well as the Ismailis and to their local traditions and literature. In 1810, Rousseau prepared a memoir on the contemporary Syrian Nusayris (and Ismailis), which contained many valuable historical, social and religious details obtained directly from the sectarians themselves.[5] Noting that the Nusayris comprised numerous tribes, a fact already known, Rousseau added that they were under the overall leadership of a single *shaykh*; and that they were hostile towards the Muslims and the Ismailis, but preferred the Christians probably because of having borrowed their doctrine of the divinity of Jesus which they had then applied to ʿAli.[6] Rousseau's memoir received much publicity in the orientalist circles of Europe mainly because of de Sacy's association with it. However, the Nusayris were then still perceived, incorrectly, as a non-Muslim sect or even as identical with the Qarmatis. The latter view was espoused by de Sacy who also allowed for the possibility of the Nusayris representing a subdivision of the Qarmatis.[7]

Subsequently, Joseph Catafago, who served during the 1840s as chancellor and dragoman at the Prussian consulate-general in Syria, was the earliest European to obtain access to Nusayri literature. He acquired a copy of a Nusayri text, the *Majmuʿ al-aʿyad* (The Book of the Festivals) of Maymun al-Tabarani (d. 426/1034), as well as the manuscript of a Nusayri catechism, the *Kitab taʿlim diyanat al-Nusayriyya*.[8] Catafago gained access to a wide selection of Nusayri texts and compiled what may be regarded as the first Western bibliography of Nusayri works.[9] Indeed, he evidently intended to write a comprehensive monograph on the Nusayri religion, on a par with de Sacy's monumental work on the Druze religion, a desideratum that was never realised. An English translation of the above-mentioned catechism, the first Nusayri work to have been recovered, as well as of another sectarian text (*Kitab al-mashyakha*) were produced by Samuel Lyde (1825–1860), an Anglican missionary who settled amongst the Nusayris of northern Syria during the 1850s.[10] Earlier, Lyde himself had written a book on the Nusayris containing inaccuracies.[11] Other European travellers of the period, such as Frederick Walpole (1822–1876), who produced a massive work on the so-called Ansayris that was devoid of any factually significant details,[12] seemed equally unaware of the true identity of the Nusayris and often confused them with the Ismailis, Druzes, Kurds or other religious and ethnic groups.

An important milestone in modern Nusayri studies was the 1864 publication in Beirut of *Kitab al-bakura al-Sulaymaniyya*, a book containing some Nusayri texts as well as descriptions of the initiation rites and various religious teachings and practices of the Nusayris. The author of this book was Sulayman Efendi al-Adhani, a renegade Nusayri.[13] Born in 1250/1834 in Adana in southern Turkey, Sulayman became learned in Nusayri teachings and even acquired the rank of a *shaykh* in his community. However, he later converted to Christianity and settled in Beirut, where he wrote his book for the purpose of refuting the Nusayris. Sulayman was eventually lured back to his native village and murdered for his apostasy by his former co-religionists. This book, which acquired much popularity, was initially brought to the attention of orientalists by Edward Salisbury (1814–1901), Professor of Arabic at Yale University, who had received a copy of it through the efforts of American missionaries in Syria. Salisbury, who in similar manner received some Ismaili-related texts from Syria, provided the English translation of a portion of Sulayman's book in his article on it.[14] The same book served as a major source for René Dussaud (1868–1958), the French orientalist with a special interest in Syria, who in 1900 published the first scholarly book on the history and religion of the Nusayris,[15] which included a comprehensive bibliography of the Nusayri sources then known in Europe as well as the various genres of studies on the subject.[16] It should be added that by the beginning of the 20th century a variety of Nusayri manuscripts had found their way into the collections of the Bibliothèque Nationale in Paris and other European libraries, providing a solid textual foundation for further progress in Nusayri studies. However, by 1939, when Louis Massignon (1883–1962) published his own Nusayri bibliography,[17] the state of the field had not progressed beyond what Dussaud had offered in his monograph. Due to his interest in the esoteric-mystical traditions in Islam, Massignon himself wrote a few short pieces on the Nusayris offering his idiosyncratic ideas on their origins.[18]

By the 1940s, however, Rudolf Strothmann (1877–1960) of Hamburg University, who was particularly interested in Shiʿi Islam and its diverse manifestations, had begun to make important contributions to Nusayri studies, also translating a number of Nusayri texts into German.[19] Nonetheless, Nusayri studies remained rather marginalised, particularly by comparison with Ismaili and Zaydi studies, which were then witnessing unprecedented breakthroughs. It is only in the last few decades that more widespread scholarly attention has started to be paid to the field of Nusayri studies on the basis of the manuscript sources that have now been made available. Amongst the limited number of scholars who have made important contributions to the field, mention may be made of H. Halm, M. Moosa, M. M. Bar-Asher, A. Kofsky and Y. Friedman.[20] In the meantime, only a handful of Nusayris, such as Muhammad Amin Ghalib al-Tawil (d. 1932),[21] and other Muslim authors have written on the Nusayris. Such works, generally speaking, are either apologetic or polemical depending on the particular religious identity of their Muslim authors. In this context it should be noted that a ten-volume collection of authentic Nusayri texts was published recently in Lebanon, in a series entitled *Silsilat al-turath al-'Alawi*.[22] The editor of this series, who has adopted the pseudonym of Abu Musa al-Hariri, has had some previous publications of his own.[23]

History of the Nusayris

The origins of the Nusayris may be traced to a certain Abu Shu'ayb Muhammad b. Nusayr al-Namiri (or al-Numayri), who hailed from the *ghulat* circles on the fringes of Imami Shi'ism. Until the 5th/11th century, the earliest Nusayris were also known as the Namiriyya (or Numayriyya) after the *nisba* of their eponym. Ibn Nusayr was a supporter of the tenth and eleventh Twelver Shi'i Imams, 'Ali al-Hadi (d. 254/868) and al-Hasan al-'Askari (d. 260/874). According to the earliest Imami heresiographers who were well-informed on developments within Imami Shi'ism, Ibn Nusayr proclaimed the divinity of the imams and also claimed the status of prophethood for himself.[24] He evidently held that Imam al-Hadi had personally designated him as a prophet. However, the Imami sources, which enumerate the Nusayriyya amongst the Shi'i *ghulat* and, as such, are hostile towards them, actually relate that Imam al-Hadi cursed and repudiated Ibn Nusayr for his exaggerated claims.[25] Imami sources further report that Ibn Nusayr taught the doctrine of metempsychosis or transmigration of souls (*tanasukh*), which has an important function in Nusayri cosmogony, also attributing various antinomian (*ibahi*) ideas to him. It has been reported that Ibn Nusayr enjoyed some favour at the Abbasid court in Samarraʾ, where he was supported by the *katib*, or secretary, Muhammad b. Musa Ibn al-Furat al-Juʿfi (d. 254/868), a brother of the famous Abbasid vizier.[26]

According to the Nusayri tradition, Ibn Nusayr was even closer, as a disciple, to the eleventh Twelver Imam al-Hasan al-ʿAskari in Samarraʾ, and was entrusted by this imam with a new revelation, which was to provide the basis of the Nusayri doctrine. It seems that Ibn Nusayr had his own original circle of disciples and supporters in Samarraʾ, led by a certain Yahya b. Muʿin al-Samarri.[27] Ibn Nusayr and his disciples enjoyed a degree of tribal support in Iraq, from Ibn Nusayr's own Banu Numayr and other tribal groups, which ensured the survival of the earliest Nusayris under adverse circumstances. It has been argued that the earliest Nusayris received protection as well as financial help from the Imami Banu'l-Furat, the eminent family of viziers and functionaries in the service of the Abbasids who had secret ties to certain extremist Shiʿi groups, especially the Nusayriyya.[28] It may be noted here that the earliest Nusayris appeared on the historical scene in Abbasid Iraq around the time when Hamdan Qarmat and ʿAbdan were successfully leading the Ismaili (Qarmati) *daʿwa* activities there.

Not much is known about the immediate successors of Ibn Nusayr, who died in 270/883. Matters are particularly complicated as the members of the radical Nusayri sect observed *taqiyya* rather strictly. The Nusayri sources that have come to light in modern times have preserved only the names of Ibn Nusayr's successors to the leadership of the group, starting with Muhammad b. Jundab, appointed by Ibn Nusayr himself. Muhammad was, in turn, succeeded by ʿAbd Allah al-Jannan al-Junbulani (d. 287/900), who was of Persian origin and was possibly responsible for incorporating the Persian festivals of the spring and autumn equinoxes, Nawruz and Mihragan, into Nusayri rituals, celebrated as the days when the divinity of ʿAli is manifested in the sun.

One Abu ʿAbd Allah al-Husayn b. Hamdan al-Khasibi, a disciple of al-Junbulani and who initially led the sect in the Shiʿi suburb of al-Karkh to the south of Baghdad, was the person responsible for propagating the Nusayri doctrines in northern Syria, which was to become the permanent stronghold of their community. With the advent of the Shiʿi Buyids in Iraq in 334/945 as the new overlords of the Abbasids, the situation of the Shiʿi communities there changed for the better. Soon afterwards, in 336/947, al-Khasibi returned to Iraq to visit the Nusayris who had lived there in secrecy. Al-Khasibi and other members of the sect, who also referred to themselves as the Muwahhidun, or Unitarians, had been obliged from early on to observe *taqiyya* mainly as Imami Shi'is. Furthermore, they were unable to dispense with their *taqiyya* practices under the Buyids, who evidently did not adhere to any particular form of Shi'ism after their Zaydi origins, and were not favourably disposed towards the various Shi'i *ghulat* groups who had persisted amongst the Imamiyya. This explains why al-Khasibi has been cited in Twelver Imami sources, such as al-Majlisi's *Bihar al-anwar*, as a transmitter of Shi'i *hadith*. Al-Khasibi returned to Aleppo in his final years to benefit from the patronage of the Hamdanids, appointing his disciple 'Ali b. 'Isa al-Jisri to lead the Nusayris of Iraq.

While dissimulating as an Imami Shi'i, al-Khasibi became a major transmitter of Nusayri teachings, including mystical and allegorical interpretations (*ta'wil*) of Qur'anic passages. Indeed, he played a key role in the development of early Nusayri doctrines and their propagation in both Iraq and northern Syria. Al-Khasibi was also a poet of some merit, serving at the courts of the Buyids in Iraq and western Persia and later at the courts of the Shi'i Hamdanids of Mawsil and Aleppo; he dedicated his *Kitab al-hidaya*, written in the Imami tradition, to Sayf al-Dawla (r. 333–356/944–967), the Shi'i Hamdanid *amir* of Aleppo.[29] Of his numerous works, his *Diwan* of collected poems has been preserved. On al-Khasibi's death in 346/957, or possibly a decade later, his tomb to the north of Aleppo, known locally under the name of Shaykh Yabraq, became a pilgrimage site for the Nusayris until at least the early decades of the 20th century.

From amongst his numerous disciples, al-Khasibi chose Muhammad b. 'Ali al-Jilli as his successor to lead the Nusayris of northern Syria.[30] It was in his time that Aleppo was recaptured by the Byzantine emperor Nicephorus Phocas in 351/962, marking the beginning of the Hamdanid dynasty's rapid decline. Under the circumstances, the Nusayris also began to address their religious propaganda to Christian communities on the Syrian coast; al-Jilli's *al-Risala al-Masihiyya*, in which Nusayri interpretations are provided for Christian doctrines, was directed particularly to the Nestorian Christians of Syria, aiming to win converts amongst them.[31] It is important to note that the contemporary Nusayri sources reiterate the sect's emphasis on the necessity of observing *taqiyya*, since in the aftermath of the downfall of the Shiʿi Hamdanids the Nusayris had lost their main protectors. In the event, secret Nusayri cells survived in Aleppo, Harran, Beirut and Tiberias, home of al-Jilli's most eminent disciple and future leader of the sect, al-Tabarani.

Muhammad al-Jilli died after 384/994, and he was succeeded by Maymun b. Qasim al-Tabarani, nicknamed Surur (Happiness) after a title of one of his books. He was learned in Shiʿi doctrines, Christianity, Greek philosophy and Iranian religions. Al-Tabarani became the real founder of the Syrian Nusayri community and teachings, with his numerous writings accounting for the bulk of the Nusayri sacred scriptures.[32] His *Majmuʿ al-aʿyad*, which contains the teachings of his predecessors, remains the most important source on the holidays and festivals observed by the Nusayris.[33] In 423/1032, due to incessant warfare in the region, al-Tabarani left Aleppo for Ladhiqiyya (Laodicea), then still under Byzantine domination. He did not encounter any Muslim hostility in Ladhiqiyya, from where he succeeded in converting the rural inhabitants of the Syrian coastal mountain range. Al-Tabarani's period of leadership coincided with the appearance of the Druzes, who also called themselves the Muwahhidun and who were to become rivals of the Nusayris in Syria. In fact Hamza b. ʿAli, founder of the Druze religious doctrine, wrote a treatise entitled *al-Risala al-damigha fi'l-fasiq al-Nusayri*, in refutation of the Nusayris.[34] Al-Tabarani died in 426/1034 at Ladhiqiyya; his tomb, located inside the Shaʿrani Mosque, is venerated by the Nusayris.[35]

The subsequent medieval history of the Nusayris is rather obscure. Henceforth, the Nusayris lacked charismatic central leaders and were mainly led in various scattered groups by their local *shaykh*s. There are, however, some vague references in the Nusayri sources to several community leaders after al-Tabarani. A number of Nusayri *shaykh*s who were not particularly distinguished in terms of their scholarship now rose to positions of leadership, including one ʿIsmat al-Dawla, a direct disciple of al-Tabarani. Meanwhile, the Nusayri community in Syria enjoyed the support of a number of local tribal families, such as the Banu Muhriz, who owned fortresses in the Jabal Ansariyya in the 5th/11th century. By the early decades of the 6th/12th century, some of these fortresses, such as Marqab, were lost to the Crusaders who were then establishing themselves in the northern part of the Jabal

Ansariyya (today known as Jabal al-ʿAlawiyyin), the heartland of the Nusayri community. The Crusaders, in due course, established four principalities in the Levant. The northern part of the Jabal Ansariyya was incorporated into the Frankish principality of Antioch. From this point onwards, the Nusayris, lacking effective military power, were subjected to Crusader rule, divided between the Latin kingdom of Jerusalem in the south and the principality of Antioch in the north.

At the same time, the Nusayris were confronted by the Nizari Ismailis who had established themselves firmly in the same mountainous region by acquiring a network of castles. In 527/1132, the Syrian Nizaris purchased Qadmus, their first fortress, from its Muslim lord who, with the assistance of the Nusayris, had recovered it from the Franks the previous year.[36] From Qadmus, which became one of their major strongholds, the Syrian Nizaris extended their dominion in the region and acquired the fortresses of Kahf and Masyaf, amongst several others. As a result of these developments, the Nusayris were intermittently brought into conflict with their Nizari Ismaili neighbours – a situation that lasted into modern times. The Nusayris may also have been influenced by certain Nizari doctrines, especially their cyclical interpretation of time and religious history.

In 584/1188, following Salah al-Din's capture of Ladhiqiyya and a number of fortresses in the region, Jabal Ansariyya was incorporated into the rapidly expanding Ayyubid sultanate. Salah al-Din had his own confrontations with the Syrian Shiʿi communities, which survived the anti-Shiʿi policies of the Sunni Ayyubids. By the end of the Ayyubid period in the 7th/13th century, the Nusayris had found a new protector in the person of *amir* al-Hasan al-Makzun al-Sinjari (d. 638/1240), who was invited to the region to help the Nusayris in their conflicts with the Nizaris and the Kurds.[37] After several attempts during 617–622/1220–1225, *amir* al-Sinjari, who hailed from the Jabal Sinjar in north-western Iraq, converted to Nusayrism and established himself in the Jabal Ansariyya. In the event, he also caused the settlement of a number of bedouin tribes who had accompanied him to the region from the Jabal Sinjar. It was from al-Makzun al-Sinjari's bedouin soldiers that a number of Nusayri tribal groups, including the Haddadiyya, Matawira, Mahaliba and Darawisa, emerged. These tribes are considered as the ancestors of the greater number of the present-day ʿAlawi clans of Syria. It is interesting to note that incessant rivalries amongst the Nusayris, the Ismailis and the Druzes of Syria, where they also confronted various Sunni adversaries, in a sense served to ensure the survival of these minority religious communities of Syria.

The establishment of Mamluk rule following the Ayyubids in Syria initiated another difficult phase in the history of the Nusayris. Sultan Baybars I (r. 658–676/1260–1277), who repelled the Mongols from Syria in 659/1260 and then subdued the Nizari Ismaili fortresses there, adopted severe persecutionary measures against the Syrian Nusayris, probably because the Nusayris had earlier allied themselves with the Mongols in their fight against Baybars. In addition to levying heavy taxes on them, Baybars made numerous attempts to convert them to Sunni Islam. Furthermore, the Mamluk sultan prohibited conversion (*khitab*) to Nusayrism, while ordering the construction of mosques in every Nusayri village. Hitherto, the Nusayris had been practising their faith in utter secrecy in private houses inaccessible to other Muslims. The anti-Nusayri policies of Baybars were essentially retained by his successor Sultan Qalawun (r. 678–689/1279–1290). The Mamluks also made efforts to destroy Nusayri books and confiscate their properties.

These persecutions elicited some brief retaliation from the Syrian Nusayris. In 717/1317, a Nusayri leader from the region of Jabala, calling himself Muhammad b. al-Hasan and claiming to be the expected Mahdi of the Twelver Shiʿis, rose in revolt. This insurrection was speedily subdued by the governor of Tripoli, who had Muhammad b. al-Hasan killed.[38] A further repercussion of this uprising was that the Mamluk sultan ordered the annihilation of the Nusayris. It was under such circumstances that Ibn Taymiyya, the radical Hanbali theologian and jurist, issued a *fatwa* or juridical ruling against the Nusayris in 728/1328 shortly before his death.[39] He condemned the Nusayris, who were presented as belonging to the Qarmatis, for being more 'heretical' than even the idolators and infidels, authorising *jihad* against them. In the event, many Nusayris were massacred in the district of Tripoli. Ibn Taymiyya's *fatwa* against the Nusayris was used by many later Sunni scholars who wanted to condemn them as heretics.

By 923/1517, Sultan Selim I had defeated the last Mamluk ruler, incorporating Syria and Egypt into the Ottoman empire. The Sunni Ottoman Turks ruled over a vast multi-ethnic empire until the end of the First World War. On the whole, the Ottomans maintained a tolerant attitude towards the religious and ethnic minorities within their dominions, designated as the *millets*. As a result, religious minorities, including the various Shiʿi communities, were not generally persecuted; and for most of the Ottoman period, the Nusayris were recognised as a distinct religious group with their own judicial apparatus and practices. By the end of the 12th/18th century, the Syrian Nusayris were governed in the Jabal Ansariyya by officials known as *muqaddams*, located near Ladhiqiyya and elsewhere, who reported to the Ottoman Pasha at Tripoli. By the second half of the 19th century, the Ottomans controlled the Nusayri territory through a local chieftain, while the Nusayri tribal leaders were often engaged in factional fighting. Subsequent to periodic invasions of the territory of the Nusayris, the Ottoman troops eventually succeeded in undermining the power of the local Nusayri tribes and establishing their own direct administration in the region.[40]

In the aftermath of the disintegration of the Ottoman empire and the imposition in 1920 of the French mandate over Syria, the French established the 'Autonomous Territory of the Alawites', consisting of the province of Ladhiqiyya, the northern part of the province of Tripoli and part of the province of Hama, while ceding Cilicia, another Nusayri (now called ʿAlawi/ʿAlawite) region, to Turkey. Two years later, in 1922, the Autonomous Territory of the Alawites was proclaimed the 'State of the Alawites' (*Dawlat al-ʿAlawiyyin*), which, with the states of Damascus and Aleppo, now formed the 'Federation of the States of Syria'. In 1930, the 'State of the Alawites' was renamed the 'Government of Lattakia' and in 1937 it was transformed into a province of the new Syrian state.[41] The Nusayris-ʿAlawis, thus, did not succeed in retaining an independent state of their own, but by the early 1970s the al-Asad ʿAlawi family had acquired the presidency of the Syrian state. Additionally, many ʿAlawis had joined the country's ruling Baʿth Socialist Party and now occupied key positions in the army and the government administration.

The Nusayri-ʿAlawi doctrines

The Nusayris changed their name to ʿAlawis in the early 1920s so as to emphasise their Shiʿi roots. The Nusayris-ʿAlawis have remained a secretive, esoteric community, observing *taqiyya* and closely guarding their religious literature and doctrines. Even within their community, Nusayri teachings are accessible only to the initiated members (*khassa*), as distinct from the uninitiated masses (*ʿamma*), while women are excluded from the initiation process. Every male member of the community has the right, on attaining adulthood, usually at the age of eighteen, to become initiated. Several sources shed light on the Nusayri process of initiation. Valuable details of this gradual initiation process are contained in al-Tabarani's *Kitab al-hawi fi ʿilm al-fatawa*,[42] composed in the form of a catechism. The process starts with the instructor (*naqib*) taking an oath (*ʿahd*) of secrecy from the would-be initiate, to safeguard the Nusayri teachings and not to divulge them to the uninitiated members of the community or to outsiders. The process of initiation, with its various stages and teaching hierarchy, seems to have continued to modern times with only minor variations.[43] The religious duties of the Nusayris-ʿAlawis, of both the initiated and uninitiated members of the community, are limited to moral obligations of a general nature. The Nusayris also participate in certain religious practices such as pilgrimages (*ziyarat*) to the tombs of Nusayri saints.

At the basis of the complex religious system of thought elaborated by the Nusayriyya is a cosmogony of a gnostic nature. The Nusayri religion draws on pagan, Christian and Islamic traditions which are amalgamated particularly with certain radical Shiʿi elements as expounded by the early Shiʿi *ghulat*. The Nusayris also resort to esoteric or allegorical interpretations of Qurʾanic passages, similarly to the Ismailis. Central to the Nusayri system of religious thought is the deification of ʿAli b. Abi Talib. Aspects of Nusayri teachings are to be found in the *Kitab al-haft waʾl-azilla*, a Mufaddali–Nusayri text that takes the form of a dialogue between Imam Jaʿfar al-Sadiq and al-Mufaddal b. ʿUmar al-Juʿfi.[44] This book, known also amongst the Tayyibi Ismailis, found its way to the manuscript collections of the Nizari Ismailis, who, in the first half of the 6th/12th century, seized the Nusayri fortresses and settlements of central Syria in addition to recruiting new converts from the Nusayri community. Indeed, modern scholarship has shown that the early Nusayri doctrines were rooted in those held by the Mukhammisa (Pentadists), especially the ʿUlaʾiyya or ʿAlbaʾiyya amongst them.[45] The members of this group of the early Shiʿi *ghulat* also upheld the divinity of ʿAli.

The cosmological and eschatological doctrines of the Nusayris are equally present in the *Umm al-kitab*, which has been preserved by the Nizari Ismailis of Central Asia.[46] Similar to the *Kitab al-haft*, the *Umm al-kitab*, which is extant in an archaic form of Persian, originated during the 2nd/8th century in the Shi'i *ghulat* milieus of southern Iraq which gave rise to the Mukhammisa and later to the Nusayriyya traditions. Containing the discourses of Imam Muhammad al-Baqir in response to questions posed by an anachronistic group of disciples, including Ja'far al-Ju'fi and Muhammad b. al-Mufaddal, the *Umm al-kitab* represents the earliest extant Shi'i record of the Mukhammisa-'Ula'iyya type, which is quite distinct from the teachings of the early Ismailis, especially regarding cosmogony. However, this syncretic text was eventually adopted into Ismaili literature and, under obscure circumstances, found its way into the private libraries of the Nizari Ismailis of Badakhshan in Central Asia, where the sectarians have claimed the book as their own even though it does not contain any Ismaili doctrine.

The Nusayris believe in metempsychosis (*tanasukh*) and incarnation (*hulul*) of the divine Essence, or *ma'na*, in certain historical and mythical figures as well as in the imams. They hold that the ineffable God has appeared, at different times, in human form. Similarly to the Ismailis, the Nusayris also espouse a cyclical view of history, which they combine with their Neoplatonised emanational cosmogony. They hold that the deity has been manifested in seven eras (*adwar* or *akwar*), each time in the form of a trinity: two entities or persons (*aqanim*) emanate from the divine Essence (*ma'na*), namely, *ism*, the Name, also called *hijab*, the Veil; and *bab*, the Gate, through which the believer may contemplate the mystery of divinity. In each era, the *ma'na* is veiled by the presence of *ism* or *hijab*, representing the prophets from Adam to Muhammad. Each prophet is, in turn, accompanied by a *bab*, the Gate through which the believer may contemplate the mystery of divinity.

The divine trinity of the Nusayriyya has been incarnated not only in historical but also in mythical persons, including biblical figures and others from the Greek, Iranian and Islamic traditions. In the first six eras of history, the *ma'na* was incarnated in Abel, Seth, Joseph, Joshua, Asaph and St Peter; and the true character of their incarnations was veiled by the presence of those eras' *ism* or *hijab*, namely, Adam, Noah, Jacob, Moses, Solomon and Jesus, each of whom was accompanied by a *bab*. The various figures representing the *bab*s include both familiar names, such as the archangel Gabriel, as well as unknown ones, including Ya'il b. Fatin and Ruzbih b. Marzuban.[47] In the seventh and final era, that of Islam or *al-qobba al-Muhammadiyya*, the divine trinity is represented by ʿAli as the *maʿna*, Muhammad as the *ism* or *hijab*, and Salman al-Farsi as the *bab*. According ʿAli primacy over Muhammad seems to have served as the precedent for the inversion of the first two persons representing the *maʿna* and *ism* in the earlier trinities as well. In Nusayri thought this divine trinity is designated symbolically by *ʿayn-mim-sin*', standing for the first letters of the names ʿAli, Muhammad and Salman and functioning as the primary initiatory expression of the Nusayris.[48]

In the era of Islam, the deity was later manifested also in the first eleven imams of the Twelver Shiʿis, ending with al-Hasan al-ʿAskari, and their disciples. The *bab*s of these eleven imams were the intermediaries between the concealed divinity and the initiated believers. For instance, Muhammad b. Nusayr himself is regarded as the *bab* of the eleventh imam, al-Hasan al-ʿAskari, whose secret revelation was preserved through him exclusively for the Nusayriyya. The Nusayri cosmogony further holds that from the divine trinity there emanated a series of other beings, starting with the five *yatim*s or *aytam*, orphans, who were identified with five of Muhammad's Companions (*sahaba*), including Abu Dharr al-Ghiffari, al-Miqdad b. Aswad al-Kindi, ʿAbd Allah b. Rawaha al-Ansari, ʿUthman b. Mazʿun al-Najashi and Qanbar b. Kadan al-Dawsi. It should be noted that these Companions also remained loyal to ʿAli. These orphans are regarded as the creators of the universe as well as the rulers of the spiritual world and its constellations.[49]

The basic ideas of the Nusayri cosmogony are to be found in the *Kitab al-haft*, which also contains a gnostic myth on the genesis and fall of the souls of the Nusayris as well as a salvational theory.[50] According to this myth, in the beginning of time, the souls of the Nusayris were lights surrounding and praising God. After a series of transgressions, including the sin of disputing His divinity, the Nusayri souls fell to the material world, where they became encased in material bodies and condemned to metempsychosis, temporal (for the elect) or eternal (for the damned) transmigration (*nasukhiyya*). In the course of their fall, as noted above, God appears to them seven times in seven eras calling for their obedience. The Nusayri believer who acknowledges the identity of the *maʿna* is saved and may be liberated from metempsychosis; the soul of such a saved Nusayri is released from its body and embarks on a journey across the heavens towards the divine light. Once again, women are excluded from this soteriological journey.

The syncretic nature of the Nusayri religion is also reflected in its complex calendar of festivals rooted in a diversity of Christian, Persian and Muslim traditions, which are all interpreted allegorically.[51] The Nusayris-ʿAlawis celebrate many of the Muslim festivals, including *ʿId al-fitr* (feast of breaking the fast at the end of the month of Ramadan) and *ʿId al-adhha* (feast of the sacrifice traditionally celebrated at the end of the *hajj* pilgrimage), but with their own interpretations. Similarly to other Shiʿi communities, they also observe *ʿId al-Ghadir*, which for the ʿAlawis represents Muhammad's proclamation of ʿAli's divinity, and the *ʿAshura'* in celebration of Imam al-Husayn's occultation, rather than commemorating his martyrdom, as he is regarded as a hidden divine figure. The ʿAlawis also celebrate a number of Persian festivals of Zoroastrian origin because of their belief in the superiority of the Persians over the Arabs, though again with different allegorical interpretations; these include the spring equinox on 21 March marking Nawruz, or Persian New Year, and the Mihragan marking the autumn equinox and the incarnation of the deity in ʿAli. From amongst a number of Christian festivals, they celebrate the Epiphany, called *ʿId al-ghutas* (feast of the baptism), Palm Sunday and Christmas (*Laylat al-milad*). The ʿAlawis also celebrate Mass, including the consecration of bread and wine, but in a Shiʿi context and maintaining that the mystery of faith is ʿAli who, as light, is manifested in the wine. The popular religion of the Nusayris-ʿAlawis also retains certain traces of pagan traditions, such as the veneration of trees and springs. The Nusayris also developed allegorical interpretations of the religious commandments and prohibitions, such as fasting in the month of Ramadan and the *hajj* pilgrimage.[52] Furthermore, they do not have mosques or other public spaces of worship, but conduct their religious ceremonies in private homes, especially the residences of their *shaykh*s.

In order to end their isolation and emphasise their Shiʿi roots, as already noted, the Nusayris changed the name of their community to ʿAlawis (Arabic, ʿAlawiyyun), the followers of ʿAli, in the early 1920s. Several contemporary ʿAlawi *shaykh*s in Syria have articulated afresh the community's Shiʿi identity while refraining from the earlier Nusayriyya designation. In fact they use the terms ʿAlawi, Shiʿi and Imami synonymously.[53] Meanwhile, the ʿAlawi *shaykh*s are increasingly receiving their education at Twelver Shiʿi institutions. Nevertheless, the contemporary ʿAlawis, at least in Syria, seem to represent two different identity trends. The more conservative members of the community, living mainly in the Jabal Ansariyya region, uphold the traditional Nusayri doctrines and rituals, while the urban ʿAlawi groups, known mainly as Jaʿfaris, are becoming progressively assimilated into Twelver Shiʿism. The latter groups have developed close relationships with the Twelver Shiʿis of Iran and the Arab lands. In spite of these developments, however, the medieval anti-Nusayri *fatwa* of Ibn Taymiyya is still influential with the Hanbali-Salafi circles in Saudi Arabia as well as with the Muslim Brotherhood (Ikhwan al-Muslimun) of Syria and elsewhere.

Glossary

Listings in the glossary are selected terms and names, chiefly of Arabic and Persian origin, appearing in the text. In this glossary, pl. and lit. are the abbreviated forms for the words 'plural' and 'literally'; q.v. (*quod vide*) is used for cross-reference within the glossary.

adhān: Muslim call to prayer. There are slight differences between the Sunni and Shiʿi calls to prayer made five times a day.

ahl al-bayt: lit., the 'people of the house'; members of the household of the Prophet, including especially Muḥammad, ʿAlī, Fāṭima, al-Ḥasan, al-Ḥusayn and their progeny. The Prophet's family is also designated as *āl Muḥammad*.

ahl al-dhimma: non-Muslim minorities in a Muslim state; as such, they were protected and accorded religious and communal rights in exchange for submission to Muslim sovereignty and the payment of a special tax known as *jizya*.

ʿAlids: descendants of ʿAlī b. Abī Ṭālib, cousin and son-in-law of the Prophet, and also the fourth caliph and the first Shiʿi imam (q.v.).The Shiʿis believed certain ʿAlids should be imams, and they acknowledged ʿAlī as the first among their imams. ʿAlī's first spouse was Fāṭima, the Prophet's daughter, and ʿAlī's descendants by Fāṭima (the only descendants of the Prophet) are in particular called Fāṭimids (q.v.). Descendants of ʿAlī and Fāṭima through their sons al-Ḥasan and al-Ḥusayn are also called

Ḥasanids and Ḥusaynids. Descendants of al-Ḥasan and al-Ḥusayn are often also designated, respectively, as *sharīf*s and *sayyid*s.

ʿālim (pl., *ʿulamāʾ*): a learned man; specifically a scholar in Islamic religious sciences.

amīr (pl., *umarāʾ*): military commander, prince; many independent rulers in the Islamic world also held this title.

amīr al-juyūsh: the 'commander of the armies'; a title used specifically by military viziers.

amr: command; specifically the divine command or volition.

anṣār: lit., helpers; name given collectively to those Medinese who supported the Prophet after his emigration (*hijra*) from Mecca to Medina, as distinct from the *muhājirūn* (q.v.).

ʿaql: intellect, intelligence, reason.

asās: lit., foundation; successor to a speaking prophet, *nāṭiq* (q.v.).

aṣlān: the two roots or principles; the original dyad of *ʿaql* and *nafs* of the pleroma in Neoplatonised cosmology.

atabeg (or *atābak*): lit., 'father-lord'; a Turkish title given to tutors or guardians of Saljūq and other Turkish rulers. The *atabeg*s became powerful officers of state and some of them founded independent dynasties in Islamic lands.

ʿawāmm (or *ʿāmma*): the common people, the masses, as distinct from the *khawāṣṣ* (q.v.).

bāb: lit., gate; the Ismaili religious term for the administrative head of the *daʿwa* (q.v.) under the Fāṭimids, sometimes also called *bāb al-abwāb;* the highest rank after the imam, in the *daʿwa* hierarchy of the Fāṭimid Ismailis; the equivalent of the official term *dāʿī al-duʿāt* (q.v.), mentioned especially in non-Ismaili sources; also the intermediary between the Twelver Shiʿis and their twelfth Imam-Mahdi during the latter's occultation; such an intermediary was also called emissary (*safīr*), deputy (*nāʾib*) or agent (*wakīl*). It is also part of the divine trinity in the emanational cosmogony of the Nuṣayrīs; also a chapter or short treatise.

Banū Hāshim: see Hāshimids.

bāṭin: the inward, hidden or esoteric meaning behind the literal wording of sacred texts and religious prescriptions, notably the Qur'an and the *sharīʿa* (q.v.), as distinct from the *ẓāhir* (q.v.); hence, Bāṭinīs, Bāṭiniyya, the groups associated with such ideas. Most of these groups were Shiʿi, particularly Ismaili.

bayʿa: recognition of authority, especially the act of swearing allegiance to a new sovereign or spiritual leader.

bidʿa (pl., *bidaʿ*): lit., innovation; a blameworthy doctrinal innovation for which there is no precedent in the Qur'an or from the time of the Prophet.

dāʿī (pl., *duʿāt*): lit., he who summons; a religious propagandist or missionary of various Muslim groups, especially amongst the Ismaili and Zaydi Shiʿis. The term *dāʿī* came to be used generically from early on by the Ismailis in reference to any authorised representative of their da'wa (q.v.); a propagandist responsible for spreading the Ismaili religious teachings and for winning suitable converts. The Zaydi Shi'is used the term in reference to their spiritual leaders who were not qualified to be recognised as full imams (q.v.).

dā'ī al-du'āt: chief *dā'ī*; a non-technical term used mainly in non-Ismaili sources; see *bāb*.

dā'ī muṭlaq: a rank in the *da'wa* (q.v.) hierarchy of the Fāṭimid Ismailis; it later became the highest rank in the Ṭayyibī Musta'lian *da'wa* organisation; the administrative head of the Ṭayyibī *da'wa* during its Yamani phase, enjoying absolute authority in the community. It was also adopted by the administrative heads of the Dā'ūdī, Sulaymānī and 'Alawī branches of the Ṭayyibī *da'wa*.

dār al-hijra: lit., 'abode of emigration'; the early Ismailis established a number of such fortified abodes in Iraq, Yaman, Bahrayn and North Africa, as places of refuge and headquarters for their *da'wa* (q.v.) activities, from which they expected to return victoriously to the Muslim society at large. The Zaydis, too, expounded a doctrine of *hijra*, defined as the obligation of the faithful Zaydis not only to support the rightful imam (q.v.), but also to emigrate from the land of injustice (*dār al-ẓulm*). The Muṭarrifī Zaydis interpreted this doctrine as a permanent obligation to emigrate to 'abodes of emigration' (*dār al-hijra*), also designated as *hijra*s, where they gathered to engage in ritual purification, worship and ascetic practices.

darwīsh (Anglicised, dervish): a term meaning 'poor' applied to a practising Sufi (q.v.), with special reference to his poor or wandering life.

daʿwa: mission or propaganda; in the religio-political sense, *daʿwa* is the invitation or call to adopt the cause of an individual or family claiming the right to the imamate; it also refers to the entire hierarchy of ranks, sometimes called *ḥudūd* (q.v.), within the particular religious organisation developed for this purpose, especially amongst the Ismailis. The Ismailis often referred to their movement simply as *al-daʿwa*, or more formally as *al-daʿwa al-hādiya*, the 'rightly guiding mission'. Any qualified person aspiring to the imamate of the Zaydis also needed to launch an open *daʿwa*, inviting the faithful to accept his leadership.

dawla: state or dynasty.

dawr (pl., *adwār*): period, era, cycle of history; the Ismailis held that the hierohistory of mankind consisted of seven *adwār*, each inaugurated by a speaking prophet, or *nāṭiq* (q.v.), who brought a revealed message in the form of a religious law. The Nuṣayrīs ('Alawīs) held a similar cyclical conception of the sacred history of mankind.

dīwān: a public financial register; a government department; also the collected poems of a poet.

faqīh (pl., *fuqahā'*): in its technical meaning it denotes an exponent of *fiqh* (q.v.); a specialist in Islamic jurisprudence; a Muslim jurist in general.

faṣl (pl., *fuṣūl*): chapter, epistle.

Fāṭimids: descendants of 'Alī b. Abī Ṭālib and the Prophet's daughter Fāṭima, corresponding to Fāṭimid 'Alids (q.v.); also the name of the Ismaili dynasty of caliph-imams, claiming

Fāṭimid descent, reigning from 297/909 to 567/1171.

fatwā (pl., *fatāwā*): a judgement on some detail of the law issued by a qualified religious scholar known as a *muftī*.

fidāʾī: one who offers his life for a cause; a term used for special devotees in several religio-political Muslim groups.

fiqh: the technical term for Islamic jurisprudence; the science of law in Islam; the discipline of elucidating the *sharīʿa* (q.v.).

ghayba: lit., absence; the word has been used in a technical sense for the condition of anyone who has been withdrawn by God from the eyes of men and whose life during that period of occultation (called his *ghayba*) may be miraculously prolonged. In this sense, a number of Shiʿi groups have recognised the *ghayba* of a particular imam (q.v.), with the implication that no further imam was to succeed him and he was to return at a foreordained time before the Day of Resurrection, *qiyāma* (q.v.), as the Mahdi (q.v.). The twelfth imam of the Twelver Shiʿis has remained in *ghayba* since 260/874.

ghulāt (pl. of *ghālī*): exaggerator, extremist; a term of disapproval for individuals accused of exaggeration (*ghuluww*) in religion and in respect to imams (q.v.); it was applied particularly to those Shiʿi personalities and groups whose doctrines were offensive to the Twelver Shiʿis.

ginān: derived from the Sanskrit word meaning meditative or contemplative knowledge; a general term used for the corpus of the indigenous religious literature of the Nizārī Ismaili

Khojas and some related groups in South Asia. Composed in a number of Indic languages, the hymn-like *ginān*s are recorded mainly in the Khojkī script developed within the Nizārī Khoja community.

ḥadd (pl., *ḥudūd*): fixed punishments in Islamic law, often stipulated in the Qur'an; also a rank in the *daʿwa* (q.v.) hierarchy of the Ismailis. See also *ḥudūd*.

ḥadīth: a report, sometimes translated as Tradition, relating an action or saying of the Prophet, or the corpus of such reports collectively, constituting one of the major sources of Islamic law, second in importance only to the Qur'an. For the Shiʿi communities, it generally also refers to the deeds and sayings of their imams (q.v.). The Shiʿis accept those *ḥadīth*s related from the Prophet which had been handed down or sanctioned by their imams in conjunction with those *ḥadīth*s related from the imams recognised by them. The Shiʿis also use the terms *riwāyāt* and *akhbār* as synonyms of *ḥadīth*.

ḥajj: the annual pilgrimage to Mecca and some other sacred localities in the Ḥijāz in the month of Dhu'l-Ḥijja, the last month of the Muslim calendar, required of every Muslim at least once in his lifetime if possible. One who has performed the *ḥajj* is called Ḥājj in Arabic and Ḥājjī in Persian and Turkish.

ḥaqāʾiq (pl. of *ḥaqīqa*): truths; as a technical term it denotes the gnostic system of Ismaili thought. In this sense, the *ḥaqāʾiq* are the unchangeable truths contained in the *bāṭin* (q.v.); while the law changes with every law-announcing prophet or *nāṭiq* (q.v.), the *ḥaqāʾiq* remain eternal.

Ḥasanids: see ʿAlids.

Hāshimids: descendants of Hāshim b. ʿAbd Manāf, the common ancestor of the Prophet, ʿAlī and al-ʿAbbās. The chief Hāshimid branches were the ʿAlids (q.v.) and the Abbasids, descendants of the Prophet's uncle al-ʿAbbās.

ḥudūd (pl. of *ḥadd*): ranks; a technical term denoting the various ranks in the *daʿwa* (q.v.) hierarchy of the Ismailis, also called *ḥudūd al-dīn*. See also *ḥadd*.

ḥujja: proof or the presentation of proof. Amongst the Shiʿis, the term has been used in different senses. Initially, it meant the proof of God's presence or will, and as such it referred to that person who at any given time served as evidence among mankind of God's will. In this sense, the application of the term was systematised by the Imāmī Shiʿis to designate the category of prophets and imams (q.v.) and, after the Prophet Muḥammad, more particularly of the imams. The original Shiʿi application of the term *ḥujja* was retained by the pre-Fāṭimid Ismailis who also used *ḥujja* in reference to a dignitary in their religious hierarchy. The *ḥujja* was also a high rank in the *daʿwa* (q.v.) hierarchy of the Fāṭimid Ismailis; there were twelve such *ḥujja*s, each one in charge of a separate *daʿwa* region called *jazīra* (q.v.). In the Nizārī Ismaili *daʿwa*, the term generally denoted the chief representative of the imam, sometimes also called *pīr* (q.v.).

ḥulūl: infusion or incarnation of the divine essence in the human body; amongst some Shiʿi groups, notably the *ghulāt* (q.v.) and the Nuṣayriyya, it referred particularly to the incarnation of the divine essence in an imam (q.v.).

Ḥusaynids: see ʿAlids.

ijmāʿ: consensus; as a technical term it denotes consensus among religious scholars, *fuqahāʾ*, on matters of jurisprudence.

ijtihād: independent legal decision or judgement arrived at by knowledge and reasoning, *ʿaql*, particularly in matters pertaining to *sharīʿa* (q.v.); one who practises *ijtihād* is called *mujtahid*; the opposite of *taqlīd* (q.v.).

ilḥād: deviation from the right religious path; heresy in religion. The Ismailis, the Nuṣayrīs and other Shiʿi groups were often accused of *ilḥād* by Sunni Muslims. A person accused of *ilḥād* is called *mulḥid* (pl., *malāḥida*).

ʿilm: knowledge, more specifically religious knowledge. Amongst the Shiʿis, it was held that every imam (q.v.) possessed a special secret knowledge, *ʿilm*, which was divinely inspired and transmitted through the *naṣṣ* (q.v.) of the preceding imam.

imam (Arabic, *imām*; pl., *aʾimma*): leader of a group of Muslims in prayer, *ṣalāt*; the supreme leader of the Muslim community. The title was used particularly by the Shiʿis in reference to the persons recognised by them as the heads of the Muslim community after the Prophet. The Shiʿis regard ʿAlī b. Abī Ṭālib and certain of his descendants as such leaders or imams, the legitimate successors to the Prophet. The imams are held to be *maʿṣūm*, fully immune from sin and error; they are generally held to be also divinely appointed, and divinely guided in the discharge of their special spiritual functions. Amongst the Sunnis, the term is used in reference to any great *ʿālim* (q.v.), especially the founder of a legal *madhhab* (q.v.). The office of imam is called imamate (Arabic, *imāma*).

iqṭāʿ: an administrative grant of land or of its revenues by a Muslim ruler to an individual, usually in recompense for service.

ʿirfān: gnosis or the way of knowledge which is the heart of Sufi (q.v.) teachings, and the means whereby man is led to the realisation of the divine through illuminative knowledge.

ʿiṣma: inerrancy, infallibility; a quality attributed to prophets and, in Shiʿi Islam, to imams (q.v.). One who is endowed with *ʿiṣma* is called *maʿṣūm*.

jamāʿa: assembly, religious congregation; pronounced *jamāʿat* in Persian.

jamāʿat-khāna: assembly house; congregation place, with a special prayer hall, used by the Nizārī Ismailis for their religious and communal activities.

jazīra (pl., *jazāʾir*): lit., island; a term denoting a particular *daʿwa* (q.v.) region. The Ismailis, specifically the Fāṭimid Ismailis, in theory divided the world into twelve regions, sometimes called *jazāʾir al-arḍ*, each *jazīra* denoting a separate region for the dissemination of their *daʿwa*, and placed under the charge of a *ḥujja* (q.v.).

kalima: word; specifically the divine word, *logos*; a synonym of *kalimat Allāh*.

kashf: manifestation, unveiling; in Ismaili doctrine, it is used specifically in reference to a period, called *dawr al-kashf*, when the imams (q.v.) were manifest, or when the *ḥaqāʾiq* (q.v.) would no longer be concealed in the *bāṭin* (q.v.), in distinction from *ghayba* (q.v.) or *satr* (q.v.).

khān: Turkish title, originally a contraction of *khāqān*, which as a title of sovereignty denoted supremacy over a group of tribes or territories. The title *khān* was used by Turkish Muslim rulers in Central Asia from the 4th/10th century onwards; in time it came to be applied to subordinate rulers and important local officials; also an honorific appellation.

khānaqāh: place for devotional gathering and meditation for the Sufis (q.v.); Sufi residential facility often linked to other functions.

khawāṣṣ (or *khāṣṣa*): the elite, the privileged people, as distinct from the *ʿawāmm* (q.v.).

Khoja: see *khwāja*.

khums: lit., one-fifth; as a technical term it denotes a religious tax originally paid to the Prophet and, by the Shiʿi Muslims, to the imams (q.v.) on certain categories of goods and income. The Twelver Shiʿis are now expected to pay *khums* to their *marjaʿ al-taqlīd* (q.v.).

khuṭba: an address or sermon delivered by a *khāṭib* at the Friday midday public prayers in the mosque; since it includes a prayer for the ruler, mention in the *khuṭba* is a mark of sovereignty in Islam.

khwāja: master; a title used in different senses in Islamic lands; it was frequently accorded to scholars, teachers, merchants and *wazīr*s (q.v.); in India it was transformed to 'Khoja', denoting an Indian caste consisting mostly of Nizārī Ismailis. In a looser sense, 'Khoja' is used in reference to Nizārī Ismailis of South Asian origins in general.

kitmān: see *taqiyya*.

kufr: unbelief; one who is accused of disbelief is called *kāfir*.

laqab (pl., *alqāb*): honorific title, sobriquet, nickname.

madhhab (pl., *madhāhib*): a system or school of religious law in Islam; in particular it is applied to the four main systems of *fiqh* (q.v.) that arose among the Sunni Muslims, namely, Ḥanafī, Mālikī, Shāfiʿī and Ḥanbalī, named after the jurists who founded them. Different Shiʿi communities have had their own *madhāhib*; the Twelver Imāmī Shiʿi *madhhab* is known as Jaʿfarī, named after Imam Jaʿfar al-Ṣādiq. In Persian, the word *madhhab* is also used to mean religion, a synonym of *dīn*.

maʾdhūn: lit., licentiate; a rank in the Ismaili *daʿwa* (q.v.) hierarchy below that of the *dāʿī* (q.v.). In the post-Fāṭimid period of Ismaili history in particular, *maʾdhūn* was used generically by the Ismailis in reference to the assistant of the *dāʿī*.

madrasa: a college or seminary of higher Muslim learning, frequently attached to a mosque.

Mahdi (Arabic, *mahdī*): 'the rightly guided one'; a name applied to the restorer of true religion and justice who, according to a widely held Muslim belief, will appear and rule before the end of the world. This name with its various messianic connotations has been applied to different individuals by Shiʿi and Sunni Muslims in the course of the centuries. Belief in the coming of the Mahdi of the family of the Prophet, the *ahl al-bayt* (q.v.), became a central aspect of the faith in Shiʿi Islam, in contrast to Sunnism. Also distinctively Shiʿi was the common belief in a temporary absence or occultation, *ghayba* (q.v.), of the Mahdi and his eventual return, *rajʿa* (q.v.), in glory. In Shiʿi teminology, at least from the 2nd/8th century, the Mahdi was commonly given the epithet *al-qāʾim* (q.v.), 'riser', also called *qāʾim āl Muḥammad*, denoting a member of the Prophet's family who would rise and restore justice on earth. Various early Shiʿi groups expected the return of the last imam (q.v.) recognised by them in the role of the *qāʾim*. The majority of the early Ismailis, including especially the Qarmaṭīs, recognised their seventh imam, Muḥammad b. Ismāʿīl, as the Mahdi. The Twelver Shiʿis have acknowledged their twelfth imam as their hidden Mahdi. The Zaydis did not generally recognise any of their imams as the Mahdi. In Imāmī and Ismaili usage, the term *qāʾim* widely replaced that of Mahdi.

majlis (pl., *majālis*): lecture, teaching session; also the space where such lectures are delivered; also a gathering for religious, scholarly or literary purposes; in modern usage it also refers to a consultative body.

malāḥida (pl. of *mulḥid*): see *ilḥād*.

marjaʿ al-taqlīd (Persian, *marjaʿ-i taqlīd*): the 'source of emulation', or the 'supreme exemplar'; as a technical term it refers to that Shiʿi religious scholar who through his learning and probity is qualified to be followed in all points of religious practice and law by the generality of the Twelver Shiʿi Muslims.

maʿṣūm: see *ʿiṣma*.

mawlā (pl., *mawālī*): master; freed slave; client of an Arab tribe; more specifically a non-Arab convert to Islam who acquired status by attachment to an Arab tribal group. In the early Islamic centuries, the term *mawālī* was applied generally to the non-Arab converts to Islam.

minbar: the pulpit in a mosque, from which the *khuṭba* (q.v.) is delivered.

muhājirūn: lit., emigrants; name given collectively to those Meccan followers of the Prophet who accompanied him in his emigration (*hijra*) from Mecca to Medina, initiating the Islamic era and calendar, as distinct from the *anṣār* (q.v.).

muḥtasham: a title used commonly in reference to the leader of the Nizārī Ismailis of Quhistān in eastern Persia during the Alamūt phase of their history.

mujtahid: see *ijtihād*.

mulḥid: see *ilḥād*.

muʾmin: believer, true believer; more specifically a Muslim or member of a particular Islamic group.

muqallid: see *taqlīd*.

murīd: disciple; specifically, disciple of a Sufi (q.v.) master; member of a Sufi order in general; also frequently used in reference to an ordinary Nizārī Ismaili in Persia and elsewhere during the post-Alamūt phase of Nizārī history.

murshid: guide, Sufi (q.v.) master; also used in reference to the imam (q.v.) of the Nizārī Ismailis during the post-Alamūt phase of their history.

nabī (pl., *anbiyāʾ*): prophet. The office of *nabī* is called *nubuwwa*.

nafs: soul, often used as a synonym of *rūḥ*.

naṣṣ: explicit designation of a successor by his predecessor, particularly relating to the Shiʿi view of succession to the imamate, whereby each imam (q.v.), under divine guidance, designates his successor. One who receives the *naṣṣ* is called *manṣūṣ*.

nāṭiq (pl., *nuṭaqāʾ*): lit., speaker, one gifted with speech; in Ismaili thought, a speaking or law- announcing prophet who brings a new religious law, *sharīʿa* (q.v.), abrogating the previous law and hence initiating a new *dawr* (q.v.) in the sacred history of humankind.

pīr: the Persian equivalent of the Arabic word *shaykh* in the sense of a spiritual guide, Sufi (q.v.) master or *murshid* (q.v.), qualified to lead disciples, *murīd*s (q.v.), on the mystical path, *ṭarīqa* (q.v.), to truth (*ḥaqīqa*); also used loosely in reference to the imam (q.v.) and the holders of the highest ranks in the *daʿwa* (q.v.) hierarchy of the post-Alamūt Nizārī Ismailis.

qāḍī (pl., *quḍāt*): a religious judge administering Islamic law, the *sharīʿa* (q.v.).

qāḍī al-quḍāt: chief *qāḍī* (q.v.); the highest judiciary officer of the Fāṭimid state.

qāʾim: ʻriser’; the eschatological Mahdi (q.v.).

qaṣīda: a poetic genre of a certain length, normally concerned with the eulogy of a personality; in Persian it is a lyric poem, most frequently panegyric.

qiyāma (Persian, *qiyāmat*): Resurrection and the Last Day, when mankind will be judged and committed forever to either Paradise or Hell.

rajʿa: lit., return; the word has been used in a technical sense to denote the return or reappearance of a messianic personality, specifically one considered as the Mahdi (q.v.). A number of early Shiʿi groups awaited the return of one or another imam (q.v.) as the Mahdi, often together with many of his supporters, from the dead or from occultation, *ghayba* (q.v.), before the Day of Resurrection, *qiyāma* (q.v.).

risāla (pl., *rasāʾil*): treatise, epistle, letter.

ṣaḥāba: companions; as a technical term it denotes the Companions of the Prophet, including the *muhājirūn* (q.v.) and the *anṣār*, amongst other categories.

ṣāmit: lit., silent one; successor to a speaking prophet, *nāṭiq* (q.v.).

satr: concealment, veiling; in Ismaili thought, it is used specifically in reference to a period, called *dawr al-satr*, when the imams (q.v.) were hidden from the eyes of their followers, or when the *ḥaqāʾiq* (q.v.) were concealed in the *bāṭin* (q.v.), as distinct from *kashf* (q.v.).

sayyid (pl., *sādāt*): lord, master; an honorific appellation for men of authority; the term has been used extensively, but not exclusively, for the descendants of the Prophet, particularly in the Ḥusaynid line; see ʿAlids.

shāh: an Iranian royal title denoting a king; it is often also added to the names of Sufi (q.v.) saints and Nizārī Ismaili imams (q.v.) of the post-Alamūt period.

sharīʿa (or *sharʿ*): the divinely revealed sacred law of Islam; the whole body of rules guiding the life of a Muslim. The provisions of the *sharīʿa* are worked out through the discipline of *fiqh* (q.v.).

sharīf (pl., *ashrāf*): noble; at first used generally of the leading Arab families, then more particularly of the descendants of the Prophet, particularly in the Ḥasanid line; see ʿAlids.

shaykh (pl., *mashāyikh*): old man, elder; the chief of a tribe; any religious dignitary; in particular, an independent Sufi (q.v.) master or spiritual guide, qualified to lead aspirants on the Sufi path, *ṭarīqa* (q.v.); in this sense called *pīr* (q.v.) in Persian; *shaykh* is also a high rank in the *daʿwa* organisation of the Dāʾūdī Ṭayyibī Ismailis; and also in the religious organisation of the Nuṣayrī (ʿAlawī) community.

Sufi: an exponent of Sufism (*taṣawwuf*), the commonest term for that aspect of Islam which is based on the mystical life; hence it denotes a Muslim mystic; more specifically, a member of an organised Sufi order, *ṭarīqa* (q.v.).

sulṭān (Anglicised, sultan): a Muslim term for sovereign; the supreme political and military authority in a Muslim state.

sunna: custom, practice; particularly that associated with the exemplary life of the Prophet, comprising his deeds, utterances and his unspoken approval; it is embodied in *ḥadīth* (q.v.).

tafsīr (pl., *tafāsīr*): lit., explanation, commentary; particularly the commentaries on the Qurʾan; the external, philological exegesis of the Qurʾan, as distinct from *taʾwīl* (q.v.). A Qurʾan commentator is called *mufasir* (pl., *mufasirūn*).

Ṭālibids: descendants of Abū Ṭālib b. ʿAbd al-Muṭṭalib, the father of ʿAlī and full-brother of the Prophet's father, ʿAbd Allāh, including particularly the ʿAlids (q.v.) and the descendants of ʿAlī's brother Jaʿfar al-Ṭayyār.

taʿlīm: teaching, instruction; in Shiʿi Islam, authoritative teaching in religion which could be carried out only by an imam (q.v.) in every age after the Prophet Muḥammad.

tanāsukh: metempsychosis, transmigration of souls; passing of the soul (*nafs* or *rūḥ*) from one body to another; reincarnation of the soul of an individual in a different human body or even in a different creature.

taqiyya: precautionary dissimulation of one's true religious beliefs, especially in times of danger, used in particular by Twelvers (Ithnāʿasharīs), Ismailis and Nuṣayrīs (ʿAlawīs). It is the equivalent of the Persian word *kitmān*.

taqlīd: lit., emulation, imitation or following; it denotes the following of the authoritative guidance of a qualified *mujtahid*; one who practises *taqlīd* is known as *muqallid*; the opposite of *ijtihād* (q.v.).

ṭarīqa: way, path; the mystical spiritual path followed by Sufis (q.v.); any one of the organised Sufi orders. It is also used by the Nizārī Ismailis in reference to their interpretation of Islam.

tashbīh: lit., 'making similar'; in Shiʿi theology, it denotes a mode of anthropomorphism by which God is regarded as similar to created beings.

tawḥīd: as an Islamic doctrine, it denotes the oneness (unicity) of God, His absolute existence, and that He has no equal.

taʾwīl: the educing of the inner meaning from the literal wording or apparent meaning of a text or a ritual, religious prescription; as a technical term among the Shiʿi Muslims, particularly the Ismailis, it denotes the method of educing the *bāṭin* (q.v.) from the *ẓāhir* (q.v.); as such it was used extensively by the Ismailis for the allegorical, symbolic or esoteric interpretation of the Qurʾan, the *sharīʿa*, historical events and the world of nature. The Nuṣayrīs-ʿAlawīs, too, have resorted to *taʾwīl*. Translated also as spiritual or hermeneutic exegesis, *taʾwīl* may be distinguished from *tafsīr* (q.v.).

ʿulamāʾ: see *ʿālim*.

umma: community, any people as followers of a particular religion or prophet; in particular, the Muslims as forming a religious community.

uṣūl (pl. of *aṣl*): lit., roots; as a technical term it refers to primary principles, either of religion, *uṣūl al-dīn*, or of jurisprudence, *uṣūl al-fiqh*.

waṣī (pl., *awṣiyāʾ*): legatee, executor of a will; the immediate successor to a prophet; in this sense, it was the function of *awṣiyāʾ* to interpret and explain the messages brought by prophets, *anbiyāʾ*; see *nāṭiq*.

wazīr (Anglicised, vizier): a high officer of state, the equivalent of a chief minister. The power and status of the office of *wazīr*, called *wizāra* (Anglicised, vizierate), varied greatly in different periods and under different Muslim dynasties.

ẓāhir: the outward, literal, or exoteric meaning of sacred texts and religious prescriptions, notably the Qurʾan and the *sharīʿa* (q.v.), as distinct from the *bāṭin* (q.v.).

Notes

Notes to Chapter 1: Introduction

1 See Abu Mansur ʿAbd al-Qahir b. Tahir al-Baghdadi, *al-Farq bayn al-firaq*, ed. M. Badr (Cairo, 1328/1910), pp. 265–299; English trans., *Moslem Schisms and Sects*, part II, tr. A. S. Halkin (Tel Aviv, 1935), pp. 107–157.

2 See, for instance, al-Hasan b. Musa al-Nawbakhti, *Kitab firaq al-Shiʿa*, ed. H. Ritter (Istanbul, 1931), pp. 37–41, 57–60; and Saʿd b. ʿAbd Allah al-Ashʿari al-Qummi, *Kitab al-maqalat wa'l-firaq*, ed. M. J. Mashkur (Tehran, 1963), pp. 50–55, 63–64, 80–83. These works represent the earliest Imami heresiographies.

3 See S. M. Stern, 'The Book of the Highest Initiation and Other Anti-Ismaʿili Travesties', in his *Studies in Early Ismaʿilism* (Jerusalem and Leiden, 1983), pp. 56–83.

4 Abu Hamid Muhammad al-Ghazali, *Fada'ih al-Batiniyya*, ed. ʿAbd al-Rahman Badawi (Cairo, 1964); partial English trans. in Richard J. McCarthy, *Freedom and Fulfillment* (Boston, 1980), pp. 175–286. See also H. Corbin, 'The Ismaʿili Response to the Polemic of Ghazali', in S. H. Nasr, ed., *Ismaʿili Contributions to Islamic Culture* (Tehran, 1977), pp. 67–98.

5 For one such Zaydi refutation of the Ismailis, written in 707/1308 by a Caspian Zaydi who settled in Yaman, see Muhammad b. al-Hasan al-Daylami, *Bayan madhhab al-Batiniyya wa-butlanih*, ed. R. Strothmann (Istanbul, 1939).

6 In modern times, several scholars have studied the various aspects of this subject, including especially the anti-Islamic polemical tradition developed in medieval Europe. See N. Daniel, *Islam and the West: The Making of an Image* (Edinburgh, 1966); Richard W. Southern, *Western Views of Islam in the Middle Ages* (Cambridge, MA, 1962); A. Hourani, *Islam in European Thought* (Cambridge, 1991), especially pp. 7–60; H. Goddard, *A History of Christian–Muslim Relations* (Edinburgh and Chicago, 2000); and John V. Tolan, *Saracens: Islam in the Medieval European Imagination* (New York, 2002).

7 Southern, *Western Views*, pp. 27–28.

8 See W. Montgomery Watt, *Muslim–Christian Encounters* (London, 1991), pp. 85–86; and his *The Influence of Islam on Medieval Europe* (Edinburgh, 1972), pp. 73–77.

9 William of Tyre, *Willelmi Tyrensis Archiepiscopi Chronicon*, ed. Robert B. C. Huygens (Turnhout, 1986), pp. 890–892; English trans., *A History of Deeds Done Beyond the Sea*, tr. Emily A. Babcock and A. C. Krey (New York, 1943), vol. 2, pp. 323–325.

10 James of Vitry (Jacobi de Vitriaco), *Historia Orientalis*, in *Gesta Dei per Francos*, ed. J. Bongars (Hanover, 1611), vol. 1, pp. 1060–1061. See also Daniel, *Islam and the West*, p. 318.

11 For a survey of these legends and their European sources, see F. Daftary, *The Assassin Legends: Myths of the Isma'ilis* (London, 1994), pp. 88–127; see also his *The Isma'ilis: Their History and Doctrines* (2nd ed., Cambridge, 2007), pp. 10–22.

12 See, for instance, Abu Shama, *Kitab al-rawdatayn fi akhbar al-dawlatayn* (Cairo, 1287–1288/1870–1871), vol. 1, pp. 240, 258.

13 See Ronald W. Ferrier, ed. and tr., *A Journey to Persia: Jean Chardin's Portrait of a Seventeenth-century Empire* (London, 1996), and J. Emerson, 'Chardin', *EIR*, vol. 5, pp. 369–377.

14 Fred M. Donner, 'Modern Approaches to Early Islamic History', in *The New Cambridge History of Islam:* Volume 1, *The Formation of the Islamic World Sixth to Eleventh Centuries*, ed. Chase F. Robinson (Cambridge, 2010), pp. 625–626.

15 Silvestre de Sacy's studies on the Druzes culminated in his posthumously published book entitled *Exposé de la religion des Druzes* (Paris, 1838; reprinted, Paris, 1964), 2 vols., with a substantial introductory chapter on the early Ismailis and a biography of the Fatimid caliph-imam al-Hakim.

16 A. I. Silvestre de Sacy, 'Mémoire sur la dynastie des Assassins, et sur l'étymologie de leur nom', *Mémoires de l'Institut Royal de France*, 4 (1818), pp. 1–84; reprinted in Bryan S. Turner, ed., *Orientalism: Early Sources,* Volume 1, *Readings in Orientalism* (London, 2000), pp. 118–169; complete English trans. in F. Daftary, *The Assassin Legends,* pp. 129–188.

17 Joseph von Hammer-Purgstall, *Die Geschichte der Assassinen aus Morgenländischen Quellen* (Stuttgart and Tübingen, 1818); French trans., *Histoire de l'ordre des Assassins*, tr. J. J. Hellert and P. A. de la Nourais (Paris, 1833; reprinted, Paris, 1961); English trans., *The History of the Assassins*, tr. O. C. Wood (London, 1835; reprinted, New York, 1968).

18 For an analysis of this work, see F. Daftary, 'The "Order of the Assassins": J. von Hammer and the Orientalist Misrepresentations of the Nizari Ismailis', *Iranian Studies*, 39 (2006), pp. 71–81.

19 The generally meagre number of Ismaili works known to orientalists by 1922 is well reflected in the first Western bibliography of Ismaili texts, both published and unpublished, which appeared in that year; see L. Massignon, 'Esquisse d'une bibliographie Qarmate', in T. W. Arnold and R. A. Nicholson, ed., *A Volume of Oriental Studies Presented to Edward G. Browne on his 60th Birthday* (Cambridge, 1922), pp. 329–338; reprinted in L. Massignon, *Opera Minora*, ed. Y. Moubarac (Paris, 1969), vol. 1, pp. 627–639.

20 See E. Kohlberg, 'Western Studies of Shiʿa Islam', in M. Kramer, ed., *Shiʿism, Resistance, and Revolution* (Boulder and London, 1987), pp. 33–39; reprinted in his *Belief and Law in Imami Shiʿism* (Aldershot, 1991), article II.

21 See especially J. Wellhausen, *The Arab Kingdom and its Fall*, tr. Margaret G. Weir (Calcutta, 1927; reprinted, Beirut, 1963), originally published in German in 1902; and his *The Religio-Political Factions in Early Islam*, tr. R. C. Ostle and S. M. Walzer (Amsterdam, 1975), published originally in German in 1901.

22 See particularly I. Goldziher, *Vorlesungen über den Islam*, ed. F. Babinger (2nd ed., Heidelberg, 1925), pp. 188–253; English trans., *Introduction to Islamic Theology and Law*, tr. A. and R. Hamori (Princeton, 1981), pp. 167–229. This book was based almost entirely on primary sources. Goldziher's significant contributions to the study of Shiʿism in the West are also scattered in his *Muhammedanische Studien* (Halle, 1889–1890); English trans., *Muslim Studies*, tr. C. R. Baber and S. M. Stern (London, 1967–1971), 2 vols.

23 R. Strothmann, *Das Staatsrecht der Zaiditen* (Strassburg, 1912); his *Kultus der Zaiditen* (Strassburg, 1912), and his *Die Zwölfer-Schiʿa* (Leipzig, 1926; reprinted, Hildesheim, 1975). Strothmann was amongst the earliest European scholars to have also edited a number of Ismaili texts, including a collection of Tayyibi works entitled *Gnosis-Texte der Ismailiten* (Göttingen, 1943).

24 D. M. Donaldson, *The Shiʿite Religion* (London, 1933).

25 D. Shayegan, 'Corbin, Henry', *EIR*, vol. 6, pp. 268–272; and his more detailed exposition of Corbin's thought in *Henry Corbin: La topographie spirituelle de l'Islam Iranien* (Paris, 1990); and Christian Jambet, 'Bibliographie générale', in *Les cahiers de l'Herne: Henry Corbin*, ed. C. Jambet (Paris, 1981), pp. 345–360. See also H. Corbin, *En Islam Iranien: Aspects spirituels et philosophiques* (Paris, 1971–1972), 4 vols., synthesising his contributions on the spiritual and philosophical aspects of Twelver Shiʿism.

26 T. Fahd, ed., *Le Shiʿisme Imamite. Colloque de Strasbourg (6–9 mai 1968)* (Paris, 1970), with contributions by H. Corbin, W. Madelung, S. H. Nasr and others.

27 See M. A. Amir-Moezzi et al., ed., *Le Shiʿisme Imamite quarante ans après. Hommage à Etan Kohlberg* (Turnhout, 2009).

28 Sayyid Muhammad Husayn Tabataba'i, *Shiʿa dar Islam* (Tehran, 1348 Sh./1969); English trans., *Shiʿite Islam*, ed. and tr. S. H. Nasr (London, 1975). This is the first authoritative introduction to Shiʿism, with special reference to its Twelver tradition, written by a traditional scholar in modern times. See also Jaʿfar Sobhani, *Manshur-i ʿaqa'id-i Imamiyya* (Qumm, 1376 Sh./1997); English trans., *Doctrines of Shiʿi Islam: A Compendium of Imami Beliefs and Practices*, ed. and tr. Reza Shah-Kazemi (London, 2001).

29 These are the *Danishnama-yi Jahan-i Islam* (*Encyclopaedia of the World of Islam*) (Tehran, 1375 Sh.–/1996–), and *Da'irat al-Maʿarif-i Buzurg-i Islami* (*The Great Islamic Encyclopaedia*), ed. K. M. Bujnurdi (Tehran, 1367 Sh.–/1989–); abridged English trans., *Encyclopaedia Islamica*, ed. W. Madelung and F. Daftary (Leiden, 2008–).

30 M. Momen, *An Introduction to Shiʿi Islam: The History and Doctrines of Twelver Shiʿism* (New Haven, 1985).

31 See F. Daftary, 'Bibliography of the Works of Wilferd Madelung', in F. Daftary and J. W. Meri, ed., *Culture and Memory in Medieval Islam: Essays in Honour of Wilferd Madelung* (London, 2003), pp. 5–40.

32 See J. van Ess, *Theologie und Gesellschaft im 2. und 3. Jahrhundert Hidschra* (Berlin and New York, 1991–1997), 6 vols.

33 See F. Daftary, 'Ivanow, Vladimir', *EIR*, vol. 14, pp. 298–300.

34 W. Ivanow, *A Guide to Ismaili Literature* (London, 1933).

35 See F. Daftary, 'Bibliography of the Publications of the late W. Ivanow', *Islamic Culture*, 45 (1971), pp. 55–67, and 56 (1982), pp. 239–240.

36 W. Ivanow, *Ismaili Literature: A Bibliographical Survey* (Tehran, 1963).

37 Ismail K. Poonawala, *Biobibliography of Ismaʿili Literature* (Malibu, CA, 1977), and F. Daftary, *Ismaili Literature: A Bibliography of Sources and Studies* (London, 2004).

38 Marshall G. S. Hodgson, *The Order of Assassins: The Struggle of the Early Nizari Ismaʿilis against the Islamic World* (The Hague, 1955; reprinted, New York, 1980; reprinted, Philadelphia, 2005).

39 F. Daftary, *The Ismaʿilis: Their History and Doctrines* (Cambridge, 1990; 2nd ed., Cambridge, 2007); and his *A Short History of the Ismailis: Traditions of a Muslim Community* (Edinburgh, 1998), translated into Arabic, Persian, Urdu, Gujarati, Tajik (Cyrillic), Chinese, Uyghur and numerous European languages. See further 'Bibliography of the Works of Farhad Daftary', in Omar Alí-de-Unzaga, ed., *Fortresses of the Intellect: Ismaili and other Islamic Studies in Honour of Farhad Daftary* (London, 2011), pp. 33–57.

40 See A. Gacek, *Catalogue of Arabic Manuscripts in the Library of The Institute of Ismaili Studies* (London, 1984–1985), 2 vols.; Delia Cortese, *Ismaili and Other Arabic Manuscripts: A Descriptive Catalogue of Manuscripts in the Library of The Institute of Ismaili Studies* (London, 2000); also her *Arabic Ismaili Manuscripts: The Zahid ʿAli Collection in the Library of The Institute of Ismaili Studies* (London, 2003); F. de Blois, *Arabic, Persian and Gujarati Manuscripts: The Hamdani Collection in the Library of The Institute of Ismaili Studies* (London, 2011); and P. E. Walker, 'Institute of Ismaili Studies', *EIR*, vol. 12, pp. 164–166.

41 For details, see Sabine Schmidtke, 'The History of Zaydi Studies: An Introduction', *Arabica*, 59 (2012), pp. 185–199.

42 R. Dussaud, *Histoire et religion des Nosairis* (Paris, 1900).

43 See especially H. Halm, *Die islamische Gnosis: Die extreme Schia und die ʿAlawiten* (Zurich and Munich, 1982).

44 See particularly Meir M. Bar-Asher and A. Kofsky, *The Nusayri-ʿAlawi Religion: An Enquiry into its Theology and Liturgy* (Leiden, 2002).

45 Y. Friedman, *The Nusayri-ʿAlawis: An Introduction to the Religion, History and Identity of the Leading Minority in Syria* (Leiden, 2010). A number of Arabic monographs on the Nusayris have also appeared, written either apologetically by members of the community or polemically by their detractors.

Notes to Chapter 2: The Origins and Early History of Shiʿi Islam

1 See P. Crone and M. Hinds, *God's Caliph: Religious Authority in the First Centuries of Islam* (Cambridge, 1986), especially pp. 4–23.

2 W. Madelung has produced an exhaustive analysis of the historiography on this subject in his *The Succession to Muhammad: A Study of the Early Caliphate* (Cambridge, 1997); see also his 'Shiʿism in the Age of the Rightly-Guided Caliphs', in L. Clarke, ed., *Shiʿite Heritage: Essays on Classical and Modern Traditions* (Binghamton, NY, 2001), pp. 9–18; reprinted in his *Studies in Medieval Shiʿism*, ed. S. Schmidtke (Farnham, UK, 2012), article II, and his 'Shiʿa', *EI2*, vol. 9, pp. 420–424. In this connection see also al-Baladhuri, *Ansab al-ashraf*, vol. 2, ed. W. Madelung (Beirut, 2003), covering the Prophet's succession and ʿAli's caliphate.

3 On the meaning and early use of this expression, see Madelung, *Succession to Muḥammad,* pp. 178–179, and M. A. Amir-Moezzi, 'Reflections on the Expression *din ʿAli*: The Origins of the Shiʿi Faith', in his *The Spirituality of Shiʿi Islam: Beliefs and Practices*, tr. H. Karmali (London, 2011), pp. 3–44.

4 See L. Veccia Vaglieri, 'Ghadir Khumm', *EI2*, vol. 2, pp. 993–994, where full references are cited.

5 See S. H. Nasr, *Ideals and Realities of Islam* (new rev. ed., Cambridge, 2001), pp. 141 ff.

6 On the roots of discontent with 'Uthman's caliphate and the circumstances of his murder, see M. A. Shaban, *Islamic History: A New Interpretation* (Cambridge, 1971–1976), vol. 1, pp. 60–70; and M. Hinds, 'The Murder of Caliph 'Uthman', *IJMES*, 3 (1972), pp. 450–469; reprinted in his *Studies in Early Islamic History*, ed. J. Bacharach et al. (Princeton, 1996), pp. 29–55.

7 For further details, see M. Hinds, 'Kufan Political Alignments and their Background in the Mid-Seventh Century A.D.', *IJMES*, 2 (1971), pp. 358–365; reprinted in his *Studies*, pp. 1–28; and G. H. A. Juynboll, 'The Qurra' in Early Islamic History', *Journal of the Economic and Social History of the Orient*, 16 (1973), pp. 113–129.

8 See P. Crone, '"Even an Ethiopian Slave": The Transformation of a Sunni Tradition', *BSOAS*, 57 (1994), pp. 59–69; reprinted in her *From Kavad to al-Ghazali: Religion, Law and Political Thought in the Near East, c.600–c.1100* (Aldershot, 2005), article VIII; and P. Crone, *Medieval Islamic Political Thought* (Edinburgh, 2004), pp. 54–64.

9 See al-Tabari, *Ta'rikh al-rusul wa'l-muluk*, ed. Michael J. de Goeje et al., series I–III (Leiden, 1879–1901), II, pp. 227–391; English trans., *The History of al-Tabari*: Volume XIX, *The Caliphate of Yazid b. Mu'awiya*, tr. I. K. A. Howard (Albany, NY, 1990), pp. 16–183. J. Wellhausen made a thorough use of the early sources; see his *Religio-Political Factions*, pp. 105–120, based mainly on al-Tabari; S. Husain M. Jafri, *Origins and Early Development of Shi'a Islam* (London, 1979), pp. 174–221; and W. Madelung, 'Hosayn b. 'Ali', *EIR*, vol. 12, pp. 493–498.

10 See M. Ayoub, *Redemptive Suffering in Islam: A Study of the Devotional Aspects of 'Ashura' in Twelver Shi'ism* (The Hague, 1978); A. Amanat, 'Meadow of Martyrs: Kashifi's Persianization of the Shi'i Martyrdom Narrative in the Late Timurid Herat', in Daftary and Meri, ed., *Culture and Memory in Medieval Islam*, pp. 250–275; reprinted in his *Apocalyptic Islam and Iranian Shi'ism* (London, 2009), pp. 91–109; P. Chelkowski, 'Ta'ziya', *EI2*, vol. 10, pp. 406–408; and F. Mehrvash, "Ashura", *EIS*, vol. 3, pp. 883–892.

11 The most detailed account of al-Mukhtar's revolt is contained in al-Tabari, *Ta'rikh*, II, pp. 520–752; English trans., *The History of al-Tabari*: Volume XX, *The Collapse of Sufyanid Authority and the Coming of the Marwanids*, tr. G. R. Hawting (Albany, NY, 1989), pp. 105–225; and *The History of al-Tabari*: Volume XXI, *The Victory of the Marwanids*, tr. M.

Fishbein (Albany, NY, 1990), pp. 1–121; see also Wellhausen, *Religio-Political Factions*, pp. 125–145, based mainly on al-Tabari.

12 See W. Madelung, 'The *Hashimiyyat* of al-Kumayt and Hashimi Shi'ism', *Studia Islamica*, 70 (1989), pp. 5–26; reprinted in his *Religious and Ethnic Movements in Medieval Islam* (Hampshire, UK, 1992), article V; reprinted also in E. Kohlberg, ed., *Shi'ism* (Aldershot, 2003), pp. 87–108. See also Claude Cahen, 'Points de vue sur la "Révolution 'Abbaside"', *Revue Historique*, 230 (1963), pp. 295–338; reprinted in his *Les peuples Musulmans dans l'histoire médiévale* (Damascus, 1977), pp. 105–160.

13 See I. Goldziher, 'Le dénombrement des sectes Musulmanes', *Revue de l'Histoire des Religions*, 26 (1892), pp. 129ff.; reprinted in his *Gesammelte Schriften*, ed. J. de Somogyi (Hildesheim, 1967–1973), vol. 2, pp. 406ff. See also W. Montgomery Watt, 'The Great Community and the Sects', in Gustave E. von Grunebaum, ed., *Theology and Law in Islam* (Wiesbaden, 1971), pp. 25–36; reprinted in his *Early Islam: Collected Articles* (Edinburgh, 1990), pp. 173–184.

14 For a survey of the changing criteria of exaggeration during the first three centuries of Islam, see W. al-Qadi, 'The Development of the Term *Ghulat* in Muslim Literature with Special Reference to the Kaysaniyya', in A. Dietrich, ed., *Akten des VII. Kongresses für Arabistik und Islamwissenschaft* (Göttingen, 1976), pp. 295–319; reprinted in Kohlberg, ed., *Shi'ism*, pp. 169–193.

15 See al-Nawbakhti, *Firaq*, pp. 32–34, 35–37; and al-Qummi, *al-Maqalat*, pp. 44–46, 48–50. Some details are to be found also in 'Abd al-Qahir b. Tahir al-Baghdadi, *al-Farq bayn al-Firaq*, ed. M. Badr (Cairo, 1328/1910), pp. 214–217, 253ff.; English trans. *Moslem Schisms and Sects*, part II, tr. Abraham S. Halkin (Tel Aviv, 1935), pp. 31–35, 91ff. See also Marshall Hodgson, 'How Did the Early Shi'a Become Sectarian?', *JAOS*, 75 (1955), pp. 4–8; reprinted in Kohlberg, ed., *Shi'ism*, pp. 6–10; and Hodgson's *The Venture of Islam: Conscience and History in a World Civilization* (Chicago, 1974), vol. 1, pp. 258–267.

16 See William F. Tucker, *Mahdis and Millenarians: Shi'ite Extremists in Early Muslim Iraq* (Cambridge, 2008), containing a collection of several of the author's earlier seminal articles.

17 Al-Nawbakhti, *Firaq*, pp. 52–53; and al-Qummi, *al-Maqalat*, pp. 74–76.

18 For an analysis of certain aspects of this process of identity formation, see N. Haider, *The Origins of the Shi'a: Identity, Ritual, and Sacred Space in Eighth-Century Kufa* (Cambridge, 2011), especially pp. 3–17, 215–253. For a similar study on the emergence of a specifically religious Shi'i communal

identity during the first two centuries of Islam, see Maria M. Dakake, *The Charismatic Community: Shiʿite Identity in Early Islam* (Albany, NY, 2007).

19 On aspects of al-Baqir's teachings, see Arzina R. Lalani, *Early Shiʿi Thought: The Teachings of Imam Muhammad al-Baqir* (London, 2000), especially pp. 84–95, 114–126.

20 For further details, see W. Madelung, "Abd Allah b. ʿAbbas and Shiʿite Law', in U. Vermeulen and J. M. F. Van Reeth, ed., *Law, Christianity and Modernism in Islamic Society* (Leuven, 1998), pp. 13–25; reprinted in his *Studies in Medieval Shiʿism*, article I.

21 See al-Qummi, *al-Maqalat*, pp. 56–59; H. Halm, *Die islamische Gnosis*, pp. 113–198, 218ff.; and Daftary, *The Ismaʿilis*, pp. 93–95, where further references are cited.

22 See Abu ʿAmr Muhammad b. ʿUmar al-Kashshi, *Ikhtiyar maʿrifat al-rijal*, as abridged by Muhammad b. al-Hasan al-Tusi, ed. H. al-Mustafawi (Mashhad, 1348 Sh./1969).

23 See Ahmad b. ʿAli al-Najashi, *Kitab al-rijal* (Bombay, 1317/1899); Abu Jaʿfar Muhammad b. al-Hasan al-Tusi, *Fihrist kutub al-Shiʿa*, ed. A. Sprenger et al. (Calcutta, 1853–1855); his *Rijal al-Tusi*, ed. M. S. Al Bahr al-ʿUlum (Najaf, 1381/1961); and Ibn Shahrashub, *Kitab maʿalim al-ʿulama'*, ed. ʿA. Iqbal (Tehran, 1353/1934); these and other similar works have been reprinted many times in Najaf, Qumm, Mashhad and Tehran.

24 Al-Nawbakhti, *Firaq*, pp. 34, 53–55; and al-Qummi, *al-Maqalat*, pp. 76–78.

25 See W. Madelung, 'Zayd b. ʿAli b. al-Husayn', *EI2*, vol. 11, pp. 473–474. Zayd and the early Zaydiyya will be covered in greater detail in Chapter 5.

26 The influence of the Muʿtazila on Zaydi Shiʿism is investigated in W. Madelung, *Der Imam al-Qasim ibn Ibrahim und die Glaubenslehre der Zaiditen* (Berlin, 1965), pp. 7–43, while a discussion of the connection between Muʿtazilism and Imami Shiʿism may be found in W. Madelung, 'Imamism and Muʿtazilite Theology', in Fahd, ed., *Le Shiʿisme Imamite*, pp. 13–30; reprinted in his *Religious Schools and Sects in Medieval Islam* (London, 1985), article VII.

27 P. Crone, 'On the Meaning of the ʿAbbasid Call to al-Rida', in C. E. Bosworth et al., ed., *The Islamic World: From Classical to Modern Times, Essays in Honor of Bernard Lewis* (Princeton, 1989), pp. 95–111; reprinted in Kohlberg, ed., *Shiʿism*, pp. 291–307, also in her *From Arabian Tribes to Islamic Empire: Army, State and Society in the Near East c.600–850* (Aldershot, 2008), article VII; see also Crone, *Medieval Islamic*, pp. 87–98.

28 See M. Sharon, *Black Banners from the East: The Establishment of the ʿAbbasid State – Incubation of a Revolt* (Jerusalem and Leiden, 1983), pp. 201–226; and G. H. Yusofi, 'Abu Moslem Korasani', *EIR*, vol. 1, pp. 340–344.

29 Al-Nawbakhti, *Firaq*, pp. 32, 41ff.; al-Qummi, *al-Maqalat*, p. 44; G. H. Sadighi, *Les mouvements religieux Iranien au IIe et au IIIe siècle de l'hégire* (Paris, 1938), especially pp. 163–280; Richard N. Frye, *The Golden Age of Persia* (London, 1975), pp. 126–137; and W. Madelung, *Religious Trends in Early Islamic Iran* (Albany, NY, 1988), pp. 1–12. For the most comprehensive treatment of the subject now, see Patricia Crone, *The Nativist Prophets of Early Islamic Iran: Rural Revolt and Zoroastrianism* (Cambridge, 2012).

30 See al-Kashshi, *al-Rijal*, pp. 133–161, 167, 185–191, 213, 251–252, 255–280, 281–285, 316–317, 345, 352, 375, 382–383; al-Najashi, *al-Rijal*, pp. 10, 92, 103–104, 148–149, 154, 176, 228, 304–305; al-Tusi, *Rijal*, pp. 142–341; al-Tusi, *Fihrist*, pp. 141–143, 212, 323, 355–356. See also Jafri, *Origins*, pp. 305–310; and W. Madelung, 'The Shiʿite and Kharijite Contribution to Pre-Ashʿarite *Kalam*', in P. Morewedge, ed., *Islamic Philosophical Theology* (Albany, NY, 1979), pp. 120–139; reprinted in his *Religious Schools*, article VIII.

31 Al-Nawbakhti, *Firaq*, pp. 37–41, 58–60; al-Qummi, *al-Maqalat*, pp. 50–55, 63–64, 81–82; al-Kashshi, *al-Rijal*, pp. 224–226, 228, 290–308, 324, 344, 352–353, 365–366, 370, 482–483, 528–529, 571; Abu'l-Hasan ʿAli b. Ismaʿil al-Ashʿari, *Kitab maqalat al-Islamiyyin*, ed. H. Ritter (Istanbul, 1929–1930), pp. 10–13; al-Baghdadi, *al-Farq*, pp. 236–237; tr. Halkin, pp. 62–66; Muhammad b. ʿAbd al-Karim al-Shahrastani, *Kitab al-milal wa'l-nihal*, ed. ʿA. M. al-Wakil (Cairo, 1387/1968), vol. 1, pp. 179–181; partial English trans., *Muslim Sects and Divisions*, tr. A. K. Kazi and J. G. Flynn (London, 1984), pp. 154–155; H. Corbin, 'Une liturgie Shiʿite du Graal', in *Mélanges d'histoire des religions offerts à Henri Charles Puech* (Paris, 1974), pp. 190–207; English trans., 'A Shiʿite Liturgy of the Grail', in H. Corbin, *The Voyage and the Messenger: Iran and Philosophy*, tr. J. Rowe (Berkeley, 1998), pp. 173–204; Halm, *Die islamische Gnosis*, pp. 199–217; and H. Ansari, 'Abu al-Khattab', *EIS*, vol. 2, pp. 203–210, where full references to the sources are cited.

32 Summary expositions, in English, of the Imami Shiʿi doctrine of the imamate are to be found in Tabataba'i, *Shiʿite Islam*, pp. 173–190; Sobhani, *Doctrines of Shiʿi Islam*, pp. 96–112; and Momen, *Introduction to Shiʿi Islam*, pp. 147–160. Many relevant arguments are also contained in M. A. Amir-Moezzi, *The Divine Guide in Early Shiʿism: The Sources of Esotericism in Islam*, tr. D. Streight (Albany, NY, 1994), especially pp. 29–97. See also W. Madelung, 'Imama', *EI2*, vol. 3, pp. 1163–1169, at pp. 1166–1167.

33 Al-Nawbakhti, *Firaq*, pp. 56–57; al-Qummi, *al-Maqalat*, pp. 78–79; Muhammad b. Yaʿqub al-Kulayni, *al-Usul min al-kafi*, ed. ʿAli Akbar al-Ghaffari (3rd ed., Tehran, 1388/1968), vol. 2, pp. 217–226. See also E. Kohlberg, 'Some Imami-Shiʿi Views on *taqiyya*', *JAOS*, 95 (1975), pp. 395–402; reprinted in his *Belief and Law*, article III; and his, 'Taqiyya in Shiʿi Theology

and Religion', in Hans G. Kippenberg and Guy G. Stroumsa, ed., *Secrecy and Concealment: Studies in the History of Mediterranean and Near Eastern Religions* (Leiden, 1995), pp. 345–380.

34 These *hadiths* are to be found in the *Kitab al-hujja*, the opening book, in al-Kulayni's *al-Usul min al-kafi*, vol. 1, pp. 168–548, and in the *Kitab al-walaya* in al-Qadi al-Nuʿman's *Daʿaʾim al-Islam*, ed. Asaf A. A. Fyzee (Cairo, 1951–1961), vol. 1, pp. 14–98; English trans., *The Pillars of Islam*, tr. Asaf A. A. Fyzee, completely revised by Ismail K. Poonawala (New Delhi, 2002–2004), vol. 1, pp. 18–122.

35 Al-Kulayni, *al-Usul*, vol. 1, pp. 376–377.

Notes to Chapter 3: The Ithnaʿasharis or Twelvers

1 On these Imami heresiographies and their common reliance on an earlier source produced by the Imami scholar Hisham b. al-Hakam, see W. Madelung, 'Bemerkungen zur imamitischen Firaq-Literatur', *Der Islam*, 43 (1967), pp. 37–52; reprinted in his *Religious Schools*, article XV; English trans., 'Some Remarks on the Imami Firaq-Literature', in Kohlberg, ed., *Shiʿism*, pp. 153–167.

2 Al-Nawbakhti, *Firaq*, pp. 57ff.; and al-Qummi, *al-Maqalat*, pp. 79ff. See also al-Ashʿari, *Maqalat*, pp. 25, 27–29; Ibn Hazm, *Kitab al-fasl fi'l-milal wa'l-ahwa' wa'l-nihal* (Cairo, 1317–1321/1899–1903), vol. 4, pp. 93, 180; al-Shahrastani, *al-Milal*, vol. 1, pp. 165–169; and Abu Hatim al-Razi, *Kitab al-zina*, part 3, ed. ʿAbd Allah Sallum al-Samarraʾi, in his *al-Ghuluww wa'l-firaq al-ghaliya* (Baghdad, 1392/1972), pp. 286ff.

3 See al-Tabari, *Taʾrikh*, III, pp. 551–568; English trans., *The History of al-Tabari*: Volume XXX, *The ʿAbbasid Caliphate in Equilibrium*, tr. C. E. Bosworth (Albany, NY, 1989), pp. 14–38; ʿAli b. al-Husayn al-Masʿudi, *Muraj al-dhahab*, ed. and tr. C. Barbier de Meynard and A. Pavet de Courteille (Paris, 1861–1876), vol. 6, pp. 266–268; and Abu'l-Faraj al-Isfahani, *Maqatil al-Talibiyyin*, ed. A. Saqr (Cairo, 1368/1949), pp. 431ff., 442–460.

4 Al-Nawbakhti, *Firaq*, pp. 67, 72 ff.; al-Qummi, *al-Maqalat*, pp. 89, 93ff.; al-Kulayni, *al-Usul*, vol. 1, pp. 311–319, 486–492; al-Kashshi, *al-Rijal*, pp. 459, 591–592; Abu'l-Faraj al-Isfahani, *Maqatil*, pp. 561–572; Muhammad b. Muhammad al-Mufid, *Kitab al-Irshad: The Book of Guidance into the Lives of the Twelve Imams*, tr. Ian K. A. Howard (London, 1981), pp. 436–479; Tabatabaʾi, *Shiʿite Islam*, pp. 63–64, 205–207; Hossein Modarressi, *Crisis and Consolidation in the Formative Period of Shiʿite Islam* (Princeton, 1993), pp. 10–14; and E. Kohlberg, 'Musa al-Kazim', *EI2*, vol. 7, pp. 645–648.

5 See F. Gabrieli, *Al-Ma'mun e gli 'Alidi* (Leipzig, 1929), pp. 35ff.; W. Madelung, 'New Documents Concerning al-Ma'mun, al-Fadl b. Sahl and 'Ali al-Rida', in W. al-Qadi, ed., *Studia Arabica et Islamica: Festschrift for Ihsan Abbas* (Beirut, 1981), pp. 333–346; reprinted in his *Religious and Ethnic Movements*, article VI; and his "Ali al-Reza', *EIR*, vol. 1, pp. 877–880. See also Said Amir Arjomand, 'The Crisis of the Imamate and the Institution of Occultation in Twelver Shi'ism: A Sociohistorical Perspective', *IJMES*, 28 (1996), pp. 491–515, at pp. 494–496; reprinted in Kohlberg, ed., *Shi'ism*, pp. 112–114.

6 Al-Nawbakhti, *Firaq*, pp. 74ff.; al-Qummi, *al-Maqalat*, pp. 93ff.; al-Kulayni, *al-Usul*, vol. 1, pp. 320–322, 492–497; al-Mufid, *al-Irshad*, pp. 480–495; and W. Madelung, 'Muhammad b. 'Ali al-Rida', *EI2*, vol. 7, pp. 396–397.

7 Al-Nawbakhti, *Firaq*, pp. 77–79; al-Qummi, *al-Maqalat*, pp. 99–101; al-Kulayni, *al-Usul*, vol. 1, pp. 323–325, 497–502; al-Mufid, *al-Irshad*, pp. 496–506; Arjomand, 'Crisis of the Imamate', pp. 498ff.; reprinted in Kohlberg, ed., *Shi'ism*, pp. 116ff.; and W. Madelung, "Ali al-Hadi', *EIR*, vol. 1, pp. 861–862.

8 Al-Nawbakhti, *Firaq*, pp. 78ff.; al-Qummi, *al-Maqalat*, pp. 101ff.; al-Kulayni, *al-Usul*, vol. 1, pp. 503–514; al-Mufid, *al-Irshad*, pp. 507–523; Tabataba'i, *Shi'ite Islam*, pp. 209–210; and H. Halm, "Askari', *EIR*, vol. 2, p. 769.

9 See al-Nawbakhti, *Firaq*, pp. 79–94; al-Qummi, *al-Maqalat*, pp. 102–116; al-Kulayni, *al-Usul*, vol. 1, pp. 498–525; al-Mufid, *al-Irshad*, pp. 524–554; and al-Razi, *Kitab al-zina*, part 3, pp. 292–293. The issues are discussed, from Shi'i perspectives, in A. A. Sachedina, *Islamic Messianism: The Idea of Mahdi in Twelver Shi'ism* (Albany, NY, 1981); and Jassim M. Hussain, *The Occultation of the Twelfth Imam: A Historical Background* (London, 1982). See also E. Kohlberg, 'From Imamiyya to Ithna-'Ashariyya', *BSOAS*, 39 (1976), pp. 521–534; reprinted in his *Belief and Law*, article XIV; and I. K. Poonawala, 'Apocalyptic: ii. In Muslim Iran', *EIR*, vol. 2, pp. 157–160.

10 See Verena Klemm, 'Die vier *Sufara'* des Zwölften Imam. Zur formativen Periode der Zwölferši'a', *Die Welt des Orients*, 15 (1984), pp. 126–143; English trans., 'The Four *Sufara'* of the Twelfth Imam: On the Formative Period of the Twelver Shi'a', in Kohlberg, ed., *Shi'ism*, pp. 135–152; S. A. Arjomand, 'Imam *Absconditus* and the Beginnings of the Theology of Occultation: Imami Shi'ism *circa* 280–90 A.H./900 A.D.', *JAOS*, 117 (1997), pp. 1–12; Modarressi, *Crisis and Consolidation*, pp. 64–105; Andrew J. Newman, *The Formative Period of Twelver Shi'ism: Hadith as Discourse Between Qum and Baghdad* (London, 2000), pp. 12–31; and H. Halm, *Shi'ism*, tr. J. Watson and M. Hill (2nd ed., Edinburgh, 2004), pp. 32–44.

11 For a detailed study on several members of Banu Nawbakht and their contributions to Shi'i Islam, see 'Abbas Iqbal, *Khandan-i Nawbakhti* (2nd ed., Tehran, 1345 Sh./1966).

12 Madelung, 'Imamism and Mu'tazilite Theology', pp. 16ff. See also Newman, *Formative Period of Twelver Shi'ism*, pp. 38 ff.

13 Halm, *Shi'ism*, pp. 48–56.

14 See, for example, W. Madelung, 'A Treatise of the Sharif al-Murtada on the Legality of Working for the Government', *BSOAS*, 43 (1980), pp. 18–31; and his 'Authority in Twelver Shi'ism in the Absence of the Imam', in *La notion d'autorité au Moyen Age: Islam, Byzance, Occident* (Paris, 1982), pp. 163–173; both articles reprinted in Madelung's *Religious Schools*, articles IX and X, respectively. See also W. Madelung, ''Alam-al-Hoda', *EIR*, vol. 1, pp. 791–795.

15 See Nasir al-Din al-Tusi, *Sayr va suluk*, ed. and tr. S. J. Badakhchani as *Contemplation and Action: The Spiritual Autobiography of a Muslim Scholar* (London, 1998), text pp. 3–7, 11–12, 17–18, 20–21, translation pp. 26–32, 38–39, 47–48, 52–53.

16 For interesting views on al-Tusi's search for different patrons who would facilitate his learned enquiries, see W. Madelung, 'Nasir ad-Din Tusi's Ethics between Philosophy, Shi'ism and Sufism', in Richard G. Hovannisian, ed., *Ethics in Islam* (Malibu, CA, 1985), pp. 85–101; and H. Dabashi, 'The Philosopher/Vizier: Khwaja Nasir al-Din al-Tusi and the Isma'ilis', in F. Daftary, ed., *Mediaeval Isma'ili History and Thought* (Cambridge, 1996), pp. 231–245. See also H. Landolt, 'Khwaja Nasir al-Din al-Tusi (597/1201–672/1274), Isma'ilism and Ishraqi Philosophy', in N. Pourjavady and Ž. Vesel, ed., *Nasir al-Din Tusi, Philosophe et savant de XIIIe siècle* (Tehran, 2000), pp. 13–30; and H. Daiber, 'Al-Tusi, Nasir al-Din', *EI2*, vol. 10, pp. 746–750.

17 Nasir al-Din al-Tusi, *al-Risala fi'l-imama*, ed. M. T. Danishpazhuh (Tehran, 1335 Sh./1956).

18 See Nasir al-Din al-Tusi, *Masari' al-musari'*, ed. W. Madelung (Tehran, 1383 Sh./2004). See also al-Shahrastani, *Kitab al-musara'a*, ed. and tr. W. Madelung and T. Mayer as *Struggling with the Philosopher: A Refutation of Avicenna's Metaphysics* (London, 2001); and T. Mayer, 'The Absurdities of Infinite Time: Shahrastani's Critique of Ibn Sina and Tusi's Defence', in R. Hansberger et al., ed., *Medieval Arabic Thought: Essays in Honour of Fritz Zimmermann* (London and Turin, 2012), pp. 105–134.

19 Al-'Allama al-Hilli, *Mabadi' al-wusul ila 'ilm al-usul*, ed. 'A. M. 'Ali (Najaf, 1390/1970), especially pp. 240–252.

20 On the Hurufis and the Nuqtawis and their doctrines, which have not yet been fully investigated, see John K. Birge, *The Bektashi Order of Dervishes*

(London, 1965); Sadiq Kiya, *Nuqtawiyan ya Pasikhaniyan* (Tehran, 1320 Sh./1941); A. Amanat, 'The Nuqtawi Movement of Mahmud Pisikhani and his Persian Cycle of Mystical-Materialism', in Daftary, ed., *Mediaeval Ismaʿili History*, pp. 281–297; reprinted in his *Apocalyptic Islam*, pp. 73–89; K. Babayan, *Mystics, Monarchs and Messiahs: Cultural Landscapes of Early Modern Iran* (Cambridge, MA, 2002), pp. 57–108; H. T. Norris, 'The Hurufi Legacy of Fadlullah of Astarabad', in L. Lewisohn, ed., *The Heritage of Sufism*: Volume II, *The Legacy of Medieval Persian Sufism (1150–1500)* (Oxford, 1999), pp. 87–97; S. Bashir, *Fazlallah Astarabadi and the Hurufis* (Oxford, 2005); H. Algar, 'Horufism', *EIR*, vol. 12, pp. 483–490; and his 'Nuktawiyya', *EI2*, vol. 8, pp. 114–117.

21 Marshall Hodgson, *Venture of Islam*, vol. 2, pp. 493ff.

22 See Said A. Arjomand, *The Shadow of God and the Hidden Imam* (Chicago, 1984), pp. 66–84; and B. Scarcia Amoretti, 'Religion in the Timurid and Safavid Periods', in *The Cambridge History of Iran:* Volume 6, *The Timurid and Safavid Periods*, ed. P. Jackson and L. Lockhart (Cambridge, 1986), pp. 610–655.

23 Claude Cahen, 'Le problème du Shiʿisme dans l'Asie Mineure turque préottomane', in Fahd, ed., *Le Shiʿisme Imamite*, pp. 115–129, at pp. 118ff.

24 On Haydar Amuli's thought and the relationship between Shiʿism and Sufism in general, see Corbin, *En Islam Iranien*, vol. 1, pp. 74–85, and vol. 3, pp. 149–213; J. van Ess, 'Haydar-i Amuli', *EI2*, vol. 12, Supplement, pp. 363–365; S. H. Nasr, 'Le Shiʿisme et le Soufisme. Leurs relations principielles et historiques', in Fahd, ed., *Le Shiʿisme Imamite*, pp. 215–233; and his *Sufi Essays* (London, 1972), pp. 104–120.

25 See, for instance, Sayyid Haydar Amuli, *Jamiʿ al-asrar wa-manbaʿ al-anwar*, ed. H. Corbin and O. Yayha, in a collection of Amuli's works entitled *La philosophie Shiʿite* (Tehran and Paris, 1969), pp. 2–617, at pp. 47, 116–117, 216–217, 220–222, 238, 388, 611–615; and Amuli's *Asrar al-shariʿa*, ed. M. Khwajawi (Tehran, 1982), pp. 5ff., 23ff.

26 See, for instance, Shaykh Husayn Pirzada Zahidi, *Silsilat al-nasab Safawiyya*, ed. H. K. Iranshahr (Berlin, 1343/1924); and Sholeh Quinn and Charles Melville, 'Safavid Historiography', in C. Melville, ed., *A History of Persian Literature:* Volume X, *Persian Historiography* (London, 2012), pp. 209–257, at pp. 232–240.

27 See V. Minorsky, 'The Poetry of Shah Ismaʿil I', *BSOAS*, 10 (1940–1942), pp. 1007–1053; and Halm, *Shiʿism*, pp. 73–78. For further details in this context, see Michel M. Mazzaoui, *The Origins of the Safawids: Šiʿism, Sufism, and the Gulat* (Wiesbaden, 1972), pp. 71–82.

28 See W. Madelung, 'Shiite Discussions on the Legality of the *Kharaj*', in R. Peters, ed., *Proceedings of the Ninth Congress of the Union Européenne*

des Arabisants et Islamisants (Leiden, 1981), pp. 193–202; reprinted in his *Religious Schools*, article XI; and his 'Al-Karaki', *EI2*, vol. 4, p. 610.

29 See H. Corbin, 'Confessions extatiques de Mir Damad', in *Mélanges Louis Massignon* (Damascus, 1956), vol. 1, pp. 331–378; his *Histoire de la philosophie Islamique* (Paris, 1986), pp. 462–475; English trans., *History of Islamic Philosophy*, tr. L. Sherrard (London, 1993), pp. 338–348; and Corbin's *En Islam Iranien*, vol. 4, pp. 9–201; and the following works by S. H. Nasr: 'The School of Ispahan', in M. M. Sharif, ed., *A History of Muslim Philosophy* (Wiesbaden, 1968), vol. 2, pp. 904–932; 'Spiritual Movements, Philosophy and Theology in the Safavid Period', in *Cambridge History of Iran*, vol. 6, pp. 656–697; and *Islamic Philosophy from its Origin to the Present* (Albany, NY, 2006), pp. 209–233. See also H. Dabashi, 'Mir Damad and the Founding of the "School of Isfahan"', in S. H. Nasr and O. Leaman, ed., *History of Islamic Philosophy* (London, 2001), vol. 1, pp. 597–634; and Sajjad H. Rizvi, 'Mysticism and Philosophy: Ibn 'Arabi and Mulla Sadra', in P. Adamson and R. C. Taylor, ed., *The Cambridge Companion to Arabic Philosophy* (Cambridge, 2005), pp. 224–246. For a number of works of the representatives of the 'School of Isfahan', including especially Mir Damad, Mir Findiriski and Mulla Sadra, see *Anthologie des philosophes Iraniens*, vol. 1, ed. S. Jalal al-Din Ashtiyani (Tehran and Paris, 1971).

30 Said A. Arjomand, 'The Office of *Mulla-bashi* in Shi'ite Iran', *Studia Islamica*, 57 (1983), pp. 135–146.

31 On the Akhbari-Usuli dispute, see G. Scarcia, 'Intorno alle controversie tra Aḫbari e Usuli presso gli Imamiti di Persia', *Rivista degli Studi Orientali*, 33 (1958), pp. 211–250; J. Cole, 'Shi'i Clerics in Iraq and Iran, 1722–1780: The Akhbari-Usuli Conflict Reconsidered', *Iranian Studies*, 18 (1985), pp. 3–34; E. Kohlberg, 'Aspects of Akhbari Thought in the Seventeenth and Eighteenth Centuries', in N. Levtzion and J. O. Voll, ed., *Eighteenth-Century Renewal and Reform in Islam* (Syracuse, NY, 1987), pp. 133–160; reprinted in his *Belief and Law*, article XVII; and his 'Astarabadi, Mohammad Amin', *EIR*, vol. 2, pp. 845–846. A. J. Newman, 'The Nature of the Akhbari/Usuli Dispute in Late Safavid Iran', *BSOAS*, 55 (1992), pp. 22–51, 250–261; R. Gleave, *Inevitable Doubt: Two Theories of Shi'i Jurisprudence* (Leiden, 2000); also his 'Compromise and Conciliation in the Akhbari-Usuli Dispute: Yusuf al-Bahrani's Assessment of 'Abd Allah al-Samahiji's *Munyat al-Mumarisin*', in Alí-de-Unzaga, ed., *Fortresses of the Intellect*, pp. 491–519; W. Madelung, 'Akhbariyya', *EI2*, vol. 12, Supplement, pp. 56–57; and E. Gheisari, 'Akhbariyya', *EIS*, vol. 3, pp. 407–412.

32 For the turbulent history of Persia during the 12th/18th century, see Laurence Lockhart, *The Fall of the Safavi Dynasty and the Afghan Occupation*

of Persia (Cambridge, 1958); also his *Nadir Shah: A Critical Study Based Mainly Upon Contemporary Sources* (London, 1938); Rudi Matthee, *Persia in Crisis: Safavid Decline and the Fall of Isfahan* (London, 2012); Michael Axworthy, *The Sword of Persia: Nader Shah from Tribal Warrior to Conquering Tyrant* (London, 2006); John R. Perry, *Karim Khan Zand: A History of Iran, 1747–1779* (Chicago, 1979); and the following three chapters: P. Avery, 'Nadir Shah and the Afsharid Legacy'; J. Perry, 'The Zand Dynasty', and Gavin R. G. Hambly, 'Agha Muhammad Khan and the Establishment of the Qajar Dynasty', in *The Cambridge History of Iran*: Volume 7, *From Nadir Shah to the Islamic Republic*, ed. P. Avery, G. Hambly and C. Melville (Cambridge, 1991), pp. 3–62, 63–103 and 104–143, respectively.

33 On the relations between the *ʿulama* and the state in modern Persia, see H. Algar, *Religion and State in Iran 1785–1906: The Role of the Ulama in the Qajar Period* (Berkeley, 1969); his 'The Oppositional Role of the Ulama in Twentieth-Century Iran', in Nikki R. Keddie, ed., *Scholars, Saints, and Sufis: Muslim Religious Institutions in the Middle East since 1500* (Berkeley, 1972), pp. 231–255; and his 'Religious Forces in Eighteenth- and Nineteenth-Century Iran', in *Cambridge History of Iran*, vol. 7, pp. 705–731.

34 See Juan R. Cole, 'Imami Jurisprudence and the Role of the Ulama: Mortaza Ansari on Emulating the Supreme Exemplar', in Nikki R. Keddie, ed., *Religion and Politics in Iran: Shiʿism from Quietism to Revolution* (New Haven, 1983), pp. 33–46; and S. Murata, 'Ansari, Mortaza', *EIR*, vol. 2, pp. 102–103. See also Ahmad Kazemi Moussavi, 'The Establishment of the Position of *Marjaʿiyyat-i Taqlid* in the Twelver-Shiʿi Community', *Iranian Studies*, 18 (1985), pp. 35–51; A. Amanat, 'In Between the Madrasa and the Marketplace: The Designation of Clerical Leadership in Modern Shiʿism', in S. Amir Arjomand, ed., *Authority and Political Culture in Shiʿism* (Albany, NY, 1988), pp. 98–132; reprinted in Amanat, *Apocalyptic Islam*, pp. 149–178; and J. Calmard, 'Mardjaʿ-i Taklid', *EI2*, vol. 6, pp. 548–556.

35 Nikki R. Keddie, *Religion and Rebellion in Iran: The Tobacco Protest of 1891–1892* (London, 1966), and Ann K. S. Lambton, 'The Tobacco Régie: Prelude to Revolution', *Studia Islamica*, 22 (1965), pp. 119–157, and 23 (1966), pp. 71–90; both articles reprinted in her *Qajar Persia: Eleven Studies* (London, 1987), pp. 223–276.

36 On these issues, see N. Calder, 'Zakat in Imami Shiʿi Jurisprudence, from the Tenth to the Sixteenth Century A.D.', *BSOAS*, 44 (1981), pp. 468–480; and his 'Khums in Imami Shiʿi Jurisprudence, from the Tenth to the Sixteenth Century A.D.', *BSOAS*, 45 (1982), pp. 39–47; both reprinted in his *Interpretation and Jurisprudence in Medieval Islam*, ed. J. Mojaddedi and A. Rippin (Aldershot, 2006), articles XVII and XVIII, respectively; A.

Sachedina, 'Al-Khums. The Fifth in the Imami Shi'i Legal System', *Journal of Near Eastern Studies*, 39 (1980), pp. 275–289; Ann K. S. Lambton, 'A Nineteenth Century View of *jihad*', *Studia Islamica*, 32 (1970), pp. 181–192; E. Kohlberg, 'The Development of the Imami Shi'i Doctrine of *jihad*', *Zeitschrift der Deutschen Morgenländischen Gesellschaft*, 126 (1976), pp. 64–86; reprinted in his *Belief and Law*, article XV; and Halm, *Shi'ism*, pp. 98–105.

37 On the Shaykhiyya, see Corbin, *En Islam Iranien*, vol. 4, pp. 205–300; also his *Spiritual Body and Celestial Earth: From Mazdean Iran to Shi'ite Iran*, tr. N. Pearson (Princeton, 1977), pp. 180–266, containing a number of Shaykhi texts in translation; M. Bayat, *Mysticism and Dissent: Socioreligious Thought in Qajar Iran* (Syracuse, NY, 1982), pp. 37–86; Juan R. Cole, 'Casting Away the Self: The Mysticism of Shaykh Ahmad al-Ahsa'i', in R. Brunner and W. Ende, ed., *The Twelver Shia in Modern Times: Religious Culture and Political History* (Leiden, 2001), pp. 25–37; M. A. Amir-Moezzi, 'An Absence Filled with Presences: Shaykhiyya Hermeneutics of the Occultation', in his *Spirituality of Shi'i Islam*, pp. 461–485; Z. Ebrahimi, 'Al-Ahsa'i', *EIS*, vol. 3, pp. 362–367; A. Eschraghi, 'Kazem Rasti', *EIR*, vol. 16, pp. 201–205; and D. M. MacEoin, 'Shaykhiyya', *EI2*, vol. 9, pp. 403–405.

38 See A. Amanat, *Resurrection and Renewal: The Making of the Babi Movement in Iran, 1844–1850* (Ithaca, NY, 1989); Bayat, *Mysticism and Dissent*, pp. 87–131; and D. M. MacEoin, 'Babism', *EIR*, vol. 3, pp. 309–317.

39 The classic treatment of the Persian Constitutional Revolution remains Edward G. Browne's *The Persian Revolution of 1905–1909* (Cambridge, 1910). See also Abdul-Hadi Hairi, *Shi'ism and Constitutionalism in Iran* (Leiden, 1977); Vanessa Martin, *Islam and Modernism: The Iranian Revolution of 1906* (London, 1989); Ann K. S. Lambton, 'The Persian 'Ulama and Constitutional Reform', in Fahd, ed., *Le Shi'isme Imamite*, pp. 245–269; reprinted in Lambton, *Qajar Persia*, pp. 277–300; M. Litvak, 'Madrasa and Learning in Nineteenth-Century Najaf and Karbala', in Brunner and Ende, ed., *Twelver Shia in Modern Times*, pp. 58–78; S. Amir Arjomand, 'The 1906–07 Iranian Constitution and the Constitutional Debate on Islam', *Journal of Persianate Studies*, 5 (2012), pp. 152–174; and H. Algar, ''Abdallah Behbahani', *EIR*, vol. 1, pp. 190–193.

40 See C. Ghani, *Iran and the Rise of Reza Shah: From Qajar Collapse to Pahlavi Rule* (London, 1998); and H. Katouzian, *State and Society in Iran: The Eclipse of the Qajars and the Emergence of the Pahlavis* (London, 2000).

41 For further highlights of the *'ulama*-state relations in Iran during the 20th century, see S. Akhavi, *Religion and Politics in Contemporary Iran: Clergy–State Relations in the Pahlavi Period* (Albany, NY, 1980); Michael M. J. Fischer, *Iran: From Religious Dispute to Revolution* (Cambridge, MA, 1980);

H. Algar, 'Religious Forces in Twentieth-Century Iran', in *Cambridge History of Iran*, vol. 7, pp. 732–764; and M. Faghfoory, 'Ulama-State Relations in Iran: 1921–1941', *IJMES*, 19 (1987), pp. 413–432.

42 A. Hairi, 'Burudjirdi', *EI2*, vol. 12, Supplement, pp. 157–158; and H. Algar, 'Borujerdi, Hosayn Tabataba'i', *EIR*, vol. 4, pp. 376–379.

43 Y. Richard, 'Ayatollah Kashani: Precursor of the Islamic Republic', in Nikki Keddie, ed., *Religion and Politics in Iran*, pp. 101–124; F. Kazemi, 'State and Society in the Ideology of the Devotees of Islam', *State, Culture and Society*, 1 (1985), pp. 118–135; and his 'Feda'ian-e Eslam', *EIR*, vol. 9, pp. 470–474. See also A. Rahnema, 'Kašani, Sayyed Abu'l-Qasem', *EIR*, vol. 15, pp. 640–647.

44 B. Moin, *Khomeini: Life of the Ayatollah* (London, 1999); and S. A. Arjomand, 'Khumayni, Sayyid Ruh Allah Musawi', *EI2*, vol. 12, Supplement, pp. 530–531.

45 Ayatullah R. Khumayni, *Hukumat-i Islami ya vilayat-i faqih* (Najaf, 1391/1971); English trans., 'Islamic Government', in R. Khumayni, *Islam and Revolution: Writings and Declarations of Imam Khomeini*, tr. H. Algar (Berkeley, 1981), pp. 25–166. For some studies on *vilayat-i faqih,* see N. Calder, 'Accommodation and Revolution in Imami Shi'i Jurisprudence: Khumayni and the Classical Tradition', *Middle Eastern Studies*, 18 (1982), pp 3–20; reprinted in his *Interpretation and Jurisprudence*, article XIX; H. Enayat, 'Iran: Khumayni's Concept of the "Guardianship of the Jurist"', in J. Piscatori, ed., *Islam and the Political Process* (Cambridge, 1982), pp. 160–180; G. Rose, '*Velayat-e Faqih* and the Recovery of Islamic Identity in the Thought of Ayatollah Khomeini', in Nikki Keddie, ed., *Religion and Politics in Iran*, pp. 166–188; Said A. Arjomand, 'Ideological Revolution in Shi'ism', in Arjomand, ed., *Authority and Political Culture in Shi'ism*, pp. 178–209; also his 'Authority in Shiism and Constitutional Development in the Islamic Republic of Iran', in Brunner and Ende, ed., *Twelver Shia in Modern Times*, pp. 301–332; A. Amanat, 'From *ijtihad* to *wilayat-i faqih*: The Evolving of the Shi'i Legal Authority into Political Power', in A. Amanat and F. Griffel, ed., *Shari'a: Islamic Law in the Contemporary Context* (Stanford, 2007), pp. 120–136; reprinted in his *Apocalyptic Islam*, pp. 179–196; and S. Akhavi, 'Contending Discourses in Shi'i Law on the Doctrine of *Wilayat al-Faqih*', *Iranian Studies*, 29 (1996), pp. 229–268.

46 The literature on the Islamic Revolution in Iran is rather extensive. In addition to the sources cited in the preceding notes, we can mention here only the following additional works in English: Said A. Arjomand, *The Turban for the Crown: The Islamic Revolution in Iran* (Oxford, 1988); E. Abrahamian, *Iran Between two Revolutions* (Princeton, 1982); Sh. Bakhash, *The Reign of the*

Ayatollahs: Iran and the Islamic Revolution (London, 1985); Nikki R. Keddie, *Roots of Revolution: An Interpretive History of Modern Iran* (New Haven, 1981); and Nikki R. Keddie and E. Hooglund, ed., *The Iranian Revolution and the Islamic Republic* (Ann Arbor, MI, 1982).

47 For further details on the Twelver communities of the Arab lands and their leadership, see Y. Nakash, *The Shiʿis of Iraq* (Princeton, 1994); his *Reaching for Power: The Shiʿa in the Modern Arab World* (Princeton, 2006); M. Litvak, *Shiʿi Scholars of Nineteenth-Century Iraq: The 'Ulama' of Najaf and Karbala'* (Cambridge, 1998); F. Ajami, *The Vanished Imam: Musa Al Sadr and the Shia of Lebanon* (London, 1986); H. Cobban, 'The Growth of Shiʿi Power in Lebanon and its Implications for the Future', and J. Goldberg, 'The Shiʿi Minority in Saudi Arabia', both in Juan R. I. Cole and Nikki R. Keddie, ed., *Shiʿism and Social Protest* (New Haven, 1986), pp. 137–155 and 230–246, respectively; Ahmad N. Hamzeh, *In the Path of Hizbullah* (Syracuse, NY, 2004); Chibli Mallat, *Shiʿi Thought from the South of Lebanon* (Oxford, 1988); R. K. Ramazani, 'Shiʿism in the Persian Gulf', in Cole and Keddie, ed., *Shiʿism*, pp. 30–54; S. Mervin, 'The Clerics of Jabal ʿAmil and the Reform of Religious Teaching in Najaf Since the Beginning of the 20th Century', and G. Steinberg, 'The Shiites in the Eastern Province of Saudi Arabia (al-Ahsa'), 1913–1953', both in Brunner and Ende, ed., *Twelver Shia in Modern Times*, pp. 79–86 and 236–254, respectively; Momen, *Introduction to Shiʿi Islam*, pp. 261–282; and Halm, *Shiʿism*, pp. 124–132.

48 For further details on Twelver Shiʿis of the Indian subcontinent, see John N. Hollister, *The Shiʿa of India* (London, 1953), especially pp. 101–194; Juan R. I. Cole, *Roots of North Indian Shiʿism in Iran and Iraq: Religion and State in Awadh, 1722–1859* (Berkeley, 1988); S. Athar A. Rizvi, *A Socio-Intellectual History of the Isnaʿ Ashari Shiʿis in India* (Canberra, 1986), 2 vols.; Nakash, *Shiʿis of Iraq*, pp. 211–229; D. Bredi, 'Profilo della communità Sciita del Pakistan', *Oriente Moderno*, 75 (1995), pp. 27–75; and A. Rieck, 'The Struggle for Equal Rights as a Minority: Shia Communal Organizations in Pakistan, 1948–1968', in Brunner and Ende, ed., *Twelver Shia in Modern Times*, pp. 268–283.

49 See F. Daftary, 'Shah Tahir and Nizari Ismaili Disguises', in T. Lawson, ed., *Reason and Inspiration in Islam: Theology, Philosophy and Mysticism in Muslim Thought, Essays in Honour of Hermann Landolt* (London, 2005), pp. 395–406.

50 H. Amiji, 'The Asian Communities', in James Kritzeck and William H. Lewis, ed., *Islam in Africa* (New York, 1969), pp. 165–177; Daftary, *The Ismaʿilis*, pp. 474ff., 485ff.; and A. Sachedina, 'Khojas', in *The Oxford Encyclopaedia of the Islamic World*, ed. John L. Esposito (Oxford, 2009), vol. 3, pp. 334–338.

Notes to Chapter 4: The Ismailis

1 This chapter is essentially based on the author's *The Isma'ilis: Their History and Doctrines* (2nd ed., Cambridge, 2007), where full references to the sources and studies are given, and *A Short History of the Ismailis: Traditions of a Muslim Community* (Edinburgh, 1998).

2 Al-Nawbakhti, *Firaq*, p. 55; al-Qummi, *al-Maqalat*, p. 78; and Sachedina, *Islamic Messianism*, pp. 153–154.

3 See al-Kulayni, *al-Usul*, vol. 1, pp. 307–311; al-Kashshi, *al-Rijal*, pp. 451, 462; al-Mufid, *al-Irshad*, pp. 436–440, 510; and Tabataba'i, *Shi'ite Islam*, pp. 75, 190, 205, 221.

4 Al-Nawbakhti, *Firaq*, pp. 57–58; al-Qummi, *al-Maqalat*, p. 80; al-Shahrastani, *al-Milal*, vol. 1, pp. 27, 167–168; tr. Kazi, pp. 23, 144; tr. D. Gimaret et al. as *Livre des religions et des sectes* (Louvain and Paris, 1986–1993), vol. 1, pp. 491–492. See also al-Razi, *Kitab al-zina*, part 3, pp. 287–289.

5 Al-Nawbakhti, *Firaq*, pp. 58, 62; and al-Qummi, *al-Maqalat*, pp. 80–81. See also al-Ash'ari, *Maqalat*, pp. 26–27; al-Baghdadi, *al-Farq*, pp. 46–47; tr. Seelye, pp. 65–66; al-Shahrastani, *al-Milal*, vol. 1, pp. 27–28, 168, 191ff.; tr. Kazi, pp. 23, 144, 163ff.; al-Mufid, *al-Irshad*, p. 431; and al-Tusi, *al-Rijal*, p. 310.

6 See al-Kashshi, *al-Rijal*, pp. 217–218, 244–245, 321, 325–326, 354–356, 390; Ja'far b. Mansur al-Yaman, *Sara'ir wa-asrar al-nutaqa'*, ed. M. Ghalib (Beirut, 1404/1984), pp. 256–257; and F. Daftary, 'Esma'il', *EIR*, vol. 8, pp. 625–626.

7 Idris 'Imad al-Din b. al-Hasan, *'Uyun al-akhbar wa-funun al-athar*, vol. 4, ed. M. al-Saghirji (Damascus, 2007), pp. 504–510; also his *Kitab zahr al-ma'ani*, ed. M. Ghalib (Beirut, 1411/1991), pp. 204–208; and F. Daftary, 'Muhammad b. Isma'il al-Maymun', *EI2*, vol. 12, Supplement, pp. 634–635.

8 Al-Nawbakhti, *Firaq*, p. 61; and al-Qummi, *al-Maqalat*, p. 83.

9 Al-Nu'man b. Muhammad, *Iftitah al-da'wa wa ibtida' al-dawla*, ed. W. al-Qadi (Beirut, 1970), pp. 32–47; ed. F. Dachraoui (Tunis, 1975), pp. 2–18; English trans., *Founding the Fatimid State: The Rise of an Early Islamic Empire*, tr. H. Haji (London, 2006), pp. 20–41.

10 Nizam al-Mulk, *Siyar al-muluk* (*Siyasat-nama*), ed. H. Darke (2nd ed., Tehran, 1347 Sh./1968), pp. 282–295, 297–305; English trans., *The Book of Government or Rules for Kings*, tr. H. Darke (2nd ed., London, 1978), pp. 208–218, 220–226. See also Samuel M. Stern, 'The Early Isma'ili Missionaries in North-West Persia and in Khurasan and Transoxania', *BSOAS*, 23 (1960), pp. 56–90; reprinted in his *Studies in Early Isma'ilism*, pp. 189–233.

11 See W. Madelung, 'Das Imamat in der frühen ismailitischen Lehre', *Der Islam*, 37 (1961), pp. 43–135, at pp. 59–65, 69ff.; reprinted in his *Studies*

in Medieval Shi'ism, article VII; and F. Daftary, 'A Major Schism in the Early Isma'ili Movement', *Studia Islamica*, 77 (1993), pp. 123–139; reprinted in his *Ismailis in Medieval Muslim Societies* (London, 2005), pp. 45–61.

12 On this letter, see Husayn F. al-Hamdani, ed. and tr., *On the Genealogy of Fatimid Caliphs* (Cairo, 1958); and A. Hamdani and F. de Blois, 'A Re-examination of al-Mahdi's Letter to the Yemenites on the Genealogy of the Fatimid Caliphs', *JRAS* (1983), pp. 173–207.

13 See H. Corbin, 'Sabian Temple and Ismailis', in his *Temple and Contemplation*, tr. Philip Sherrard (London, 1986), pp. 132–138, 170–182; and Ismail K. Poonawala, 'Isma'ili *ta'wil* of the Qur'an', in A. Rippin, ed., *Approaches to the History of the Interpretation of the Qur'an* (Oxford, 1988), pp. 199–222.

14 Ja'far b. Mansur al-Yaman, *Kitab al-'alim wa'l-ghulam*, ed. and tr. James W. Morris as *The Master and the Disciple: An Early Islamic Spiritual Dialogue* (London, 2001), text pp. 1–95, translation pp. 63–171. See also H. Corbin, 'L'initiation Ismaélienne ou l'ésotérisme et le Verbe', *Eranos Jahrbuch*, 39 (1970), pp. 41–142, containing also a summary French translation of this text; reprinted in H. Corbin, *L'homme et son ange. Initiation et chevalerie spirituelle* (Paris, 1983), pp. 81–205.

15 See H. Corbin, 'Cyclical Time in Mazdaism and Ismailism', in his *Cyclical Time and Ismaili Gnosis*, tr. R. Manheim and J. W. Morris (London, 1983), pp. 30–58; Paul E. Walker, 'Eternal Cosmos and the Womb of History: Time in Early Ismaili Thought', *IJMES*, 9 (1978), pp. 355–366; reprinted in his *Fatimid History and Ismaili Doctrine* (Aldershot, 2008), article XII; F. Daftary, 'Cyclical Time and Sacred History in Medieval Ismaili Thought', in K. D'hulster and J. Van Steenbergen, ed., *Continuity and Change in the Realms of Islam: Studies in Honour of Professor Urbain Vermeulen* (Leuven, 2008), pp. 151–158; and his 'Dawr', *EIR*, vol. 7, pp. 151–153.

16 This early Ismaili cosmology has been reconstructed in modern times mainly on the basis of fragmentary evidence contained in later works, notably a treatise by Abu 'Isa al-Murshid, a *da'i* of the 4th/10th century. See S. M. Stern, 'The Earliest Cosmological Doctrine of Isma'ilism', in his *Studies*, pp. 3–29; H. Halm, *Kosmologie und Heilslehre der frühen Isma'iliya: Eine Studie zur islamischen Gnosis* (Wiesbaden, 1978), pp. 18–127; and his 'The Cosmology of the Pre-Fatimid Isma'iliyya', in F. Daftary, ed., *Mediaeval Isma'ili History and Thought* (Cambridge, 1996), pp. 75–83.

17 The Fatimid period is the best documented phase in Ismaili history; see Paul E. Walker, *Exploring an Islamic Empire: Fatimid History and its Sources* (London, 2002). Taqi al-Din Ahmad b. 'Ali al-Maqrizi (d. 845/1442) was the only Sunni historian of medieval times to devote an independent work to the Fatimids; see his *Itti'az al-hunafa' bi-akhbar al-a'imma al-Fatimiyyin*

al-khulafa', ed. J. al-Shayyal and M. H. M. Ahmad (Cairo, 1387–1393/1967–1973), 3 vols.; ed. Ayman F. Sayyid (Damascus, 2010), 4 vols. For general modern surveys of Ismaili history and thought during this phase, see H. Halm, *The Empire of the Mahdi: The Rise of the Fatimids*, tr. M. Bonner (Leiden, 1996); his *Die Kalifen von Kairo: Die Fatimiden in Ägypten 973–1074* (Munich, 2003); F. Dachraoui, *Le califat Fatimide au Maghreb (296–365 H./909–975 Jc.)* (Tunis, 1981); M. Brett, *The Rise of the Fatimids: The World of the Mediterranean and the Middle East in the Fourth Century of the Hijra, Tenth Century CE* (Leiden, 2001); and Ayman F. Sayyid, *al-Dawla al-Fatimiyya fi Misr: tafsir jadid* (2nd ed., Cairo, 2000).

18 S. M. Stern, 'Cairo as the Centre of the Isma'ili Movement', in *Colloque international sur l'histoire du Caire* (Cairo, 1972), pp. 437–450; reprinted in his *Studies*, pp. 234–256; A. Hamdani, 'Evolution of the Organisational Structure of the Fatimi Da'wah: The Yemeni and Persian Contribution', *Arabian Studies*, 3 (1976), pp. 85–114; and F. Daftary, 'The Ismaili *Da'wa* outside the Fatimid *Dawla*', in M. Barrucand, ed., *L'Égypte Fatimide, son art et son histoire* (Paris, 1999), pp. 29–43; reprinted in his *Ismailis in Medieval Muslim Societies*, pp. 62–88.

19 Taqi al-Din al-Maqrizi, *Kitab al-mawa'iz wa'l-i'tibar fi dhikr al-khitat wa'l-athar* (Bulaq, 1270/1853–1854), vol. 1, pp. 390–391, 458–460, and vol. 2, pp. 341–342; H. Halm, 'The Isma'ili Oath of Allegiance (*'ahd*) and the "Sessions of Wisdom" (*majalis al-hikma*) in Fatimid Times', in Daftary, ed., *Mediaeval Isma'ili History and Thought*, pp. 91–115; also his *The Fatimids and their Traditions of Learning* (London, 1997), pp. 23–29, 41–45, 71–78; and Paul E. Walker, 'Fatimid Institutions of Learning', *Journal of the American Research Center in Egypt*, 34 (1997), pp. 179–200; reprinted in his *Fatimid History*, article I.

20 For a rare Ismaili text on the attributes and methods of operation of an ideal *da'i*, see Ahmad b. Ibrahim al-Nisaburi, *al-Risala al-mujaza al-kafiya fi adab al-du'at*, ed. and tr. Verena Klemm and Paul E. Walker as *A Code of Conduct: A Treatise on the Etiquette of the Fatimid Ismaili Mission* (London, 2011).

21 W. Ivanow, *Ismaili Literature: A Bibliographical Survey* (Tehran, 1963), pp. 21–50; and Ismail K. Poonawala, *Biobibliography of Isma'ili Literature* (Malibu, CA, 1977), pp. 31–132.

22 Abu Ya'qub al-Sijistani, *Kitab al-yanabi'*, ed. and tr. H. Corbin, in his *Trilogie Ismaélienne* (Tehran and Paris, 1961), text pp. 1–97, partial French translation, pp. 5–127; English trans., *The Book of Wellsprings*, tr. Paul E. Walker in his *The Wellsprings of Wisdom* (Salt Lake City, 1994), pp. 37–111. See also Paul E. Walker, *Early Philosophical Shiism: The Ismaili Neoplatonism*

of Abu Ya'qub al-Sijistani (Cambridge, 1993), pp. 67–142; his *Abu Ya'qub al-Sijistani: Intellectual Missionary* (London, 1996), pp. 26–103; W. Madelung, 'Aspects of Isma'ili Theology: The Prophetic Chain and the God Beyond Being', in S. H. Nasr, ed., *Isma'ili Contributions to Islamic Culture* (Tehran, 1977), pp. 51–65; reprinted in his *Religious Schools*, article XIV; D. de Smet, *La philosophie Ismaélienne: un ésotérisme chiite entre néoplatonisme et gnose* (Paris, 2012), pp. 15–173; and Ismail K. Poonawala, 'An Early Doctrinal Controversy in the Iranian School of Isma'ili Thought and its Implications', *Journal of Persianate Studies*, 5 (2012), pp. 17–34.

23 All of Nasir-i Khusraw's works are relevant for studying his metaphysical system; see, for instance, his *Kitab jami' al-hikmatayn*, ed. H. Corbin and M. Mu'in (Tehran and Paris, 1953); English trans., *Between Reason and Revelation: Twin Wisdoms Reconciled*, tr. E. Ormsby (London, 2012). For Nasir's other published works, see Daftary, *Ismaili Literature*, pp. 134–140.

24 Hamid al-Din al-Kirmani, *Rahat al-'aql*, ed. M. Kamil Husayn and M. M. Hilmi (Cairo, 1953). For studies of al-Kirmani's metaphysical system, see Daniel de Smet, *La quiétude de l'intellect: Néoplatonisme et gnose Ismaélienne dans l'oeuvre de Hamid ad-Din al-Kirmani (Xe/XIe s.)* (Leuven, 1995); and Paul E. Walker, *Hamid al-Din al-Kirmani: Ismaili Thought in the Age of al-Hakim* (London, 1999).

25 W. Madelung, 'The Sources of Isma'ili Law', *Journal of Near Eastern Studies*, 35 (1976), pp. 29–40; reprinted in his *Religious Schools*, article XVIII; I. K. Poonawala, 'Al-Qadi al-Nu'man and Isma'ili Jurisprudence', in Daftary, ed., *Mediaeval Isma'ili History and Thought*, pp. 117–143; and F. Daftary, 'Al-Qadi al-Nu'man, Isma'ili Law and Imami Shi'ism', in M. A. Amir-Moezzi et al., ed., *Le Shi'isme Imamite quarante ans après. Hommage à Etan Kohlberg* (Turnhout, 2009), pp. 179–186. See also Sumaiya A. Hamdani, *Between Revolution and State: The Path to Fatimid Statehood, Qadi al-Nu'man and the Construction of Fatimid Legitimacy* (London, 2006).

26 Much valuable material on Druze history, religion and literature may still be found in A. I. Silvestre de Sacy's classic study entitled *Exposé de la religion des Druzes* (Paris, 1838), 2 vols. See also David R. W. Bryer, 'The Origins of the Druze Religion', *Der Islam*, 52 (1975), pp. 47–84, 239–262, and 53 (1976), pp. 5–27; Nejla M. Abu-Izzeddin, *The Druzes: A New Study of their History, Faith and Society* (Leiden, 1984); and Kais M. Firro, *A History of the Druzes* (Leiden, 1992).

27 In this context, see especially Hamid al-Din al-Kirmani's *al-Masabih fi ithbat al-imama*, ed. and tr. Paul E. Walker as *Master of the Age: An Islamic Treatise on the Necessity of the Imamate* (London, 2007). See also I.

K. Poonawala, 'Hamid al-Din al-Kirmani and the Proto-Druze', *Journal of Druze Studies*, 1 (2000), pp. 71–94.

28 For a critical edition, French translation and analysis of the first two volumes, see Daniel de Smet, *Les Épîtres sacrées des Druzes: Rasa'il al-Hikma* (Leuven, 2007), 2 vols.

29 See W. Madelung, 'The Fatimids and the Qarmatis of Bahrayn', in Daftary, ed., *Mediaeval Isma'ili History*, pp. 21–73; and F. Daftary, 'Carmatians', *EIR*, vol. 4, pp. 823–832.

30 See H. Corbin, 'Nasir-i Khusrau and Iranian Isma'ilism', in *The Cambridge History of Iran*: Volume 4, *The Period from the Arab Invasion to the Saljuqs*, ed. R. N. Frye (Cambridge, 1975), pp. 520–542; and Alice C. Hunsberger, *Nasir Khusraw, The Ruby of Badakhshan: A Portrait of the Persian Poet, Traveller and Philosopher* (London, 2000).

31 See S. M. Stern, 'The Succession to the Fatimid Imam al-Amir, the Claims of the Later Fatimids to the Imamate, and the Rise of Tayyibi Ismailism', *Oriens*, 4 (1951), pp. 193–255; reprinted in his *History and Culture in the Medieval Muslim World* (London, 1984), article XI.

32 Hatim b. Ibrahim al-Hamidi, *Tuhfat al-qulub wa furjat al-makrub*, ed. A. Hamdani (Beirut, 2012). See also A. Hamdani, 'The Da'i Hatim Ibn Ibrahim al-Hamidi (d. 596 H./1199 A.D.) and his Book *Tuhfat al-Qulub*', *Oriens*, 23–24 (1970–1971), pp. 258–300; and F. Daftary, 'Sayyida Hurra: The Isma'ili Sulayhid Queen of Yemen', in Gavin R. G. Hambly, ed., *Women in the Medieval Islamic World* (New York, 1998), pp. 117–130; reprinted in his *Ismailis in Medieval Muslim Societies*, pp. 89–103.

33 See Poonawala, *Biobibliography*, pp. 133–177.

34 See Hollister, *The Shi'a of India*, pp. 265–305; Sh. T. Lokhandwalla, 'The Bohras, a Muslim Community of Gujarat', *Studia Islamica*, 3 (1955), pp. 117–135; Asghar Ali Engineer, *The Bohras* (New Delhi, 1980); J. Blank, *Mullas on the Mainframe: Islam and Modernity among the Daudi Bohras* (Chicago, 2001); Saifiyah Qutbuddin, 'History of the Da'udi Bohra Tayyibis in Modern Times: The *Da'i*s, the *Da'wa* and the Community'; and Tahera Qutbuddin, 'The Da'udi Bohra Tayyibis: Ideology, Literature, Learning and Social Practice', both in F. Daftary, ed., *A Modern History of the Ismailis* (London, 2011), pp. 297–330 and 331–354, respectively. See also T. Qutbuddin, 'Bohras', *EI3*, 2013–2, pp. 56–66

35 See Daftary, *The Isma'ilis*, pp. 295–300; Tahera Qutbuddin, 'A Brief Note on Other Tayyibi Communities: Sulaymanis and 'Alawis', in Daftary, ed., *A Modern History of the Ismailis*, pp. 355–358; I. K. Poonawala, 'Sulaymanis', *EI2*, vol. 9, p. 829; and W. Madelung, 'Makramids', *EI2*, vol. 6, pp.

191–192. For lists of Da'udi, Sulaymani and 'Alawi *da'is*, see Daftary, *The Isma'ilis*, pp. 510–513; and his *Ismaili Literature*, pp. 447–450.

36 Ivanow, *Ismaili Literature*, pp. 127–136; and Poonawala, *Biobibliography*, pp. 251–263.

37 F. Daftary, 'Persian Historiography of the Early Nizari Isma'ilis', *Iran, Journal of the British Institute of Persian Studies*, 30 (1992), pp. 91–97; reprinted in his *Ismailis in Medieval Muslim Societies*, pp. 107–123.

38 'Ata-Malik b. Muhammad Juwayni, *Ta'rikh-i jahan-gusha*, ed. M. Qazvini (Leiden and London, 1912–1937), vol. 3, pp. 186–278; English trans., *The History of the World-Conqueror*, tr. John A. Boyle (Manchester, 1958), vol. 2, pp. 666–725; Rashid al-Din Fadl Allah, *Jami' al-tawarikh: qismat-i Isma'iliyan*, ed. M. T. Danishpazhuh and M. Mudarrisi Zanjani (Tehran, 1338 Sh./1959), pp. 97–195; ed. M. Rawshan (Tehran, 1387 Sh./2008), pp. 97–191; and Abu'l-Qasim 'Abd Allah Kashani, *Zubdat al-tawarikh: bakhsh-i Fatimiyan va Nizariyan*, ed. M. T. Danishpazhuh (2nd ed., Tehran, 1366 Sh./1987), pp. 133–237.

39 For modern surveys of Nizari history during this period, see Marshall G. S. Hodgson, *The Order of Assassins: The Struggle of the Early Nizari Isma'ilis against the Islamic World* (The Hague, 1955; reprinted, New York, 1980; reprinted, Philadelphia, 2005); his 'The Isma'ili State', in *The Cambridge History of Iran*: Volume 5, *The Saljuq and Mongol Periods*, ed. J. A. Boyle (Cambridge, 1968), pp. 422–482; B. Lewis, *The Assassins: A Radical Sect in Islam* (London, 1967); and Daftary, *The Isma'ilis*, pp. 301–402, 614–642.

40 F. Daftary, 'Hasan-i Sabbah and the Origins of the Nizari Isma'ili Movement', in Daftary, ed. *Mediaeval Isma'ili History*, pp. 181–204; reprinted in his *Ismailis in Medieval Muslim Societies*, pp. 124–148.

41 For the best descriptions of the medieval Nizari strongholds, see P. Willey, *Eagle's Nest: Ismaili Castles in Iran and Syria* (London, 2005).

42 Carole Hillenbrand, 'The Power Struggle between the Saljuqs and the Isma'ilis of Alamut, 487–518/1094–1124: The Saljuq Perspective', in Daftary, ed., *Mediaeval Isma'ili History*, pp. 205–220.

43 Al-Shahrastani, *al-Milal*, vol. 1, pp. 195–198; tr. Kazi, pp. 167–170; tr. Gimaret et al., vol. 1, pp. 560–565.

44 See 'Ali b. Muhammad Ibn al-Walid, *Damigh al-batil wa-hatf al-munadil*, ed. M. Ghalib (Beirut, 1403/1982), 2 vols. See also H. Corbin, 'The Isma'ili Response to the Polemic of Ghazali', in Nasr, ed., *Isma'ili Contributions*, pp. 67–98.

45 See especially Nasir al-Din al-Tusi, *Rawda-yi taslim*, ed. and tr. S. Jalal Badakhchani as *Paradise of Submission: A Medieval Treatise on Ismaili Thought* (London, 2005); French trans., *La convocation d'Alamût. Somme de*

philosophie Ismaélienne, tr. Ch. Jambet (Lagrasse, 1996); and al-Tusi's *Shi'i Interpretations of Islam: Three Treatises on Theology and Eschatology*, ed. and tr. S. J. Badakhchani (London, 2010).

46 F. Daftary, 'Sinan and the Nizari Ismailis of Syria', in Daniela Bredi et al., ed., *Scritti in onore di Biancamaria Scarcia Amoretti* (Rome, 2008), pp. 489–500; and his 'Rashid al-Din Sinan', *EI2*, vol. 8, pp. 442–443.

47 Sa'd al-Din Nizari Quhistani, *Safar-nama*, ed. Chingiz G. A. Bayburdi (Tehran, 1391 Sh./2012); and Nadia Eboo Jamal, *Surviving the Mongols: Nizari Quhistani and the Continuity of Ismaili Tradition in Persia* (London, 2002), especially pp. 108–146. See also L. Lewisohn, 'Sufism and Isma'ili Doctrine in the Persian Poetry of Nizari Quhistani (645–721/1247–1321)', *Iran, Journal of the British Institute of Persian Studies*, 41 (2003), pp. 229–251; and Shafique N. Virani, *The Ismailis in the Middle Ages* (Oxford, 2007), pp. 60–70.

48 F. Daftary, 'Ismaili–Sufi Relations in Early Post-Alamut and Safavid Persia', in L. Lewisohn and D. Morgan, ed., *The Heritage of Sufism*: Volume III, *Late Classical Persianate Sufism (1501–1750)* (Oxford, 1999), pp. 275–289; reprinted in his *Ismailis in Medieval Muslim Societies*, pp. 183–203.

49 W. Ivanow, 'Tombs of Some Persian Ismaili Imams', *Journal of the Bombay Branch of the Royal Asiatic Society*, New Series, 14 (1938), pp. 49–62.

50 Mustansir bi'llah II, *Pandiyat-i jawanmardi*, ed. and tr. W. Ivanow (Leiden, 1953). See also Virani, *Ismailis in the Middle Ages*, pp. 122–126, 140ff., 159–164, 180–182.

51 Muhammad Qasim Hindu Shah Astarabadi, better known as Firishta, *Ta'rikh-i Firishta*, ed. J. Briggs (Bombay, 1832), especially vol. 2, pp. 213–231; F. Daftary, 'Shah Tahir and Nizari Ismaili Disguises', in Lawson, ed., *Reason and Inspiration in Islam*, pp. 395–406; and I. K. Poonawala, 'Shah Tahir', *EI2*, vol. 9, pp. 200–201.

52 On the Satpanthi tradition of the Nizari Khojas and their *ginans*, see A. Nanji, *The Nizari Isma'ili Tradition in the Indo-Pakistan Subcontinent* (Delmar, NY, 1978); Ali Asani's studies collected in his *Ecstasy and Enlightenment: The Ismaili Devotional Literature of South Asia* (London, 2002); his 'Creating Tradition through Devotional Songs and Communal Script: The Khojah Isma'ilis of South Asia', in R. Eaton, ed., *India's Islamic Traditions 711–1750, Themes in Indian History* (New Delhi, 2003), pp. 285–310; and his 'From Satpanthi to Ismaili Muslim: The Articulation of Ismaili Khoja Identity in South Asia', in Daftary, ed., *A Modern History of the Ismailis*, pp. 95–128.

53 See C. Shackle and Z. Moir, *Ismaili Hymns from South Asia: An Introduction to the Ginans* (London, 1992); and Tazim R. Kassam, *Songs of Wisdom and Circles of Dance: Hymns of the Satpanth Isma'ili Muslim Saint,*

Pir Shams (Albany, NY, 1995), both containing selections of *ginans* in English translation.

54 For a rare anthropological study of this complex phenomenon, see Dominique-Sila Khan, *Conversions and Shifting Identities: Ramdev Pir and the Ismailis of Rajasthan* (New Delhi, 1997); her *Crossing the Threshold: Understanding Religious Identities in South Asia* (London, 2004) is also relevant in this context.

55 On the renewed association between this Sufi order and the Nizari imams in Persia, see Maʿsum ʿAli Shah, *Taraʾiq al-haqaʾiq*, ed. M. J. Mahjub (Tehran, 1339–1345 Sh./1960–1966), vol. 3, pp. 170–192; N. Pourjavady and P. L. Wilson, *Kings of Love: The Poetry and History of the Niʿmatullahi Sufi Order* (Tehran, 1978), pp. 93–135; and L. Lewisohn, 'An Introduction to the History of Modern Persian Sufism, Part I: The Niʿmatullahi Order: Persecution, Revival and Schism', *BSOAS*, 61 (1998), pp. 439–453.

56 See H. Algar 'The Revolt of Agha Khan Mahallati and the Transference of the Ismaʿili Imamate to India', *Studia Islamica*, 29 (1969), pp. 55–81; and his 'Mahallati, Agha Khan', *EI2*, vol. 5, pp. 1221–1222. See also Daftary, *The Ismaʿilis*, pp. 463–476, 659–663, where full references are cited.

57 Asaf A. A. Fyzee, *Cases in the Muhammadan Law of India and Pakistan* (Oxford, 1965), pp. 504–549; A. Shodan, *A Question of Community: Religious Groups and Colonial Law* (Calcutta, 1999), pp. 82–116; and T. Purohit, *The Aga Khan Case: Religion and Identity in Colonial India* (Cambridge, MA, 2012), reflecting a biased perspective. See also James C. Masselos, 'The Khojas of Bombay: The Defining of Formal Membership Criteria during the Nineteenth Century', in I. Ahmad, ed., *Caste and Social Stratification among Muslims in India* (New Delhi, 1973), pp. 1–20.

58 See M. Ruthven, 'Aga Khan III and the Ismaʿili Renaissance', in Peter B. Clarke, ed., *New Trends and Developments in the World of Islam* (London, 1998), pp. 371–395; M. Boivin, 'The Reform of Islam in Ismaili Shiʿism from 1885 to 1957', in Françoise 'Nalini' Delvoye, ed., *Confluences of Cultures: French Contributions to Indo-Persian Studies* (New Delhi, 1994), pp. 197–216; M. Boivin, *La rénovation du Shîʿisme Ismaélien en Inde et au Pakistan. D'après les ecrits et les discours de Sultan Muhammad Shah Aga Khan (1902–1954)* (London, 2003); Shiraz Thobani, 'Communities of Tradition and the Modernizing of Education in South Asia: The Contribution of Aga Khan III', and Zayn R. Kassam, 'The Gender Policies of Aga Khan III and Aga Khan IV', both in Daftary, ed., *A Modern History of the Ismailis*, pp. 161–185 and 247–264, respectively; and Daftary, *The Ismaʿilis*, pp. 480–496.

59 Aga Khan III, *The Memoirs of Aga Khan: World Enough and Time* (London, 1954).

60 M. Ruthven, 'The Aga Khan Development Network and Institutions', in Daftary, ed., *A Modern History of the Ismailis*, pp. 189–220; W. Frischauer, *The Aga Khans* (London, 1970), pp. 206–272; and Daftary, *The Ismaʿilis*, pp. 496–504.

61 See F. Daftary and Z. Hirji, *The Ismailis: An Illustrated History* (London, 2008), pp. 176–245.

Notes to Chapter 5: The Zaydis

1 For the earliest Western survey of Zaydi literature, see R. Strothmann, 'Die Literatur der Zaiditen', *Der Islam*, 1 (1910), pp. 354–368, and 2 (1911), pp. 49–78. For the most recent account of Zaydi studies, including recovered manuscript sources, see S. Schmidtke, 'The History of Zaydi Studies: An Introduction', *Arabica*, 59 (2012), pp. 185–199. See also H. Ansari and S. Schmidtke, 'The Literary-Religious Tradition among 7th/13th Century Yemeni Zaydis: The Formation of the Imam al-Mahdi li-Din Allah Ahmad b. al-Husayn b. al-Qasim (d. 656/1258)', *Journal of Islamic Manuscripts*, 2 (2011), pp. 165–222.

2 This chapter draws extensively on the work of Professor W. Madelung, especially his *Der Imam al-Qasim ibn Ibrahim und die Glaubenslehre der Zaiditen* (Berlin, 1965), the only major study of early Zaydi history and thought, and amongst his numerous other studies and entries in *EI2* and *EIR*. See F. Daftary, 'Bibliography of the Works of Wilferd Madelung', in Daftary and Meri, ed., *Culture and Memory*, pp. 5–40.

3 On Zayd's revolt, see al-Tabari, *Ta'rikh*, II, pp. 1667–1688, 1698–1716; English trans., *The History of al-Tabari:* Volume XXVI, *The Waning of the Umayyad Caliphate*, tr. Carole Hillenbrand (Albany, NY, 1989), pp. 3–23, 36–54; Abu'l-Faraj al-Isfahani, *Maqatil al-Talibiyyin*, ed. A. Saqr (Cairo, 1368/1949), pp. 133–151; C. van Arendonk, *Les débuts de l'Imamat Zaidite au Yémen*, tr. J. Ryckmans (Leiden, 1960), pp. 28–33, 307–312; Madelung, *Der Imam al-Qasim*, pp. 52–61; and his 'Zayd b. ʿAli b. al-Husayn', *EI2*, vol. 11, pp. 473–474.

4 Al-Tabari, *Ta'rikh*, II, pp. 1710, 1770–1774; English trans., *History of al-Tabari:* Volume XXVI, pp. 48, 120–125; Abu'l-Faraj al-Isfahani, *Maqatil*, pp. 142–143, 152–158; Wellhausen, *Arab Kingdom*, pp. 338–339, 359, 499–500; his *Religio-Political Factions*, pp. 163–164; Arendonk, *Les débuts*, pp. 33–35; his 'Yahya b. Zaid al-Husaini', *EI*, vol. 4, pp. 1151–1152; and W. Madelung, 'Yahya b. Zayd', *EI2*, vol. 11, pp. 249–250.

5 For the heresiographical tradition on early Zaydi Shiʿism and its Batriyya and Jarudiyya currents, see al-Nawbakhti, *Firaq al-Shiʿa*, pp. 18–19, 48–52;

al-Qummi, *al-Maqalat*, pp. 17–19, 70–74; al-Ashʿari, *Maqalat al-Islamiyyin*, pp. 65–75; al-Baghdadi, *al-Farq bayn al-firaq*, pp. 16, 23–26; tr. Seelye, pp. 35, 43–47; al-Shahrastani, *al-Milal*, vol. 1, pp. 154–162; tr. Kazi, pp. 132–138; tr. Gimaret, vol. 1, pp. 457–475. For an early Ismaili (Qarmati) view, see Abu Tammam Yusuf b. Muhammad al-Nisaburi, *An Ismaili Heresiography: The 'Bab al-shaytan' from Abu Tammam's Kitab al-shajara*, ed. and tr. W. Madelung and P. E. Walker (Leiden, 1998), pp. 88–94. See also Madelung, *Der Imam al-Qasim*, pp. 44–51; and his 'Batriyya', *EI2*, vol. 12, Supplement, pp. 129–130. See also E. Kohlberg, 'Some Zaydi Views on the Companions of the Prophet', *BSOAS*, 39 (1976), pp. 91–98.

6 For an alternative historical narrative of early Zaydism, holding that initially the Zaydiyya were comprised almost exclusively of the Batriyya and that only later the Jarudiyya emerged as the dominant current, and emphasising that Zaydism gradually evolved from one orientation to another in the course of the 2nd/8th century, see Haider, *Origins of the Shiʿa*, especially pp. 3–23, 189–214.

7 Al-Nawbakhti, *Firaq*, pp. 29–32, 35; al-Qummi, *al-Maqalat*, pp. 26–27, 39–40, 56; al-Baghdadi, *al-Farq*, p. 234; tr. Halkin, p. 56; al-Tabari, *Ta'rikh*, II, pp. 1879–1887, 1947–1948, 1976–1981; English trans., *The History of al-Tabari:* Volume XXVI, tr. Hillenbrand, pp. 254–263; and *The History of al-Tabari:* Volume XXVII, *The ʿAbbasid Revolution*, tr. J. A. Williams (Albany, NY, 1985), pp. 59, 85–90; Wellhausen, *Arab Kingdom*, pp. 383–386, 393–395; his *Religio-Political Factions*, pp. 164–165; C. Edmund Bosworth, *Sistan under the Arabs, from the Islamic Conquest to the Rise of the Saffarids (30–250/651–864)* (Rome, 1968), pp. 76–77; William W. Tucker, ' ʿAbd Allah ibn Muʿawiya and the Janahiyya: Rebels and Ideologues of the Late Umayyad Period', *Studia Islamica*, 51 (1980), pp. 39–56; reprinted in his *Mahdis and Millenarians*, pp. 88–108; and D. M. Dunlop, 'ʿAbdallah b. Moʿavia', *EIR*, vol. 1, pp. 183–184.

8 See the following works of W. Madelung: *Der Imam al-Qasim*, pp. 138–140; 'The Origins of the Yemenite *Hijra*', in A. Jones, ed., *Arabicus Felix: Luminosus Britannicus. Essays in Honour of A. F. L. Beeston on his Eightieth Birthday* (Reading, 1991), pp. 25–44; reprinted in his *Religious and Ethnic Movements*, article XIII, and his 'A Mutarrifi Manuscript', in *Proceedings of the VIth Congress of Arabic and Islamic Studies* (Stockholm and Leiden, 1975), pp. 75–83; reprinted in his *Religious Schools*, article XIX.

9 See Madelung, *Der Imam al-Qasim*, pp. 80ff.

10 Al-Tabari, *Ta'rikh*, II, pp. 552–562, 612–624, 669–672; English trans., *The History of al-Tabari:* Volume XXX, *The ʿAbbasid Caliphate in Equilibrium*, tr. C. E. Bosworth (Albany, NY, 1989), pp. 16–30, 113–131, 205–208; Abu'l-Faraj al-Isfahani, *Maqatil*, pp. 463–486; *Arabic Texts Concerning the*

History of the Zaydi Imams of Tabaristan, Daylaman and Gilan, ed. W. Madelung (Beirut, 1987), pp. 55–70, 79–84, 173–208, containing extracts from a number of Zaydi works on Imam Yahya b. ʿAbd Allah; Arendonk, *Les débuts*, pp. 65–70, 317–319; and W. Madelung, 'Yahya b. ʿAbd Allah', *EI2*, vol. 11, pp. 242–243.

11 In particular, mention should be made of Ibn Isfandiyar, *Taʾrikh-i Tabaristan*, ed. ʿAbbas Iqbal (Tehran, 1320 Sh./1941); Zahir al-Din Marʿashi, *Taʾrikh-i Tabaristan va Ruyan va Mazandaran*, ed. M. H. Tasbihi (Tehran, 1345 Sh./1966); his *Taʾrikh-i Gilan va Daylamistan*, ed. H. L. Rabino (Rasht, 1330/1912); ed. M Sutuda (Tehran, 1347 Sh./1968); Awliyaʾ Allah Amuli, *Taʾrikh-i Ruyan*, ed. M. Sutuda (Tehran, 1348 Sh./1969); and the Zaydi works of the Caspian region collected in *Arabic Texts Concerning the History of the Zaydi Imams*, ed. Madelung. See also Hyacinth L. Rabino di Borgomale, 'Les dynasties Alaouides du Mazandéran', *Journal Asiatique*, 210 (1927), pp. 253–277; the following works by W. Madelung: 'The Alid Rulers of Tabaristan, Dayalaman and Gilan', in *Atti del III Congresso di Studi Arabi e Islamici, Ravello, 1966* (Naples, 1967), pp. 483–492; 'Abu Ishaq al-Sabi on the Alids of Tabaristan and Gilan', *Journal of Near Eastern Studies*, 26 (1967), pp. 17–57; reprinted in his *Religious and Ethnic Movements*, article VII; his 'The Minor Dynasties of Northern Iran', in *The Cambridge History of Iran:* Volume 4, *The Period from the Arab Invasion to the Saljuqs*, ed. R. N. Frye (Cambridge, 1975), pp. 198–249, at pp. 206–212, 219–222; and his "Alids', in *EIR*, vol. 1, pp. 881–886. See also A. Hakimiyan, *ʿAlawiyan-i Tabaristan* (Tehran, 1348 Sh./1969), especially pp. 74–118; and M. S. Khan, 'The Early History of Zaydi Shiʿism in Daylaman and Gilan', *Zeitschrift der Deutschen Morgenländischen Gesellschaft*, 125 (1975), pp. 301–314; reprinted in Kohlberg, ed., *Shiʿism*, pp. 221–234.

12 The chief study on Imam al-Qasim's life and teachings is Madelung's *Der Imam al-Qasim*, pp. 86–152. See also Madelung's following studies: 'Imam al-Qasim ibn Ibrahim and Muʿtazilism', in *On Both Sides of al-Mandab: Ethiopian, South-Arabic and Islamic Studies Presented to Oscar Löfgren on his Ninetieth Birthday 13 May 1988 by Colleagues and Friends* (Stockholm, 1989), pp. 39–48; 'Al-Qasim ibn Ibrahim and Christian Theology', *Aram*, 3 (1991), pp. 35–44; both reprinted in Madelung's *Studies in Medieval Shiʿism*, articles IV and V, respectively; and his 'Al-Rassi, al-Kasim b. Ibrahim', *EI2*, vol. 8, pp. 453–454. See also al-Qasim b. Ibrahim al-Rassi, *Majmuʿ kutub wa-rasaʾil al-imam al-Qasim b. Ibrahim al-Rassi 169–246 H*, ed. ʿAbd al-Karim A. Jadban (Sanaa, 1423/2001); his *Al-Kasim b. Ibrahim on the Proof of God's Existence. Kitab al-Dalil al-Kabir*, ed. and tr. B. Abrahamov (Leiden, 1990), and

B. Abrahamov, 'Al-Kasim Ibn Ibrahim's Theory of the Imamate', *Arabica*, 34 (1987), pp. 80–105.

13 Al-Tabari, *Ta'rikh*, III, pp. 1524–1532, 1583–1585, 1683, 1698, 1736–1738, 1840, 1883–1885; English trans., *The History of al-Tabari:* Volume XXXV, *The Crisis of the 'Abbasid Caliphate*, tr. G. Saliba (Albany, NY, 1985), pp. 21–26, 63–65, 142, 156; and Volume XXXVI, *The Revolt of the Zanj*, tr. D. Waines (Albany, NY, 1992), pp. 24–26, 116, 158–161; Ibn Isfandiyar, *Ta'rikh*, vol. 1, pp. 94–96, 224–258; Mar'ashi, *Ta'rikh-i Tabaristan*, pp. 126–142; Amuli, *Ta'rikh*, pp. 86–104; and F. Buhl, 'Al-Hasan b. Zayd b. Muhammad', *EI2*, vol. 3, p. 245.

14 Al-Tabari, *Ta'rikh*, III, p. 2292; English trans., *The History of al-Tabari:* Volume XXXVIII, *The Return of the Caliphate to Baghdad*, tr. F. Rosenthal (Albany, NY, 1985), pp. 204–205. See also *Arabic Texts Concerning the History of the Zaydi Imams*, ed. Madelung, pp. 17–43, 71–75, 85–101, 209–242; Ibn Isfandiyar, *Ta'rikh*, vol. 1, pp. 268–275; Mar'ashi, *Ta'rikh-i Tabaristan*, pp. 143–148; Amuli, *Ta'rikh*, pp. 104–110; and R. Strothmann, 'Hasan al-Utrush', *EI2*, vol. 3, pp. 254–255.

15 Ibn Isfandiyar, *Ta'rikh*, vol. 1, pp. 275–298; Mar'ashi, *Ta'rikh-i Tabaristan*, pp. 68–72, 149–153; Amuli, *Ta'rikh*, pp. 111–115; al-Mas'udi, *Muruj*, vol. 9, pp. 6–19; Hamza al-Isfahani, *Ta'rikh sini muluk al-ard*, ed. J. Irani Tabrizi (Berlin, 1340/1921), pp. 152–153, 241; al-Baghdadi, *al-Farq*, p. 267; tr. Halkin, pp. 112–113; and Madelung, 'Abu Ishaq al-Sabi on the Alids of Tabaristan', pp. 32–43.

16 Ibn Isfandiyar, *Ta'rikh*, vol. 1, pp. 106, 298–301; *Arabic Texts*, ed. Madelung, pp. 38–43; S. M. Stern, 'The Coins of Amul', *Numismatic Chronicle*, 7th series, 6 (1967), pp. 205–278, at pp. 216–220, 227–231, 269–278; reprinted in his *Coins and Documents from the Medieval Middle East*, ed. F. W. Zimmermann (London, 1986), article III; Madelung, 'Abu Ishaq al-Sabi', pp. 43–52; and his 'Hawsam', *EI2*, vol. 12, Supplement, p. 363.

17 See *Arabic Texts*, ed. Madelung, pp. 261–321; and Madelung, *Der Imam al-Qasim*, pp. 177–181.

18 Abu'l-Qasim al-Busti, *Min kashf asrar al-Batiniyya wa-'iwar madhhabihim*, ed. 'Adil Salim al-'Abd al-Jadir, in his *al-Isma'iliyyun: kashf al-asrar wa-naqd al-afkar* (Kuwait, 2002), pp. 187–369. See also al-Busti's *Kitab al-bahth 'an adillat al-takfir wa'l-tafsiq*, ed. W. Madelung and S. Schmidtke (Tehran, 1382 Sh./2003), another Mu'tazili Zaydi work discussing the criteria for charging Muslims with unbelief (*kufr*) and grave offence (*fisq*); and S. M. Stern, 'Abu'l-Qasim al-Busti and his Refutation of Isma'ilism', *JRAS* (1961), pp. 14–35; reprinted in his *Studies*, pp. 299–320.

19 See Hamid al-Din al-Kirmani, *al-Risala al-kafiya fi'l-radd 'ala'l-Haruni al-Husayni*, in *Majmu'at rasa'il al-Kirmani*, ed. M. Ghalib (Beirut, 1403/1983), pp.

148–182. For another Zaydi *fatwa* against the Ismailis issued by Imam al-Mansur bi'llah ʻAbd Allah b. Hamza, see *Arabic Texts*, ed. Madelung, pp. 165–170.

20 For an extract of this treatise, see *Arabic Texts*, ed. Madelung, pp. 293–305. For further details on Zaydi perspectives on Sufism, see W. Madelung, 'Zaydi Attitudes to Sufism', in F. de Jong and B. Radtke, ed., *Islamic Mysticism Contested: Thirteen Centuries of Controversies and Polemics* (Leiden, 1999), pp. 124–144; reprinted in Madelung's *Studies in Medieval Shiʻism*, article VI.

21 See *Arabic Texts*, ed. Madelung, pp. 146, 329.

22 For the fullest Nizari account of this event, see Kashani, *Zubdat al-tawarikh*, pp. 175–179.

23 Abu'l-Qasim ʻAbd Allah Kashani, *Ta'rikh-i Uljaytu*, ed. M. Hambly (Tehran, 1348 Sh./1969), p. 60; with the relevant extract in H. L. Rabino di Borgomale, 'Deux descriptions du Gîlân du temps des Mongols', *Journal Asiatique*, 238 (1950), pp. 331–332.

24 Marʻashi, *Ta'rikh-i Gilan*, ed. Rabino, pp. 14, 38–39; ed. Sutuda, pp. 16, 40–41.

25 See Marʻashi, *Ta'rikh-i Gilan*, ed. Rabino, pp. 50–51, 64–68; ed. Sutuda, pp. 52–53, 66–70, and the following works by H. L. Rabino di Borgomale: 'Rulers of Lahijan and Fuman, in Gilan, Persia', *JRAS* (1918), pp. 85–92; 'Les dynasties locales du Gîlân et du Daylam', *Journal Asiatique*, 237 (1949), pp. 301–350, at pp. 316–317, 322–327; and his 'Les dynasties Alaouides', pp. 263–265. See also Daftary, *The Ismaʻilis*, pp. 415–417.

26 On Imam al-Hadi, see his biography in ʻAli b. Muhammad al-ʻAbbasi al-ʻAlawi, *Sirat al-Hadi ila'l-Haqq Yahya b. al-Husayn*, ed. Suhayl Zakkar (Beirut, 1392/1972). See also Yahya b. al-Husayn b. al-Qasim, *Ghayat al-amani fi akhbar al-qutr al-Yamani*, ed. S. ʻA. ʻAshur (Cairo, 1388/1968), vol. 1, pp. 166–201; Arendonk, *Les débuts*, pp. 127–305; P. Dresch, *Tribes, Government and History in Yemen* (Oxford, 1993), pp. 167–183; and W. Madelung, 'Al-Hadi ila'l-Hakk', *EI2*, vol. 12, Supplement, pp. 334-335. For a list of the Zaydi imams in Yaman, see Ayman F. Sayyid, *Masadir ta'rikh al-Yaman fi'l-ʻasr al-Islami* (Cairo, 1974), pp. 404–416. See also Muhammad b. Muhammad Zabara, *A'immat al-Yaman* (Taʻizz, 1952); and his *A'immat al-Yaman bi'l-qarn al-rabiʻ ʻashar li'l-hijra* (Cairo, 1376/1956), 3 vols.

27 See Musallam b. Muhammad al-Lahji, *The Sira of Imam Ahmad b. Yahya al-Nasir li-Din Allah, from Musallam al-Lahji's Kitab Akhbar al-Zaydiyya bi l-Yaman*, ed. W. Madelung (Exeter, 1990), text pp. 1–119; and J. R. Blackburn 'Al-Nasir li-Din Allah', *EI2*, vol. 7, p. 996.

28 Yahya b. al-Husayn b. al-Qasim, *Ghayat al-amani*, vol. 1, pp. 227–334; al-Maqrizi, *Ittiʻaz al-hunafa'*, ed. al-Shayyal, vol. 1, pp. 278, 281–282; ed.

Sayyid, vol. 1, pp. 319, 322–324; Madelung, *Der Imam al-Qasim*, pp. 194–197; and his 'Al-Mansur Bi'llah, al-Kasim b. 'Ali', *EI2*, vol. 6, pp. 435–436.

29 On al-Husayn al-Mahdi and the Husayniyya Zaydis, see Yahya b. al-Husayn, *Ghayat al-amani*, vol. 1, pp. 233–270; and W. Madelung, 'The *Sirat al-Amirayn al-Ajallayn al-Sharifayn al-Fadilayn al-Qasim wa-Muhammad ibnay Ja'far ibn al-Imam al-Qasim b. 'Ali al-'Iyani* as a Historical Source', in *Studies in the History of Arabia*, I: *Sources for the History of Arabia*, part 2, *Proceedings of the First International Symposium on Studies in the History of Arabia* (Riyad, 1979), pp. 69–87; reprinted in his *Religious and Ethnic Movements*, article XII.

30 Abu'l-Fath al-Daylami hailed from the Caspian region, and evidently first claimed the Zaydi imamate in his native land around 430/1039, before arriving in Yaman where he launched his *da'wa* in 437/1046. He succeeded in capturing Sa'da and establishing himself there. His extant works include a Qur'an commentary, a manuscript copy of which is kept at the Great Mosque (*al-Jami' al-kabir*) in San'a'. See W. Madelung, 'Abu'l-Fath al-Daylami', *EI2*, vol. 12, Supplement, p. 22; and S. Muhaqqeq, 'Abu al-Fath al-Daylami', *EIS*, vol. 1, pp. 756–758.

31 On the Mutarrifiyya, see the following works of W. Madelung: *Der Imam al-Qasim*, pp. 202ff., 212–216; 'The Origins of the Yemenite *Hijra*', especially pp. 30–39; and his 'Mutarrifiyya', *EI2*, vol. 7, pp. 772–773.

32 On Zaydi–Sufi relations in Yaman, which have remained generally hostile, see 'Abd Allah b. Muhammad al-Hibshi, *al-Sufiyya wa'l-fuqaha' fi'l-Yaman* (Sanaa, 1396/1976). See also Madelung, 'Zaydi Attitudes to Sufism', especially pp. 127 ff.; and Muhammad Ali Aziz, *Religion and Mysticism in Early Islam: Theology and Sufism in Yemen* (London, 2011), especially pp. 165–182.

33 The relevant passage is quoted in Madelung, 'Zaydi Attitudes to Sufism', pp. 136–137. On Imam al-Mansur al-Qasim, other than his unpublished *sira*s, see his great-grandson Yahya b. al-Husayn b. al-Qasim (d. ca. 1100/1688) *Ghayat al-amani*, vol. 2, pp. 770–814; Arthur S. Tritton, *The Rise of the Imams of Sanaa* (London, 1925), based on a partial *sira* of this imam by Ahmad b. Muhammad al-Sharafi (d. 1055/1645); and J. R. Blackburn, 'Al-Mansur Bi'llah', *EI2*, vol. 6, pp. 436–437. See also G. Rex Smith, 'Some Arabic Sources Concerning the First Ottoman Occupation of the Yemen (945–1045/1538–1636)', in J. Hathaway, ed., *The Arab Lands in the Ottoman Era: Essays in Honor of Professor Caesar Farah* (Minneapolis, MN, 2009), pp. 19–39.

34 See S. Traboulsi, 'The Ottoman Conquest of Yemen: The Ismaili Perspective', in Hathaway, ed., *The Arab Lands*, pp. 41–60.

35 See *Arabic Texts*, ed. Madelung, pp. 165–170; and Madelung, 'Zaydi Attitudes to Sufism', pp. 138–142.

36 See A. Rouaud, 'Al-Mutawakkil 'ala Allah Yahya, fondateur du Yémen moderne', *L'Afrique et l'Asie modernes*, 141 (1984), pp. 56–73; and his 'Yahya b. Muhammad', *EI2*, vol. 11, pp. 247–248. For a detailed history of modern Yaman, under Yahya and his successors through the 1980s, see P. Dresch, *A History of Modern Yemen* (Cambridge, 2002).

37 Michael Cook, *Commanding Right and Forbidding Wrong in Islamic Thought* (Cambridge, 2000), pp. 247–251.

38 See 'Abd Allah b. Muhammad al-Hibshi, *Mu'allafat hukkam al-Yaman*, ed. E. Niewöhner-Eberhard (Wiesbaden, 1979), pp. 126–143.

39 On al-Shawkani's teachings within the changing intellectual and ideological milieu of Yaman, see B. Haykel, *Revival and Reform in Islam: The Legacy of Muhammad al-Shawkani* (Cambridge, 2003); B. Haykel and A. Zysow, 'What Makes a *Madhab* a *Madhab*: Zaydi Debates on the Structure of Legal Authority', *Arabica*, 59 (2012), pp. 332–371; and B. Haykel, 'al-Shawkani, Muhammad b. 'Ali (1760-1834)', in *The Princeton Encyclopedia of Islamic Political Thought*, ed. G. Bowering (Princeton, 2013), pp. 506–507.

40 Haykel, *Revival and Reform*, p. 231.

41 For the underlying issues and challenges, see James R. King, 'Zaydi Revival in a Hostile Republic: Competing Identities, Loyalties and Visions of State in Republican Yemen', *Arabica*, 59 (2012), pp. 404–445.

Notes to Chapter 6: The Nusayris or 'Alawis

1 See M. Aringberg-Laanatza, 'Alevis in Turkey – Alawites in Syria: Similarities and Differences', in T. Olsson et al, ed., *Alevi Identity: Cultural, Religious and Social Perspectives*. Papers Read at a Conference Held at the Swedish Research Institute in Istanbul, 25–27 November 1996 (Istanbul, 1998), pp. 151–165. See also D. Shankland, 'Are the Alevis Shi'ite?', in L. Ridgeon, ed., *Shi'i Islam and Identity* (London, 2012), pp. 210–228; M. Moosa, ''Alawiyah', and D. Shankland, 'Alevis', both entries in *The Oxford Encyclopedia of the Islamic World*, ed. John L. Esposito (Oxford, 2009), vol. 1, pp. 105–107 and 112–113, respectively.

2 Barthélemy d'Herbelot de Molainville, *Bibliothèque orientale* (Paris, 1697), with four later editions.

3 Carsten Niebuhr, *Reisebeschreibung nach Arabien und andern umliegenden Länden* (Zurich, 1992), vol. 2, pp. 736–742; French trans., *Voyage en Arabie* (Amsterdam, 1780), vol. 2, pp. 357–361.

4 Constantine F. C. de Volney, *Travels through Syria and Egypt* (London, 1787), vol. 2, pp. 1–8.

5 See Jean Baptiste L. J. Rousseau, 'Mémoire sur l'Ismaélis et les Nosaïris de Syrie, adressé à M. Silvestre de Sacy', *Annales des Voyages*, 14 (1811), pp. 271–303 (with the Nusayris covered on pp. 292–303), which also contains some explanatory notes by de Sacy himself. This memoir was later incorporated into Rousseau's expanded work entitled *Mémoire sur les trois plus fameuses sectes du Musulmanisme; les Wahabis, les Nosaïris et les Ismaélis* (Paris, 1818). See also John L. Burckhardt, *Travels in Syria and the Holy Land* (London, 1822), pp. 150–156.

6 Rousseau, 'Mémoire' (1811), pp. 300–301.

7 See de Sacy's notes in Rousseau, 'Mémoire' (1811), pp. 292–293, 303, a view reiterated later in his magisterial work on the Druzes, which contained a short section on the Nusayris; see de Sacy's *Exposé de la religion des Druzes* (Paris, 1838), vol. 2, pp. 560–586.

8 See J. Catafago, 'Notice sur les Ansériens', *Journal Asiatique*, 4th series, 11 (1848), pp. 149–168; and his 'Lettre de M. Catafago à M. Mohl', *Journal Asiatique*, 4th series, 12 (1848), pp. 72–78.

9 See J. Catafago, 'Nouvelles mélanges', *Journal Asiatique*, 7th series, 8 (1876), pp. 523–525, listing some forty Nusayri works.

10 See S. Lyde, *The Asian Mystery: Illustrated in the History, Religion, and Present State of the Ansaireeh or Nusairis of Syria* (London, 1860), pp. 233–269 (*Kitab al-mashyakha*), and pp. 271–281 (*Kitab ta'lim*). For the full text and English translation of the Nusayri catechism in question, see Bar-Asher and Kofsky, *Nusayri-'Alawi Religion*, pp. 163–221.

11 S. Lyde, *The Ansyreeh and the Ismaeleeh* (London, 1853).

12 F. Walpole, *The Ansayrii, (or Assassins) with Travels in the Further East, in 1850–51* (London, 1851), 3 vols.

13 Sulayman Efendi al-Adhani, *Kitab al-bakura al-Sulaymaniyya fi kashf asrar al-diyana al-Nusayriyya* (Beirut, [1864]; reprinted, Beirut, 1988; reprinted, Cairo, 1410/1990).

14 Edward E. Salisbury, 'The Book of Sulaimân's First Ripe Fruit, Disclosing the Mysteries of the Nusairian Religion, by Sulaimân Effendi of Adhanah: with Copious Extracts', *JAOS*, 8 (1866), pp. 227–308.

15 R. Dussaud, *Histoire et religion des Nosairis* (Paris, 1900).

16 Ibid., pp. xiii–xxxv.

17 L. Massignon, 'Esquisse d'une bibliographie Nusayrie', in *Mélanges Syriens offerts à M. René Dussaud par ses amis et ses élèves* (Paris, 1939), vol. 2, pp. 913–922; reprinted in L. Massignon, *Opera Minora*, ed. Y. Moubarac (Paris, 1969), vol. 1, pp. 640–649. See also M. Boivin, 'Ghulat et Chi'isme

Salmanien chez Louis Massignon', in Ève Pierunek and Y. Richard, ed., *Louis Massignon et l'Iran* (Paris and Leuven, 2000), pp. 61–75.

18 See L. Massignon, 'Les Nusayris', in *L'Élaboration de l'Islam* (Paris, 1961), pp. 109–114; reprinted in his *Opera Minora*, vol. 1, pp. 619–624; and his 'Nusairi', *EI*, vol. 3, pp. 963–967.

19 See the following works by R. Strothmann: 'Festkalender der Nusairier', *Der Islam*, 27 (1944), pp. 1–60, and 27 (1946), pp. 161–273; 'Die Nusairi im heutigen Syrien', in *Nachrichten der Akademie der Wissenschaften zu Göttingen*, Philologisch-historische Klasse, 4 (1950), pp. 29–64; 'Die Nusairi nach MS. arab. Berlin 4291', in *Documenta Islamica Inedita. Festschrift R. Hartmann* (Berlin, 1952), pp. 173–187; and 'Seelenwanderung bei den Nusairi', *Oriens*, 12 (1959), pp. 89–114, amongst his other works.

20 See the following publications of H. Halm: '"Das Buch der Schatten". Die Mufaddal-Tradition der Gulat und die Ursprünge des Nusairiertums', *Der Islam*, 55 (1978), pp. 219–266, and 58 (1981), pp. 15–86; *Die islamische Gnosis: Die extreme Schia und die ʿAlawiten* (Zurich and Munich, 1982), especially pp. 240–274, 284–355; and 'Nusayriyya', *EI2*, vol. 8, pp. 145–148. See also M. Moosa, *Extremist Shiites: The Ghulat Sects* (Syracuse, NY, 1987), especially pp. 255–418; M. M. Bar-Asher has numerous publications on the Nusayris, and several studies in collaboration with Aryeh Kofsky; see the works cited in their *Nusayri-ʿAlawi Religion*, pp. 224–225; and M. M. Bar-Asher, 'The Iranian Components of the Nusayri Religion', *Iran, Journal of the British Institute of Persian Studies*, 41 (2003), pp. 217–227.

21 Muhammad A. G. al-Tawil, *Ta'rikh al-ʿAlawiyyin* (Ladhiqiyya, 1924; 4th ed., Beirut, 1401/1981), originally written in Ottoman Turkish in Adana, Turkey. See also Munir al-Sharif, *ʿAlawiyyun: man hum wa ayna hum* (Damascus, 1946), another apologetic work written by a Nusayri author.

22 On this series and its contents, see Friedman, *The Nusayri-ʿAlawis*, pp. 2–3.

23 See, for instance, Abu Musa al-Hariri, *al-ʿAlawiyyun al-Nusayriyyun* (Beirut, 1980).

24 Al-Nawbakhti, *Firaq al-Shiʿa*, p. 78; and al-Qummi, *al-Maqalat*, pp. 100–101. See also al-Ashʿari, *Maqalat*, p. 15; al-Baghdadi, *al-Farq*, pp. 239–242; tr. Halkin, pp. 70–74; Ibn Hazm, *Kitab al-fasl*, vol. 4, p. 188; al-Shahrastani, *al-Milal*, vol. 1, pp. 188–189; tr. Kazi, pp. 161–162; and Halm, *Die islamische Gnosis*, pp. 282–283.

25 See, for instance, al-Kashshi, *Ikhtiyar*, pp. 520–521.

26 Ibid., pp. 302, 554.

27 See Friedman, *The Nusayri-ʿAlawis*, pp. 8–12, with references to the Nusayri sources.

28 See L. Massignon, 'Les origines Shî'ites de la famille vizirale des Banû'l-Furât', in *Mélanges Gaudefroy-Demombynes* (Cairo, 1935–1945), pp. 25–29; reprinted in his *Opera Minora*, vol. 1, pp. 484–487. See also Claude Cahen, 'Note sur les origines de la communauté Syrienne des Nusayris', *Revue des Études Islamiques*, 38 (1970), pp. 243–249.

29 Al-Husayn b. Hamdan al-Khasibi, *Kitab al-hidaya al-kubra* (Beirut, 1986); also in *Silsilat al-turath al-'Alawi*, vol. 7, pp. 17–397. See also al-Tawil, *Ta'rikh*, pp. 260, 318; Friedman, *The Nusayri-'Alawis*, pp. 33–34, 250–253; and Y. Friedman, 'Al-Husayn ibn Hamdan al-Khasibi: A Historical Biography of the Founder of the Nusayri-'Alawite Sect', *Studia Islamica*, 93 (2001), pp. 91–112.

30 Al-Tawil, *Ta'rikh* (4th ed., Beirut, 1401/1981), p. 259.

31 See Friedman, *The Nusayri-'Alawis*, pp. 35–40, 254–257.

32 Ibid., pp. 40ff., 260–263.

33 Abu Sa'id Maymun b. al-Qasim al-Tabarani, *Kitab majmu' al-a'yad*, ed. R. Strothmann in his 'Festkalender der Nusairier', in *Der Islam*, 27 (1944), pp. 1–60, and 27 (1946), pp. 161–273; also in *Silsilat al-turath al-'Alawi*, vol. 3, pp. 207–412.

34 Edited by R. Strothmann, in his 'Drusen-Antwort auf Nusairi-Angriff', *Der Islam*, 25 (1939), pp. 269–281.

35 Al-Tawil, *Ta'rikh*, pp. 263–265.

36 Ibn al-'Adim, *Zubdat al-halab min ta'rikh Halab*, ed. S. al-Dahhan (Damascus, 1951–1968), vol. 2, pp. 251–252; Ibn Fadl Allah al-'Umari, *Masalik al-absar fi mamalik al-amsar*, ed. Ayman F. Sayyid (Cairo, 1985), pp. 132–133; and Willey, *Eagle's Nest*, pp. 228–230.

37 Al-Tawil, *Ta'rikh*, pp. 358ff.; As'ad 'Ali, *Ma'rifat Allah wa'l-Makhzum al-Sinjari* (Beirut, 1972), vol. 2, pp. 328–349; and Friedman, *The Nusayri-'Alawis*, pp. 51–56.

38 See Ibn Kathir, *al-Bidaya wa'l-nihaya* (Beirut, 1988), vol. 14, p. 83; Taqi al-Din al-Maqrizi, *al-Suluk li-ma'rifat duwal al-muluk* (Cairo, 1971), vol. 2, pp. 174–175; Moosa, *Extremist Shiites*, pp. 272–273; and U. Vermeulen, 'Some Remarks on a Rescript of an-Nasir Muhammad b. Qala'un on the Abolition of Taxes and the Nusayris (Mamlaka of Tripoli, 717/1317)', *Orientalia Lovaniensia Periodica*, 1 (1970), pp. 195–201.

39 See S. Guyard, 'Le Fetwa d'Ibn Taimiyyah sur les Nosairis', *Journal Asiatique*, 6th series, 18 (1871), pp. 158–198; Y. Friedman, 'Ibn Taymiyya's *Fatawa* against the Nusayri-'Alawi Sect', *Der Islam*, 82 (2005), pp. 349–363; and his *The Nusayri-'Alawis*, pp. 187–199 and 299–309, containing a complete English translation of Ibn Taymiyya's *fatwa*.

40 Al-Tawil, *Ta'rikh*, pp. 405–461; Dussaud, *Histoire*, pp. 32–40; and Moosa, *Extremist Shiites*, pp. 276–279.

41 For further details, see al-Tawil, *Ta'rikh*, pp. 469–534; and Moosa, *Extremist Shiites*, pp. 280–310.

42 Al-Tabarani, *Kitab al-hawi*, in *Silsilat al-turath al-ʿAlawi*, vol. 3, pp. 45–116. See also Moosa, *Extremist Shiites*, pp. 372–381; Friedman, *The Nusayri-ʿAlawis*, pp. 210–222; and B. Tendler Krieger, 'Marriage, Birth, and *batini ta'wil*: A Study of Nusayri Initiation Based on the *Kitab al-Hawi fi ʿilm al-fatawa* of Abu Saʿid Maymun al-Tabarani', *Arabica*, 58 (2011), pp. 53–75.

43 See Friedman, *The Nusayri-ʿAlawis*, pp. 210–222.

44 This is the most famous of the works attributed to al-Mufaddal b. ʿUmar al-Juʿfi, a follower of Imam Jaʿfar al-Sadiq and, later, of Imam Musa al-Kazim. See *Kitab al-haft wa'l-azilla*, ed. ʿArif Tamir and I. ʿA. Khalifa (Beirut, 1960); ed. M. Ghalib (Beirut, 1964); also in *Silsilat al-turath al-ʿAlawi*, vol. 6, pp. 290–423. See also H. Halm, '"Das Buch der Schatten". Die Mufaddal-Tradition der Gulat', *Der Islam*, 55 (1978), pp. 219–266, and 58 (1981), pp. 15–86; Halm, *Die islamische Gnosis*, pp. 240–274, containing a partial German translation of the *Kitab al-haft*; and M. Asatryan, 'Heresy and Rationalism in Early Islam: The Origins and Evolution of the Mufaddal-Tradition' (Ph.D. thesis, Yale University, 2012), pp. 140–241.

45 See al-Qummi, *al-Maqalat*, pp. 59–60, 63; al-Kashshi, *al-Rijal*, pp. 305, 398–401; Ibn Hazm, *al-Fasl*, vol. 4, p. 186; al-Shahrastani, *al-Milal*, vol. 1, pp. 175–176; tr. Kazi, pp. 151–152; Halm, *Die islamische Gnosis*, pp. 218–232; and W. Madelung, 'Mukhammisa', *EI2*, vol. 7, pp. 517–518.

46 *Umm al-kitab*, ed. W. Ivanow, in *Der Islam*, 23 (1936), pp. 1–132; Italian trans., *Ummu'l-Kitab*, tr. P. Filippani-Ronconi (Naples, 1966); partial German trans., in Halm, *Die islamische Gnosis*, pp. 113–198; Turkish trans., in I. Kaygusuz, *Bir Proto-Alevi Kaynaği, Ummü'l-Kitab*, tr. A. Selman (Istanbul, 2009), pp. 121–258. See also W. Ivanow, 'Notes sur l'Ummu'l-kitab des Ismaëliens de l'Asie Centrale', *Revue des Études Islamiques*, 6 (1932), pp. 419–481; and P. Filippani-Ronconi, 'The Soteriological Cosmology of Central-Asiatic Ismaʿilism', in Nasr, ed., *Ismaʿili Contributions*, pp. 99–120.

47 See the Nusayri catechism entitled *Kitab taʿlim diyanat al-Nusayriyya*, in Bar-Asher and Kofsky, *Nusayri-ʿAlawi Religion*, pp. 163–199.

48 See Friedman, *The Nusayri-ʿAlawis*, pp. 72–84; and Moosa, *Extremist Shiites*, pp. 311–323 and 342–351.

49 Dussaud, *Histoire*, pp. 68ff., 188; Moosa, *Extremist Shiites*, pp. 357–361; and Friedman, *The Nusayri-ʿAlawis*, pp. 85–101.

50 Bar-Asher and Kofsky, *Nusayri-ʿAlawi Religion*, pp. 75–83. See also M. M. Bar-Asher and A. Kofsky, 'L'ascension céleste du gnostique Nusayrite

et le voyage nocturne du Prophète Muhammad', in M. A. Amir-Moezzi, ed., *Le voyage initiatique en terre d'Islam* (Louvain and Paris, 1996), pp. 133–148.

51 For details, see Bar-Asher and Kofsky, *Nusayri-'Alawi Religion*, pp. 111–151, based on al-Tabarani's *Majmu' al-a'yad*; Dussaud, *Histoire*, pp. 136–152; Friedman, *The Nusayri-'Alawis*, pp. 152–173; Moosa, *Extremist Shiites*, pp. 382–397; and Halm, *Die islamische Gnosis*, pp. 315–355.

52 See Moosa, *Extremist Shiites*, pp. 409–418; and Friedman, *The Nusayri-'Alawis*, pp. 130–152.

53 For instance, see Shaykh Mahmud al-Salih, *al-Naba' al-yaqin 'an al-'Alawiyyin* (Ladhiqiyya, 1997), pp. 47–49.

Bibliography

1. Works of reference

Āghā Buzurg, Muḥammad Muḥsin al-Ṭihrānī. *al-Dharīʿa ilā taṣānīf al-Shīʿa*. Tehran and Najaf, 1357–1398/1938–1978.

Amir-Moezzi, Mohammad-Ali (ed.). *Dictionnaire du Coran*. Paris, 2007.

Bāmdād, Mahdī. *Sharḥ-i ḥāl-i rijāl-i Īrān*. Tehran, 1347–1350 Sh./1968–1971.

Blois, François de. *Arabic, Persian and Gujarati Manuscripts: The Hamdani Collection in the Library of The Institute of Ismaili Studies*. London, 2011.

Bosworth, C. Edmund. *The New Islamic Dynasties: A Chronological and Genealogical Manual*. Edinburgh, 1996. Persian trans., *Silsilahā-yi Islāmī-yi jadīd*, tr. F. Badraʾī. Tehran. 1381 Sh./2002.

Brockelmann, Carl. *Geschichte der arabischen Litteratur*. Weimar, 1898–1902; 2nd ed., Leiden, 1943–1949. *Supplementbände*. Leiden, 1937–1942.

Choueiri, Youssef (ed.). *A Companion to the History of the Middle East*. Chichester, UK, 2008.

Conflict and Conquest in the Islamic World: A Historical Encyclopedia, ed. A. Mikaberidze. Santa Barbara, CA, 2011.

Cortese, Delia. *Ismaili and Other Arabic Manuscripts: A Descriptive Catalogue of Manuscripts in the Library of The Institute of Ismaili Studies*. London, 2000.

____ *Arabic Ismaili Manuscripts: The Zāhid ʿAlī Collection in the Library of The Institute of Ismaili Studies*. London, 2003.

Daftary, Farhad. *Ismaili Literature: A Bibliography of Sources and Studies*. London, 2004.

____ *Historical Dictionary of the Ismailis*. Lanham, MD and Toronto, 2012.

Encyclopaedia Iranica, ed. E. Yarshater. London and New York, 1982–.

Encyclopaedia Islamica, ed. W. Madelung and F. Daftary. Leiden, 2008–.

The Encyclopaedia of Islam, ed. M. Th. Houtsma et al. 1st ed., Leiden and London, 1913–1938; reprinted, Leiden, 1987.

The Encyclopaedia of Islam, ed. Hamilton A. R. Gibb et al. New (2nd) ed., Leiden, 1954–2004.

The Encyclopaedia of Islam, Three, ed. M. Gaborieau et al. 3rd ed., Leiden, 2007–.
Encyclopaedia of the World of Islam (Dānishnāma-yi Jahān-i Islām), ed. Gholām-ʿAlī Ḥaddād ʿĀdel et al. Tehran, 1375 Sh.– /1996– .
Encyclopedia of Religion, ed. M. Eliade. London and New York, 1987; second edition, ed. Lindsay Jones. Farmington Hills, MI, 2005.
Gacek, Adam. *Catalogue of Arabic Manuscripts in the Library of The Institute of Ismaili Studies*. London, 1984–1985.
The Great Islamic Encyclopaedia (Dāʾirat al-Maʿārif-i Buzurg-i Islāmī), ed. K. Mūsavī Bujnūrdī. Tehran, 1367 Sh.–/1989–.
An Historical Atlas of Islam, ed. Hugh Kennedy. Leiden, 2002.
al-Ḥusaynī, S. Aḥmad. *Muʾallafāt al-Zaydiyya*. Qumm, 1413/1993.
Ivanow, Wladimir. *A Guide to Ismaili Literature*. London, 1933.
____ *Ismaili Literature: A Bibliographical Survey*. Tehran, 1963.
Khanbagi, Ramin. *Shiʿi Islam: A Comprehensive Bibliography*. New York, 2006.
Lane-Poole, Stanley. *The Mohammadan Dynasties*. London, 1894. Persian trans., *Ṭabaqāt-i salāṭīn-i Islām*, tr. ʿA. Iqbāl. Tehran, 1312 Sh./1933. Arabic trans. (from the Persian trans.), *Ṭabaqāt salāṭīn al-Islām*, tr. M. Ṭāhir al-Kaʿabī. Baghdad, 1388/1968.
Leaman, Oliver (ed.). *The Biographical Encyclopaedia of Islamic Philosophy*. London, 2006.
Medieval Islamic Civilization: An Encyclopedia, ed. Josef W. Meri. New York and London, 2006.
Modarressi Tabātabāʾi, Hossein. *An Introduction to Shīʿī Law: A Bibliographical Study*. London, 1984.
The Oxford Encyclopedia of the Islamic World, ed. John L. Esposito. Oxford, 2009.
The Oxford Encyclopedia of the Modern Islamic World, ed. John L. Esposito. Oxford, 1995.
Poonawala, Ismail K. *Biobibliography of Ismāʿīlī Literature*. Malibu, CA, 1977.
The Princeton Encyclopedia of Islamic Political Thought, ed. Gerhard Bowering. Princeton, 2013.
Sayyid, Ayman F. *Maṣādir taʾrīkh al-Yaman fiʾl-ʿaṣr al-Islāmī*. Cairo, 1974.
Sezgin, Fuat. *Geschichte des arabischen Schrifttums*. Leiden, 1967– .
Shorter Encyclopaedia of Islam, ed. Hamilton A. R. Gibb and J. H. Kramers. Leiden, 1953.
Storey, Charles A. *Persian Literature: A Bio-bibliographical Survey*. London, 1927–.
Swayd, Samy S. *The Druzes: An Annotated Bibliography*. Kirkland, WA, 1998.
Türkiye Diyanet Vakfi Islām Ansiklopedisi. Istanbul, 1988–.

Zambaur, Eduard K. M. von. *Manuel de généalogie et de chronologie pour l'histoire de l'Islam*. Hannover, 1927; reprinted, Osnabrück, 1976.

2. Primary sources

al-ʿAbbāsī al-ʿAlawī, ʿAlī b. Muḥammad. *Sīrat al-Hādī ila'l-Ḥaqq Yaḥyā b. al-Ḥusayn*, ed. Suhayl Zakkār. Beirut, 1392/1972.

ʿAbd al-Jabbār b. Aḥmad al-Hamadhānī. *Tathbīt dalā'il nubuwwat Sayyidnā Muḥammad*, ed. ʿAbd al-Karīm ʿUthmān. Beirut, 1966–1969.

Abu'l-Faraj al-Iṣfahānī, ʿAlī b. al-Ḥusayn. *Maqātil al-Ṭālibiyyīn*, ed. A. Ṣaqr. Cairo, 1368/1949.

Abu'l-Fidā, Ismāʿīl b. ʿAlī. *al-Mukhtaṣar fī akhbār al-bashar*. Cairo, 1325/1907.

Abū Shāma, Shihāb al-Dīn ʿAbd al-Raḥmān b. Ismāʿīl. *Kitāb al-rawḍatayn fī akhbār al-dawlatayn*. Cairo, 1287–1288/1870–1871.

Abū Tammām Yūsuf b. Muḥammad al-Nīsābūrī, *An Ismaili Heresiography: The 'Bāb al-shayṭān' from Abū Tammām's Kitāb al-shajara*, ed. and tr. W. Madelung and P. E. Walker. Leiden, 1998.

al-Adhanī, Sulaymān. *Kitāb al-bākūra al-Sulaymāniyya fī kashf asrār al-diyāna al-Nuṣayriyya*. Beirut, [1864]; reprinted, Beirut, 1988; reprinted, Cairo, 1410/1990. Partial English trans. in Edward E. Salisbury, 'The Book of Sulaimân's First Ripe Fruit, Disclosing the Mysteries of the Nusairian Religion, by Sulaimân Effendi of Adhanah: with Copious Extracts', *JAOS*, 8 (1866), pp. 227–308.

Akhbār al-Qarāmiṭa, ed. S. Zakkār. 2nd ed., Damascus, 1982.

Āmulī, Awliyā' Allāh. *Ta'rīkh-i Rūyān*, ed. M. Sutūda. Tehran, 1348 Sh./1969.

Āmulī, Sayyid Ḥaydar. *Asrār al-sharīʿa*, ed. M. Khwājawī. Tehran, 1982.

____. *Jāmiʿ al-asrār wa-manbaʿ al-anwār*, in his *La philosophie Shiʿite*, ed. H. Corbin and O. Yahya. Tehran and Paris, 1969, pp. 2–617.

Anthologie des philosophes Iraniens, vol. 1, ed. S. Jalāl al-Dīn Āshtiyānī. Tehran and Paris, 1971.

An Anthology of Philosophy in Persia: Volume 2, *Ismaili Thought in the Classical Age*, ed. S. Hossein Nasr and M. Aminrazavi. London, 2008.

Arabic Texts Concerning the History of the Zaydī Imāms of Ṭabaristān, Daylamān and Gīlān, ed. W. Madelung. Beirut, 1987.

ʿArīb b. Saʿd al-Qurṭubī. *Ṣilat ta'rīkh al-Ṭabarī*, ed. Michael J. de Goeje. Leiden, 1897.

al-Ashʿarī, Abu'l-Ḥasan ʿAlī b. Ismāʿīl. *Kitāb maqālāt al-Islāmiyyīn*, ed. H. Ritter. Istanbul, 1929–1930.

al-Astarābādī, Muḥammad Amīn. *al-Fawā'id al-madaniyya*, ed. Nūr al-Dīn Mūsawī. Qumm, 2003.

Badr al-Dīn Muḥammad b. Ḥātim al-Yāmī al-Hamdānī. *Kitāb al-simṭ al-ghālī al-thaman*, ed. G. Rex Smith, in his *The Ayyūbids and Early Rasūlids in Yemen*, vol. 1. London, 1974.

al-Baghdādī, Abū Manṣūr ʿAbd al-Qāhir b. Ṭāhir. *al-Farq bayn al-firaq*, ed. M. Badr. Cairo, 1328/1910. English trans., *Moslem Schisms and Sects*, part I, tr. K. C. Seelye. New York, 1919; part II, tr. Abraham S. Halkin. Tel Aviv, 1935.

al-Balādhurī, Aḥmad b. Yaḥyā. *Ansāb al-ashrāf*, vol. 2, ed. W. Madelung. Beirut, 2003.

al-Bustī, Abu'l-Qāsim Ismāʿīl b. Aḥmad. *Min kashf asrār al-Bāṭiniyya wa-ʿiwār madhhabihim*, ed. ʿĀdil Sālim al-ʿAbd al-Jādir, in his *al-Ismāʿīliyyūn: kashf al-asrār wa-naqd al-afkār*. Kuwait, 2002, pp. 187–369.

al-Daylamī, Muḥammad b. al-Ḥasan. *Bayān madhhab al-Bāṭiniyya wa-buṭlānih*, ed. R. Strothmann. Istanbul, 1939.

Fidā'ī Khurāsānī, Muḥammad b. Zayn al-ʿĀbidīn. *Kitāb-i hidāyat al-mu'minīn al-ṭālibīn*, ed. Aleksandr A. Semenov. Moscow, 1959.

Firishta, Muḥammad Qāsim Hindū Shāh Astarābādī. *Ta'rīkh-i Firishta*, ed. J. Briggs. Bombay, 1832.

Fūmanī, ʿAbd al-Fattāḥ. *Ta'rīkh-i Gīlān*, ed. M. Sutūda. Tehran, 1349 Sh./1970.

Gardīzī, Abū Saʿīd ʿAbd al-Ḥayy b. al-Ḍaḥḥāk. *Zayn al-akhbār*, ed. ʿA. Ḥabībī. Tehran, 1347 Sh./1968. Partial English trans., *The Ornament of Histories: A History of the Eastern Islamic Lands, AD 650–1041*, tr. C. Edmund Bosworth. London, 2011.

al-Ghazālī, Abū Ḥāmid Muḥammad b. Muḥammad. *Faḍā'iḥ al-Bāṭiniyya*, ed. ʿAbd al-Raḥmān Badawī. Cairo, 1383/1964. Partial English trans., in Richard J. McCarthy, *Freedom and Fulfillment*. Boston, 1980, pp. 175–286.

Gīlānī, Mullā Shaykh ʿAlī. *Ta'rīkh-i Māzandarān*, ed. M. Sutūda. Tehran, 1352 Sh./1973.

Gnosis-Texte der Ismailiten, ed. R. Strothmann. Göttingen, 1943.

Ḥāfiẓ Abrū, ʿAbd Allāh b. Luṭf Allāh al-Bihdādīnī. *Majmaʿ al-tawārīkh al-sulṭāniyya: qismat-i khulafā'-i ʿAlawiyya-i Maghrib va Miṣr va Nizāriyān va rafīqān*, ed. M. Mudarrisī Zanjānī. Tehran, 1364 Sh./1985.

Ḥamd Allāh Mustawfī Qazwīnī. *Ta'rīkh-i guzīda*, ed. ʿA. Navā'ī. Tehran, 1339 Sh./1960.

al-Ḥāmidī, Ḥātim b. Ibrāhīm. *Tuḥfat al-qulūb wa furjat al-makrūb*, ed. A. Hamdani. Beirut, 2012.

al-Ḥāmidī, Ibrāhīm b. al-Ḥusayn. *Kitāb kanz al-walad*, ed. M. Ghālib. Wiesbaden, 1971.

Hidāyat, Riḍā Qulī Khān. *Rawḍat al-ṣafā-yi Nāṣirī*. Tehran, 1339 Sh./1960.

al-Ḥillī, al-ʿAllāma Jamāl al-Dīn al-Ḥasan Ibn al-Muṭahhar. *Mabādi' al-wuṣūl ilā ʿilm al-uṣūl*, ed. ʿA. M. ʿAlī. Najaf, 1390/1970.

al-Ḥurr al-ʿĀmilī, Muḥammad b. al-Ḥasan. *ʿAmal al-ʿāmil fī dhikr ʿulamāʾ Jabal ʿĀmil*. Tehran, 1306 Sh./1927.

____ *Wasāʾil al-Shīʿa*, ed. ʿA. al-Rabbānī al-Shīrāzī and M. al-Rāzī. Tehran, 1376–1389/1956–1969.

al-Ḥusaynī, Ṣadr al-Dīn ʿAlī b. Nāṣir. *Akhbār al-dawla al-Saljūqiyya*, ed. M. Iqbāl. Lahore, 1933. English trans., *The History of the Seljuq State*, tr. C. Edmund Bosworth. London and New York, 2011.

Ibn al-ʿAdīm, Kamāl al-Dīn ʿUmar. *Zubdat al-ḥalab min taʾrīkh Ḥalab*, ed. S. al-Dahhān. Damascus, 1951–1968.

Ibn al-Athīr, ʿIzz al-Dīn Abuʾl-Ḥasan ʿAlī b. Muḥammad. *al-Kāmil fiʾl-taʾrīkh*, ed. Carl J. Tornberg. Leiden, 1851–1876; reprinted, Beirut, 1965–1967.

Ibn Bābawayh, Abū Jaʿfar Muḥammad b. ʿAlī al-Ṣadūq. *Man lā yahḍuruhuʾl-faqīh*, ed. Ḥ. M. al-Kharsān. Najaf, 1957; ed. ʿAlī Akbar al-Ghaffārī. Tehran, 1392–1394/1972–1975.

Ibn al-Dawādārī, Abū Bakr b. ʿAbd Allāh. *Kanz al-durar wa-jāmiʿ al-ghurar*, vol. 6, ed. Ṣ. al-Munajjid. Cairo, 1961.

Ibn Faḍl Allāh al-ʿUmarī, Shihāb al-Dīn Aḥmad. *Masālik al-abṣār fī mamālik al-amṣār*, ed. Ayman F. Sayyid. Cairo, 1985.

Ibn Ḥawqal, Abuʾl-Qāsim Muḥammad b. ʿAlī. *Kitāb ṣūrat al-arḍ*, ed. J. H. Kramers. 2nd ed., Leiden, 1938–1939. French trans., *Configuration de la terre*, tr. J. H. Kramers and G. Wiet. Paris, 1964.

Ibn Ḥazm, Abū Muḥammad ʿAlī b. Aḥmad. *Kitāb al-faṣl fiʾl-milal waʾl-ahwāʾ waʾl-niḥal*. Cairo, 1317–1321/1899–1903.

Ibn ʿInaba, Jamāl al-Dīn Aḥmad b. ʿAlī. *ʿUmdat al-ṭālib fī ansāb āl Abī Ṭālib*, ed. M. Ḥ. Āl al-Ṭāliqānī. Najaf, 1961.

Ibn Isfandiyār, Muḥammad b. al-Ḥasan. *Taʾrīkh-i Ṭabaristān*, ed. ʿAbbās Iqbāl. Tehran, 1320 Sh./1941.

Ibn al-Jawzī, ʿAbd al-Raḥmān b. ʿAlī al-Ḥanbalī. *Kitāb al-muntaẓam fī taʾrīkh al-mulūk waʾl-umam*, ed. F. Krenkow. Hyderabad, 1357–1362/1938–1943.

Ibn Kathīr, ʿImād al-Dīn Ismāʿīl. *al-Bidāya waʾl-nihāya*. Beirut, 1988.

Ibn Khallikān, Abuʾl-ʿAbbās Aḥmad b. Muḥammad. *Wafayāt al-aʿyān wa-anbāʾ abnāʾ al-zamān*, ed. Iḥsān ʿAbbās. Beirut, 1968–1972.

Ibn Mujāwir, Jamāl al-Dīn Yūsuf b. Yaʿqūb. *Taʾrīkh al-Mustabṣir*, ed. O. Löfgren. Leiden, 1951–1954.

Ibn al-Murtaḍā, Aḥmad b. Yaḥyā. *Kitāb al-azhār fī fiqh al-aʾimmat al-aṭhār*. N. p., 1982.

____ *Sharḥ al-azhār fī fiqh al-aʾimmat al-aṭhār*. Sanaa, 1973.

Ibn Muyassar, Tāj al-Dīn Muḥammad b. ʿAlī. *Akhbār Miṣr*, ed. Ayman F. Sayyid. Cairo, 1981.

Ibn al-Nadīm, Abu'l-Faraj Muḥammad b. Isḥāq al-Warrāq. *Kitāb al-fihrist*, ed. Gustav Flügel. Leipzig, 1871–1872; ed. M. Riḍā Tajaddud. 2nd ed., Tehran, 1973. English trans.,*The Fihrist of al-Nadīm*, tr. Bayard Dodge. New York, 1970.

Ibn al-Qalānisī, Abū Yaʿlā Ḥamza b. Asad. *Dhayl ta'rīkh Dimashq*, ed. Henry F. Amedroz. Leiden, 1908. French trans., *Damas de 1075 à 1154*, tr. Roger Le Tourneau. Damascus, 1952.

Ibn Shahrāshūb, Abū Jaʿfar Muḥammad b. ʿAlī. *Kitāb maʿālim al-ʿulamā'*, ed. ʿAbbās Iqbāl. Tehran, 1353/1934.

____ *Manāqib āl Abī Ṭālib*. Bombay, 1313/1896.

Ibn al-Walīd, ʿAlī b. Muḥammad. *Dāmigh al-bāṭil wa-ḥatf al-munāḍil*, ed. M. Ghālib. Beirut, 1403/1982.

____ *Kitāb al-dhakīra fi'l-ḥaqīqa*, ed. Muḥammad Ḥasan al-Aʿẓamī. Beirut, 1341/1971.

____ *Tāj al-ʿaqā'id wa-maʿdin al-fawā'id*, ed. ʿĀrif Tāmir. Beirut, 1967.

Idrīs ʿImād al-Dīn b. al-Ḥasan. *Kitāb zahr al-maʿānī*, ed. M. Ghālib. Beirut, 1411/1991.

____ *ʿUyūn al-akhbār wa-funūn al-āthār*, vols. 1-7, ed. A. Chleilat et al. Damascus, 2007–2012. Partial English trans., *The Founder of Cairo: The Fatimid Imam-Caliph al-Muʿizz and his Era*, tr. S. Jiwa. London, 2013.

Jaʿfar b. Manṣūr al-Yaman. *Kitāb al-ʿālim wa'l-ghulām*, ed. and tr. James W. Morris as *The Master and the Disciple: An Early Islamic Spiritual Dialogue*. London, 2001.

al-Janadī, Bahā' al-Dīn Muḥammad b. Yūsuf. *Akhbār al-Qarāmiṭa bi'l-Yaman*, ed. and tr. H. C. Kay, in his *Yaman, its Early Mediaeval History*. London, 1892, text pp. 139–152, translation pp. 191–212.

al-Jawdharī, Abū ʿAlī Manṣūr al-ʿAzīzī. *Sīrat al-ustādh Jawdhar*, ed. M. Kāmil Ḥusayn and M. ʿA. Shaʿīra. Cairo. 1954; ed. and tr. H. Haji as *Inside the Immaculate Portal: A History from Early Fatimid Archives*. London, 2012. French trans., *Vie de l'ustadh Jaudhar*, tr. M. Canard. Algiers, 1958.

Juwaynī, ʿAlā' al-Dīn ʿAṭā-Malik b. Muḥammad. *Ta'rīkh-i jahān-gushā*, ed. M. Qazvīnī. Leiden and London, 1912–1937. English trans., *The History of the World-Conqueror*, tr. John A. Boyle. Manchester, 1958.

Kāshānī, Abu'l-Qāsim ʿAbd Allāh b. ʿAlī. *Zubdat al-tawārīkh: bakhsh-i Fāṭimiyān va Nizāriyān*, ed. M. T. Dānishpazhūh. 2nd ed., Tehran, 1366 Sh./1987.

al-Kashshī, Abū ʿAmr Muḥammad b. ʿUmar. *Ikhtiyār maʿrifat al-rijāl*, as abridged by Muḥammad b. al-Ḥasan al-Ṭūsī, ed. Ḥ. al-Muṣṭafawī. Mashhad, 1348 Sh./1969.

al-Khaṣībī, al-Ḥusayn b. Ḥamdān. *Kitāb al-hidāya al-kubrā*. Beirut, 1986; also in *Silsilat al-turāth al-ʿAlawī*, vol. 7, pp. 17–397.

Khayrkhwāh-i Harātī, Muḥammad Riḍā b. Khwāja Sulṭān Ḥusayn. *Taṣnīfāt*, ed. W. Ivanow. Tehran, 1961.

al-Kirmānī, Ḥamīd al-Dīn Aḥmad b. ʿAbd Allāh. *Kitāb al-riyāḍ*, ed. ʿĀrif Tāmir. Beirut, 1960.

____ *Majmūʿat rasāʾil al-Kirmānī*, ed. M. Ghālib. Beirut, 1403/1983.

____ *al-Maṣābīḥ fī ithbāt al-imāma*, ed. and tr. Paul E. Walker as *Master of the Age: An Islamic Treatise on the Necessity of the Imamate*. London, 2007.

____ *Rāḥat al-ʿaql*, ed. M. Kāmil Ḥusayn and M. Muṣṭafā Ḥilmī. Cairo, 1953.

al-Kulaynī, Abū Jaʿfar Muḥammad b. Yaʿqūb. *al-Uṣūl min al-kāfī*, ed. ʿAlī Akbar al-Ghaffārī. 3rd ed., Tehran, 1388/1968.

Lāhījī, ʿAlī b. Shams al-Dīn. *Taʾrīkh-i Khānī*, ed. M. Sutūda. Tehran, 1352 Sh./1973.

al-Laḥjī, Musallam b. Muḥammad. *The Sīra of Imām Aḥmad b. Yaḥyā al-Nāṣir li-Dīn Allāh, from Musallam al-Laḥjī's Kitāb Akhbār al-Zaydiyya bi l-Yaman*, ed. W. Madelung. Exeter, 1990.

Lisān al-Mulk Sipihr, Muḥammad Taqī. *Nāsikh al-tawārīkh: taʾrīkh-i Qājāriyya*, ed. Muḥammad Bāqir Bihbūdī. Tehran, 1344 Sh./1965.

al-Majdūʿ, Ismāʿīl b. ʿAbd al-Rasūl. *Fahrasat al-kutub waʾl-rasāʾil*, ed. ʿAlī Naqī Munzavī. Tehran, 1966.

al-Majlisī, Muḥammad Bāqir b. Muḥammad Taqī. *Biḥār al-anwār*. Tehran, 1376–1392/1956–1972. 110 vols.

al-Maqrīzī, Taqī al-Dīn Aḥmad b. ʿAlī. *Ittiʿāẓ al-ḥunafāʾ bi-akhbār al-aʾimma al-Fāṭimiyyīn al-khulafāʾ*, ed. J. al-Shayyāl and Muḥammad Ḥ. M. Aḥmad. Cairo, 1387–1393/1967–1973; ed. Ayman F. Sayyid. Damascus, 2010. Partial English trans., *Towards a Shiʿi Mediterranean Empire: Fatimid Egypt and the Founding of Cairo, The Reign of the Imam-Caliph al-Muʿizz*, tr. S. Jiwa. London, 2009.

____ *Kitāb al-mawāʿiẓ waʾl-iʿtibār fī dhikr al-khiṭaṭ waʾl-āthār*. Būlāq, 1270/1853–1854.

____ *al-Sulūk li-maʿrifat duwal al-mulūk*. Cairo, 1971.

Marʿashī, Mīr Tīmūr. *Taʾrīkh-i khāndān-i Marʿashī-yi Māzandarān*, ed. M. Sutūda. 1356 Sh./1977.

Marʿashī, Ẓahīr al-Dīn. *Taʾrīkh-i Gīlān va Daylamistān*, ed. H. L. Rabino. Rasht, 1330/1912; ed. M. Sutūda. Tehran, 1347 Sh./1968.

____ *Taʾrīkh-i Ṭabaristān va Rūyān va Māzandarān*, ed. M. Ḥ. Tasbīḥī. Tehran, 1345 Sh./1966.

al-Masʿūdī, Abuʾl-Ḥasan ʿAlī b. al-Ḥusayn. *Murūj al-dhahab*, ed. and French tr. C. Barbier de Meynard and A. Pavet de Courteille. Paris, 1861–1876.

Maʿṣūm ʿAlī Shāh, Muḥammad Maʿṣūm Shīrāzī. *Ṭarāʾiq al-ḥaqāʾiq*, ed. Muḥammad Jaʿfar Maḥjūb. Tehran, 1339–1345 Sh./1960–1966.

Mīrkhwānd, Muḥammad b. Khwāndshāh. *Rawḍat al-ṣafāʾ*. Tehran, 1338–1339 Sh./1960.

Miskawayh, Abū ʿAlī Aḥmad b. Muḥammad. *Tajārib al-umam*, ed. and tr. Henry F. Amedroz and D. S. Margoliouth as *The Eclipse of the ʿAbbāsid Caliphate*. Oxford and London, 1920–1921.

al-Muʾayyad fiʾl-Dīn al-Shīrāzī, Abū Naṣr Hibat Allāh. *al-Majālis al-Muʾayyadiyya*, vols. 1 and 3, ed. M. Ghālib. Beirut, 1974–1984; vols. 1–3, ed. Ḥātim Ḥamīd al-Dīn. Bombay and Oxford, 1975–2005.

al-Mufaḍḍal b. ʿUmar al-Juʿfī (attributed). *Kitāb al-haft waʾl-aẓilla*, ed. ʿĀrif Tāmir and I. ʿA. Khalīfa. Beirut, 1960; ed. M. Ghālib. Beirut, 1964; also in *Silsilat al-turāth al-ʿAlawī*, vol. 6, pp. 290–423.

al-Mufīd, Abū ʿAbd Allāh Muḥammad b. Muḥammad. *Kitāb al-Irshād: The Book of Guidance into the Lives of the Twelve Imams*, tr. Ian K. A. Howard. London, 1981.

Mustanṣir biʾllāh II. *Pandiyāt-i jawānmardī*, ed. and tr. W. Ivanow. Leiden, 1953.

al-Najāshī, Aḥmad b. ʿAlī. *Kitāb al-rijāl*. Bombay, 1317/1899.

Nāṣir-i Khusraw, Ḥakīm Abū Muʿīn. *Kitāb jāmiʿ al-ḥikmatayn*, ed. H. Corbin and M. Muʿīn. Tehran and Paris, 1953. English trans., *Between Reason and Revelation: Twin Wisdoms Reconciled*, tr. E. Ormsby. London, 2012. French trans., *Le livre réunissant les deux sagesses*, tr. Isabelle de Gastines. Paris, 1990.

____ *Safar-nāma*, ed. and tr. Wheeler M. Thackston Jr. as *Book of Travels*. Costa Mesa, CA, 2001.

____ *Wajh-i dīn*, ed. G. R. Aʿvānī. Tehran, 1977.

al-Nawbakhtī, Abū Muḥammad al-Ḥasan b. Mūsā. *Firaq al-Shīʿa*, ed. H. Ritter. Istanbul, 1931. English trans., *Shīʿa Sects*, tr. Abbas K. Kadhim. London, 2007.

al-Nīsābūrī, Aḥmad b. Ibrāhīm. *Kitāb ithbāt al-imāma*, ed. and tr. Arzina R. Lalani as *Degrees of Excellence: A Fatimid Treatise on Leadership in Islam*. London, 2009.

____ *al-Risāla al-mūjaza al-kāfiya fī ādāb al-duʿāt*, ed. and tr. Verena Klemm and Paul E. Walker as *A Code of Conduct: A Treatise on the Etiquette of the Fatimid Ismaili Mission*. London, 2011.

Niẓām al-Mulk, Abū ʿAlī Ḥasan b. ʿAlī. *Siyar al-mulūk (Siyāsat-nāma)*, ed. H. Darke. 2nd ed., Tehran, 1347 Sh./1968. English trans., *The Book of Government or Rules for Kings*, tr. H. Darke. 2nd ed., London, 1978.

Nizārī Quhistānī, Ḥakīm Saʿd al-Dīn b. Shams al-Dīn. *Safar-nāma*, ed. Chingiz G. A. Bayburdi. Tehran, 1391 Sh./2012.

al-Nuʿmān b. Muḥammad, al-Qāḍī Abū Ḥanīfa. *Daʿāʾim al-Islām* ed. Asaf A. A. Fyzee. Cairo, 1951–1961. English trans., *The Pillars of Islam.*, tr. Asaf A. A. Fyzee, completely revised by Ismail K. Poonawala. New Delhi, 2002–2004.

____ *Iftitāḥ al-daʿwa wa-ibtidāʾ al-dawla*, ed. W. al-Qāḍī. Beirut, 1970; ed. F. Dachraoui. Tunis, 1975. English trans., *Founding the Fatimid State: The Rise of an Early Islamic Empire*, tr. H. Haji. London, 2006.

____ *Taʾwīl al-daʿāʾim*, ed. Muḥammad Ḥasan al-Aʿẓamī. Cairo, 1967–1972.

al-Nuwayrī, Shihāb al-Dīn Aḥmad b. ʿAbd al-Wahhāb. *Nihāyat al-arab fī funūn al-adab*, vol. 25, ed. M. Jābir ʿAbd al-ʿĀl al-Ḥīnī. Cairo, 1404/1984.

al-Qāsim b. Ibrāhīm al-Rassī. *Al-Ḳāsim b. Ibrāhīm on the Proof of God's Existence. Kitāb al-Dalīl al-Kabīr*, ed. and tr. B. Abrahamov. Leiden, 1990.

____ *Majmūʿ kutub wa-rasāʾil al-imām al-Qāsim b. Ibrāhīm al-Rassī, 169–246 H*, ed. ʿAbd al-Karīm A. Jadbān. Sanaa, 1423/2001.

al-Qummī, Saʿd b. ʿAbd Allāh al-Ashʿarī. *Kitāb al-maqālāt waʾl-firaq*, ed. Muḥammad J. Mashkūr. Tehran, 1963.

Rashīd al-Dīn Faḍl Allāh. *Jāmiʿ al-tawārīkh: qismat-i Ismāʿīliyān*, ed. M. T. Dānishpazhūh and M. Mudarrisī Zanjānī. Tehran, 1338 Sh./1959; ed. M. Rawshan. Tehran, 1387 Sh./2008.

____ *Jāmiʿ al-tawārīkh: taʾrīkhi-i āl-i Saljūq*, ed. A. Ateş. Ankara, 1960; ed. M. Rawshan. Tehran, 1386 Sh./2007. English trans., *The History of the Seljuq Turks from the Jāmiʿ al-Tawārīkh*, tr. Kenneth A. Luther, ed. C. Edmund Bosworth. Richmond, UK, 2001.

al-Rāwandī, Muḥammad b. ʿAlī. *Rāḥat al-ṣudūr*, ed. M. Iqbāl. London, 1921.

al-Rāzī, Abū Ḥātim Aḥmad b. Ḥamdān. *Kitāb al-iṣlāḥ*, ed. Ḥ. Mīnūchihr and M. Muḥaqqiq. Tehran, 1377 Sh./1998.

al-Shahrastānī, Abuʾl-Fatḥ Muḥammad b. ʿAbd al-Karīm. *Kitāb al-milal waʾl-niḥal*, ed. ʿA. M. al-Wakīl. Cairo, 1387/1968. Partial English trans., *Muslim Sects and Divisions*, tr. A. K. Kazi and J. G. Flynn. London, 1984. French trans., *Livre des religions et des sectes*, tr. D. Gimaret, G. Monnot and J. Jolivet. Louvain and Paris, 1986–1993.

al-Shawkānī, Muḥammad b. ʿAlī. *Nayl al-awṭār fī sharḥ muntaqa al-akhbār*. Beirut, 1989.

____ *al-Sayl al-jarrār al-mutadaffiq ʿalā ḥadāʾiq al-azhār*, ed. M. Zayid. Beirut, 1985.

Shihāb al-Dīn Shāh al-Ḥusaynī. *Khiṭābāt-i ʿāliya*, ed. H. Ujāqī. Bombay, 1963.

al-Shūshtarī, Qāḍī Nūr Allāh. *Majālis al-muʾminīn*. Tehran, 1375–1376/1955–1956.

al-Sijistānī, Abū Yaʿqūb Isḥāq b. Aḥmad. *Kashf al-maḥjūb*, ed. H. Corbin. Tehran and Paris, 1949. Partial English trans., *Unveiling of the Hidden*, tr. H. Landolt, in *An Anthology of Philosophy in Persia*: Volume 2, *Ismaili Thought in the Classical Age*, ed. S. H. Nasr and M. Aminrazavi. London, 2008, pp. 71–129. French trans., *Le dévoilement des choses cachées*, tr. H. Corbin. Lagrasse, 1988.

____ *Kitāb al-yanābīʿ*, ed. and tr. H. Corbin, in his *Trilogie Ismaélienne*. Tehran and Paris, 1961, text pp. 1–97, French translation, pp. 5–127. English trans., *The Book of Wellsprings*, tr. Paul E. Walker in his *The Wellsprings of Wisdom*. Salt Lake City, 1994, pp. 37–111.

Silsilat al-turāth al-ʿAlawī, ed. Abū Mūsā al-Ḥarīrī and Shaykh Mūsā. Lebanon, 2006–2010. 10 vols.

al-Ṭabarānī, Abū Saʿīd Maymūn b. al-Qāsim. *Kitāb al-ḥāwī fī ʿilm al-fatāwā*, in *Silsilat al-turāth al-ʿAlawī*, vol. 3, pp. 45–116.

____ *Kitāb majmūʿ al-aʿyād*, ed. R. Strothmann in his 'Festkalender der Nuṣairier', *Der Islam*, 27 (1944), pp. 1–60, and 27 (1946), pp. 161–273; also in *Silsilat al-turāth al-ʿAlawī*, vol. 3, pp. 207–412.

al-Ṭabarī, Abū Jaʿfar Muḥammad b. Jarīr. *Taʾrīkh al-rusul waʾl-mulūk*, ed. Michael J. de Goeje et al. Series I-III. Leiden, 1879–1901. English trans. by various scholars as *The History of al-Ṭabarī*. Albany, NY, 1985–1999.

Taʾrīkh-i Sīstān, ed. M. T. Bahār. Tehran, 1314 Sh./1935. English trans., *The Tārīkh-i Sīstān*, tr. M. Gold. Rome, 1976.

Trilogie Ismaélienne, ed. and tr. H. Corbin. Tehran and Paris, 1961.

al-Ṭūsī, Abū Jaʿfar Muḥammad b. al-Ḥasan. *Fihrist kutub al-Shīʿa*, ed. A. Sprenger et al. Calcutta, 1853–1855.

____ *al-Istibṣār*, ed. Ḥasan al-Mūsawī al-Kharsān. Najaf, 1375–1376/1955–1957.

____ *Rijāl al-Ṭūsī*, ed. Muḥammad Ṣādiq Āl Baḥr al-ʿUlūm. Najaf, 1381/1961.

____ *Tahdhīb al-aḥkām*. Najaf, 1380/1960.

al-Ṭūsī, Khwāja Naṣīr al-Dīn Muḥammad b. Muḥammad. *Akhlāq-i Nāṣirī*, ed. M. Mīnuvī and ʿA. Ḥaydarī. Tehran, 1360 Sh./1981. English trans., *The Nasirean Ethics*, tr. George M. Wickens. London, 1964.

____ *Rawḍa-yi taslīm*, ed. and tr. S. J. Badakhchani as *Paradise of Submission: A Medieval Treatise on Ismaili Thought*. London, 2005. French trans., *La convocation d'Alamût. Somme de philosophie Ismaélienne*, tr. Christian Jambet. Lagrasse, 1996.

____ *al-Risāla fiʾl-imāma*, ed. M. T. Dānishpazhūh. Tehran, 1335 Sh./1956.

____ *Sayr va sulūk*, ed. and tr. S. J. Badakhchani as *Contemplation and Action: The Spiritual Autobiography of a Muslim Scholar*. London, 1998.

____ *Shiʿi Interpretations of Islam: Three Treatises on Theology and Eschatology*, ed. and tr. S. J. Badakhchani. London, 2010.

____ *Tajrīd al-iʿtiqād*, ed. ʿAbbās M. Ḥ. Sulaymān. Cairo, 1996.

ʿUmāra al-Yamanī, Najm al-Dīn b. ʿAlī al-Ḥakamī. *Taʾrīkh al-Yaman*, ed. and tr. Kay, in *Yaman*, text pp. 1–102, translation, pp. 1–137.

Umm al-kitāb, ed. W. Ivanow, in *Der Islam*, 23 (1936), pp. 1–132. Italian trans., *Ummu'l-Kitāb*, tr. P. Filippani-Ronconi. Naples, 1966. Partial German trans., in Halm, *Die islamische Gnosis*, pp. 113–198. Turkish trans., in İsmail Kaygusuz, *Bir Proto-Alevi Kaynağı, Ummü'l-Kitab*, tr. A. Selman. Istanbul, 2009, pp. 121–258.

Vazīrī, Aḥmad ʿAlī Khān. *Ta'rīkh-i Kirmān*, ed. M. I. Bāstānī Pārīzī. 2nd ed., Tehran, 1364 Sh./1985.

William of Tyre. *Willelmi Tyrensis Archiepiscopi Chronicon*, ed. Robert B. C. Huygens. Turnhout, 1986. English trans., *A History of Deeds Done Beyond the Sea*, ed. Emily A. Babcock and A. C. Krey. New York, 1943.

Yaḥyā b. al-Ḥusayn b. al-Qāsim. *Ghāyat al-amānī fī akhbār al-quṭr al-Yamānī*, ed. Saʿīd ʿA. ʿĀshūr. Cairo, 1388/1968.

Yaman, its Early Medieval History, ed. and tr. Henry C. Kay. London, 1892.

Ẓahīr al-Dīn Nīshāpūrī. *Saljūq-nāma*, ed. Ismāʿīl Afshār. Tehran, 1332 Sh./1953; ed. A. H. Morton. Chippenham, 2004.

3. Studies

Abrahamian, Ervand. *Iran Between Two Revolutions*. Princeton, 1982.

Abrahamov, Binyamin. 'Al-Ḳāsim Ibn Ibrāhīm's Theory of the Imamate', *Arabica*, 34 (1987), pp. 80–105.

Abu-Izzeddin, Nejla M. *The Druzes: A New Study of their History, Faith and Society*. Leiden, 1984.

Aga Khan III, Sultan Muhammad (Mahomed) Shah. *The Memoirs of Aga Khan: World Enough and Time*. London, 1954.

____ *Aga Khan III: Selected Speeches and Writings of Sir Sultan Muhammad Shah*, ed. K. K. Aziz. London, 1997–1998.

Ajami, Fouad. *The Vanished Imam: Musa Al Sadr and the Shia of Lebanon*. London, 1986.

Akhavi, Shahrough. *Religion and Politics in Contemporary Iran: Clergy–State Relations in the Pahlavī Period*. Albany, NY, 1980.

____ 'Contending Discourses in Shiʿi Law on the Doctrine of *Wilāyat al-Faqīh*', *Iranian Studies*, 29 (1996), pp. 229–268.

Algar, Hamid. *Religion and State in Iran, 1785–1906: The Role of the Ulama in the Qajar Period*. Berkeley, 1969.

____ 'The Revolt of Āghā Khān Maḥallātī and the Transference of the Ismāʿīlī Imamate to India', *Studia Islamica*, 29 (1969), pp. 55–81.

____ 'The Oppositional Role of the Ulama in Twentieth-Century Iran', in Nikki R. Keddie, ed., *Scholars, Saints, and Sufis: Muslim Religious Institutions in the Middle East since 1500*. Berkeley, 1972, pp. 231–255.

____ 'Religious Forces in Eighteenth- and Nineteenth-Century Iran', in *The Cambridge History of Iran*: Volume 7, pp. 705–731.

____ 'Religious Forces in Twentieth-Century Iran', in *The Cambridge History of Iran*, Volume 7, pp. 732–764.

____ 'Maḥallātī, Āghā Khān', *EI2*, vol. 5, pp. 1221–1222.

____ 'Nuḳtawiyya', *EI2*, vol. 8, pp. 114–117.

____ 'Āqā Khan', *EIR*, vol. 2, pp. 170–175.

____ 'Borūjerdī, Ḥosayn Ṭabāṭabā'ī', *EIR*, vol. 4, pp. 376–379.

____ 'Horufism', *EIR*, vol. 12, pp. 483–490.

Ali, S. Mujtaba. *The Origin of the Khojāhs and their Religious Life Today*. Würzburg, 1936.

Alí-de-Unzaga, Omar (ed.). *Fortresses of the Intellect: Ismaili and Other Islamic Studies in Honour of Farhad Daftary*. London, 2011.

Amanat, Abbas. 'In Between the Madrasa and the Marketplace: The Designation of Clerical Leadership in Modern Shi'ism', in S. Amir Arjomand, ed., *Authority and Political Culture in Shi'ism*. Albany, NY, 1988, pp. 98–132.

____ 'The Nuqṭawī Movement of Maḥmūd Pisīkhānī and his Persian Cycle of Mystical-Materialism', in Daftary, ed., *Mediaeval Isma'ili History*, pp. 281–297.

____ *Apocalyptic Islam and Iranian Shi'ism*. London, 2009.

Amiji, Hatim M. 'The Asian Communities', in James Kritzeck and William H. Lewis, ed., *Islam in Africa*. New York, 1969, pp. 141–181.

Amir-Moezzi, Mohammad-Ali.*The Divine Guide in Early Shi'ism: The Sources of Esotericism in Islam*, tr. D. Streight. Albany, NY, 1994.

____ *The Spirituality of Shi'i Islam: Beliefs and Practices*, tr. Hafiz Karmali. London, 2011.

Amir-Moezzi, Mohammad-Ali and Christian Jambet. *Qu'est-ce que le Shî'isme?* Paris, 2004.

Amir-Moezzi, Mohammad-Ali et al. (ed.). *Le Shī'isme Imāmite quarante ans après. Hommage à Etan Kohlberg*. Turnhout, 2009.

Amoretti, Biancamaria Scarcia. 'Religion in the Timurid and Safavid Periods', in *The Cambridge History of Iran*: Volume 6, pp. 610–655.

____ *Sciiti nel mondo*. Rome, 1994.

al-'Amrī, Ḥusayn 'Abdullāh. *The Yemen in the 18th and 19th Centuries: A Political and Intellectual History*. London, 1985.

Ansari, Hassan, 'Abū al-Khaṭṭāb', *EIS*, vol. 2, pp. 203–210.

Ansari, Hassan and Sabine Schmidtke. 'The Literary-Religious Tradition among 7th/13th Century Yemenī Zaydīs: The Formation of the Imam al-Mahdī li-Dīn Allāh Aḥmad b. al-Ḥusayn b. al-Qāsim (d. 656/1258)', *Journal of Islamic Manuscripts*, 2 (2011), pp. 165–222.

Arendonk, Cornelis van. *Les débuts de l'Imāmat Zaidite au Yémen*, tr. J. Ryckmans. Leiden, 1960.

Aringberg-Laanatza, Marianne. 'Alevis in Turkey – Alawites in Syria: Similarities and Differences', in Olsson et al., ed., *Alevi Identity*, pp. 151–165.

Arjomand, Said Amir. 'The Office of *Mullā-bāshī* in Shi'ite Iran', *Studia Islamica*, 57 (1983), pp. 135–146.

____ *The Shadow of God and the Hidden Imam*. Chicago, 1984.

____ *The Turban for the Crown: The Islamic Revolution in Iran*. Oxford, 1988.

____ 'The Crisis of the Imamate and the Institution of Occultation in Twelver Shi'ism: A Sociohistorical Perspective', *IJMES*, 28 (1996), pp. 491–515; reprinted in Kohlberg, ed., *Shī'ism*, pp. 109–133.

____ 'Imam *Absconditus* and the Beginning of a Theology of Occultation: Imami Shi'ism *circa* 280–90 A.H./900 A.D.', *JAOS*, 117 (1997), pp. 1–12.

____ 'Authority in Shiism and Constitutional Development in the Islamic Republic of Iran', in Brunner and Ende, ed., *Twelver Shia*, pp. 301–332.

____ 'The 1906–07 Iranian Constitution and the Constitutional Debate on Islam', *Journal of Persianate Studies*, 5 (2012), pp. 152–174.

____ 'Khumaynī, Sayyid Rūḥ Allāh Mūsawī', *EI2*, vol. 12, Supplement, pp. 530–531.

____ (ed.). *Authority and Political Culture in Shi'ism*. Albany, NY, 1988.

Asani, Ali S. *Ecstasy and Enlightenment: The Ismaili Devotional Literature of South Asia*. London, 2002.

____ 'Creating Tradition through Devotional Songs and Communal Script: The Khojah Isma'ilis of South Asia', in Richard Eaton, ed., *India's Islamic Traditions 711–1750, Themes in Indian History*. New Delhi, 2003, pp. 285–310.

____ 'From Satpanthi to Ismaili Muslim: The Articulation of Ismaili Khoja Identity in South Asia', in Daftary, ed., *A Modern History of the Ismailis*, pp. 95–128.

Axworthy, Michael. *The Sword of Persia: Nader Shah from Tribal Warrior to Conquering Tyrant*. London, 2006.

Ayoub, Mahmoud. *Redemptive Suffering in Islam: A Study of the Devotional Aspects of 'Āshūrā' in Twelver Shī'ism*. The Hague, 1978.

Aziz, Muhammad Ali. *Religion and Mysticism in Early Islam: Theology and Sufism in Yemen*. London, 2011.

Babayan, Kathryn. *Mystics, Monarchs and Messiahs: Cultural Landscapes of Early Modern Iran*. Cambridge, MA, 2002.

Bakhash, Shaul.*The Reign of the Ayatollahs: Iran and the Islamic Revolution*. London, 1985.

Bar-Asher, Meir M. 'Sur les éléments Chrétiens de la religion Nuṣayrite-'Alawite', *Journal Asiatique*, 289 (2001), pp. 185–216.

____ 'The Iranian Components of the Nuṣayrī Religion', *Iran, Journal of the British Institute of Persian Studies*, 41 (2003), pp. 217–227.

____ 'Nusayris', in *Medieval Islamic Civilization: An Encyclopedia,* ed. Josef W. Meri. London and New York, 2006, vol. 2, pp. 569–570.

____ 'Le rapport de la religion Nuṣayrite-ʿAlawite au Shiʿisme Imamite', in M. A. Amir-Moezzi et al., ed., *Le Shīʿisme Imāmite quarante ans après. Hommage à Etan Kohlberg*. Turnhout, 2009, pp. 73–93.

Bar-Asher, Meir M. and A. Kofsky. *The Nuṣayrī-ʿAlawī Religion: An Enquiry into its Theology and Liturgy*. Leiden, 2002.

____ 'The Nuṣayrī Doctrine of ʿAlī's Divinity and the Nuṣayrī Trinity according to an Unpublished Treatise from the 7th/13th Century', in Ahmet Y. Ocak, ed., *From History to Theology, Ali in Islamic Beliefs*. Ankara, 2005, pp. 111–147.

Barrucand, Marianne (ed.). *L'Égypte Fatimide, son art et son histoire.* Paris, 1999.

Bashir, Shahzad. *Fazlallah Astarabadi and the Hurufis*. Oxford, 2005.

Bayat, Mangol. *Mysticism and Dissent: Socioreligious Thought in Qajar Iran.* Syracuse, NY, 1982.

Berkey, Jonathan P. *The Formation of Islam: Religion and Society in the Near East, 600–1800*. Cambridge, 2003.

Bertel's, Andrey E. *Nasir-i Khosrov i ismailizm*. Moscow, 1959. Persian trans., *Nāṣir-i Khusraw va Ismāʿīliyān*, tr. Y. Āriyanpūr. Tehran, 1346 Sh./1967.

Birge, John. *The Bektashi Order of Dervishes*. London, 1965.

Blank, Jonah. *Mullas on the Mainframe: Islam and Modernity among the Daudi Bohras*. Chicago, 2001.

Bloom, Jonathan M. *Arts of the City Victorious: Islamic Art and Architecture in Fatimid North Africa and Egypt*. New Haven, 2007.

Boivin, Michel. 'The Reform of Islam in Ismaili Shīʿism from 1885 to 1957', in Françoise 'Nalini' Delvoye, ed., *Confluences of Cultures: French Contributions to Indo-Persian Studies*. New Delhi, 1994, pp. 197–216.

____ 'Ghulât et Chiʿisme Salmanien chez Louis Massignon', in Ève Pierunek and Yann Richard, ed., *Louis Massignon et l'Iran*. Paris and Leuven, 2000, pp. 61–75.

____ *La rénovation du Shîʿisme Ismaélien en Inde et au Pakistan. D'après les ecrits et les discours de Sulṭān Muḥammad Shah Aga Khan (1902–1954).* London, 2003.

Bosworth, C. Edmund. *Sīstān under the Arabs, from the Islamic Conquest to the Rise of the Ṣaffārids (30–250/651–864).* Rome, 1968.

____ *The History of the Saffarids of Sistan and the Maliks of Nimruz (247/861 to 949/1542–3).* Costa Mesa, CA and New York, 1994.

Bredi, Daniela. 'Profilo della communità Sciita del Pakistan', *Oriente Moderno*, 75 (1995), pp. 27–75.

Brett, Michael. *The Rise of the Fatimids: The World of the Mediterranean and the Middle East in the Fourth Century of the Hijra, Tenth Century CE.* Leiden, 2001.

Browne, Edward G. *The Persian Revolution of 1905–1909*. Cambridge, 1910.

____ *A Literary History of Persia*. London and Cambridge, 1902–1924.

Brunner, Rainer and W. Ende (ed.). *The Twelver Shia in Modern Times: Religious Culture and Political History*. Leiden, 2001.

Bryer, David R. W. 'The Origins of the Druze Religion', *Der Islam*, 52 (1975), pp. 47–84, 239–262, and 53 (1976), pp. 5–27.

Cahen, Claude. 'Points de vue sur la "Révolution Abbāside"', *Revue Historique*, 230 (1963), pp. 295–338; reprinted in his *Les Peuples Musulmans dans l'histoire médiévale*. Damascus, 1977, pp. 105–160.

____ 'Le problème du Shî'isme dans l'Asie Mineure turque préottomane', in Fahd, ed., *Le Shî'isme Imâmite*, pp. 115–129.

____ 'Note sur les origines de la communauté Syrienne des Nuṣayris', *Revue des Études Islamiques*, 38 (1970), pp. 243–249.

Calder, Norman. 'Zakāt in Imāmī Shī'ī Jurisprudence, from the Tenth to the Sixteenth Century A.D.', *BSOAS*, 44 (1981), pp. 468–480.

____ 'Accommodation and Revolution in Imami Shi'i Jurisprudence: Khumayni and the Classical Tradition', *Middle Eastern Studies*, 18 (1982), pp. 3–20.

____ 'Khums in Imāmī Shī'ī Jurisprudence, from the Tenth to the Sixteenth Century A.D.', *BSOAS*, 45 (1982), pp. 39–47.

____ 'Doubt and Prerogative: The Emergence of an Imāmī Shī'ī Theory of *Ijtihād*', *Studia Islamica*, 70 (1989), pp. 57–78.

____ *Interpretation and Jurisprudence in Medieval Islam*, ed. J. Mojaddedi and A. Rippin. Aldershot, 2006.

Calmard, Jean. 'Mardja'-i Taḳlīd', *EI2*, vol. 6, pp. 548–556.

The Cambridge History of Iran: Volume 4, *The Period from the Arab Invasion to the Saljuqs*, ed. Richard N. Frye. Cambridge, 1975.

The Cambridge History of Iran: Volume 5, *The Saljuq and Mongol Periods*, ed. John A. Boyle. Cambridge, 1968.

The Cambridge History of Iran: Volume 6, *The Timurid and Safavid Periods*, ed. P. Jackson and L. Lockhart. Cambridge, 1986.

The Cambridge History of Iran: Volume 7, *From Nadir Shah to the Islamic Republic*, ed. P. Avery, G. Hambly and C. Melville. Cambridge, 1991.

Canard, Marius. *Miscellanea Orientalia*. London, 1973.

____ 'Fāṭimids', *EI2*, vol. 2, pp. 850–862.

Catafago, Joseph. 'Notice sur les Ansériens', *Journal Asiatique*, 4th series, 11 (1848), pp. 149–168.

Chittick, William. 'Ibn ʿArabī and his School', in S. H. Nasr, ed., *Islamic Spirituality: Manifestations*. London, 1991, pp. 49–79.

Cilardo, Agostino. *Diritto ereditario Islamico delle scuole giuridiche Ismailita e Imamita*. Rome and Naples, 1993.

____ *Diritto ereditario Islamico delle scuole giuridiche Sunnite (Ḥanafita, Mālikita, Šāfiʿita e Ḥanbalita) e delle scuole giuridiche Zaydita, Ẓāhirita e Ibāḍita*. Rome and Naples, 1994.

Cobban, Helena. 'The Growth of Shiʿi Power in Lebanon and its Implications for the Future', in Cole and Keddie, ed., *Shiʿism and Social Protest*, pp. 137–155.

Cole, Juan R. 'Imami Jurisprudence and the Role of the Ulama: Mortaza Ansari on Emulating the Supreme Exemplar', in Keddie, ed., *Religion and Politics in Iran*, pp. 33–46.

____ 'Shiʿi Clerics in Iraq and Iran, 1722–1780: The Akhbari-Usuli Conflict Reconsidered', *Iranian Studies*, 18 (1985), pp. 3–34.

____ *Roots of North Indian Shīʿism in Iran and Iraq: Religion and State in Awadh, 1722–1859*. Berkeley, 1988.

____ 'Casting Away the Self: The Mysticism of Shaykh Aḥmad al-Aḥsāʾī', in Brunner and Ende, ed.,*Twelver Shia*, pp. 25–37.

____ *Sacred Space and Holy War: The Politics, Culture and History of Shiʿite Islam*. London, 2002.

Cole, Juan R. and Nikki R. Keddie (ed.). *Shiʿism and Social Protest*. New Haven, 1986.

Cook, Michael. *Commanding Right and Forbidding Wrong in Islamic Thought*. Cambridge, 2000.

Corbin, Henry. 'Confessions extatiques de Mīr Dāmād', in *Mélanges Louis Massignon*. Damascus, 1956, vol. 1, pp. 331–378.

____ 'Au pays de l'imām caché', *Eranos Jahrbuch*, 32 (1963), pp. 31–87.

____ 'L'initiation Ismaélienne ou l'ésotérisme et le Verbe', *Eranos Jahrbuch*, 39 (1970), pp. 41–142; reprinted in his *L'homme et son ange. Initiation et chevalerie spirituelle*. Paris, 1983, pp. 81–205.

____ *En Islam Iranien: Aspects spirituels et philosophiques*. Paris, 1971–1972.

____ *Spiritual Body and Celestial Earth: From Mazdean Iran to Shīʿite Iran*, tr. N. Pearson. Princeton, 1977.

____ 'The Ismāʿīlī Response to the Polemic of Ghazālī', in Nasr, ed., *Ismāʿīlī Contributions*, pp. 67–98.

____ *Cyclical Time and Ismaili Gnosis*, tr. R. Manheim and James W. Morris. London, 1983.

____ *Temple and Contemplation*, tr. Philip Sherrard. London, 1986.

____ *Histoire de la philosophie Islamique*. Paris, 1986. English trans., *History of Islamic Philosophy*, tr. L. Sherrard. London, 1993.

____ *L'Imâm caché*. Paris, 2003.

Cortese, Delia and Simonetta Calderini. *Women and the Fatimids in the World of Islam*. Edinburgh, 2006.

Crone, Patricia. *Medieval Islamic Political Thought*. Edinburgh, 2004.

____ *From Kavād to al-Ghazālī: Religion, Law and Political Thought in the Near East, c.600–c.1100*. Aldershot, 2005.

____ *From Arabian Tribes to Islamic Empire: Army, State and Society in the Near East c. 600–850*. Aldershot, 2008.

____ *The Nativist Prophets of Early Islamic Iran: Rural Revolt and Local Zoroastrianism*. Cambridge, 2012.

____ 'Mawlā: II. In Historical and Legal Usage', *EI2*, vol. 6, pp., 874–882.

____ "Uthmāniyya', *EI2*, vol. 10, pp. 952–954.

Crone, Patricia and M. Hinds. *God's Caliph: Religious Authority in the First Centuries of Islam*. Cambridge, 1986.

Dabashi, Hamid. 'The Philosopher/Vizier: Khwāja Naṣīr al-Dīn al-Ṭūsī and the Isma'ilis', in Daftary, ed., *Mediaeval Isma'ili History*, pp. 231–245.

____ 'Mīr Dāmād and the Founding of the "School of Isfahan"', in S. H. Nasr and O. Leaman, ed., *History of Islamic Philosophy*. London, 2001, vol. 1, pp. 597–634.

Dachraoui, Farhat. *Le califat Fatimide au Maghreb (296–365 H./909–975 Jc.)*. Tunis, 1981.

Daftary, Farhad. *The Ismāʿīlīs: Their History and Doctrines*. 2nd ed., Cambridge, 2007.

____ 'The Earliest Ismāʿīlīs', *Arabica*, 38 (1991), pp. 214–245; reprinted in Kohlberg, ed., *Shīʿism*, pp. 235–266; also in P. Luft and C. Turner, ed., *Shiʿism: Critical Concepts in Islamic Studies*, Volume I: *Origins and Evolution*. London, 2008, pp. 132–157.

____ 'A Major Schism in the Early Ismāʿīlī Movement', *Studia Islamica*, 77 (1993), pp. 123–139.

____ *The Assassin Legends: Myths of the Ismaʿilis*. London, 1994. French trans., *Légendes des Assassins*, tr. Z. Rajan-Badouraly. Paris, 2007. Persian trans., *Afsānahā-yi ḥashāshīn*, tr. F. Badra'ī. Tehran, 1376 Sh./1997. Russian trans., *Legendy ob Assasinakh*, tr. L. R. Dodykhudoeva. Moscow, 2009. Turkish trans., *Alamut Efsanelari*, tr. Ö. Çelebi. Ankara, 2008.

____ *A Short History of the Ismailis: Traditions of a Muslim Community*. Edinburgh, 1998. Arabic trans., *Mukhtaṣar ta'rīkh al-Ismāʿīliyyīn*, tr. S. al-Qaṣīr. Damascus and Beirut, 2001. French trans., *Les Ismaéliens*, tr. Z. Rajan-Badouraly. Paris, 2003. German trans., *Kurze Geschichte der Ismailiten*, tr. K. Maier. Würzburg, 2003. Italian trans., *Gli Ismailiti*, tr. A. Straface. Venice, 2011. Persian trans., *Mukhtaṣarī dar taʾrīkh-i Ismāʿīliyya*, tr. F. Badraʾī. Tehran, 1378 Sh./1999. Portuguese trans., *Breve história dos Ismaelitas*, tr. P. J. de Sousa Pinto. Lisbon, 2003. Russian trans., *Kratkaya istoriya ismaʿilizma*, tr. L. R. Dodykhudoeva and L. N. Dodkhudoeva. Moscow, 2003.

____ 'Sayyida Ḥurra: The Ismāʿīlī Ṣulayḥid Queen of Yemen', in Gavin R. G. Hambly, ed., *Women in the Medieval Islamic World*. New York, 1998, pp. 117–130.

____ 'Ismāʿīlī–Sufi Relations in Early Post-Alamūt and Safavid Persia', in L. Lewisohn and D. Morgan, ed., *The Heritage of Sufism*: Volume III, *Late Classical Persianate Sufism (1501–1750)*. Oxford, 1999, pp. 275–289.

____ 'Intellectual Life among the Ismailis: An Overview', in F. Daftary, ed., *Intellectual Traditions in Islam*. London, 2000, pp. 87–111.

____ *Ismailis in Medieval Muslim Societies*. London, 2005.

____ 'ʿAlī in Classical Ismaili Theology', in Ahmet Y. Ocak, ed., *From History to Theology, Ali in Islamic Beliefs*. Ankara, 2005, pp. 59–82.

____ 'The "Order of the Assassins": J. von Hammer and the Orientalist Misrepresentations of the Nizari Ismailis', *Iranian Studies*, 39 (2006), pp. 71–81.

____ 'Ismaili History and Literary Traditions', in H. Landolt, S. Sheikh and K. Kassam, ed., *An Anthology of Ismaili Literature*. London, 2008, pp. 1–29.

____ 'Sinān and the Nizārī Ismailis of Syria', in Daniela Bredi et al., ed., *Scritti in onore di Biancamaria Scarcia Amoretti*. Rome, 2008, pp. 489–500.

____ 'Al-Qāḍī al-Nuʿmān, Ismāʿīlī Law and Imāmī Shīʿism', in M. A. Amir-Moezzi et al., ed., *Le Shīʿisme Imāmite quarante ans après. Hommage à Etan Kohlberg*. Turnhout, 2009, pp. 179–186.

____ 'Religious Identity, Dissimulation and Assimilation: The Ismaili Experience', in Y. Suleiman, ed., *Living Islamic History: Studies in Honour of Professor Carole Hillenbrand*. Edinburgh, 2010, pp. 47–61.

____ 'Hidden Imams and Mahdis in Ismaili History', in Bruce D. Craig, ed., *Ismaili and Fatimid Studies in Honor of Paul E. Walker*. Chicago, 2010, pp. 1–22.

____ 'Varieties of Islam', in *The New Cambridge History of Islam:* Volume 4, *Islamic Culture and Societies to the End of the Eighteenth Century*, ed. R. Irwin. Cambridge, 2010, pp. 105–141.

____ 'Rāshid al-Dīn Sinān', *EI2*, vol. 8, pp. 442–443.

____ 'ʿAlids', *EI3*, 2008–2, pp. 78–81.

____ 'Carmatians', *EIR*, vol. 4, pp. 823–832.

____ 'Ḥasan Ṣabbāḥ', *EIR*, vol. 12, pp. 34–37.

____ 'Ismaʿilism', *EIR*, vol. 14, pp. 173–195.

____ 'Assassins', *EIS*, vol. 3, pp. 911–914.

____ 'Assassins', in *The Oxford Encyclopedia of the Islamic World*, ed. John L. Esposito. Oxford, 2009, vol. 1, pp. 227–229.

____ 'Aga Khan', in *The Princeton Encyclopedia of Islamic Political Thought*, ed. G. Bowering. Princeton, 2013, pp. 22–23.

____ (ed.). *Mediaeval Isma'ili History and Thought*. Cambridge, 1996.

____ (ed.). *A Modern History of the Ismailis: Continuity and Change in a Muslim Community*. London, 2010.

____ and Zulfikar Hirji. *The Ismailis: An Illustrated History*. London, 2008.

____ and Joseph W. Meri (ed.). *Culture and Memory in Medieval Islam: Essays in Honour of Wilferd Madelung*. London, 2003.

____ and Azim Nanji. 'What is Shiite Islam?', in Vincent J. Cornell, ed., *Voices of Islam:* Volume 1, *Voices of Tradition*. Westport, CT, 2007, pp. 217–244.

Daiber, Hans. 'Al-Ṭūsī, Naṣīr al-Dīn', *EI2*, vol. 10, pp. 746–750.

Dakake, Maria M. *The Charismatic Community: Shi'ite Identity in Early Islam*. Albany, NY, 2007.

Daniel, Elton L. *The Political and Social History of Khurasan under Abbasid Rule, 747–820*. Minneapolis, MN, 1979.

Daniel, Norman. *Islam and the West: The Making of an Image*. Edinburgh, 1966.

De Smet, Daniel. *La quiétude de l'intellect: Néoplatonisme et gnose Ismaélienne dans l'oeuvre de Ḥamîd ad-Dîn al-Kirmânî (Xe/XIes.)*. Leuven, 1995.

____ *La philosophie Ismaélienne: un ésotérisme chiite entre néoplatonisme et gnose*. Paris, 2012.

Donaldson, Dwight M. *The Shi'ite Religion*. London, 1933.

Donner, Fred M. 'Modern Approaches to Early Islamic History', in *The New Cambridge History of Islam:* Volume 1, *The Formation of the Islamic World Sixth to Eleventh Centuries*, ed. Chase F. Robinson. Cambridge, 2010, pp. 625–647.

Dresch, Paul. *Tribes, Government, and History in Yemen*. Oxford, 1993.

____ *A History of Modern Yemen*. Cambridge, 2002.

Dumasia, Naoroji M. *The Aga Khan and His Ancestors: A Biographical and Historical Sketch*. Bombay, 1939; reprinted, New Delhi, 2008.

Dussaud, René. *Histoire et religion des Noṣairîs*. Paris, 1900.

Eboo Jamal, Nadia. *Surviving the Mongols: Nizārī Quhistānī and the Continuity of Ismaili Tradition in Persia*. London, 2002.

Ebrahimi, Zeinolabedin. 'al-Aḥsā'ī', *EIS*, vol. 3, pp. 362–367.

El-Bizri, Nader (ed.). *The Ikhwān al-Ṣafā' and their Rasā'il: An Introduction*. Oxford, 2008.

Emerson, John, 'Chardin', *EIR*, vol. 5, pp. 369–377.

Enayat, Hamid. 'Iran: Khumayni's Concept of the "Guardianship of the Jurist"', in J. Piscatori, ed., *Islam and the Political Process*. Cambridge, 1982, pp. 160–180.

Engineer, Ali Asghar. *The Bohras*. New Delhi, 1980.

Eschragi, Armin. 'Kāẓem Rašti', *EIR*, vol. 16, pp. 201–205.

van Ess, Josef. *Theologie und Gesellschaft im 2. und 3. Jahrhundert Hidschra*. Berlin and New York, 1991–1997.

Faghfoory, Mohammad. 'Ulama-State Relations in Iran: 1921–1941', *IJMES*, 19 (1987), pp. 413–432.

Fahd, Toufic (ed.). *Le Shîʿisme Imâmite. Colloque de Strasbourg (6–9 mai 1968)*. Paris, 1970.

Filippani-Ronconi, Pio. *Ismaeliti ed 'Assassini'*. Milan, 1973.

Firro, Kais. *A History of the Druzes*. Leiden, 1992.

Fischer, Michael M. J. *Iran: From Religious Dispute to Revolution*. Cambridge, MA, 1980.

Friedman, Yaron. 'al-Ḥusayn ibn Hamdān al-Khaṣībī: A Historical Biography of the Founder of the Nuṣayrī-'Alawite Sect', *Studia Islamica*, 93 (2001), pp. 91–112.

____ 'Ibn Taymiyya's *Fatāwa* against the Nuṣayrī-'Alawī Sect', *Der Islam*, 82 (2005), pp. 349–363.

____ *The Nuṣayrī-ʿAlawīs: An Introduction to the Religion, History and Identity of the Leading Minority in Syria*. Leiden, 2010.

Frischauer, Willi. *The Aga Khans*. London, 1970.

Frye, Richard N. *The Golden Age of Persia*. London, 1975.

Fyzee, Asaf A. A. *Cases in the Muhammadan Law of India and Pakistan*. Oxford, 1965.

____ 'The Ismāʿīlīs', in Arthur J. Arberry, ed., *Religion in the Middle East: Volume 2, Islam*. Cambridge, 1969, pp. 318–329.

____ 'Bohorās', *EI2*, vol. 1, pp. 1254–1255.

Gabrieli, Francesco. *Al-Ma'mūn e gli 'Alidi*. Leipzig, 1929.

Ghani, Cyrus. *Iran and the Rise of Reza Shah: From Qajar Collapse to Pahlavi Rule*. London, 1998.

Gheisari, Ehsan. 'Akhbāriyya', *EIS*, vol. 3, pp. 407–412.

Gleave, Robert. *Inevitable Doubt: Two Theories of Shīʿī Jurisprudence*. Leiden, 2000.

____ *Scripturalist Islam: The History and Doctrine of the Akhbārī Shīʿī School*. Leiden, 2007.

____ 'Shīʿism', in Choueiri, ed., *A Companion to the History of the Middle East*, pp. 87–105.

____ 'Compromise and Conciliation in the Akhbārī-Uṣūlī Dispute: Yūsuf al-Baḥrānī's Assessment of 'Abd Allāh al-Samāhījī's *Munyat*

al-Mumārisīn', in Alí-de-Unzaga, ed., *Fortresses of the Intellect*, pp. 491–519.
____ "Alī b. Abī Ṭālib', *EI3*, 2008–2, pp. 62–71.
Gobillot, Geneviève. *Les Chiites*. Turnhout, 1998.
Goddard, Hugh. *A History of Christian–Muslim Relations*. Edinburgh and Chicago, 2000.
Goldberg, Jacob. 'The Shiʿi Minority in Saudi Arabia', in Cole and Keddie, ed., *Shiʿism and Social Protest*, pp. 230–246.
Goldziher, Ignaz. *Introduction to Islamic Theology and Law*, tr. A. and R. Hamori. Princeton, 1981.
Guyard, Stanislas. 'Le Fetwa d'Ibn Taimiyyah sur les Nosairis', *Journal Asiatique*, 6th series, 18 (1871), pp. 158–198.
Haider, Najam. *The Origins of the Shīʿa: Identity, Ritual and Sacred Space in Eighth-Century Kūfa*. Cambridge, 2011.
Hairi, Abdul-Hadi. *Shīʿism and Constitutionalism in Iran*. Leiden, 1977.
____ 'Burūdjirdī', *EI2*, vol. 12, Supplement, pp. 157–158.
Ḥakīmiyān, Abu'l-Fatḥ. *ʿAlawiyān-i Ṭabaristān*. Tehran, 1348 Sh./1969.
Halm, Heinz. *Kosmologie und Heilslehre der frühen Ismāʿīlīya: Eine Studie zur islamischen Gnosis*. Wiesbaden, 1978.
____ '"Das Buch der Schatten". Die Mufaḍḍal-Tradition der Ġulāt und die Ursprünge des Nuṣairiertums', *Der Islam*, 55 (1978), pp. 219–266.
____ *Die islamische Gnosis: Die extreme Schia und die ʿAlawiten*. Zurich and Munich, 1982.
____ *The Empire of the Mahdi: The Rise of the Fatimids*, tr. M. Bonner. Leiden, 1996.
____ 'The Ismaʿili Oath of Allegiance (*ʿahd*) and the "Sessions of Wisdom" (*majālis al-ḥikma*) in Fatimid Times', in Daftary, ed., *Mediaeval Ismaʿili History*, pp. 91–115.
____ *The Fatimids and their Traditions of Learning*. London, 1997.
____ *Shiʿa Islam: From Religion to Revolution*, tr. A. Brown. Princeton, 1997.
____ *Die Kalifen von Kairo: Die Fatimiden in Ägypten 973–1074*. Munich, 2003.
____ *Shiʿism*, tr. J. Watson and M. Hill. 2nd ed., Edinburgh, 2004.
____ 'Nuṣayriyya', *EI2*, vol. 8, pp. 145–148.
Hamblin, William and Daniel C. Peterson. 'Zaydīyah', in *The Oxford Encyclopedia of the Islamic World*, ed. John L. Esposito. Oxford, 2009, vol. 6, pp. 45–47.
Hamdani, Abbas. 'The Dāʿī Ḥātim Ibn Ibrāhīm al-Ḥāmidī (d. 596 H./1199 A.D.) and his Book *Tuḥfat al-Qulūb*', *Oriens*, 23–24 (1970–1971), pp. 258–300.

____ 'Evolution of the Organisational Structure of the Fāṭimī Daʿwah: The Yemeni and Persian Contribution', *Arabian Studies*, 3 (1976), pp. 85–114.

al-Hamdānī, Ḥusayn F. *al-Ṣulayḥiyyūn wa'l-ḥaraka al-Fāṭimiyya fi'l-Yaman*. Cairo, 1955.

____ (ed. and tr.). *On the Genealogy of Fatimid Caliphs*. Cairo, 1958.

Hamdani, Sumaiya A. *Betweeen Revolution and State: The Path to Fatimid Statehood, Qadi al-Nuʿman and the Construction of Fatimid Legitimacy*. London, 2006.

al-Ḥarīrī, Abū Mūsā. *al-ʿAlawiyyūn al-Nuṣayriyyūn*. Beirut, 1980.

Hawting, Gerald R. *The First Dynasty of Islam: The Umayyad Caliphate AD 661–750*. 2nd ed., London, 2000.

____ 'al-Mukhtār b. Abī 'Ubayd', *EI2*, vol. 7, pp. 521–524.

Haykel, Bernard. *Revival and Reform in Islam: The Legacy of Muhammad al-Shawkani*. Cambridge, 2003.

____ 'al-Shawkani, Muhammad b. 'Ali (1760–1834)', in *The Princeton Encyclopedia of Islamic Political Thought*, ed. G. Bowering. Princeton, 2013, pp. 506–507.

Haykel, Bernard and A. Zysow. 'What Makes a *Maḏhab* a *Maḏhab*: Zaydī Debates on the Structures of Legal Authority', *Arabica*, 59 (2012), pp. 332–371.

Heine, Peter. 'Aspects of the Social Structure of Shiite Society in Modern Iraq', in Brunner and Ende, ed., *Twelver Shia*, pp. 87–93.

al-Ḥibshī, 'Abd Allāh. *al-Ṣūfiyya wa'l-fuqahā' fi'l-Yaman*. Sanaa, 1396/1976.

____ *Mu'allafāt ḥukkām al-Yaman*, ed. Elke Niewöhner-Eberhard. Wiesbaden, 1979.

Hillenbrand, Carole. 'The Power Struggle between the Saljuqs and the Ismaʿilis of Alamūt, 487–518/1094–1124: The Saljuq Perspective', in Daftary, ed., *Mediaeval Ismaʿili History*, pp. 205–220.

____ *The Crusades: Islamic Perspectives*. Edinburgh, 1999.

Hinds, Martin. *Studies in Early Islamic History*, ed. J. Bacharach et al. Princeton, 1996.

Hodgson, Marshall G. S. 'How Did the Early Shīʿa Become Sectarian?', *JAOS*, 75 (1955), pp. 1–13; reprinted in Kohlberg, ed., *Shīʿism*, pp. 3–15.

____ *The Order of Assassins: The Struggle of the Early Nizārī Ismāʿīlīs against the Islamic World*. The Hague, 1955; reprinted, New York, 1980; reprinted, Philadelphia, 2005.

____ 'The Ismāʿīlī State', in *The Cambridge History of Iran:* Volume 5, pp. 422–482.

____ *The Venture of Islam: Conscience and History in a World Civilization*. Chicago, 1974.

____ 'Durūz', *EI2*, vol. 2, pp. 631–634.

Hollister, John N. *The Shi'a of India*. London, 1953; reprinted, New Delhi, 1979.

Hourani, Albert. *Islam in European Thought*. Cambridge, 1991.

Howard, Ian K. A. 'Shī'ī Theological Literature', in M. J. L. Young et al., ed., *Religion, Learning and Science in the 'Abbasid Period*. Cambridge, 1990, pp. 16–32.

Hunsberger, Alice C. *Nasir Khusraw, The Ruby of Badakhshan: A Portrait of the Persian Poet, Traveller and Philosopher*. London, 2000.

Hussain, Jassim M. *The Occultation of the Twelfth Imam: A Historical Background*. London, 1982.

Iqbāl, 'Abbās. *Khāndān-i Nawbakhtī*. 2nd ed., Tehran, 1345 Sh./1966.

Ivanow, Wladimir. 'Notes sur l'Ummu'l-kitab des Ismaëliens de l'Asie Centrale', *Revue des Études Islamiques*, 6 (1932), pp. 419–481.

____ *Ismaili Tradition Concerning the Rise of the Fatimids*. London, etc., 1942.

____ *The Alleged Founder of Ismailism*. Bombay, 1946.

____ 'Ismā'īlīya', in *Shorter Encyclopaedia of Islam*, pp. 179–183.

Ja'fariyān, Rasūl. *Ta'rīkh-i tashayyu' dar Īrān*. Tehran, 1386 Sh./2007.

Jafri, S. Husain M. *Origins and Early Development of Shī'a Islam*. London, 1979.

____ 'Twelver-Imam Shī'ism', in S. Hossein Nasr, ed., *Islamic Spirituality: Foundations*. London, 1987, pp. 160–178.

Jambet, Christian. *La grande résurrection d'Alamût. Les formes de la liberté dans le Shî'isme Ismaélien*. Lagrasse, 1990.

Juynboll, G. H. A. 'The Qurrā' in Early Islamic History', *Journal of the Economic and Social History of the Orient*, 16 (1973), pp. 113–129.

Kassam, Tazim R. *Songs of Wisdom and Circles of Dance: Hymns of the Satpanth Ismā'īlī Muslim Saint, Pīr Shams*. Albany, NY, 1995.

Kassam, Zayn R. 'The Gender Policies of Aga Khan III and Aga Khan IV', in Daftary, ed., *A Modern History of the Ismailis*, pp. 247–264.

Katouzian, Homa. *State and Society in Iran: The Eclipse of the Qajars and the Emergence of the Pahlavis*. London, 2000.

Kazemi, Farhad. 'State and Society in the Ideology of the Devotees of Islam', *State, Culture and Society*, 1 (1985), pp. 118–135.

____ 'Fedā'īān-e Eslām', *EIR*, vol. 9, pp. 470–474.

Kazemi Moussavi, Ahmad. 'The Establishment of the Position of *Marja'iyyat-i Taqlid* in the Twelver-Shi'i Community', *Iranian Studies*, 18 (1985), pp. 35–51.

____ *Religious Authority in Shi'ite Islam*. Kuala Lumpur, 1996.

Keddie, Nikkie R. *Religion and Rebellion in Iran: The Tobacco Protest of 1891–1892*. London, 1966.

____ *Roots of Revolution: An Interpretative History of Modern Iran.* New Haven, 1981.

____ (ed.). *Religion and Politics in Iran: Shiʿism from Quietism to Revolution.* New Haven, 1983.

Keddie, Nikki R. and E. Hooglund (ed.). *The Iranian Revolution and the Islamic Republic.* Ann Arbor, MI, 1982.

Kennedy, Hugh. *The Prophet and the Age of the Caliphates.* London, 1989.

Khan, Dominique-Sila. *Conversions and Shifting Identities: Ramdev Pir and the Ismailis in Rajasthan.* New Delhi, 1997.

____ *Crossing the Threshold: Understanding Religious Identities in South Asia.* London, 2004.

Khan, M. S. 'The Early History of Zaydī Shīʿism in Daylamān and Gīlān', *Zeitschrift der Deutschen Morgenländischen Gesellschaft*, 125 (1975), pp. 301–314; reprinted in Kohlberg, ed., *Shīʿism*, pp. 221–234.

Khumaynī, Āyatullāh Rūḥullāh. *Ḥukūmat-i Islāmī yā vilāyat-i faqīh.* Najaf, 1391/1971. English trans., 'Islamic Government', in R. Khumaynī, *Islam and Revolution: Writings and Declarations of Imam Khomeini*, tr. H. Algar. Berkeley, 1981, pp. 25–166.

King, James R. 'Zaydī Revival in a Hostile Republic: Competing Identities, Loyalties and Visions of State in Republican Yemen', *Arabica*, 59 (2012), pp. 404–445.

Kiyā, Ṣādiq. *Nuqṭawiyān yā Pasīkhāniyān.* Tehran, 1320 Sh./1941.

Klemm, Verena. 'Die vier *Ṣufarāʾ* des Zwölften Imām. Zur formativen Periode der Zwölferšīʿa', *Die Welt des Orients*, 15 (1984), pp. 126–143. English trans., 'The Four *Ṣufarāʾ* of the Twelfth Imam: On the Formative Period of the Twelver Shīʿa', in Kohlberg, ed., *Shīʿism*, pp. 135–152.

____ *Memoirs of a Mission: The Ismaili Scholar, Statesman and Poet al-Muʾayyad fiʾl-Dīn al-Shīrāzī.* London, 2003.

Kohlberg, Etan. 'Some Imāmī-Shīʿī Views on *taqiyya*', *JAOS*, 95 (1975), pp. 395–402.

____ 'The Development of the Imāmī Shīʿī Doctrine of *jihād*', *Zeitschrift der Deutschen Morgenländischen Gesellschaft*, 126 (1976), pp. 64–86.

____ 'From Imāmiyya to Ithnā-ʿAshariyya', *BSOAS*, 39 (1976), pp. 521–534.

____ 'Some Zaydī Views on the Companions of the Prophet', *BSOAS*, 39 (1976), pp. 91–98.

____ 'Aspects of Akhbari Thought in the Seventeenth and Eighteenth Centuries', in N. Levtzion and J. O. Voll, ed., *Eighteenth-Century Renewal and Reform in Islam.* Syracuse, NY, 1987, pp. 133–160.

____ *Belief and Law in Imāmī Shīʿism.* Aldershot, 1991.

____ 'Taqiyya in Shīʿī Theology and Religion', in Hans G. Kippenberg and Guy G. Stroumsa, ed., *Secrecy and Concealment: Studies in the History of Mediterranean and Near Eastern Religions*. Leiden, 1995, pp. 345–380.

____ 'Mūsā al-Kāẓim', *EI2*, vol. 7, pp. 645–648.

____ (ed.). *Shīʿism*. Aldershot, 2003.

Krieger, Bella Tendler 'Marriage, Birth, and *bāṭinī taʾwīl*: A Study of Nuṣayrī Initiation Based on the *Kitāb al-Ḥāwī fī ʿilm al-fatāwī* of Abū Saʿīd Maymūn al-Ṭabarānī', *Arabica*, 58 (2011), pp. 53–75.

Lalani, Arzina R. *Early Shīʿī Thought: The Teachings of Imam Muḥammad al-Bāqir*. London, 2000.

Lambton, Ann K. S. 'The Tobacco Régie: Prelude to Revolution', *Studia Islamica*, 22 (1965), pp. 119–157, and 23 (1966), pp. 71–90.

____ 'A Nineteenth Century View of *jihād*', *Studia Islamica*, 32 (1970), pp. 181–192.

____ 'The Persian ʿUlamā and Constitutional Reform', in Fahd, ed., *Le Shîʿisme Imâmite*, pp. 245–269.

____ *Qajar Persia: Eleven Studies*. London, 1987.

Landolt, Hermann. 'Khwāja Naṣīr al-Dīn al-Ṭūsī (597/1201–672/1274), Ismāʿīlism and Ishrāqī Philosophy', in N. Pourjavady and Ž. Vesel, ed., *Naṣīr al-Dīn Ṭūsī, philosophe et savant du XIIIe siècle*. Tehran, 2000, pp. 13–30.

____ "Aṭṭār, Sufism, and Ismailism', in L. Lewisohn and Ch. Shackle, ed., *ʿAṭṭār and the Persian Sufi Tradition: The Art of Spiritual Flight*. London, 2006, pp. 3–26.

Laoust, Henri. *Les schismes dans l'Islam*. Paris, 1965.

Lewis, Bernard. *The Assassins: A Radical Sect in Islam*. London, 1967.

____ *Studies in Classical and Ottoman Islam (7th–16th Centuries)*. London, 1976.

Lewisohn, Leonard. 'An Introduction to the History of Modern Persian Sufism, Part I: The Niʿmatullāhī Order: Persecution, Revival and Schism', *BSOAS*, 61 (1998), pp. 439–453.

____ 'Sufism and Ismāʿīlī Doctrine in the Persian Poetry of Nizārī Quhistānī (645–721/1247–1321)', *Iran, Journal of the British Institute of Persian Studies*, 41 (2003), pp. 229–251.

Lewisohn, Leonard and David Morgan (ed.). *The Heritage of Sufism*: Volume III, *Late Classical Persianate Sufism (1501–1750)*. Oxford, 1999.

Litvak, Meir. *Shiʿi Scholars of Nineteenth-Century Iraq: The ʿUlamaʾ of Najaf and Karbalaʾ*. Cambridge, 1998.

____ 'Madrasa and Learning in Nineteenth-Century Najaf and Karbalā'', in Brunner and Ende, ed., *Twelver Shia*, pp. 58–78.

Lockhart, Laurence. *The Fall of the Ṣafavī Dynasty and the Afghan Occupation of Persia.* Cambridge, 1958.

Lokhandwalla, Sh. T. 'The Bohras, a Muslim Community of Gujarat', *Studia Islamica*, 3 (1955), pp. 117–135.

MacEoin, D. 'Shaykhiyya', *EI2*, vol. 9, pp. 403–405.

Madelung, Wilferd. 'Das Imamat in der frühen ismailitischen Lehre', *Der Islam*, 37 (1961), pp. 43–135.

____ *Der Imam al-Qāsim ibn Ibrāhīm und die Glaubenslehre der Zaiditen.* Berlin, 1965.

____ 'Abū Isḥāq al-Ṣābī on the Alids of Ṭabaristān and Gīlān', *Journal of Near Eastern Studies*, 26 (1967), pp. 17–56.

____ 'The Alid Rulers of Ṭabaristān, Daylamān and Gīlān', in *Atti del III Congresso di Studi Arabi e Islamici, Ravello, 1966.* Naples, 1967, pp. 483–492.

____ 'Bemerkungen zur imamitischen Firaq-Literatur', *Der Islam*, 43 (1967), pp. 37–52. English trans., 'Some Remarks on the Imāmī Firaq-Literature', in Kohlberg, ed., *Shīʿism*, pp. 153–167.

____ 'Imāmism and Muʿtazilite Theology', in Fahd, ed., *Le Shîʿisme Imâmite*, pp. 13–30.

____ 'The Minor Dynasties of Northern Iran', in *The Cambridge History of Iran:* Volume 4, pp. 198–249.

____ 'The Sources of Ismāʿīlī Law', *Journal of Near Eastern Studies*, 35 (1976), pp. 29–40.

____ 'Aspects of Ismāʿīlī Theology: The Prophetic Chain and the God Beyond Being', in Nasr, ed., *Ismāʿīlī Contributions*, pp. 51–65.

____ 'The Shiite and Khārijite Contribution to Pre-Ashʿarite *Kalām*', in P. Morewedge, ed., *Islamic Philosophical Theology*. Albany, NY, 1979, pp. 120–139.

____ 'New Documents Concerning al-Ma'mūn, al-Faḍl b. Sahl and ʿAlī al-Riḍā', in W. al-Qāḍī, ed., *Studia Arabica et Islamica: Festschrift for Iḥsān ʿAbbās*. Beirut, 1981, pp. 333–346

____ 'Shiite Discussions on the Legality of the *Kharāj*', in R. Peters, ed., *Proceedings of the Ninth Congress of the Union Européenne des Arabisants et Islamisants*. Leiden, 1981, pp. 193–202.

____ 'Authority in Twelver Shiism in the Absence of the Imam', in *La notion d'autorité au Moyen Age: Islam, Byzance, Occident*. Paris, 1982, pp. 163–173.

____ 'Naṣīr ad-Dīn Ṭūsī's Ethics between Philosophy, Shiʿism, and Sufism', in Richard G. Hovannisian, ed., *Ethics in Islam*. Malibu, CA, 1985, pp. 85–101.

____ *Religious Schools and Sects in Medieval Islam*. London, 1985.

____ *Religious Trends in Early Islamic Iran*. Albany, NY, 1988.
____ 'Imam al-Qāsim ibn Ibrāhīm and Muʿtazilism', in *On Both Sides of al-Mandab: Ethiopian, South-Arabic and Islamic Studies Presented to Oscar Löfgren on his Ninetieth Birthday 13 May 1988 by Colleagues and Friends*. Stockholm, 1989, pp. 39–48.
____ 'The *Hāshimiyyāt* of al-Kumayt and Hāshimī Shiʿism', *Studia Islamica*, 70 (1989), pp. 5–26; reprinted in Kohlberg, ed., *Shīʿism*, pp. 87–108.
____ 'The Origins of the Yemenite *Hijra*', in A. Jones, ed., *Arabicus Felix: Luminosus Britannicus. Essays in Honour of A. F. L. Beeston on his Eightieth Birthday*. Reading, 1991, pp. 25–44.
____ *Religious and Ethnic Movements in Medieval Islam*. Hampshire, UK, 1992.
____ 'The Fatimids and the Qarmaṭīs of Baḥrayn', in Daftary, ed., *Mediaeval Ismaʿili History*, pp. 21–73.
____ *The Succession to Muḥammad: A Study of the Early Caliphate*. Cambridge, 1997.
____ "ʿAbd Allāh b. ʿAbbās and Shiʿite Law', in U. Vermeulen and J. M. F. Van Reeth, ed., *Law, Christianity and Modernism in Islamic Society*. Leuven, 1998, pp. 13–25.
____ 'Zaydī Attitudes to Sufism', in F. de Jong and B. Radtke, ed., *Islamic Mysticism Contested: Thirteen Centuries of Controversies and Polemics*. Leiden, 1999, pp. 124–144.
____ 'Shīʿism in the Age of the Rightly-Guided Caliphs', in L. Clarke, ed., *Shīʿite Heritage: Essays on Classical and Modern Traditions* . Binghamton, NY, 2001, pp. 9–18.
____ 'Al-Mahdī al-Ḥaqq, al-Ḫalīfa ar-Rašīd und die Bekehrung der Dailamiten zur Šīʿa', in H. Biesterfeldt and V. Klemm, ed., *Differenz und Dynamik im Islam. Festschrift für Heinz Halm zum 70. Geburtstag*. Würzburg, 2012, pp. 115–123.
____ *Studies in Medieval Shiʿism*, ed. S. Schmidtke. Farnham, UK, 2012.
____ 'Imāma', *EI2*, vol. 3, pp. 1163–1169.
____ 'Ismāʿīliyya', *EI2*, vol. 4, pp. 198–206.
____ 'Ḳarmaṭī', *EI2*, vol. 4, pp. 660–665.
____ 'al-Mahdī', *EI2*, vol. 5, pp. 1230–1238.
____ 'Makramids', *EI2*, vol. 6, pp. 191–192.
____ 'al-Manṣūr Bi'llāh, al-Ḳāsim b. ʿAlī', *EI2*, vol. 6, pp. 435–436.
____ 'Muṭarrifiyya', *EI2*, vol. 7, pp. 772–773.
____ 'al-Rassī, al-Ḳāsim b. Ibrāhīm', *EI2*, vol. 8, pp. 453–454.
____ 'Shīʿa', *EI2*, vol. 9, pp. 420–424.
____ 'Zayd b. ʿAlī', *EI2*, vol. 11, pp. 473–474.
____ 'Zaydiyya', *EI2*, vol. 11, pp. 477–481.

____ 'Akhbāriyya', *EI2*, vol. 12, Supplement, pp. 56–57.
____ 'al-Hādī ila'l-Ḥaḳḳ', *EI2*, vol. 12, Supplement, pp. 334–335.
____ ''Alī al-Reżā', *EIR*, vol. 1, pp. 877–880.
____ ''Alids', *EIR*, vol. 1, pp. 881–886.
____ 'Dāʿī ela'l-Ḥaqq', *EIR*, vol. 6, pp. 595–597.
____ 'Daylamites: ii. In the Islamic Period', *EIR*, vol. 7, pp. 343–347.
____ 'Ḥosayn b. 'Alī', *EIR*, vol. 12, pp. 493–498.
Mallat, Chibli. *Shiʿi Thought from the South of Lebanon*. Oxford, 1988.
Marquet, Yves. 'Ikhwān al-Ṣafā'', *EI2*, vol. 3, pp. 1071–1076.
Martin, Vanessa. *Islam and Modernism: The Iranian Revolution of 1906*. London, 1989.
Masselos, James C. 'The Khojas of Bombay: The Defining of Formal Membership Criteria during the Nineteenth Century', in I. Ahmad, ed., *Caste and Social Stratification among Muslims in India*. New Delhi, 1973, pp. 1–20.
Massignon, Louis. 'Esquisse d'une bibliographie Qarmaṭe', in Thomas W. Arnold and R. A. Nicholson, ed., *A Volume of Oriental Studies Presented to Edward G. Browne on his 60th Birthday*. Cambridge, 1922, pp. 329–338; reprinted in L. Massignon, *Opera Minora*, ed. Y. Moubarac. Paris, 1969, vol. 1, pp. 627–639.
____ 'Les origines Shîʿites de la famille vizirale des Banû'l-Furât', in *Mélanges Gaudefroy-Demombynes*. Cairo, 1935–1945, pp. 25–29; reprinted in Massignon, *Opera Minora*, vol. 1, pp. 484–487.
____ 'Esquisse d'une bibliographie Nuṣayrie', in *Mélanges Syriens offerts à M. René Dussaud par ses amis et ses élèves*. Paris, 1939, vol. 2, pp. 913–922; reprinted in Massignon, *Opera Minora*, vol. 1, pp. 640–649.
____ 'Les Nusayris', in *L'Élaboration de l'Islam*. Paris. 1961, pp. 109–114; reprinted in Massignon, *Opera Minora*, vol. 1, pp. 619–624.
____ 'Ḳarmaṭians', *EI*, vol. 2, pp. 767–772.
____ 'Nuṣairī', *EI*, vol. 3, pp. 963–967.
Matthee, Rudi. *Persia in Crisis: Safavid Decline and the Fall of Isfahan*. London, 2012.
Mauriello, Raffaele. *Descendants of the Family of the Prophet: A Case Study, the Šīʿī Religious Establishment of Nağaf (Iraq)*. Pisa and Rome, 2011 (*Rivista degli Studi Orientali*, New Series, 83, Supplement 1).
Mazzaoui, Michel M. *The Origins of the Ṣafawids: Šīʿism, Ṣūfism, and the Ġulāt*. Wiesbaden, 1972.
Mehrvash, Farhang. ''Āshūrā'', *EIS*, vol. 3, pp. 883–892.
Mervin, Sabrina. 'The Clerics of Jabal 'Āmil and the Reform of Religious Teaching in Najaf Since the Beginning of the 20th Century', in Brunner and Ende, ed., *Twelver Shia*, pp. 79–86.
Minorsky, Vladimir. *La domination des Dailamites*. Paris, 1932.

____ 'The Poetry of Shāh Ismā'īl I', *BSOAS*, 10 (1940–1942), pp. 1007–1053.

____ 'Daylam', *EI2*, vol. 2, pp. 189–194.

Misra, Satish C. *Muslim Communities in Gujarat*. Bombay, 1964.

Mitha, Farouk. *Al-Ghazālī and the Ismailis: A Debate on Reason and Authority in Medieval Islam*. London, 2001.

Modarressi, Hossein. *Crisis and Consolidation in the Formative Period of Shi'ite Islam*. Princeton, 1993.

Moin, Baqer. *Khomeini: Life of the Ayatollah*. London, 1999.

Momen, Moojan. *An Introduction to Shi'i Islam: The History and Doctrines of Twelver Shi'ism*. New Haven, 1985.

Moosa, Matti. *Extremist Shiites: The Ghulat Sects*. Syracuse, NY, 1987.

____ ''Alawīyah', in *The Oxford Encyclopedia of the Islamic World*, ed. John L. Esposito. Oxford, 2009, vol. 1, pp. 105–107.

Nakash, Yitzhak. *The Shi'is of Iraq*. Princeton, 1994.

____ *Reaching for Power: The Shi'a in the Modern Arab World*. Princeton, 2006.

Nanji, Azim. *The Nizārī Ismā'īlī Tradition in the Indo-Pakistan Subcontinent*. Delmar, NY, 1978.

____ 'Ismā'īlism', in S. Hossein Nasr, ed., *Islamic Spirituality: Foundations*. London, 1987, pp. 179–198.

____ 'Ismā'īlī Philosophy', in S. H. Nasr and O. Leaman, ed., *History of Islamic Philosophy*. London, 1996, vol. 1, pp. 144–154.

Nasr, Seyyed Hossein. 'The School of Iṣpahān', in M. M. Sharif, ed., *A History of Muslim Philosophy*. Wiesbaden, 1968, vol. 2, pp. 904–932.

____ 'Le Shî'isme et le Soufisme. Leurs relations principielles et historiques', in Fahd, ed., *Le Shî'isme Imâmite*, pp. 215–233.

____ *Sufi Essays*. London, 1972.

____ 'Spiritual Movements, Philosophy and Theology in the Safavid Period', in *The Cambridge History of Iran*: Volume 6, pp. 656–697.

____ *Ideals and Realities of Islam*. New rev. ed., Cambridge, 2001.

____ *Islamic Philosophy from its Origins to the Present*. Albany, NY, 2006.

____ 'Ithnā'ashariyya', *EI2*, vol. 4, pp. 277–279.

____ (ed.). *Ismā'īlī Contributions to Islamic Culture*. Tehran, 1977.

____ (ed.). *Islamic Spirituality: Manifestations*. London, 1991.

____ et al. (ed.). *Shi'ism: Doctrines, Thought, and Spirituality*. Albany, NY, 1988.

Netton, Ian R. *Allāh Transcendent: Studies in the Structure and Semiotics of Islamic Philosophy, Theology and Cosmology*. London, 1989.

Newman, Andrew J. 'The Nature of the Akhbārī/Uṣūlī Dispute in Late Ṣafavid Iran', *BSOAS*, 55 (1992), pp. 22–51, and 250–261.

____ *The Formative Period of Twelver Shī'ism: Ḥadīth as Discourse Between Qum and Baghdad*. London, 2000.

____ 'Safavids and "Subalterns": The Reclaiming of Voices', in Alí-de-Unzaga, ed., *Fortresses of the Intellect*, pp. 473–490.

Niyāzmand, S. Riḍā. *Shīʿa dar taʾrīkh-i Īrān*. Tehran, 1383 Sh./2004.

Olsson, Tord et al. (ed.). *Alevi Identity: Cultural, Religious and Social Perspectives*. Papers Read at a Conference Held at the Swedish Research Institute in Istanbul, 25–27 November 1996. Istanbul, 1998.

Perry, John R. *Karim Khan Zand: A History of Iran, 1747–1779*. Chicago, 1979.

Petersen, Erling R. *ʿAlī and Muʿāwiya in Early Arabic Tradition*. Copenhagen, 1964.

Poonawala, Ismail K. 'Ismāʿīlī *taʾwīl* of the Qurʾān', in Andrew Rippin, ed., *Approaches to the History of the Interpretation of the Qurʾān*. Oxford, 1988, pp. 199–222.

____ 'Al-Qāḍī al-Nuʿmān and Ismaʿili Jurisprudence', in Daftary, ed., *Mediaeval Ismaʿili History*, pp. 117–143.

____ 'Hamid al-Din al-Kirmani and the Proto-Druze', *Journal of Druze Studies*, 1 (2000), pp. 71–94.

____ 'Sources for al-Qāḍī al-Nuʿmān's Works and Their Authenticity', in Bruce D. Craig, ed., *Ismaili and Fatimid Studies in Honor of Paul E. Walker*. Chicago, 2010, pp. 87–99.

____ 'An Early Doctrinal Controversy in the Iranian School of Ismaʿili Thought and its Implications', *Journal of Persianate Studies*, 5 (2012), pp. 17–34.

____ 'Sulaymānīs', *EI2*, vol. 9, p. 829.

Poonawala, Ismail K. and E. Kohlberg. "Alī b. Abī Ṭāleb', *EIR*, vol. 1, pp. 838–848.

Pourjavady, Nasrollah and Peter L. Wilson. 'Ismāʿīlīs and Niʿmatullāhīs', *Studia Islamica*, 41 (1975), pp. 113–135.

____ *Kings of Love: The Poetry and History of the Niʿmatullāhī Sufi Order*. Tehran, 1978.

al-Qāḍī, Wadād. 'The Development of the Term *Ghulāt* in Muslim Literature with Special Reference to the Kaysāniyya', in A. Dietrich, ed., *Akten des VII. Kongresses für Arabistik und Islamwissenschaft*. Göttingen, 1976, pp. 295–319; reprinted in Kohlberg, ed., *Shīʿism*, pp. 169–193.

Quinn, Sholeh and Charles Melville, 'Safavid Historiography', in C. Melville, ed., *A History of Persian Literature:* Volume X, *Persian Historiography*. London, 2012, pp. 209–257.

Qutbuddin, Saifiyah. 'History of the Daʾudi Bohra Tayyibis in Modern Times: The *Daʿis*, the *Daʿwa* and the Community', in Daftary, ed., *A Modern History of the Ismailis*, pp. 297–330.

Qutbuddin, Tahera. 'The Da'udi Bohra Tayyibis: Ideology, Literature, Learning and Social Practice', in Daftary, ed., *A Modern History of the Ismailis*, pp. 331–354.

____ 'Bohras', *EI3*, 2013–2, pp. 56–66.

Rabino di Borgomale, Hyacinth L. 'Rulers of Lahijan and Fuman, in Gilan, Persia', *JRAS* (1918), pp. 85–100.

____ 'Les dynasties Alaouides du Mazandéran', *Journal Asiatique*, 210 (1927), pp. 253–277.

____ 'Les dynasties locales du Gîlân et du Daylam', *Journal Asiatique*, 237 (1949), pp. 301–350.

Rahnema, Ali. 'Kāšānī, Sayyed Abu'l-Qāsem', *EIR*, vol. 15, pp. 640–647.

Ramazani, R. K. 'Shiʿism in the Persian Gulf', in Cole and Keddie, ed., *Shiʿism and Social Protest*, pp. 30–54.

Richard, Yann. *Le Shiʿisme en Iran*. Paris, 1980.

____ *Shiʿite Islam: Polity, Ideology, and Creed*, tr. A. Nevill. Oxford, 1995.

Rieck, Andreas. 'The Struggle for Equal Rights as a Minority: Shia Communal Organization in Pakistan, 1948–1968', in Brunner and Ende, ed., *Twelver Shia*, pp. 268–283.

Rizvi, Sajjad H. 'Mysticism and Philosophy: Ibn ʿArabī and Mullā Ṣadrā', in Peter Adamson and Richard C. Taylor, ed., *The Cambridge Companion to Arabic Philosophy*. Cambridge, 2005, pp. 224–246.

Rizvi, S. Athar A. *A Socio-Intellectual History of the Isnā ʿAsharī Shīʿīs in India*. Canberra, 1986.

Rizvi, S. Athar A. and Noel Q. King. 'The Khoja Shia Ithna-Asheriya Community in East Africa (1840–1967)', *Muslim World*, 64 (1974), pp. 194–204.

Rose, Gregory. '*Velayat-i Faqih* and the Recovery of Islamic Identity in the Thought of Ayatollah Khomeini', in Keddie, ed., *Religion and Politics in Iran*, pp. 166–188.

Rouaud, R. 'Al-Mutawakkil ʿalā Allāh Yaḥyā, fondateur du Yémen moderne', *L'Afrique et l'Asie modernes*, 141 (1984), pp. 56–73.

Ruthven, Malise. 'Aga Khan III and the Ismaʿili Renaissance', in Peter B. Clarke, ed., *New Trends and Developments in the World of Islam*. London, 1998, pp. 371–395.

____ 'The Aga Khan Development Network and Institutions', in Daftary, ed., *A Modern History of the Ismailis*, pp. 189–220.

Rypka, Jan. *History of Iranian Literature*, ed. K. Jahn. Dordrecht, 1968.

Sachedina, Abdulaziz A. *Islamic Messianism: The Idea of Mahdi in Twelver Shiʿism*. Albany, NY, 1981.

____ *The Just Ruler (al-sultan al-ʿādil) in Shīʿite Islam: The Comprehensive Authority of the Jurist in Imamite Jurisprudence*. Oxford, 1988.

____ 'Khojas', in *The Oxford Encyclopedia of the Islamic World*, ed. John L. Esposito. Oxford, 2009, vol. 3, pp. 334–338.

Sadighi, Gholam Hossein. *Les mouvements religieux Iraniens au IIe et IIIe siècle de l'hégire*. Paris, 1938.

Sayyid, Ayman F. *al-Dawla al-Fāṭimiyya fī Miṣr: tafsīr jadīd*. 2nd ed., Cairo, 2000.

Scarcia, Gianroberto. 'Intorno alle controversie tra Aḫbārī e Uṣūlī presso gli Imāmītī di Persia', *Rivista degli Studi Orientali*, 33 (1958), pp. 211–250.

Schmidtke, Sabine. *The Theology of al-ʿAllāma al-Ḥillī (d. 726/1325)*. Berlin, 1991.

____ 'The History of Zaydī Studies: An Introduction', *Arabica*, 59 (2012), pp. 185–199.

Serjeant, Robert B. 'The Zaydīs', in Arthur J. Arberry, ed., *Religion in the Middle East*: Volume 2, *Islam*. Cambridge, 1969, pp. 285–301.

Shaban, M. A. *Islamic History: A New Interpretation*. Cambridge, 1971–1976.

Shackle, Christopher and Z. Moir. *Ismaili Hymns from South Asia: An Introduction to the Ginans*. London, 1992.

Shah-Kazemi, Reza. *Justice and Remembrance: Introducing the Spirituality of Imam ʿAlī*. London, 2006.

Shah-Kazemi, Reza et al. "Alī b. Abī Ṭālib', *EIS*, vol. 3, pp. 477–583.

Shankland, David. 'Are the Alevis Shiʿite?', in L. Ridgeon, ed., *Shiʿi Islam and Identity*. London, 2012, pp. 210–228.

____ 'Alevis', in *The Oxford Encyclopedia of the Islamic World*, ed. John L. Esposito. Oxford, 2009, vol. 1, pp. 112–113.

al-Sharīf, Munīr. *ʿAlawiyyūn: man hum wa ayna hum*. Damascus, 1946.

Sharon, Moshe. *Black Banners from the East: The Establishment of the ʿAbbāsid State – Incubation of a Revolt*. Jerusalem and Leiden, 1983.

Shayegan, Daryush. *Henry Corbin: La topographie spirituelle de l'Islam Iranien*. Paris, 1990.

Shodan, Amrita. *A Question of Community: Religious Groups and Colonial Law*. Calcutta, 1999.

Silvestre de Sacy, Antoine I. 'Mémoire sur la dynastie des Assassins, et sur l'étymologie de leur nom', *Mémoires de l'Institut Royal de France*, 4 (1818), pp. 1–84; reprinted in Bryan S. Turner, ed., *Orientalism: Early Sources*, Volume 1, *Readings in Orientalism*. London, 2000, pp. 118–169. English trans., 'Memoir on the Dynasty of the Assassins', in Daftary, *The Assassin Legends*, pp. 129–188.

____ *Exposé de la religion des Druzes*. Paris, 1838; reprinted, Paris, 1964.

Smith, G. Rex. 'Some Arabic Sources Concerning the First Ottoman Occupation of the Yemen (945–1045/1538–1636)', in J. Hathaway, ed., *The Arab*

Lands in the Ottoman Era: Essays in Honor of Professor Caesar Farah. Minneapolis, MN, 2009, pp. 19–39.

____ 'Ṣulayḥids', *EI2*, vol. 9, pp. 815–817.

Sobhani, Ja'far. *Doctrines of Shi'i Islam: A Compendium of Imami Beliefs and Practices*, ed. and tr. Reza Shah-Kazemi. London, 2001.

Southern, Richard W. *Western Views of Islam in the Middle Ages*. Cambridge, MA, 1962.

Steinberg, Guido. 'The Shiites in the Eastern Province of Saudi Arabia (al-Aḥsā'), 1913–1953', in Brunner and Ende, ed., *Twelver Shia*, pp. 236–254.

Stern, Samuel M. 'The Succession to the Fatimid Imam al-Āmir, the Claims of the Later Fatimids to the Imamate, and the Rise of Ṭayyibī Ismailism', *Oriens*, 4 (1951), pp. 193–255; reprinted in his *History and Culture in the Medieval Muslim World*. London, 1984, article XI.

____ 'The Early Ismā'īlī Missionaries in North-West Persia and in Khurāsān and Transoxania', *BSOAS*, 23 (1960), pp. 56–90.

____ 'The Coins of Āmul', *Numismatic Chronicle*, 7th series, 6 (1967), pp. 205–278; reprinted in his *Coins and Documents from the Medieval Middle East*, ed. F. W. Zimmermann. London, 1986, article III.

____ 'Cairo as the Centre of the Ismā'īlī Movement', in *Colloque international sur l'histoire du Caire*. Cairo, 1972, pp. 437–450.

____ *Studies in Early Ismā'īlism*. Jerusalem and Leiden, 1983.

Strothmann, Rudolf. 'Die Literatur der Zaiditen', *Der Islam*, 1 (1910), pp. 354–368, and 2 (1911), pp. 49–78.

____ *Das Staatsrecht der Zaiditen*. Strassburg, 1912.

____ *Kultus der Zaiditen*. Strassburg, 1912.

____ *Die Zwölfer-Schī'a*. Leipzig, 1926; reprinted, Hildesheim, 1975.

____ 'Drusen-Antwort auf Nuṣairī-Angriff', *Der Islam*, 25 (1939), pp. 269–281.

____ 'Seelenwanderung bei den Nuṣairī', *Oriens*, 12 (1959), pp. 89–114.

____ 'Zaydīya', *EI*, vol. 4, pp. 1196–1198.

____ 'Ḥasan al-Uṭrūsh', *EI2*, vol. 3, pp. 254–255.

Ṭabāṭabā'ī, Sayyid Muḥammad Ḥusayn. *Shi'ite Islam*, ed. and tr. S. Hossein Nasr. London, 1975.

al-Ṭawīl, Muḥammad Amīn Ghālib. *Ta'rīkh al-'Alawiyyīn*. 4th ed., Beirut, 1401/1981.

Thobani, Shiraz. 'Communities of Tradition and the Modernizing of Education in South Asia: The Contribution of Aga Khan III', in Daftary, ed., *A Modern History of the Ismailis*, pp. 161–185.

Tolan, John V. *Saracens: Islam in the Medieval European Imagination*. New York, 2002.

Trimingham, J. Spencer. *The Sufi Orders in Islam*. Oxford, 1971.

Tritton, Arthur S. *The Rise of the Imams of Sanaa*. London, 1925.

Tucker, William F. *Mahdis and Millenarians: Shīʿite Extremists in Early Muslim Iraq*. Cambridge, 2008.

Vermeulen, Urbain. 'Some Remarks on a Rescript of an-Nāṣir Muḥammad b. Qalā'ūn on the Abolition of Taxes and the Nuṣayrīs (Mamlaka of Tripoli, 717/1317)', *Orientalia Lovaniensia Periodica*, 1 (1970), pp. 195–201.

Virani, Shafique. *The Ismailis in the Middle Ages*. Oxford, 2007.

Walbridge, Linda S. (ed.). *The Most Learned of the Shiʿa: The Institution of the Marjaʿ Taqlid*. Oxford, 2001.

Walker, Paul E. *Early Philosophical Shiism: The Ismaili Neoplatonism of Abū Yaʿqūb al-Sijistānī*. Cambridge, 1993.

____ *Abū Yaʿqūb al-Sijistānī: Intellectual Missionary*. London, 1996.

____ 'Fatimid Institutions of Learning', *Journal of the American Research Center in Egypt*, 34 (1997), pp. 179–200.

____ *Ḥamīd al-Dīn al-Kirmānī: Ismaili Thought in the Age of al-Ḥākim*. London, 1999.

____ *Exploring an Islamic Empire: Fatimid History and its Sources*. London, 2002.

____ 'The Ismāʿīlīs', in Peter Adamson and Richard C. Taylor, ed., *The Cambridge Companion to Arabic Philosophy*. Cambridge, 2005, pp. 72–91.

____ *Fatimid History and Ismaili Doctrine*. Aldershot, 2008.

____ 'Institute of Ismaili Studies', *EIR*, vol. 12, pp. 164–166.

Watt, William Montgomery. 'The Great Community and the Sects', in Gustave E. von Grunebaum, ed., *Theology and Law in Islam*. Wiesbaden, 1971, pp. 25–36.

____ *The Influence of Islam on Medieval Europe*. Edinburgh, 1972.

____ *The Formative Period of Islamic Thought*. Edinburgh, 1973.

____ *Early Islam: Collected Articles*. Edinburgh, 1990.

____ *Muslim–Christian Encounters*. London, 1991.

Wellhausen, Julius. *The Arab Kingdom and its Fall*, tr. Margaret G. Weir. Calcutta, 1927; reprinted, Beirut, 1963.

____ *The Religio-Political Factions in Early Islam*, tr. R. C. Ostle and S. M. Walzer. Amsterdam, 1975.

Weulersee, Jacques. *Le pays des Alaouites*. Tours, 1940.

Willey, Peter. *Eagle's Nest: Ismaili Castles in Iran and Syria*. London, 2005.

Zabāra, Muḥammad b. Muḥammad. *A'immat al-Yaman*. Taʿizz, 1952.

____ *A'immat al-Yaman bi'l-qarn al-rābiʿ ʿashar li'l-hijra*. Cairo, 1376/1956.

Zarrīnkūb, ʿAbd al-Ḥusayn. *Ta'rīkh-i Īrān baʿd az Islām*. 2nd ed., Tehran, 1355 Sh./1976.

Index

Page numbers in *italics* refer to lists and tables.

Abaqa, Ilkhanid, 76
al-ʿAbbas b. ʿAbd al-Muttalib, uncle of the Prophet, 36, 45, 52, 209
Abbas I, Safawid *shah*, 84, 139
Abbasids, 5–6, 36, 39, 48–50, 59–60, 115, 124, 147, 180
  became Sunnis, 50
  versus Fatimids, 5–6
  repressed Shiʿism, 50, 63, 108
  revolt of, 48–9
  social order under, 49
ʿAbd ʿAli Sayf al-Din, Daʾudi *daʿi*, 129
ʿAbd Allah b. al-ʿAbbas, Abbasid, 45, 52, 63, 108
ʿAbd Allah b. al-Hasan al-Muthanna b. al-Hasan, ʿAlid, 47, 48, 52
ʿAbd Allah b. Jaʿfar al-Aftah, ʿAlid, 52, 58, 59, 107, 108
ʿAbd Allah b. Jaʿfar al-Tayyar, Talibid, 36, 52, 209
ʿAbd Allah al-Mahd *see* ʿAbd Allah b. al-Hasan al-Muthanna b. al-Hasan
ʿAbd Allah al-Mahdi *see* al-Mahdi, ʿAbd Allah
ʿAbd Allah b. Muʿawiya, Talibid, leader of anti-Umayyad revolt, 52, 149
ʿAbd Allah b. Muhammad b. Ismaʿil (al-Akbar), concealed Ismaili imam, 109
ʿAbd Allah b. Muhammad al-Makrami, Sayyidna, Sulaymani *daʿi*, 130
ʿAbd Allah al-Nawus, 58
ʿAbd Allah b. Rawaha al-Ansari, 188
ʿAbd Allah b. Sabaʾ 40
ʿAbd al-ʿAziz II, king of Saudi Arabia, *116*, 164
ʿAbd al-Jabbar al-Hamadhani, al-Qadi, Muʿtazili scholar, 71, 159
ʿAbd al-Majid al-Hafiz *see* al-Hafiz
ʿAbd al-Malik b. ʿAttash, Ismaili *daʿi* in Persia, 124
ʿAbdan, Qarmati leader, 109, 110, 112, 180
Abel, 187
Abraham (Ibrahim), 114
Abu ʿAbd Allah Muhammad b. ʿAli al-ʿAlawi, Zaydi scholar, 151
Abu ʿAbd Allah Muhammad al-Mahdi li-Din Allah *see* al-Mahdi li-Din Allah, Abu ʿAbd Allah Muhammad
Abu ʿAbd Allah al-Shiʿi, early Ismaili *daʿi* in North Africa, 111, 115
Abu Ahmad al-Tahir al-Musawi, ʿAlid, father of al-Sharif al-Murtada, 71
Abu ʿAli al-Mansur al-Hakim bi-Amr Allah *see* al-Hakim, Fatimid caliph

Abu Bakr, first caliph, 25–7, 29, 45, 83, 148, 163, 168
Abu Dharr al-Ghiffari, 188
Abu Hanifa al-Nuʿman (al-Qadi al-Nuʿman) *see* al-Nuʿman b. Muhammad, al-Qadi Abu Hanifa
Abu Hashim ʿAbd Allah, Hanafid ʿAlid, eponym of Hashimiyya, 39, 52, 147
Abu Hashim ʿAlawi, Zaydi pretender in Daylam, 161
Abu Hatim al-Razi, early Ismaili (Qarmati) *daʿi* and author, 111, 119, 120, 123, 157
Abu Ishaq-i Quhistani, Nizari author, 139
Abu Jaʿfar Muhammad, ʿAlid, last Zaydi ruler of Tabaristan, 157
Abu Jaʿfar Muhammad b. Yaʿqub al-Kulayni *see* al-Kulayni, Abu Jaʿfar Muhammad
Abu Mansur al-ʿIjli, eponym of Mansuriyya, 40, 42
Abu Mansur Nizar al-ʿAziz bi'llah *see* al-ʿAziz
Abu Mikhnaf, historian, 33
Abu Muhammad al-Hasan b. ʿAli al-Utrush *see* al-Utrush, Abu Muhammad al-Hasan b. ʿAli al-Nasir li'l-Haqq
Abu Muslim al-Isfahani, Muʿtazili theologian, 153
Abu Muslim al-Khurasani, 48, 49
Abu Saʿid, Ilkhanid, 80
Abu Saʿid al-Jannabi *see* al-Jannabi, Abu Saʿid
Abu Shama, 17
Abu Tahir Ismaʿil al-Mansur bi'llah *see* al-Mansur, Fatimid caliph
Abu Tahir Sulayman al-Jannabi *see* al-Jannabi, Abu Tahir
Abu Talib, uncle of the Prophet, 36, 52, 149, 209
Abu Talib Akhir, Zaydi imam, 160–1
Abu Talib Yahya b. al-Husayn al-Natiq bi'l-Haqq *see* al-Natiq bi'l-Haqq, Abu Talib Yahya b. al-Husayn
Abu Tamim Maʿadd al-Muʿizz li-Din Allah *see* al-Muʿizz
Abu Yaʿqub al-Sijistani *see* al-Sijistani, Abu Yaʿqub Ishaq b. Ahmad
Abu'l-ʿAbbas al-Saffah, Abbasid caliph, 49
Abu'l-Fadl Jaʿfar b. Muhammad, al-Tha'ir fi'llah, ʿAlid, 158
Abu'l-Hasan ʿAli, *beglerbegi*, Nizari imam, 141, *142*
Abu'l-Husayn Ahmad b. al-Husayn, Zaydi imam *see* al-Mu'ayyad bi'llah, Abu'l-Husayn Ahmad b. al-Husayn b. Harun
Abu'l-Jarud Ziyad b. al-Mundhir, eponym of Jarudiyya, 148
Abu'l-Khattab al-Asadi, eponym of Khattabiyya, 51, 107
Abu'l-Maymun ʿAbd al-Majid *see* al-Hafiz
Abu'l-Qasim Ahmad al-Mustaʿli *see* al-Mustaʿli
Abu'l-Qasim Muhammad al-Qa'im bi-Amr Allah *see* al-Qa'im, Fatimid caliph
Abu'l-Qasim Shahanshah *see* al-Afdal b. Badr al-Jamali
al-Abwa', near Medina, 47–8
Acre *see* ʿAkka
Adam, 114, 187, 188
Adana, in southern Turkey, 176, 178
adhan (Muslim call to prayer), 45, 191
al-Adhani, Sulayman, Efendi, Nusayri author, 178
Adharbayjan, region in northwestern Persia, 76, 81, 82, 92, 123, 137
al-ʿAdid, Fatimid caliph, *116*, 125

'Adil-Shahis, of Bijapur, 101
adwar see dawr
al-Afdal b. Badr al-Jamali, Fatimid vizier, 124
Afghanistan, Afghans, 1, 21, 23, 88, 137, 138, 141
Africa, 1, 103, 104, 144
see also East Africa; North Africa
Afsharid dynasty, of Persia, 88
Aftahiyya, subgroup of Imamiyya, 58
Aga Khan, 1, 105, 141
Aga Khan Award for Architecture, 144
Aga Khan Development Network (AKDN), 143
Aga Khan I, Hasan 'Ali Shah, Nizari imam, 141–2, *142*, 143
Aga Khan II, Aqa 'Ali Shah, Nizari imam, *142*, 143
Aga Khan III, Sultan Muhammad (Mahomed) Shah, Nizari imam, 21, 22, *142*, 143
Aga Khan IV, Shah Karim al-Husayni, Nizari imam, 23, *142*, 143–4
Aga Khan Museum, Toronto, 144
Aga Khan Trust for Culture (AKTC), 144
Aga Khan University, Karachi, 144
Agha Khan *see* Aga Khan
Agha Muhammad Khan Qajar, founder of the Qajar dynasty of Persia, 88
Aghlabids, of Ifriqiya, 115
'ahd (oath), 113, 118, 186
see also bay'a; *mithaq*
ahl al-bayt, 4, 27, 28, 29, 31, 32, 33, 36, 42, 48, 49, 53, 120, 148, 149, 150, 166, 191
see also al Muhammad
ahl al-dhimma, 35, 191
ahl al-kitab (people of the book), 3
see also Christians; Jews; Zoroastrians
Ahmad, 'Alid, son of al-Utrush, 156, 157
Ahmad b. 'Isa b. Zayd, Zaydi imam, 147, 151
Ahmad b. Musa al-Kazim, 61
Ahmad al-Nasir li-Din Allah, 'Alid, Zaydi imam *see* al-Nasir li-Din Allah Ahmad b. Yahya
Ahmad Shah Qajar, 94
Ahmadnagar, in the Deccan, 101–2
al-Ahsa', capital of the Qarmati state of Bahrayn, 80, 123
as province in Saudi Arabia, 100
Ahsa'i, Shaykh Ahmad, eponymous founder of Shaykhiyya, 91–2
Aiglemont, near Paris, Secretariat of Aga Khan IV, 144
akhbar, 69, 71, 72, 86, 87 *see also hadith*
Akhbari, Mirza Muhammad Amin, Twelver scholar, 89
Akhbari school, of Twelver jurisprudence, 72, 86, 87–8, 89
Akhlaq-i muhtashami, of Nasir al-Din al-Tusi, 76
Akhlaq-i Nasiri, of Nasir al-Din al-Tusi, 76
al-Akhram, al-Hasan b. Haydara, Druze leader, 121
'Akka (Acre), 10, 93
Akkar, in Lebanon, 176
al Muhammad, 31, 48, 191
see also ahl al-bayt
'Ala' al-Din Muhammad, Nizari imam and lord of Alamut, *131*, 135
Alamut, fortress and seat of Nizari state, 130–6
destruction by Mongols, 136
Ismaili library at, 131
as Safawid prison, 86
Saljuq attempts to take, 133–134
qiyama proclaimed at, 134, 135
seat of Justanids, 153
as seat of Nizari state, taken by Hasan-i Sabbah, 131, 132

ʿAlawis *see* Nusayris
ʿAlawis, ʿAlawiyya, subgroup of Da'udi Bohras, 129
ʿAlawites *see* Nusayris
ʿAlawiyyun *see* Nusayris
ʿAlba'iyya *see* ʿUla'iyya
Alburz mountains, in Persia, 151, 154
Aleppo (Halab), in northern Syria, 74, 176, 181, 182, 185
Alevis, of Turkey, 175
Algeria, 111, 115
ʿAli b. Abi Talib, first Shiʿi imam and fourth caliph, 27, 28, 29, 30–31, 32, 39, 52, 57, *66*, *142*, 149, 168
  assassination of, 31
  caliphate of, 26–27, 30–31
  investiture by the Prophet, 28
  as Muhammad's *wasi*, 28, 53, 55, 113, 148
  in Nusayri doctrine, 186, 188
  primacy in Sufi doctrine, 79
  shrine at Najaf, 72, 154
  significance for Shiʿs, 26, 39, 57, 71
  in Zaydi doctrine, 148
ʿAli al-Aʿla, Hurufi propagandist, 78
ʿAli b. al-Fadl, early Ismaili *daʿi* in Yaman, 110–11, 163
ʿAli b. al-Husayn, Zayn al-ʿAbidin, imam, 33, 43, 52, *66*, 145–6, 150
ʿAli b. Ibrahim, founder of the ʿAlawi subgroup of Da'udi Bohras, 129
ʿAli b. Muhammad al-Hadi (al-Naqi), Twelver imam, 62, *67*, 179
ʿAli b. Musa al-Rida, Twelver imam, 60, 61, *67*
ʿAli al-Naqi, Twelver imam *see* ʿAli b. Muhammad al-Hadi
ʿAli al-Rida, Twelver imam *see* ʿAli b. Musa al-Rida
ʿAlid loyalism, 79
ʿAlids, 36, 42, 43, 50, 154, 191–2
  suppressed by Abbasid al-Mansur, 53
  venerated by Sufis, 79, 138
  see also Fatimids; Hanafids; Hasanids; Husaynids
allegorical interpretation *see ta'wil*
alphabet *see huruf*
Amal movement, in Lebanon, 100
al-ʿAmili, Shaykh Baha' al-Din, Twelver theosopher, 85
al-Amin, Abbasid caliph, 60
al-Amir, Fatimid caliph, *116*, 125, 126
Amir Kabir, Mirza Taqi Khan, Qajar chief minister, 92
Amir (Kar) Kiya'i Sayyids, Zaydi Alid dynasty in Gilan, 161–2
al-Amir, Muhammad b. Ismaʿil, 173
Amir-Moezzi, M. A., 21
ʿamma see ʿawamm
ʿAmmar b. Yazid *see* Khidash
Amr b. al-Layth, Saffarid, 154
amr (divine command), 192
al-ʿAmri, Abu ʿAmr ʿUthman b. Saʿid, representative of the Twelver Mahdi, 64
al-ʿAmri, Abu Jaʿfar Muhammad b. ʿUthman, representative of the Twelver Mahdi, 64
Amu Darya *see* Oxus river
Amul, in Tabaristan, 152, 153, 154, 155–6, 157, 158, 161, 162
Amuli, Sayyid Haydar *see* Haydar Amuli, Sayyid
Anatolia *see* Rum
Anjudan, village near Mahallat, 137, 138–41
ansar (Helpers), Medinese Companions of the Prophet, 192
Ansari, Shaykh Murtada, 90
Antakya (Antioch), in Turkey, 176
anthropomorphism *see tashbih*
Antioch *see* Antakya
Aq Qoyunlu, dynasty of Persia and eastern Anatolia, 81, 82
Aqa Khan *see* Aga Khan

'aql (intellect, reason), 69, 70, 71, 77, 85, 119, 120, 192
Arabia, 25, 74, 100, 168
Arabic (language), 22, 130, 132, 140
Arak, in central Persia, 95
Aramaeans, 34
Ardabil, in Persia, 81
Arendonk, C. van, orientalist, 24
Aristotle (Aristutalis or Aristu), 85, 120
Arwa, Sulayhid queen of Yaman, 125, 126
al-Asad 'Alawi family, of Syria, 185
al-Asad, Hafiz, 175
Asaf al-Dawla, Nawwab of Awadh, 102
Asani, Ali S., 23
Asaph, 187
asas, 114, 192
al-Asfar al-arba'a, of Mulla Sadra, 85
Asfar b. Shirawayh al-Daylami, Daylami commander, 157
al-Ash'ari, Abu'l-Hasan 'Ali b. Isma'il, Sunni theologian and heresiographer, 37
Ashkawar, in Daylaman, 162
ashraf, 31, 68, 208
ashraf al-qaba'il, 31
'Ashura', in commemoration of al-Husayn b. 'Ali, 33, 189
Asia, 1, 144
al-'Askari, al-Hasan *see* al-Hasan al-'Askari
Assassin legends, 14, 17, 18
Assassins, 12, 131
  origins of the name, 13–14
  variants of the term, 17
al-Astarabadi, Fadl Allah, founder of the Hurufi movement, 78
al-Astarabadi, Mir Muhammad Baqir *see* Mir Damad
al-Astarabadi, Muhammad Amin b. Muhammad, founder of the Akhbari school, 72, 87–8
'atabat, Shi'i shrine cities in Iraq, 84, 88, 90
Atatürk, Mustafa Kemal, 94
'Attar, 138
Autonomous Territory of the 'Alawites, in Syria, 185
Awadh (Oudh), 102, 103
'awamm (*'amma*), 113, 193
Awsaf al-ashraf, of Nasir al-Din al-Tusi, 80
'ayn-mim-sin, of Nusayri doctrine, 188
Ayyubids, 125, 168, 183, 184
Azalis, Azalism, 92, 93
Azhar Park, Cairo, 144
al-'Aziz, Fatimid caliph, *116*, 164

bab (gate), in Nusayri doctrine, 187–8
bab (gate), rank in the Ismaili *da'wa* hierarchy, 118
bab (gate), representative of the Twelver Mahdi, 64
bab al-abwab, 118, 193
  see also da'i al-du'at
Bab, Sayyid Ali Muhammad Shirazi, eponym of Babis, 92
Babis, Babism, 92–3
  see also Azalis; Bahais
bada' (change in God's will or command), 40
Badakhshan, in Central Asia, 119, 124, 137, 187
  see also Afghanistan; Central Asia; Tajikistan; Transoxania
Badr, in Najran, 129
Baghdad, 6, 59, 61, 62, 64, 65, 66, 74, 77, 99, 152, 159
al-Baghdadi, Abu Mansur 'Abd al-Qahir b. Tahir, Sunni jurist and heresiographer, 6, 37
Baha' Allah, Mirza Husayn Nuri, eponym of Bahais, 93
Bahais, Bahaism, 92–3
  see also Azalis; Babis

Bahmanids, of the Deccan, 101
al-Bahrani, Yusuf b. Ahmad, Twelver scholar, 88
Bahrayn, eastern Arabia, 1, 80, 87, 100, 110, 112, 122–3
balagh (initiation), 113
Balkh, in Central Asia, 73, 74
al-Balkhi, Abu'l-Qasim, Mu'tazili theologian, 153, 163
Bangladesh, 1
Banu 'Ammar, of Tripoli, 74
Banu Hamdan, of Yaman, 127, 165
Banu Hashim *see* Hashimids
Banu Himyar, of Yaman, 165
Banu Muhriz, of Syria, 182
Banu Nawbakht, of Iraq, 65–6, 70
Banu Numayr, 180
Banu Shihab, of Yaman, 166
Banu Umayya *see* Umayyads
Banu al-Walid al-Anf, of Yaman, 127
Banu Yam, of Yaman, 130
Banu'l-Furat, 180
Baqi' cemetery, in Medina, 56, 101
al-Baqir, imam *see* Muhammad al-Baqir
Baqiriyya, subgroup of Imamiyya, 46
Bar-Asher, Meir M., 179
Barid-Shahis, of Bidar, 101
Baroda (Vadodara), in Gujarat, 129
Basra, in southern Iraq, 30, 59, 89, 99, 120
Basran school of Imami Theology, 70, 71, 159, 166
Ba'th Socialist Party, of Syria, 185
batin, 7, 55, 127
  in doctrine of pre-Fatimid Ismailis, 113, 114
  in Nizari doctrine of *qiyama*, 134
Batinis, Batiniyya (the Esotericists), 6, 120, 169
al-Batr, Kathir al-Nawwa, eponym of Batriyya, 148
Batris, Batriyya, branch of Zaydis, 147–8
Bawandids, of Daylam, 80, 152
bay'a (oath of allegiance), 26, 193
  see also 'ahd; *mithaq*
Bayan b. Sam'an al-Tamimi, eponym of Bayaniyya, 42
Baybars I, Mamluk sultan, 184
Beirut, 97, 178, 182
Bektashis, Bektashiyya, Sufi order, 2, 78–9
Berar, in the Deccan, 101
Berbers, 34, 111, 115,116
Bible, 9
Bibliothèque Nationale, Paris, 24, 178
bid'a (innovation), 40, 193
Bidar, in the Deccan, 101
Bihar al-anwar, of Muhammad Baqir al-Majlisi, 86, 181
Bihbahani, 'Abd Allah, 93
al-Bihbahani, Muhammad Baqir, Twelver scholar, 88–9, 102
Bijapur, in the Deccan, 101
Biqa' valley, in Jabal 'Amil, 83, 99
Biyapish, in Gilan, 162
Black Stone of the Ka'ba (*al-hajar al-aswad*), 122–3
Bohras, 1, 21, 104, 128, 130
  see also 'Alawis; Da'udis; Sulaymanis
Bombay (Mumbai), 21, 22, 23, 103, 129, 141
Bombay High Court, 142
Brethren of Purity *see* Ikhwan al-Safa'
Brett, Michael, 23
Britain, British *see* England
Bu Sa'id dynasty, of 'Uman and Zanzibar, 103
Bukhara (now in Uzbekistan), 111, 154, 157
Burhan I Nizam Shah, 101–2
Burujurdi, Ayatullah Husayn Tabataba'i, 95–6
al-Busti, Abu'l-Qasim Isma'il, Mu'tazili scholar, 159

Buyids (Buwayhids), of Persia and Iraq, 2, 68, 72, 73, 74, 124, 157, 180
Buzurg-Umid, Kiya, Nizari leader and lord of Alamut, *131*, 161
Byzantine empire, 116, 181, 182

Cahen, Claude, 79
Cairo (al-Qahira), 99, 117, 118, 120, 121, 125, 132, 164
Calcutta, 141
Canada, 144
  see also North America
Carmatians *see* Qarmatis
Caspian provinces, region, in northern Persia, 151–2, 153, 159, 160
  Nizaris in, 160–1
  under Safawids, 161–2
  Zaydi Shiʿis of, 151–162
  see also Daylam; Gilan; Gurgan; Ruyan; Tabaristan
Caspian Sea, 151
Catafago, Joseph, dragoman at Prussian consulate in Syria, 177
Central Asia, 18, 21, 45, 73, 74, 111, 117, 118, 121, 122, 124, 136, 137–8, 187, 201
  see also individual countries
chadur, traditional Persian veil, 94
Chalus, in northern Persia, 153, 160
Chardin, John, French traveller, 15
Chingiz Khan, 74–5
Christians, Christianity, 7–9, 11, 38, 113, 177, 181, 186, 189
Christmas, 189
Cilicia, region, in Turkey, 185
Collège de France, Paris, 15, 16
Companions of the Prophet (*sahaba*), 25–6, 39, 148, 168
Constitutional Revolution, in Persia, 93
Corbin, Henry, 19, 22, 84
cosmogony *see* creation
cosmology
  in doctrine of early Ismailis, 115
  in doctrine of Hamid al-Din al-Kirmani, 119–120
  in doctrine of Nusayris, 186, 187
  in doctrine of Tayyibis, 127
  Ismaili Neoplatonic doctrine, 115, 119, 120
Cossack Brigade, in Persia, 94
creation, 179, 186, 193
Crusaders, Crusades, 9–10, 11, 12, 13–14, 17, 136, 176, 182
cyclical history, 41, 114, 126, 187–8
  see also dawr
Cyprus, 93

Daʿaʾim al-Islam, of al-Qadi al-Nuʿman, 54, 120–1, 128
Dabuyid Ispahbads, dynasty of northern Persia, 151
daʿi (summoner)
  Abbasid, 48–9
  of Daylam, 111
  early Ismaili, 109–12, 113
  Fatimid, 115–16, 117–19
  Nizari, 105
  Sulayhids as, 126–7
  Tayyibi, 125–8
  Zaydi, 149, 150, 160, 161–2
  see also daʿwa
daʿi al-duʿat (chief *daʿi*), 117, 118, 194
al-daʿi al-kabir, Zaydi *daʿi*, 153, 156
al-daʿi al-mutlaq, 127–8, 129, 130, 194
al-daʿi al-saghir, Zaydi *daʿi*, 153, 156
Damascus (Dimashq), 42, 47, 176, 185
dar al-hijra (abode of emigration), 194–5
Dar al-ʿIlm (Dar al-Hikma), Cairo, 118
dar al-zulm, 166, 194
Dar es Salaam, in Tanzania, 103
al-Darazi, Muhammad b. Ismaʿil, Druze leader, 121
Daraziyya *see* Druzes

darwish (dervish), 195
dassondh (tithe), 141
Da'ud b. 'Ajabshah, Tayyibi *da'i mutlaq*, 128
Da'ud Burhan al-Din b. Qutbshah, first Da'udi *da'i mutlaq*, 128, 129
Da'udi-Sulaymani schism *see* Da'udis
Da'udis, Da'udiyya, branch of Tayyibis, 128–9
  schism with Sulaymanis, 126, 128–9
  see also Bohras
da'wa (Persian, *da'wat*), 195
  Abbasid, 48–9
  early Ismaili, 109–12, 113
  Fatimid, 115–16, 117–18, 119, 120, 121–2, 124, 125
  Nizari, 131–2, 138–40
  Da'udi, 129
  Sulaymani, 129
  Tayyibi, 125–8
  Zaydi, 149, 150, 160, 162–3
al-da'wa al-hadiya (the rightly guiding mission), 109, 195
da'wat see da'wa
da'wat al-haqq, 109
dawla, 115, 125, 195
al-dawla al-Qasimiyya, in Yaman, 169
dawr, *adwar* (cycles, eras), 41, 114, 187, 195
  see also cyclical history; *dawr al-kashf*; *dawr al-satr*; *qobba*
dawr al-kashf (period of manifestation), 126
  see also dawr
dawr al-satr (period of concealment), 108, 109, 126, 132, 207
  see also dawr
Day of Judgement, 41, 67
  see also qiyama
Daylam, Daylaman, region, in northern Persia, 68, 106, 111, 123, 147, 152–3, 154, 155, 157, 161, 162, 163
Daylaman *see* Daylam
de Sacy *see* Silvestre de Sacy
Deccan, the, 101, 102
dervish *see darwish*
dhimmis see ahl al-dhimma
al-Dhu'ayb b. Musa al-Wadi'i al-Hamdani, first Tayyibi *da'i mutlaq* in Yaman, 126, 127
Dhu'l-Sharafayn Muhammad b. Ja'far, leader of the Husayniyya Zaydis, 165
din 'Ali, 27, 31
Diwan, of al-Husayn b. Hamdan al-Khasibi, 181
Donaldson, Dwight M., 19, 21
Druzes, Druses, 2, 17, 39, 83, 121–2, 177, 182, 184
Duruz *see* Druzes
Dussaud, René, orientalist, 24, 178

East Africa, 103–4, 129, 143
École des Langues Orientales Vivantes, Paris, 16
education, 94, 143
  religious, 103, 118, 128, 129, 143–4, 145, 190
Egypt, Egyptians, 12, 16, 17, 112, 117, 122, 124, 125, 132, 184
Encyclopaedia Iranica, 17
Encyclopaedia of Islam, 17, 21
Encyclopaedia Islamica, 17
England, 22
Epistles of the Brethren of Purity see Rasa'il Ikhwan al-Safa'
eras of human history *see* cyclical history; *dawr*
eschatology, 38, 39, 40, 42, 57, 63, 114–15, 121, 122, 127, 150, 187
  see also qiyama
Esmail, Aziz, 23
esoteric interpretation *see ta'wil*
esotericism
  Fatimids and, 118
  Khattabis and, 51

Nusayris and, 178, 185, 186
Twelver Shiʿism and, 91
Zaydi attitude towards, 159, 160
see also batin
Ess, Josef van, 21
Eulogius, bishop of Toledo, 9
Euphrates river, 31, 74
Europe, Europeans
dispersal of Ismailis, 1
laws as models, 94
medieval perceptions of Islam, 7–16, 131
modern scholarship, 18–24
Nizari imams in, 137, 143, 144
Nusayri studies, 176–9
orientalists, 16–18
exaggeration in religion *see ghulat; ghuluww*

al-Fadil al-Qasim b. Jaʿfar, *amir*, leader of Husayniyya Zaydis, 165
Fadl Allah, Shaykh Muhammad Husayn, founder of Hizbullah, 100
al-Fa'iz, Fatimid caliph, 16
al-Farabi, Abu Nasr Muhammad, philosopher, 85, 120
Fara'id al-usul, of Shaykh Murtada Ansari, 90
Fars, region in southwestern Persia, 104, 110, 124, 162
Fasiyya Shadhiliyya, Sufi brotherhood in Yaman, 170
Fath ʿAli Shah Qajar, 91, 141
Fathiyya *see* Aftahiyya
Fatima, daughter of the Prophet, 26, 27, 34, 45, 50, 52, 55, 116, *142*, 191–2, 196
Fatima, al-Maʿsuma, daughter of Musa al-Kazim, 61
Fatima, wife of Jaʿfar al-Sadiq, 107
Fatimid caliphate, 5, 112, 115–25
Fatimids
as a branch of ʿAlids, 36, 50, 149, 150, 191–2, 196
genealogy, 6, *116*
fatwa(s), 90, 196
against Ismailis, 159, 160, 170
against Nusayris, 184, 190
al-Fawa'id al-madaniyya, of Muhammad Amin al-Astarabadi, 87
Fayd Kashani, Mulla Muhsin, Twelver scholar, 86, 87
Faydiya Madrasa, Qumm, 97
Federation of the States of Syria, 185
fida'is (*fidawis*) (self-sacrificing devotees), 14, 196
Fida'iyan-i Islam (the 'Devotees of Islam'), 96
fiqh (jurisprudence), 44, 51, 69, 71, 196
see also usul al-fiqh
First World War, 99, 170, 184
France, 11, 15, 16
Franks *see* Crusaders
Friedman, Y., 179
Fundgruben des Orients, 16
al-Fusul al-arbaʿa, of Hasan-i Sabbah, 133
Fusus al-hikam, of Ibn al-ʿArabi, 170
Fyzee, Asaf A. A., 21

Gabriel *see* Jibra'il
Germany, 16
Ghadir Khumm, 28
see also ʿId al-Ghadir
ghaliya see ghulat
ghayba (occultation), 38, 40, 122, 150
of the Twelver Mahdi, 63–4
Greater, 66, 67
Lesser, 64–66, 67
al-ghayba al-kubra, 67
al-ghayba al-sughra, 67
al-Ghazali, Abu Hamid Muhammad, Sunni scholar, 6–7, 133, 168

Ghaznawids, of Afghanistan and Khurasan, 73
ghulat, *ghaliya*, 24, 36, 40–3, 45, 48, 51, 80, 81, 121, 179, 181, 186, 187, 197
ghuluww (exaggeration in religion), 40, 197
Ghuzz *see* Oghuz Turks
Gilan, region in northern Persia, 151, 152, 153, 154, 155, 158, 160–1
Gilis, 154, 155, 157
see also Gilan
ginan, 23, 139–40, 197
see also Khojas; Satpanth Ismailism
Gleave, Robert, 21
Global Center for Pluralism, Ottawa, 144
Gnostic traditions, 85, 113, 127
gnosticism (*ʿirfan*), 80, 87, 91, 114, 115, 160, 186, 188, 198
Golconda, in the Deccan, 101
Goldziher, Ignaz, orientalist, 18–19, 37
Great Resurrection *see qiyama*
Greek philosophy, 182
see also Neoplatonism; philosophical Ismailism
Griffini, E., 24
Gujarat, in western India, 103, 128, 129, 139, 140, 141
Gulpayagani, Ayatullah Sayyid Muhammad Rida, 98
Gurgan, in northern Persia, 73, 153, 154, 156, 157

Hadawiyya, Zaydi legal school, 164, 165, 171, 172, 173
Haddadiyya, Nusayri tribe, 183
al-Hadi, Abbasid caliph, 59
al-Hadi, ʿAli b. Muhammad *see* ʿAli b. Muhammad al-Hadi
al-Hadi ilaʾl-Haqq, Yahya b. al-Husayn, Zaydi imam *see* Yahya b. al-Husayn, al-Hadi ilaʾl-Haqq
al-Hadi Sharaf al-Din, Zaydi imam in Yaman, 170
hadith, 28,44, 54, 60, 68, 69–70, 71, 77, 85, 86–7, 91, 106, 148
see also akhbar
al-Hafiz, Fatimid caliph, *116*, 125
Hafizis, Hafiziyya, branch of Mustaʿlians, 125
Hafizi-Tayyibi schism, 125–6
see also Bohras
Haʾiri Yazdi, Shaykh ʿAbd al-Karim, Twelver scholar, 95–6
al-hajar al-aswad see Black Stone of the Kaʿba
hajj (pilgrimage to Mecca), 189, 197–8
al-Hakim, Ayatullah Sayyid Muhsin, 99
al-Hakim, Fatimid caliph, *116*, 118, 121–2
Halm, Heinz, 23, 24, 179
Hama, in Syria, 176, 185
Hamadan, in Persia, 73
Hamdan Qarmat, Qarmati leader in Iraq, 109, 110, 112, 180
Hamdani, Abbas, 22, 23
al-Hamdani, Husayn F., 21
Hamdanids, of Iraq and Syria, 2, 74, 165, 181, 182
Hamid al-Din al-Kirmani *see* al-Kirmani, Hamid al-Din Ahmad b. ʿAbd Allah
Hamid al-Din, clan of Qasimi Zaydis, 170
al-Hamidi, Ibrahim b. al-Husayn, Tayyibi *daʿi*, 127
Hammer(-Purgstall), Josef von, orientalist and diplomat, 17–18, 22
Hamza b. ʿAli b. Ahmad, Druze leader, 121, 122, 182
Hanafi Sunnism, 74, 202
Hanafids, branch of ʿAlids, 36, 38
Hanbali Sunnism, 172, 184, 190, 202

haqa'iq, 198
for early Ismailis, 113, 114
in Nizari doctrine, 134
in Tayyibi doctrine, 127, 128
haqiqa (religious truth), 80, 134, 198
Haraz, mountainous region in Yaman, 127, 165
al-Hariri, Abu Musa (Père Joseph Azzi), 'Alawi author, 179
Harran, in Iraq, 182
Harun al-Rashid, Abbasid caliph, 59, 61, 108, 152
al-Hasan b. 'Ali b. Abi Talib, imam, 32, 36, 39, 52, 107, 149
Hasan 'Ali Shah, Aga Khan I *see* Aga Khan I
al-Hasan b. 'Ali al-Utrush *see* al-Utrush, Abu Muhammad al-Hasan b. 'Ali al-Nasir li'l-Haqq
al-Hasan al-'Askari, Twelver imam, 62–3, 64, 66, *67*, 110, 179, 180, 188
al-Hasan al-Da'i, 'Alid *see* al-Hasan b. Qasim
Hasan II *'ala dhikrihi'l-salam*, Nizari imam and lord of Alamut, 131, 134
al-Hasan b. Qasim, 'Alid, Zaydi ruler in Tabaristan, 156, 158
Hasan b. al-Sabbah *see* Hasan-i Sabbah
al-Hasan b. Yahya b. al-Husayn, 'Alid, Zaydi imam, 151
al-Hasan b. Zayd, al-Da'i ila'l-Haqq, founder of the 'Alid Zaydi dynasty in Tabaristan, 153, 154
Hasan-i Sabbah, Nizari leader and founder of the Nizari state, 6, 124, 131–3, 160
Hasanids, branch of 'Alids, 36, 46, 48, 50, 59, 147, 149, 152, 153, 156, 158–9, 162, 192
Hashim b. 'Abd Manaf, the Prophet's great-grandfather, 27, 52, 198
Hashimids, the Prophet's clan of the Quraysh, 27, 36, 38, 42, 47–8, 52, 54, 60, 109, 198
Hashimiyya, early Shi'i group, 39, 43, 46, 48
hashishis, *hashishiyya*, 13–14, 17, 160
see also Assassin legends; Assassins
Hawsam, in eastern Gilan, 155, 158, 160
Haydar, Safawi *shaykh*, 81–2
Haydar Amuli, Sayyid, Twelver scholar, 80
Haykel, B., 172–3
Hell, 206
denied by *ghulat*, 41
d'Herbelot, Barthélemy, early orientalist, 176
hidden imams
agents of Twelver Mahdi, 64–66
for early Ismailis, 108–109, 112, 114
identification with Mahdi, 38, 40, 46, 58, 59, 67
for Nizaris, 132
persons claiming to be:
Bab, 92
early Ismaili imams, 110
Isma'il I Safawid, 82
Qarmati, 108
for Tayyibis, 125–6
for Zaydis, 165
see also dawr al-satr; *ghayba*; *satr*
hijab (veil), 187, 188
Hijaz, the, 59, 147, 164, 197
hijra (emigration), of the Prophet, 25, 192, 205
hijra, in Zaydi doctrine, 150, 166, 167, 194–5
hikma (wisdom), 118
al-hikma al-ilahiyya (Persian, *hikmat-i ilahi*), 85
al-hikma al-muta'aliya, 85
see also al-hikma al-ilahiyya
Hilla, in Iraq, 74, 77, 79, 83, 87

al-Hilli, al-ʿAllama al-Hasan Ibn al-Mutahhar, Twelver theologian, 75, 77, 87
al-Hilli, Jaʿfar b. al-Hasan (al-Muhaqqiq al-Awwal), Twelver theologian, 77
Hims (Homs), in Syria, 176
Hindus, Hinduism, 103, 128, 130, 136, 139, 140, 142
Hisham b. ʿAbd al-Malik, Umayyad caliph, 47, 146
Hisham b. al-Hakam, Imami scholar, 51, 59
Historic Cities Support Programme, 144
historiography, 131, 145, 177
Hizbullah (the Party of God), 100
Hodgson, Marshall G. S., 22, 79
Holy Land, 9, 10
  see also Middle East; Outremer
hudud (punishment), 91, 197
hudud, *hudud al-din*, ranks in Ismaili *daʿwa* organization, 113, 117, 197
hujja (proof), *131*
  Hasan-i Sabbah as, 132
  in Imami doctrine, 55, 198
  in Ismaili doctrine, 112
  in Nizari doctrine, 132, 199
  as rank in Ismaili *daʿwa* organization, 117
hujjat Allah, 55
Hukumat-i Islami, of Ayatullah (Imam) Ruhullah Khumayni, 97
Hülegü (Hulagu), founder of the Ilkhanid dynasty of Persia and Iraq, 75–6, 136
hulul (incarnation), 40, 41, 187, 199
Humayma, in Palestine, 48, 49
al-Hurr al-ʿAmili, Muhammad b. al-Hasan, Twelver scholar, 87
huruf (letters of the alphabet), 79
Hurufis, Hurufiyya, 78–9
al-Husayn b. ʿAli, Sahib Fakhkh, ʿAlid leader of anti-Abbasid revolt, 59, 147
al-Husayn b. ʿAli b. Abi Talib, imam, 32–3, 36, 39, 52, *66*, 68, 107, 146, 149, 154
  commemorated on *ʿAshuraʾ*, 33, 94
  in Nusayri doctrine, 189
al-Husayn al-Mahdi, ʿAlid, Zaydi Mahdi *see* al-Mahdi li-Din Allah al-Husayn b. al-Qasim
al-Husayn b. al-Mansur biʾllah al-Qasim *see* al-Mahdi li-Din Allah al-Husayn b. al-Qasim
al-Husayn al-Shaʿir, al-Utrush's brother, 158
Husaynids, branch of ʿAlids, 36, 43, 45–6, 51, 53, 55, 68, 116, 149, 156, 192
Husayniyya, Zaydi sect in Yaman, 165–6, 167
Hyderabad (Haydarabad), in Gujarat, 102

Ibadis, Ibadiyya, subgroup of Kharijis, 103
ibaha (antinomianism), 42
Ibn ʿAbbad, Abbasid vizier, 159
Ibn Abi Jumhur, Twelver scholar, 80
Ibn al-ʿArabi, Sufi master, 77, 80, 85, 159
Ibn ʿAttash *see* ʿAbd al-Malik b. ʿAttash
Ibn Babawayh, Imami scholar, 69–70, 87
Ibn Falah, founder of Mushaʿshaʿ, 79
Ibn al-Furat, Abbasid vizier, 65, 66
Ibn al-Furat al-Juʿfi, Muhammad b. Musa, 180
Ibn al-Hanafiyya, ʿAlid *see* Muhammad b. al-Hanafiyya
Ibn Hawshab, Mansur al-Yaman, early Ismaili *daʿi* in Yaman, 110–11, 114, 163

Ibn Hazm, ʿAli b. Ahmad, Sunni heresiographer, 37
Ibn al-Mutahhar al-Hilli *see* al-Hilli, al-ʿAllama al-Hasan Ibn al-Mutahhar
Ibn Nusayr, Abu Shuʿayb Muhammad b. Nusayr al-Namiri, eponym founder of Nusayriyya, 179–80
Ibn Rizam, Abu ʿAbd Allah Muḥammad, anti-Ismaili author, 6
Ibn Sina (Avicenna), 76, 80, 85
Ibn Tabataba, Muhammad b. Ibrahim, ʿAlid, leader of a revolt, 147
Ibn Taymiyya, Hanbali jurist, 172, 184, 190
Ibn al-Wazir, Muhammad b. Ibrahim, Sayyid, founder of the neo-Sunni school of Zaydism in Yaman, 172, 173
Ibrahim *see* Abraham
Ibrahim b. ʿAbd Allah b. al-Hasan, ʿAlid, brother of al-Nafs al-Zakiyya, 48, 52, 147
Ibrahim b. Muhammad b. ʿAli (Ibrahim al-Imam), Abbasid, 49
Ibrahim b. Muhammad b. al-Fahd al-Makrami, Sulaymani *daʿi*, 129
Ibrahim b. al-Walid I, Umayyad caliph, 47
Ibrahimi family, Shaykhi leaders, 92
ʿId al-adhha, feast of the sacrifice, 189
ʿId al-fitr, feast of breaking the fast, 189
ʿId al-Ghadir, 189
ʿId al-ghutas (Epiphany), 189
Idlib, in Syria, 176
Idris ʿImad al-Din b. al-Hasan, Tayyibi *daʿi al-mutlaq* and historian, 107, 127
  see also *ʿUyun al-akhbar*; *Zahr al-maʿani*
Ifriqiya, 115,116
  see also Maghrib; Morocco; North Africa; Tunisia
Ihyaʾ ʿulum al-din, of al-Ghazali, 168
ijmaʿ (consensus), 71, 78, 199
ijtihad, 71, 77–8, 87, 89, 97, 148, 149, 155, 158, 173, 199
  see also *marjaʿ al-taqlid*; *taqlid*
al-Ijtihad waʾl-akhbar, of Muhammad Baqir al-Bihbahani, 88–9
Ikhwan al-Muslimun *see* Muslim Brotherhood
Ikhwan al-Safaʾ (Brethren of Purity), 120
  see also *Rasaʾil Ikhwan al-Safaʾ*
Ilkhanids, Mongol dynasty of Persia and Iraq, 75, 77, 80–1, 131, 161
ʿilm (religious knowledge), 28, 29, 53–4, 55, 61, 150, 199–200
ʿImad-Shahis, of Berar, 101
imam
  absent during *dawr al-satr*, 108–109, 126, 132
  and *akhbar* (*hadith*), 54, 69–70, 72, 86–7
  attributes of, 44
  authority, 28–29
  designation of successor, 53, 55
  devotion to, 41, 55
  evolution of Twelver line of, 57, 60, 65
  infallibility, 41, 54
  intermediary role of, 70
  and *khums*, 59, 62, 91
  none after Mahdi/*qaʾim*, 38
  in Zaydi doctrine, 149–150
  see also hidden imams; imamate; *muhtasibun*; *muqtasida*
imam-qaʾim, 134
  see also Mahdi; *qaʾim*; *qiyama*
Imam-Shahis, of South Asia, 140
imamate
  in early Ismaili doctrine, 106–109
  in Imami doctrine, 53–6

principle of *ʿilm*, 54–5
principle of *nass*, 53
in Qarmati doctrine, 112
in teachings of Jaʿfar al-Sadiq, 53–55
in Zaydi doctrine, 150
see also hidden imams; *ʿilm*; imam; *nass*
Imamiyya, 43–45, 146, 151
and the *ghulat*, 45, 51
and the Muʿtazila, 47, 70, 71, 146, 151
recognized Musa al-Kazim, 59
school of law, 51
and Zaydism, 149, 151
see also Twelvers
incarnation *see hulul*
India, Indians, 74, 99, 101–102, 103, 124, 128, 139, 140, 143
see also Gujarat; Sind; South Asia
Indian subcontinent *see* India
Institute for the Study of Muslim Civilisations, London, 144
Institute of Ismaili Studies, London, 23, 143
intellect *see ʿaql*
Iran, Iranians, xv, xvii, 1, 20–1, 38, 73, 78, 81, 85, 88, 93, 95–100, 112, 119–20, 124, 138, 187
see also Persia
Iranian school of philosophical Ismailism *see* philosophical Ismailism
Iraq, 1, 30, 31, 73, 89, 90, 91, 98–9
Buyids in, 68
as centre of Imami learning, 70–72, 77
conquered by Saljuqs, 73, 124
early Ismaili *daʿwa* in, 110, 112
in the first civil war, 31
and later Kaysani sects, 39
mawali of, 35
and Nusayriyya, 180, 181
seat of Abbasid caliphate, 48, 49
versus Syria, 31
Zaydis in, 46
ʿIsa *see* Jesus
ʿIsa b. Zayd b. ʿAli, Zaydi imam, 52, 147
Isfahan, in central Persia, 20, 73, 79, 85, 86, 124
see also 'school of Isfahan'
al-Isharat wa'l-tanbihat, of Ibn Sina, 76
Iskenderun, in Turkey, 176
Islam
converts (non-Arabs) *see mawali*
and Crusaders, 8, 9, 10, 12, 13
era of, would be ended by Mahdi, 114–5
European perceptions of, 7–16
non-Muslim subjects *see ahl al-dhimma*
and other religions *see ahl al-kitab*
Shiʿi perspective, 4
Sunni–Shiʿi division, 25–29
Islamic Revolution, in Iran, 20, 95, 98
ism, the Name in Nusayri doctrine, 187–8
ʿisma (perfect immunity from error and sin), 41, 54, 149, 200
Ismaʿil b. Jaʿfar, al-Mubarak, Ismaili imam, 52, 106, 107
Ismaʿil I, founder of the Safawid dynasty, 82
Ismaili Society, Bombay, 22, 23
Ismaili studies, 21–23
Ismailis, Ismaʿiliyya, 1, 13, 17, 105–6
daʿwa, 109–111
early doctrine, 112, 114
as a movement of social protest, 109–110
organization and hierarchy, 117–8
origin of the name, 106
see also Bohras; Da'udis; Hafizis; Khojas; Nizaris; Satpanth Ismailism; Sulaymanis; Tayyibis

al-Isma'iliyya al-khalisa, early Ismaili group, 107
al-Isma'iliyya al-waqifa, 107
isnad (chain of transmitters of *hadith*), 51
al-Istibsar, of Abu Ja'far Muhammad al-Tusi, 71
Ivanow, Wladimir, 21, 22, 131
'Iyan, in Yaman, 164, 165

Jabal 'Amil, in Lebanon, 79, 83, 99, 100
Jabal Ansariyya (today's Jabal 'Alawiyyin), in Syria, 133, 176, 182–3, 185, 190
  see also Jabal Bahra'
Jabal Bahra' (today's Jabal 'Alawiyyin), in Syria, 133
Jabal al-Rass, near Medina, 152
Jabal Sinjar, in northwestern Iraq, 183
Jabala, region, in Syria, 184
Jabir al-Ju'fi, 45
Jacob, 188
Ja'far, 'Alid, son of al-Utrush, 156, 157
Ja'far b. Abi Talib, al-Tayyar, Talibid, 36, 52, 149
Ja'far b. 'Ali al-Hadi, 'Alid, brother of the eleventh Twelver imam, 62, 63
Ja'far al-Ju'fi, 187
Ja'far b. Mansur al-Yaman, Ismaili author, 114
Ja'far b. al-Qasim al-'Iyani, Zaydi leader in Yaman, 165
Ja'far al-Sadiq, imam, 42, 46, 50, 51, 52, 57, *66*, 106, 112, 146, 152
  and doctrine of imamate, 44, 46, 53–55
  and the *ghulat*, 43, 186
  hadiths of, 51
  his circle of associates, 51
  his interpretation of the law, 51, 151
Ja'faris, 190
  see also Nusayris
Ja'fariyya *see* Muhammad-Shahi Nizaris
Jahangir, Mughal emperor, 102
Jalal al-Din Hasan, Nizari imam and lord of Alamut, *131*, 134–5, *142*
Jalal al-Din Khwarazmshah, 75
Jalal al-Din Rumi, Mawlana, Sufi poet, 138
Jalayirids, of Adharbayjan, Kurdistan and Iraq, 81
jama'at (the community), 104, 200
jama'at-khana (assembly house), 140, 210
James of Vitry, bishop of Acre and Crusader historian, 10, 12, 13
Jami' al-asrar, of Haydar Amuli, 80
Janahiyya, subgroup of Kaysaniyya, 149
al-Jannabi, Abu Sa'id, founder of the Qarmati state of Bahrayn, 109, 110, 112, 122
al-Jannabi, Abu Tahir, Qarmati ruler of Bahrayn, 122–3
al-Jannan al-Junbulani, 'Abd Allah, Nusayri leader, 180
Jarudis, Jarudiyya, branch of Zaydis, 147–8, 148–9, 163
jazira, *jaza'ir*, 117, 118, 201
Jerusalem, 9
Jesus ('Isa), 114, 177, 188
Jews, 93
Jibal, region, in Persia, 111, 123, 157
Jibra'il (Gabriel), archangel, 13, 188
jihad (war), 91, 184
al-Jilli, Muhammad b. 'Ali, Nusayri leader, 181–2
al-Jisri, 'Ali b. 'Isa, Nusayri leader, 181
jizya (tribute, poll tax), 35, 191
Joseph, 187
Joshua, 187
Judaeo-Christian traditions, 38, 113, 114
Judaism, 3, 35, 113

Junayd, Safawi *shaykh*, 81
jurisprudence *see fiqh*
Jurjan *see* Gurgan
Justan, founder of the Justanid dynasty, 152
Justan III b. Marzuban, Justanid, 154
Justanids, of Daylam, 152, 153, 154, 157
Juwayni, ʿAta-Malik, historian and Mongol administrator, 131, 133

al-Kafi, of al-Kulayni, 69
kafir see kufr
Kahak, village near Mahallat in central Persia, 141
Kahf, castle in Syria, 133, 183
kalam (theology), 51, 69–70, 78, 119
  Muʿtazili school of, 47, 71, 163
  Imami Shiʿi adoption of Muʿtazili, 47, 70, 151
  Zaydi adoption of Muʿtazili, 146, 149, 151, 152, 153, 159, 173
Kalar, in northern Persia, 153
Karachi, 103, 129, 144
al-Karaki al-ʿAmili, Shaykh ʿAli (al-Muhaqqiq al-Thani), Twelver scholar, 83, 85
karamat (miracles), 168
Karbala, in Iraq, 33, 35, 43, 46, 62, 68, 84, 88, 92, 94, 95, 98, 99, 102, 103
Karim Khan Zand, founder of the Zand dynasty of Persia, 88, 141
al-Karkh, Shiʿi suburb of Baghdad, 180
Kashan, in central Persia, 73, 79
Kashani, Abu'l-Qasim ʿAbd Allah b. ʿAli, historian, 131, 133, 161
Kashani, Ayatullah Sayyid Abu'l-Qasim, 96
kashf see dawr al-kashf
Kashf al-asrar, of Ayatullah (Imam) Ruhullah Khumayni, 96
al-Kashshi, Muḥammad b. ʿUmar, Imami scholar, 45, 46
al-Kaynaʿi, Ibrahim b. Ahmad, founder of a Zaydi Sufi order in Yaman, 168–9
Kaysan, Abu ʿAmra, eponym of Kaysaniyya, 36
Kaysaniyya, 4, 36, 37–40, 41, 43, 46
Kenya, 104
khabar see akhbar
khalifa, khulafa' (successor), 26, 60, 137
al-Khalifa family, of Bahrayn, 100
khalifat rasul Allah, 26
Khamana'i, Ayatullah Sayyid ʿAli, 98, 100
Kharijis, Khawarij, 4, 31–2, 116
al-Khasibi, Abu ʿAbd Allah al-Husayn b. Hamdan, Nusayri leader, 180–1
khassa see khawass
khatam al-anbiya' ('seal of the prophets'), 25
Khattabis, extremist Shiʿi group, 24, 51
Khatunabadi, Mulla Muhammad Baqir, Twelver scholar, 86
khawass (*khassa*), 113, 186, 201
Khawla, mother of Muhammad b. al-Hanafiyya, 34, 36
Khayrkhwah-i Harati, Muhammad Rida b. Khwaja Sultan Husayn, Nizari *daʿi* and author, 139
Khidash (ʿAmmar b. Yazid), 48
khitab, conversion to Nusayrism, 184
Khojas, 1, 23, 103–4, 139–41, 142, 197, 202
  see also ginan; Nizaris; Satpanth Ismailism
Khojki, script, 23, 139, 197
Khu'i, Ayatullah Sayyid Abu'l-Qasim, 98
al-khulafa' al-rashidun (the 'rightly-guided caliphs'), 26–7

Khumayni, Imam (Ayatullah) Ruhullah, leader of the Islamic Revolution in Iran, 20, 95, 96–8, 100
khums, 27, 59, 62, 90, 202
Khurasan, region in northeastern Persia, 39, 46, 48–9, 50, 60, 71, 73, 74, 75, 111, 117, 119, 123, 124, 133, 146–7, 152, 162
Khurasaniyya, army, 49
Khurramdiniyya, Khurramiyya, 50
khuruj (insurrection), 149
Khusraw Firuz, Buyid *see* al-Malik al-Rahim Khusraw Furuz
khutba, 91, 125, 154, 202
Khuzistan, region in southwestern Persia, 73, 79, 89, 108, 109
Khwarazm, in Central Asia, 73, 74
Khwarazmians, Khwarazmshahs, 74–5
Kirman, city and province in Persia, 92, 141
Kirmani, Hajj Muhammad Karim Khan, Shaykhi leader, 92
al-Kirmani, Hamid al-Din Ahmad b. ʿAbd Allah, Ismaili *daʿi* and author, 119, 120, 121–2, 159
Kitab al-ahkam, of Yahya b. al-Husayn al-Hadi, 163
Kitab al-ʿalim, of Jaʿfar b. Mansur al-Yaman, 113–4
Kitab al-azhar fi fiqh, of al-Mahdi Ahmad b. Yahya al-Murtada, 173
Kitab al-bakura al-Sulaymaniyya, of Sulayman al-Adhani, 178
Kitab al-dhakira fi'l-haqiqa, of ʿAli Ibn al-Walid, 127
Kitab al-haft wa'l-azilla, attributed to al-Mufaddal b. ʿUmar al-Juʿfi, 186, 188
Kitab al-hawi fi ʿilm al-fatawa, of Maymun b. al-Qasim al-Tabarani, 186
Kitab al-hidaya, of al-Husayn b. Hamdan al-Khasibi, 181
Kitab al-hijra, of al-Qasim b. Ibrahim al-Rassi, 150
Kitab al-jamiʿ al-kafi, of Abu ʿAbd Allah Muhammad al-ʿAlawi, 151
Kitab kanz al-walad, of Ibrahim b. al-Husayn al-Hamidi, 127
Kitab al-mahsul, of Muhammad b. Ahmad al-Nasafi, 123
Kitab al-mashyakha, a Nusayri catechism, 177
Kitab al-mujli, of Ibn Abi Jumhur, 80
Kitab al-muntakhab, of Yahya b. al-Husayn al-Hadi, 163
Kitab al-riyad, of Hamid al-Din al-Kirmani, 120
Kitab taʿlim diyanat al-Nusayriyya, a Nusayri work, 177
Kiya Sayf al-Din Kushayji, Nizari ruler of Daylaman, 162
Kofsky, A., 179
Kohlberg, Etan, 19, 21
Kraus, Paul, orientalist, 19
Kuchispahan, in eastern Gilan, 161
Kufa, in southern Iraq, 31, 39, 48, 69, 106, 111, 146
  centre of Shiʿism, 28, 30, 32, 33
  mawali of, 35
  Qarmati centre, 109–110
  in revolt of al-Mukhtar, 35–36
  support for ʿAli, 29, 30–1, 32
kufr (unbelief), 4, 40, 55, 91, 161, 169, 202
Kuhdum, in northern Persia, 162
Kuhistan *see* Quhistan
al-Kulayni, Abu Jaʿfar Muhammad, Imami scholar, 54, 69, 87
al-Kumayt b. Zayd al-Asadi, Arab poet, 45
al-Kunduri, Saljuq vizier, 73
Kurdistan, Kurds, 177, 183
Kushayji *amirs*, Nizari dynasty in Daylaman, 162
Kutama Berbers, 111, 115, 116

al-kutub al-arbaʿa, the 'four books' of Imami Shiʿis, 69, 87
Kuwait, 101

Ladhiqiyya (Laodicea), in Syria, 176, 182, 183, 185
Lahijan, in eastern Gilan, 158, 161, 162
Lahiji, ʿAbd al-Razzaq, 86
Lahiji, Qadi Shams al-Din, Twelver scholar, 84
Lahore, 102, 103
Lamak b. Malik al-Hammadi, chief *qadi* and Ismaili *daʿi* in Yaman, 126
Langa, in northern Persia, 160
Last Judgement *see* eschatology; *qiyama*
Latakia, in Syria, 2
Latin (language), 11
Laylat al-milad see Christmas
Lebanon, 1, 2, 19, 79, 83, 88, 99–100, 122, 175, 176, 179
Leiden, 15
Levant 14, 183
  see also Holy Land; Outremer
Lewis, Bernard, 22
libertinism *see ibaha*
literature
  Ismaili, 21–23, 108, 119, 127, 131
  Nusayri, 24, 176–7, 179
  Zaydi, 23, 145
Lohana, Hindu caste, 139
London, 143
Lucknow, in northern India, 102, 103
Lyde, Samuel, Anglican missionary in Syria, 177

Maʿarrat al-Nuʿman, in Syria, 176
Mabadi' al-wusul, of ʿAllama al-Hilli, 77
Mabasim al-bisharat, of Hamid al-Din al-Kirmani, 121
Madelung, Wilferd, 21, 22, 24, 170
madhhab (school of religious law), 51, 120, 151, 164–5
  see also Hanafi Sunnism; Hanbali Sunnism; Shafiʿi Sunnism
ma'dhun, rank in Ismaili *daʿwa* hierarchy, 117, 128, 203
Maghrib, 111
  see also Ifriqiya; Morocco; North Africa; Tunisia
Mahaliba, Nusayri tribe, 183
Mahallat, in central Persia, 141
Mahdi, the
  in ʿAbd Allah al-Mahdi's reform, 112
  al-Hasan al-ʿAskari as, 63
  Ismaʿil b. Jaʿfar as, 106–7
  Jaʿfar al-Sadiq as, 58
  Muhammad b. al-Hanafiyya as, 38
  Muhammad b. Ismaʿil as, 108
  al-Mukhtar introduced idea, 38
  for the Qarmatis, 112
  Shah Ismaʿil I as, 82
  the twelfth imam of the Twelvers as, 63–64, 67
  in Zaydi doctrine, 150, 165
  see also qa'im
al-Mahdi, ʿAbd Allah, first Fatimid caliph, 109, 111–112, 114, 115, *116*, 120, 123, 126
al-Mahdi, Abu ʿAbd Allah Muhammad, Abbasid caliph, 50
al-Mahdi, Muhammad b. al-Hasan, twelfth imam of the Twelvers, 57
  his Greater Occultation, 66, 67
  his Lesser Occultation, 63, 67
  his representatives, 64–66
Mahdi b. Khusraw Firuz (Firuzan), Siyahchashm, Justanid, 157
al-Mahdi li-Din Allah, Abu ʿAbd Allah Muhammad, Zaydi imam, 155
al-Mahdi li-Din Allah al-Husayn b. al-Qasim, Zaydi Mahdi, 165
Mahdism *see* Mahdi; *qa'im*
majalis, 118, 204

majalis al-hikma ('sessions of wisdom'), 118
al-Majalis al-Mu'ayyadiyya, of al-Mu'ayyad fi'l-Din al-Shirazi, 118
al-Majlisi, Muhammad Baqir, Twelver scholar, 86, 181
al-Majlisi, Muhammad Taqi, Twelver scholar, 87
Majmu' al-a'yad, of Maymun b. Qasim al-Tabarani, 177, 182
Majorca, 11
Makan b. Kaki, Daylami commander, 157
Makrami, family of Sulaymani *da'is*, 129–30
al-Makzum al-Sinjari, al-Hasan, *amir*, 183
malahida see mulhid
Malati Sayyids *see* Amir (Kar) Kiya'i Sayyids
Malik al-Ashtar, 31
al-Malik al-Rahim Khusraw Firuz, Buyid, 73
al-Malika al-Sayyida, Sulayhid queen *see* Arwa
Maliki Sunnism, 116
Malikshah I, Saljuq sultan, 160
Mamluks, dynasty of Egypt and Syria, 136, 184
al-Ma'mun, Abbasid caliph, 58, 60–61
Man la yahduruhu'l-faqih, of Ibn Babawayh, 69
ma'na, divine Essence in Nusayri doctrine, 187
Mangu Khan *see* Möngke
Manichaeism, 42
Ma'nid, dynasty of Druze amirs, 122
al-Mansur, Abu Ja'far, Abbasid caliph, 53, 147
al-Mansur, Fatimid caliph, 116
al-Mansur bi'llah 'Abd Allah b. Hamza, Zaydi imam in Yaman, 161, 167
al-Mansur bi'llah al-Qasim b. 'Ali al-'Iyani, Zaydi imam in Yaman, 164–5
al-Mansur Muhammad b. Yahya Hamid al-Din, Zaydi imam in Yaman, 170
al-Mansur al-Qasim b. Muhammad, founder of the Qasimi dynasty of Zaydi imams in Yaman, 169, 171
Mansur al-Yaman *see* Ibn Hawshab, Mansur al-Yaman
al-Maqbali, Salih b. Mahdi, 173
Maragha, in Adharbayjan, 76
Mar'ashi, Sayyid 'Abd al-Husayn, 103
Mar'ashi, Sayyid Qiwam al-Din, Imami ruler of Tabaristan, 161
Mar'ashi, Sayyid Shihab al-Din Muhammad, 98
Mar'ashi Sayyids, of Tabaristan (Mazandaran), 162
Marco Polo, Venetian traveller, 12, 14
Mardawij b. Ziyar, founder of the Ziyarid dynasty of Persia, 157
marja' al-taqlid, 89, 100, 103, 204
marja'-i taqlid see marja' al-taqlid
Marqab, castle in Syria, 182
Marw, in Khurasan, 48, 60, 75
Marwan II, al-Himar, Umayyad caliph, 47
Mashhad, in Khurasan, 20, 61, 80, 84, 88
massacres, 33, 35, 51, 136, 184
Massignon, Louis, orientalist, 19, 24, 178
ma'sum see 'isma
Masyaf, castle in Syria, 133, 183
Matawira, Nusayri tribe, 183
mawali (clients), non-Arab Muslims, 33, 34–6, 38, 39, 42, 49–50, 204
Mawsil, in Iraq, 181
Mazandaran *see* Tabaristan
Mazandarani, Shaykh Zayn al-'Abidin, Twelver scholar, 103

Mazdakism, 170
Mazyadids, of Iraq, 74
Mecca (Makka), 25, 26, 59, 122, 123, 164, 192, 197, 205
Medina (Madina), 25, 30, 51, 59, 61, 106, 108, 147, 148, 154, 162
Memoirs, of Aga Khan III, 143
metempsychosis *see tanasukh*
Middle East, 1, 2, 12, 93, 144
see also Holy Land; Near East; Outremer
Mihragan, autumn equinox, 180, 189
millenarian, 82–3, 84, 114
see also eschatology; Mahdi; *qiyama*
millet(s), ethnic minorities in Ottoman empire, 185
al-Miqdad b. Aswad al-Kindi, 188
Mir Damad (Mir Muhammad Baqir al-Astarabadi), founder of the school of Isfahan in Twelver theosophy, 85
miʿraj (the Prophet's ascension), 91
Mirdasids, of northern Syria, 74
mithaq (oath), 113
see also ʿahd; *bayʿa*
Mombasa, in Kenya, 103
Möngke (Mangu Khan), Great Khan, 75
Mongols, 74–75, 132, 135–6, 161
Moosa, M., 179
Morocco 52, 115
see also Maghrib; North Africa
Moses (Musa), 114, 188
Mozarabs, 8
Muʿawiya I b. Abi Sufyan, founder of the Umayyad dynasty, 30, 32
al-Mu'ayyad bi'llah, Abu'l-Husayn Ahmad b. al-Husayn b. Harun, Zaydi imam, 159, 161
al-Mu'ayyad bi'llah al-Buthani *see* al-Mu'ayyad bi'llah, Abu'l-Husayn Ahmad b. al-Husayn b. Harun
al-Mu'ayyad bi'llah Yahya b. Hamza, Zaydi imam in Yaman, 168
al-Mu'ayyad fi'l-Din al-Shirazi, Ismaili *daʿi* and author, 118, 124
al-Mu'ayyad Muhammad b. Ismaʿil, Zaydi imam in Yaman, 171
al-Mu'ayyad Muhammad b. al-Qasim, Zaydi imam in Yaman, 169
Mu'ayyadiyya, school of Zaydi law in Caspian region, 159
al-Mubarak, epithet of Ismaʿil b. Jaʿfar, 107
Mubarakiyya, designation of early Ismailis, 107, 108, 109
Mudarris, Sayyid Hasan, 95
al-Mufaddal b. ʿUmar al-Juʿfi, eponym of Mufaddaliyya, 107, 186, 187
al-Mufid, Muhammad b. Muhammad al-Harithi, Imami scholar, 70, 71, 87
Muflih, Abbasid commander, 153
Mughal empire, 102, 128, 129
al-Mughira b. Saʿid, eponym of Mughiriyya, 40, 42
muhajirun (Emigrants), 205
Muhammad, the Prophet, 10, 25, 52, 113
ʿAli as his successor, 27–28
Companions of, 25–26
death of, 25
definition of his family, 28
era of, 114
seal of the prophets, 25
as sixth *natiq*, 114
in Nusayri doctrine, 187
see also ahl al-bayt; al Muhammad
Muhammad b. ʿAbd Allah al-Nafs al-Zakiyya *see* al-Nafs al-Zakiyya, Muhammad b. ʿAbd Allah
Muhammad b. ʿAli b. ʿAbd Allah b. al-ʿAbbas, Abbasid, 39

Muhammad b. ʿAli al-Ahsaʾi *see* Ibn Abi Jumhur
Muhammad b. ʿAli al-Baqir *see* Muhammad al-Baqir
Muhammad b. ʿAli al-Jawad (al-Taqi), Twelver imam, 61–2, *67*
Muhammad al-Badr Hamid al-Din, last Zaydi ruler in Yaman, 171
Muhammad al-Baqir, imam, 43–46, 52, *66*, 145–6, 148, 151, 187
Muhammad Burhan al-Din b. Tahir Sayf al-Din, Sayyidna, Daʾudi *daʿi*, 129
Muhammad b. Buzurg-Umid, Nizari leader and lord of Alamut, *131*
Muhammad al-Dibaj, ʿAlid, son of Jaʿfar al-Sadiq, 52, 58
Muhammad b. al-Hanafiyya, ʿAlid, son of ʿAli b. Abi Talib, 34, 35–6, 38, 43, 52
Muhammad b. al-Hasan, al-Mahdi, Nusayri Mahdi, 184
Muhammad b. al-Hasan, Twelver Mahdi *see* al-Mahdi, Muhammad b. al-Hasan
Muhammad b. Ibrahim al-Wazir *see* Ibn al-Wazir, Muhammad b. Ibrahim
Muhammad b. Ismaʿil b. Jaʿfar al-Sadiq, al-Maymun, 107, 110, 111–12, 114–15, 122, 123
Muhammad b. Jundab, Nusayri leader, 180
Muhammad Khudabanda, Ilkhanid *see* Öljeitü
Muhammad b. Mansur al-Muradi, Zaydi jurist, 151
Muhammad b. al-Mufaddal, 187
Muhammad al-Murtada, Zaydi imam in Yaman *see* al-Murtada Muhammad b. Yahya
Muhammad b. Nusayr, eponym of Nusayriyya *see* Ibn Nusayr, Abu Shuʿayb Muhammad b. Nusayr al-Namiri
Muhammad b. al-Qasim, Sahib al-Taliqan, ʿAlid, leader of a revolt, 147
Muhammad Rida b. Khwaja Sultan Husayn Ghuriyani Harati *see* Khayrkhwah-i Harati, Muhammad Rida b. Khwaja Sultan Husayn
Muhammad Rida Shah *see* Pahlavi, Muhammad Rida Shah
Muhammad Shah Qajar, 141
Muhammad b. Zayd, al-Daʿi ilaʾl-Haqq, ʿAlid ruler in Tabaristan, 153–4, 162
Muhammad-Shahi Nizaris *see* Muhammad-Shahis
Muhammad-Shahis (or Muʾminiyya), branch of Nizaris, 101, 137, 139
al-Muhaqqiq al-Awwal *see* al-Hilli, Jaʿfar b. al-Hasan
al-Muhaqqiq al-Thani *see* al-Karaki al-ʿAmili, Shaykh ʿAli
muhtasham, Nizari leader in Quhistan, 75, 76, 205
muhtasibun, Zaydi imams with restricted status, 150
al-Muʿizz, Fatimid caliph, *116*, 117, 119, 120
mujtahid see ijtihad
mukasir, rank in Ismaili *daʿwa* hierarchy, 128
Mukhammisa (the Pentadists), early extremist Shiʿi group, 45, 186, 187
al-Mukhtar b. Abi ʿUbayd al-Thaqafi, leader of anti-Umayyad revolt, 33–4, 35–6, 37, 40, 43, 46, 49
Mukhtariyya, 36
see also Kaysaniyya

mulhid, *malahida* (heretics), 84, 160, 199
Mulla Sadra, Twelver scholar, 85–6
mulla-bashi, 86
Multan, in Sind, 117, 140
Mumbai *see* Bombay
mu'min (believer), 42–55, 205
al-mu'min al-mumtahan (believer put to the test), 80
Mu'min al-Taq, Imami scholar, 59
muqaddams, Ottoman officials, 185
muqallid see taqlid
al-Muqtadir, Abbasid caliph, 65
al-Muqtana, Baha' al-Din, Druze leader, 122
muqtasida, Zaydi imams with restricted status, 150
murid, *muridan*, 138, 205
murshid, 205
  see also pir; *shaykh*
al-Murtada Muhammad b. Yahya, Zaydi imam in Yaman, 163, 164
Musa *see* Moses
Musa al-Kazim, Twelver imam, 52, 58, 59, 60, 62, *66*, 71, 81, 82, 106, 108, 110
Musafirids, of Daylam and Adharbayjan, 123
Musawi Isfahani, Sayyid Abu'l-Hasan, 95
Muscat (Masqat), in 'Uman, 103
Musha'sha', 79
Muslim Brotherhood (Ikhwan al-Muslimun), 190
Musta'lawiyya *see* Musta'lians
al-Musta'li, Fatimid caliph, *116*, 124, 132
Musta'lians, Musta'liyya (or Musta'lawiyya), 125
  see also Bohras; Da'udis; Hafizis; Nizari–Musta'lian schism; Sulaymanis; Tayyibis
al-Mustansir, Fatimid caliph, *116*, 118, 124, 132
Mustansir bi'llah II, Nizari imam, 138
al-Musta'sim, Abbasid caliph, 75
al-Mustazhir, Abbasid caliph, 6, 133
al-Mustazhiri, of al-Ghazali, 7, 133
mut'a (temporary marriage), 45, 155
al-Mu'tadid, Abbasid caliph, 64
al-Mu'tamid, Abbasid caliph, 63
Mutarrif b. Shihab al-Shihabi, eponymous founder of Mutarrifiyya Zaydis, 166
Mutarrifiyya, Zaydi sect in Yaman, 166–7, 167–8, 194–5
al-Mu'tasim, Abbasid caliph, 61
al-Mutawakkil, Abbasid caliph, 62, 154
al-Mutawakkil Ahmad b. Sulayman, Zaydi imam in Yaman, 167
al-Mutawakkil 'ala'llah Ahmad, Zaydi imam *see* al-Mutawakkil Ahmad b. Sulayman
al-Mutawakkil Isma'il b. al-Qasim, Zaydi imam in Yaman, 170
al-Mutawakkil al-Mutahhar b. Muhammad, Zaydi imam in Yaman, 169
al-Mutawakkil Sharaf al-Din Yahya b. Shams al-Din, Zaydi imam in Yaman, 169
al-Mutawakkil Yahya, Zaydi imam in Yaman, 170–1
Mu'tazilis, Mu'tazila, school of theology, 70, 71
  impact on Imamiyya, 47, 69, 70, 151
  impact on Zaydi doctrine, 47, 146, 149, 151, 152, 159, 166
  and Nawbakhtis, 65–6, 70
Muwahhidun *see* Druzes; Nusayris

nabi, *anbiya'* (prophets), 25, 205
  see also natiq
Nadir Shah Afshar, founder of the Afsharid dynasty of Persia, 88
nafs (soul), 41, 120, 192, 205, 209

al-Nafs al-Zakiyya, Muhammad b. ʿAbd Allah, Hasanid leader of anti-Abbasid revolt, 46, 48, 50, 52, 59, 147, 151
Nahj al-balagha, of ʿAli b. Abi Talib, 71
Na'ini, Mirza Muhammad Husayn, 95
Najaf, in Iraq, 72, 80, 83, 84, 90, 95, 97, 98, 99
al-Najashi, Ahmad b. ʿAli, Imami scholar, 46, 72
Najran, in northeastern Yaman, 129–30, 163, 167, 171
Namiriyya, early designation of Nusayriyya, 179
  see also Nusayris
Nanji, Azim, 23
naqib, *nuqaba'*
  Abbasid, 48
  ʿAlid, 68
  Nusayri, 186
al-Nasafi, Muhammad b. Ahmad, Ismaili (Qarmati) *daʿi* and author, 111, 119, 120, 123, 156
al-Nasir, Abbasid caliph, 135
al-Nasir Ahmad b. Yahya Hamid al-Din, Zaydi imam in Yaman, 171
al-Nasir al-Daylami, Abu'l-Fath, Zaydi imam in Yaman, 165
al-Nasir al-Din ʿAbd al-Rahim b. Abi Mansur, Nizari *muhtasham* in Quhistan, 75
Nasir al-Din Shah Qajar, 90, 92
Nasir al-Din al-Tusi *see* al-Tusi, Nasir al-Din Muhammad b. Muhammad
al-Nasir li-Din Allah Ahmad b. Yahya, Zaydi imam in Yaman, 163, 164
al-Nasir li'l-Haqq, Zaydi ruler in Tabaristan *see* al-ʿUtrush, Abu Muhammad al-Hasan b. ʿAli al-Nasir li'l-Haqq
al-Nasir Salah al-Din Muhammad b. ʿAli, Zaydi imam in Yaman, 169
al-Nasir al-ʿUtrush *see* al-ʿUtrush, Abu Muhammad al-Hasan b. ʿAli al-Nasir li'l-Haqq
Nasir-i Khusraw, Ismaili *daʿi* and author, 119, 124
Nasirabadi, Sayyid Dildar ʿAli, 102
Nasirids, Zaydi ʿAlid dynasty of northern Persia, 156, 157, 158, 160
Nasiriyya, branch of Zaydis, 155, 158, 161
Nasr, Seyyed Hossein, 20, 84
Nasr Allah, Sayyid Hasan, leader of Hizbullah, 100
Nasr II, Samanid *amir*, 101, 155–6
Nasr b. Sayyar, Umayyad governor, 147
nass (designation), 28, 46, 53–4, 55, 60, 106, 128, 148, 149, 150, 205–6
  see also imamate
natiq, *nutaqa'* (speaking or law-announcing prophets), 114, 115, 122, 206
  see also dawr
al-Natiq bi'l-Haqq, Abu Talib Yahya b. al-Husayn, Zaydi imam, 159
al-Nawbakhti, Abu Muhammad al-Hasan b. Musa, Imami scholar and heresiographer, 6, 37, 57, 65, 68, 106–7, 108
al-Nawbakhti, Abu Sahl Ismaʿil b. ʿAli, 65
al-Nawbakhti, Abu'l-Qasim al-Husayn b. Ruh, representative of Twelver Mahdi, 65, 66
al-Nawbakhti, al-Husayn b. ʿAli, Abbasid vizier, 65
Nawbakhtis *see* Banu Nawbakht
Nawruz, spring equinox, Persian New Year, 180, 189
Nawusiyya, early Shiʿi sect, 58
Nawwabs, of Awadh, 102
Near East, 9–10, 12–13
  see also Middle East; Outremer

Neoplatonism, 85, 111, 115, 119
  see also philosophical Ismailism; 'school of Isfahan'
neo-Sunni school, in Yaman, 172–3
Nestorian Christians, 181
Newman, Andrew, 21
Nicephorus Phocas, Byzantine emperor, 181
Niebuhr, Carsten, Danish traveller, 176
Niʿmat Allahiyya (Niʿmat Allahi), Sufi order, 79, 84, 141
Nishapur (Nisabur), in Khurasan, 73, 75, 154
Nizam al-Mulk, Saljuq vizier, 111
Nizam-Shahis, of Ahmadnagar, 101
Nizar b. al-Mustansir, Nizari imam, eponym of Nizariyya, 124, 132, 134
Nizari Quhistani, Hakim Saʿd al-Din b. Shams al-Din, Nizari poet, 137
Nizari–Mustaʿlian schism of 487/1094, 124–5, 131–2
Nizaris, Nizariyya, 1, 6–7, 17
  Alamut period, 130–136
  against Crusaders, 12–13
  daʿwa see under daʿwa
  literature *see under* literature
  methods of struggle, 132–3
  origins, 124–5
  post-Alamut period, 136
    Anjudan revival, 138–141
    modern period, 141–144
  Qasim-Shahi/Muhammad-Shahi schism, 137
  qiyama, 134
  and Sufism, 138–9
  see also Assassins; Ismailis; Khojas; Nizari–Mustaʿlian schism; Qasim-Shahi Nizaris; Satpanth Ismailism
Noah (Nuh), 114, 188
North Africa, 2, 111, 112, 115, 123, 194
  see also Algeria; Ifriqiya; Maghrib; Morocco; Tunisia
North America, 1, 144
nubuwwa (prophecy), 40–1, 205
  see also cyclical history; *dawr*
al-Nuʿman b. Muhammad, al-Qadi Abu Hanifa, Ismaili jurist and author, 54, 118, 120, 121, 128
nuqabaʾ see *naqib*
Nuqtawis, Nuqtawiyya, 78, 79
Nur al-Din Muhammad b. Hasan, Nizari imam and lord of Alamut, *131*, 134
Nurbakhshiyya, Sufi order, 79
Nuri, Mirza Yahya *see* Subh-i Azal, Mirza Yahya Nuri
Nuri, Shaykh Fadl Allah, 90
Nusayris (ʿAlawis), Nusayriyya, 2, 13, 136, 175
  origins, 179–181
  calendar of festivals, 189
  doctrines, 185–9
    Christian influences, 186
    Iranian influences, 180, 189
  early history, 181–4
  *fatwa*s against, 184, 190
  later, modern, history, 184–5

oath of allegiance *see* ʿ*ahd*; *bayʿa*; *mithaq*
occultation *see ghayba*
Ögedei, Great Khan, 75
Oghuz Turks, 73
Old Man of the Mountain, 13
  see also Assassin legends; Assassins
Old Testament, 9
Öljeitü (Uljaytu), Ilkhanid, 77, 161
Oman *see* ʿUman
orientalism, 16
Ottoman Turks, 8, 15, 88, 92, 99, 100, 130, 136, 169, 170, 185
Ottomans *see* Ottoman Turks
Outremer, 9, 11, 12

see also Holy Land; Middle East; Near East
Oxus (Amu Darya) river, 74

pagan tradition, 186, 189
Pahlavi, Muhammad Rida Shah, 95–6, 97, 98
Pahlavi, Rida Shah, 93–5
Pahlavis, dynasty of Iran (Persia), 94, 97–8
Pakistan, 1, 102, 103, 139–40, 143
see also South Asia
Palestine, 48, 93
Pandiyat-i jawanmardi, of Mustansir bi'llah II, 138
Paradise
denied by *ghulat*, 41
in Nizari doctrine of *qiyamat*, 134, 206
of the Old Man in Marco Polo's narrative, 14
parda see chadur
Paris, 15, 16, 19, 24, 144, 178
Pasikhani, Mahmud, Nuqtawi leader, 78, 79
Penitents *see* Tawwabun
Persia (Iran), 1
Afghan invasion, 88
Anjudan revival, 138–9
Aga Khan I's campaigns, 141–2
during Constitutional Revolution, 93
Iranian school of philosophical Ismailism, 119–120
Islamic Revolution of 1979, 97–8
Ismailis in, 110–111, 117, 122
Kaysani sects in, 38–9
mawali of, 34
Mongol conquest of, 74–5
Nizaris of, 130
establishment of Nizari state, 132–3
proclamation of *qiyama* at Alamut, 134
under Saljuqs, 73, 131
under Khwarazmshahs, 75
under Ilkhanids and Timurids, 75–6
under Safawids, 82–6
under Zand dynasty, 88
under Qajar dynasty, 88, 92
under Pahlavis, 93–96
Shiʿism in, 65, 69–72, 73, 82
Twelver Shiʿism in, 82–3
Zaydis in, 145, 151–5, 161, 162
Persian (language), 16, 21, 22, 45, 130, 132, 133, 138, 140, 187
Persian Gulf, 74, 101
Peter the Venerable, abbot of Cluny, 11
philosophical Ismailism, 119, 120
see also cosmology; Neoplatonism
pilgrimage to Mecca *see hajj*
pir, 137, 140, 206
see also murshid
Pir Sadr al-Din *see* Sadr al-Din, Pir
Pir Shams al-Din *see* Shams al-Din, Pir
Polo, Marco *see* Marco Polo
Poonawala, Ismail K., 22, 23
Punjab, now in Pakistan, 102–3, 139

Qadariyya, 151
Qadi Saʿid al-Qummi, 86
Qadiri, Qadiriyya, Sufi order, 140
Qadmus, castle in Syria, 133, 183
qa'im, 63, 108, 134
see also Mahdi; *qiyama*
al-Qa'im, Abbasid caliph, 73
al-Qa'im, Fatimid caliph, *116*
qa'im al-qiyama, 134
see also Mahdi; *qa'im*
Qajar dynasty, of Persia, 88–9, 91, 92–3
Qalawun, Mamluk sultan, 184
Qanbar b. Kadan al-Dawsi, 188
Qara Qoyunlu dynasty, of Persia, 81

Qaramita *see* Qarmatis
Qarmatis, 22, 105, 108, 119
of Bahrayn, 109, 115, 122–3, 124
as dissident Ismailis in schism of 286/899, 112
Mahdism of Muhammad b. Ismaʿil, 114–115
origins of the name, 110
al-Qasim b. Ibrahim al-Rassi, Zaydi imam, 148, 150, 151, 152, 155, 162, 164, 166
al-Qasim al-Mansur, Zaydi imam in Yaman, 169–70, 171
Qasim-Shahi Nizaris, 137, 138, 139, 140
Qasimi *sharifs*, 166
Qasimi Zaydis of Yaman *see* Qasimiyya
Qasimiyya, school of Zaydi law, 151, 155, 160, 161, 164
Qatar, 101
Qawaʿid al-ʿaqaʾid, of Nasir al-Din al-Tusi, 76
Qayrawan (Kairouan), 116
Qazwin (in Persia), 73, 79, 91, 153, 162
qilaʿ al-daʿwa, Nizari castles, in Syria, 133
qiyama (resurrection), 91
in doctrine of *ghulat*, 41
proclamation at Alamut, 134
in Twelver doctrine, 67
see also eschatology; *qaʾim al-qiyama*
Qizilbash, 82–3, 84
al-qobba al-Muhammadiyya, era of Islam, 188
qobba, era in Nusayri doctrine, 188
Quhistan (Kuhistan), region in southeastern Khurasan, 75, 133, 205
Qumis, region in northern Persia, 133, 153
Qumm, in central Persia, 20, 61, 69–70, 72, 73, 74, 86, 95, 96, 97, 141
al-Qummi, Saʿd b. ʿAbd Allah al-Ashʿari, Imami scholar and heresiographer, 37, 57, 68, 106–7, 108
Qurʾan, 5, 11, 27, 28, 29, 38, 40, 51, 54, 55, 85, 91, 113, 114, 120
Quraysh, Meccan tribe, 26–7, 30, 59, 127
qurraʾ, in early Islam, 29, 30, 31
Qutb-Shahis, of Golconda, 101, 102

al-Radi, Abbasid caliph, 65
Rafida, 146
Rahat al-ʿaql, of Hamid al-Din al-Kirmani, 119, 127
rajʿa (return), 38, 40, 57, 67, 122, 150
see also ghayba; Mahdi; *qaʾim*
Ranikuh, in northern Persia, 161
Rasaʾil al-hikma, scriptures of the Druzes, 122
Rasaʾil Ikhwan al-Safaʾ, of the Brethren of Purity, 120
Rashid al-Din Fadl Allah, historian and Ilkhanid vizier, 131, 133
Rashid al-Din Sinan, Nizari leader in Syria, 13, 136
Rashti, Sayyid Kazim, Shaykhi leader, 92
al-Rassi, al-Qasim b. Ibrahim *see* al-Qasim b. Ibrahim al-Rassi
Rassids, dynasty of Zaydi imams in Yaman, 164, 165
rasul Allah, 25
Rasulids, of Yaman, 169
raʾy, 148
Raymond of Lull, 11
Rayy, in Persia, 69, 70, 71, 73, 153, 157, 159, 160, 162
al-Razi, Abu Hatim *see* Abu Hatim al-Razi
religious dues *see dassondh*; *khums*
resurrection *see qiyama*
al-Rida, ʿAli b. Musa *see* ʿAli b. Musa al-Rida

al-rida min al Muhammad, 48
Rida Shah Pahlavi *see* Pahlavi, Rida Shah
al-Risala al-damigha fi'l-fasiq al-Nusayri, of Hamza b. ʿAli, 182
al-Risala al-Masihiyya, of Muhammad b. ʿAli al-Jilli, 181
al-Risala al-waʿiza, of Hamid al-Din al-Kirmani, 121
Risalat siyasat al-muridin, of al-Mu'ayyad bi'llah, Abu'l-Hasan Ahmad, 159
ritual ablution, 45, 155
Rousseau, Jean Baptiste L. J., French consul in Aleppo, 176–7
Rudbar, region in northern Persia *see* Daylam
ruh see nafs
Rukn al-Dawla, Buyid ruler, 70
Rukn al-Din Khurshah, Nizari imam and last lord of Alamut, *131*, 136, 137
Rum (Anatolia), 73, 74, 78, 79, 81
Rumi, Jalal al-Din *see* Jalal al-Din Rumi
Russia, 91, 94
Ruyan, in northern Persia, 153, 155, 160
Ruzbih b. Marzuban, 188

Sabʿiyya (Seveners), 108
Saʿda, in northern Yaman, 162, 164, 165, 167, 168
sadat-i ʿAlawi (ʿAlid Sayyids), 152
Saddam Hussain, 99
al-Sadiq, imam *see* Jaʿfar al-Sadiq
sadr, 83–4
al-Sadr, Ayatullah Muhammad Baqir, 99
al-Sadr, Imam Musa, 99–100
Sadr al-Din, Pir, Nizari preacher-saint in India, 140
Sadr al-Din Muhammad Shirazi *see* Mulla Sadra
Safar-nama, of Nizari Quhistani, 137
Safawi, Safawiyya, Sufi order, 79, 81, 82
Safawid dynasty, of Persia, 81, 82–3, 84, 86, 88, 139, 161, 162
al-Saffah, Abu'l-ʿAbbas, Abbasid caliph, 49, 52
Saffarids, of Sistan and eastern Afghanistan, 153, 154
Safi al-Din, Safawi *shaykh*, 81
Safidrud, in Gilan, 154, 162
safir, sufara', representative of the Twelver Mahdi, 64, 66, 193
sahaba see Companions of the Prophet
Saladin *see* Salah al-Din
Salafis, Salafiyya, 101, 145, 173, 190
see also Wahhabis
Salah al-Din (Saladin), founder of the Ayyubid dynasty, 125, 183
Salamiyya, in central Syria, 109, 110, 111–12, 115
Salarids *see* Musafirids
Salisbury, Edward, orientalist, 178
Saljuqs, 73, 74, 111, 124, 132–3, 160
Salman al-Farsi, 188
salvation *see* eschatology
samaʿ, 159, 168
al-Samahiji al-Bahrani, ʿAbd Allah, Twelver scholar, 88
Samanids, of Khurasan and Transoxania, 111, 124, 154, 155, 157, 158
Samarqand, in Central Asia (now in Uzbekistan), 73
Samarra', in Iraq, 62–3, 64, 180
al-Samarri, Abu'l-Husayn ʿAli b. Muhammad, representative of the Twelver Mahdi, 66
samit, 55, 114, 207
Sanʿa', in Yaman, 163, 164, 165, 166, 167, 168, 170, 171
Sanjar, Saljuq sultan, 74
Saracens, 9, 10

Satpanth Ismailism, 139, 140
see also ginan; Khojas
satr, 126, 207
see also dawr al-satr; *ghayba*
Saudi Arabia, 1, 2, 56, 100–1, 130, 145, 173, 190
Saʿudis (Al Saʿud), 171
Sawa, near Qumm, 73
Sawad, of Kufa, 109
Sayf al-Dawla, Hamdanid, 181
Sayfi Dars (Jamiʿat Sayfiyya), Surat, 129
al-Sayl al-jarrar, of al-Shawkani, 173
Sayyid ʿAli Kiya b. Sayyid Amir Kiya al-Malati, founder of the dynasty of Amir Kiyaʾi Sayyids, 162
Sayyid Muhammad Kiya b. Sayyid Haydar Kiya, Zaydi ruler, 161
Sayyid Saʿid b. Sultan, Al Bu Saʿidi sultan of ʿUman and Zanzibar, 103
al-Sayyida Hurra bint Ahmad al-Sulayhi *see* Arwa
Sayyidna Hasan-i Sabbah *see* Hasan-i Sabbah
'school of Isfahan', 80, 84–5, 86, 91
see also Mir Damad; Mulla Sadra
Second World War, 95
Selim I, Ottoman sultan, 184
Seth, 187
shafaʿa (intercession), 70
Shafiʿi Sunnism, 81, 168, 171, 173, 202
Shah Khalil Allah, Nizari imam, 141, *142*
Shah Nizar, Nizari imam, 140
Shah Sayyid Nasir *see* Nasir-i Khusraw
Shah Tahir, Dakkani (Shah Tahir b. Radi al-Din), Muhammad-Shahi Nizari imam, 101–2, 139
Shahara, stronghold of the Husayniyya Zaydis in Yaman, 166
Shahr-i Babak, in Kirman, 141
al-Shahrastani, Muhammad b. ʿAbd al-Karim, heresiographer and Ashʿari theologian, 37, 76–7, 107, 133
Shahrukh, Timurid, 81
Sham *see* Syria
Shams al-Din, Pir, 140
Shams al-Din Jaʿfar b. Abi Yahya, Zaydi jurist, 167
Shams al-Din Muhammad, Nizari imam, 137
Sharaf al-Din, Sayyid ʿAbd al-Husayn, 99
Shaʿrani Mosque, in Ladhiqiyya, 182
sharh (commentary), 75
shariʿa (sacred law of Islam), 7, 41, 80, 113, 114, 120–1, 134, 208
al-Sharif al-Murtada, ʿAlam al-Huda, Imami theologian, 70–1
al-Sharif al-Radi, Imami theologian, 71
al-Shawkani, Muhammad b. ʿAli, chief judge in Yaman, 172–4
shaykh, *mashayikh*, 137, 168, 170, 177, 182, 189, 190
Shaykh Bahaʾi *see* al-ʿAmili, Shaykh Bahaʾ al-Din
shaykh al-Islam, 84, 85
Shaykh Jiwanji Awrangabadi, ancestor of some Daʾudi *daʿis*, 129
Shaykh al-Mufid *see* al-Mufid, Muhammad b. Muhammad al-Harithi
Shaykh al-Saduq *see* Ibn Babawayh
Shaykh al-Taʾifa *see* al-Tusi, Abu Jaʿfar Muhammad b. al-Hasan
Shaykh Yabraq *see* al-Khasibi, Abu ʿAbd Allah al-Husayn b. Hamdan
Shaykhis, Shaykhiyya, 91–2, 93
Shiʿa *see* Shiʿis
al-Shiʿa al-Husayniyya see Husayniyya
shiʿat ʿAli see Shiʿis
shiʿat al-Mahdi, 35

Shihabid, dynasty of Druze *amirs*, 122
Shiʿis, Shiʿism
  Arab, unified phase, 33
  conception of religious authority, 28
  contribution of *ghulat*, 40–1
  definition of *ahl al-bayt*, 27, 29, 36
  during imamate of Jaʿfar al-Sadiq, 46, 51
  martyrology, 33
  mawali: their effect on Shiʿism, 34–5
  and Muʿtazilis, 69, 70, 151
  origins, 25, 27, 28
  repressed by Abbasids, 50
  revolt of al-Mukhtar, 35–6
  significance of *nass* imamate, 53
  as state religion of Safawids, 82
  use of the term *hujja*, 55
  and Zaydiyya, 46–7, 145–7
  see also imamate; Ismailis; Nusayris; Qarmatis; Twelvers; Zaydis
Shiraz, in Fars, 79, 86, 92, 104
Shumaytiyya, subgroup of Imamiyya, 58
al-Shushtari, Mulla ʿAbd al-Husayn, 84
al-Shushtari, Nur Allah, Qadi, Twelver scholar, 102
Siffin, battle of, 31
Sijilmasa, in Morocco, 115
al-Sijistani, Abu Yaʿqub Ishaq b. Ahmad, Ismaili *daʿi* and author, 111, 117, 119
Sikhs, 103
silsila, chain of spiritual masters in Sufism, 79
Silsilat al-turath al-ʿAlawi, collected Nusayri texts, 179
Silvestre de Sacy, Antoine Isaac, orientalist, 16, 176–7
Sinan, Nizari leader in Syria *see* Rashid al-Din Sinan
Sind, now in Pakistan, 111, 112, 117, 137, 138, 139, 140, 141
al-Sistani, Ayatullah ʿAli, 98, 99
Siyahchashm *see* Mahdi b. Khusraw Firuz
Solomon, 188
soteriology *see* eschatology; *qiyama*
soul *see nafs*
South Asia, 1, 21, 23, 102, 130, 136, 139–40, 197, 202
  see also individual countries
Southern, Richard W., 10
Spain, 8, 9, 11, 116
St John of Damascus, 8
St Peter, 187
Stern, Samuel M., 22
Strothmann, Rudolf, 19, 24, 178
Subh-i Azal, Mirza Yahya Nuri, eponym of Azalis, 93
Sufis, Sufism
  and Ismaili Shiʿism, 136–8, 140
  role in spreading Shiʿism in Persia, 79–80
  and 'school of Isfahan', 84–85
  suppressed by Safawids, 82–3
  and Twelver Shiʿism, 80
  and Zaydi Shiʿism, 159–160, 163, 166, 168
al-Suhrawardi, Shihab al-Din Yahya, 80, 85
Suhrawardiyya, Sufi order, 140
Sulayhi, Muhammad b. ʿAli, founder of the Sulayhid dynasty of Yaman, 165
Sulayhids, of Yaman, 124, 125, 126–7, 165–6
Sulayman b. ʿAbd Allah, Tahirid governor, 153
Sulayman b. Hasan, Sulaymani *daʿi mutlaq*, 129
Sulayman b. Ismaʿil, Thaʾirid, 161
Sulayman b. Surad al-Khuzaʿi, 33
Sulaymanis, Sulaymaniyya, branch of Tayyibis, 126, 128–30, 194

Sultan Ahmad Khan, Zaydi Malati Sayyid, 162
Sultan 'Ali, Safawi *shaykh*, 82
Sultan Husayn I, Safawid *shah*, 86
Sultan Muhammad (Mahomed) Shah, Aga Khan III *see* Aga Khan III
sunna, 26, 27, 44, 120, 121, 208
Sunnis, Sunnism, 4, 5–7, 12, 16, 25–7, 31, 44, 47, 50, 73, 79, 81, 88, 101, 117, 120, 124, 128, 133, 135, 140, 142, 148, 151, 154, 168, 171, 173, 184
  Abbasids as, 50, 68, 105
  acceptance of Ja'far al-Sadiq, 51
  Afghans as, 88
  Arabs as, 116
  Ayyubids as, 125, 168, 183
  conversions to, 140, 142
  conversions to Shi'ism, 102
  Gujarat as a Sunni sultanate, 128
  heresiographies, 37, 40
  Jalal al-Din Hasan's reaction towards, 135
  legal schools, 78, 88, 148, 172, 173
  medieval perceptions of Shi'i Islam, 4, 5–7
  Mughals as, 102
  Nizaris in Sunni guise, 135, 136
  Ottomans as, 88, 99, 184–5
  in Persia, 150, 151
  reaction to *ta'lim*, 133
  repression of Shi'is in Bahrayn, 100
  Saljuqs as, 73–4, 124, 132, 160
  Shi'i use of legal methodology, 77
  Shi'is in Sunni areas, 78, 82, 98–9, 140, 168, 183–4
  stance, 3, 3–4, 4, 16, 17–18, 19, 25, 40, 83, 108, 109, 117, 120, 123, 160, 166, 184
  Sufism and, 79, 81, 83, 160
  in Tabaristan, 154, 160
  in Yaman, 168–9, 171–4
  see also Hanafi Sunnism; Hanbali Sunnism; Shafi'i Sunnism; Wahhabis
Surat, in Gujarat, 23, 129
symbolic exegesis *see ta'wil*
Syria, 2, 12, 21, 24, 109, 110, 133, 137, 175, 180, 190
  Crusaders in, 13, 14
  Druze in, 122
  Ismailis in, 109, 125
  manuscripts from, 18, 21, 24
  Nizaris in, 1, 13, 17, 105, 130, 132, 133, 136, 137, 160
  Nusayris ('Alawis) in, 2, 12, 24, 175–90
  Siffin arbitration proposal, 31
  Twelvers in, 74
  Umayyad *coup*, 47

al-Tabarani, Maymun b. Qasim, Nusayri leader, 177, 182, 186
al-Tabari, Abu Ja'far Muhammad, historian, 33, 156
Tabaristan (Mazandaran), region in northern Persia, 73, 80, 151, 152, 154, 155-8, 160, 161–2
Tabataba'i, Sayyid Muhammad, 93
Tabataba'i, Sayyid Muhammad Husayn, Twelver scholar, 20
Tabriz, in Adharbayjan, 82, 84, 92, 137
tafsir (Qur'an commentary), 209
Tahdhib al-ahkam, of Abu Ja'far Muhammad al-Tusi, 71
Tahir b. Radi al-Din, Shah *see* Shah Tahir
Tahir Sayf al-Din, Sayyidna, Da'udi *da'i*, 129
Tahirids, of Khurasan, 152, 153
Tahmasp I, Safawid *shah*, 82, 83, 162
ta'iban, Zaydi Sufi penitents, 161
Tajikistan, 1, 23, 144
  see also Badakhshan; Central Asia
Tajrid al-'aqa'id, of Nasir al-Din al-Tusi, 76

takfir (charge of unbelief), 91, 92, 101
Talibids, branch of Hashimids, 36, 146, 149, 209
Talibiyya, early Zaydi sect, 149
ta'lim, 133, 209
Ta'limiyya, 133
tanasukh (metempsychosis), 41, 122, 179, 187, 209
Tanga, in East Africa, 103
Tanzania, 104
taqiyya (precautionary dissimulation), 44, 54, 69, 76, 101, 109, 112, 122, 135, 136, 150, 180, 181, 182, 185, 209
taqlid (emulation), 78, 83, 87, 89–90, 209
  see also ijtihad; *marja' al-taqlid*
tariqa, 80, 81, 209
Tarsus, in Turkey, 176
Tarum, in northern Persia, 162
tasawwuf see Sufis
Tasfiyat al-qulub, of al-Mu'ayyad bi'llah Yahya, 168
tashbih (anthropomorphism), 40, 70, 210
tawba (penitence), 166
ta'wil (esoteric interpretation), 51, 113
  in Ismaili doctrine, 112–3
  in Nizari doctrine of *qiyama*, 134
  in Nusayri doctrine, 181, 189
al-Tawil, Muhammad Amin Ghalib, 'Alawi author, 179
Ta'wil al-da'a'im, of al-Qadi al-Nu'man, 118
Tawwabun (the Penitents), 33
taxation, 35, 91, 184, 191, 202
al-Tayyib, son of the Fatimid caliph al-Amir, eponym of the Tayyibiyya, 125–6
Tayyibis, Tayyibiyya, branch of Musta'lians, 125, 126, 169
  see also 'Alawis; Bohras; Da'udis; Sulaymanis
ta'ziya (popular religious play), 33
Tehran, 19, 93, 97, 98
Tehran University, 94
Tha'irid dynasty, of Zaydi 'Alids in northern Persia, 158, 160–1
Tiberias, 182
Tigris river, 62
Tihama, in Yaman, 168
Timur (Temür), founder of the Timurid dynasty, 80–1
Timurids, of Persia and Transoxania, 81
Tobacco Protest, 90
Toledo, in Spain, 9, 11
tolerance, racial and religious, 102, 103, 168, 185
Toluy, 74
Toronto, 144
trade, 103, 128
transmigration of souls *see tanasukh*
Transoxania (Ma wara' al-nahr), 73, 111, 117, 123
  see also Badakhshan; Central Asia
Tripoli (Tarablus), in Syria, 74, 184, 185
Tughril I, Saljuq sultan, 73
Tuhfat al-qulub, of Hatim b. Ibrahim al-Hamidi, 127
Tunisia, 115
  see also Ifriqiya; Maghrib; North Africa
Tunukabun, in northern Persia, 161
Turkey, 2, 79, 94, 95, 97, 175, 176, 178, 185
Turkomans, 81, 82, 83, 88
Tus, in Khurasan, 61, 71, 73, 75
  see also Mashhad
al-Tusi, Abu Ja'far Muhammad b. al-Hasan, Shaykh al-Ta'ifa, Twelver scholar, 71–2
al-Tusi, Nasir al-Din Muhammad b. Muhammad, Khwaja, Shi'i scholar, 72, 75–7, 80, 135

Twelvers, Twelver Shiʿism, 1, 15, 58, 142
- Mahdi concept, 63, 67–8
- as majority branch of the Shiʿa, 57
- and Muʿtazilis *see under* Imamiyya
- Nasir al-Din al-Tusi as, 75–7
- practices developed under Buyids, 68
- proclaimed as state religion in Nizam-Shahi Deccan, 101–2
- proclaimed as state religion under Safawids, 81, 139
- spread by Sufi orders, 79
- and Sufism, 80
- supported imamate of Musa al-Kazim, 59, 106
- use of the term *hujja*, 55
- *see also* Imamiyya

Tyre, 9

ʿUbayd Allah al-Mahdi *see* al-Mahdi, ʿAbd Allah
Ucch, in Sind, 140
Uganda, 104
ʿUla'iyya, early Shiʿi sect, 186, 187
ʿUman, 103, 104
ʿUmar b. al-Khattab, second caliph, 25–6, 168
Umayyads, Banu Umayya, 30, 31, 33, 39, 47–8, 116, 146, 149
ʿUmdat al-Islam Jaʿfar, *amir*, leader of the Husayniyya Zaydis, 165
Umm al-kitab, anonymous Shiʿi work, 45, 187
umma (community of believers), 3, 25, 210
United Arab Emirates, 1, 101
United States of America, 178
- *see also* North America

University of Central Asia, in Tajikistan, 144
ʿUqaylids, of Iraq and northern Syria, 74
usul al-fiqh (principles of jurisprudence), 70, 77, 87, 89, 210
- *see also fiqh*

Usuli school, of Twelver jurisprudence, 86, 87, 89, 91, 102
Usulis, 86, 87, 88, 88–9
- and Shaykhism, 91

ʿUthman b. ʿAffan, third caliph, 26, 30, 31, 148, 168
ʿUthman b. Mazʿun al-Najashi, 188
ʿUthmaniyya, 31
al-Utrush, Abu Muhammad al-Hasan b. ʿAli al-Nasir li'l-Haqq, Zaydi ruler in Tabaristan and founder of the Nasiriyya Zaydi school, 154–6, 157, 158, 160, 161
ʿUyun al-akhbar, of Idris ʿImad al-Din, 127–8

Vadodara *see* Baroda
vali-yi faqih (the 'guardian jurist'), 98
Vienna, 11, 18
vilayat-i faqih (the 'guardianship of the jurist'), 20, 96–8
vizier, vizierate, 211
Volney, Constantine de, French traveller, 176

Wadi Waqash, seat of Mutarrifi Zaydis in Yaman, 166
Wahhabis, Wahhabiyya, 56, 100–1
wahy (divine revelation), 85
wakil, wukala', representative of the Twelver Mahdi, 59, 64, 66, 140, 193
al-Walid II, Umayyad caliph, 47
Walker, Paul E., 23
Walpole, Frederick, 177
waqf, awqaf (religious endowments), 91, 94, 95
Waqifiyya, early Shiʿi sect, 60, 61, 68
wasi, awsiya' (legatees), 28, 53, 55, 113, 114, 148, 211

Wasil b. 'Ata', reputed founder of the Mu'tazila, 47, 146
wazir see vizier
Wellhausen, Julius, orientalist, 18, 47
wilayat-i faqih see vilayat-i faqih
William of Tyre, archbishop and Crusader historian, 9–10, 12, 13
World War I *see* First World War
World War II *see* Second World War

Yahya b. 'Abd Allah, younger brother of al-Nafs al-Zakiyya, Zaydi imam, 147, 152
Yahya b. Abi'l-Shumayt, 58
Yahya b. al-Husayn, al-Hadi ila'l-Haqq, Zaydi imam in Yaman, 155, 162
Yahya b. Lamak al-Hammadi, Ismaili *da'i* in Yaman, 126
Yahya b. al-Mansur Muhammad Hamid al-Din, Zaydi imam in Yaman *see* al-Mutawakkil Yahya
Yahya b. Mu'in al-Samarri, Nusayri leader, 180
Yahya b. 'Umar b. Yahya, 'Alid, leader of a revolt, 146–7
Yahya b. Zayd b. 'Ali, Zaydi imam, 52, 146–7
Ya'il b. Fatin, 188
Yale University, New Haven, 178
Yaman, 124–7, 128–9, 145, 163, 165, 169–70
  Ismaili *da'wa* to, 110–111, 118, 122
  Sulayhids, 124
  Sulaymanis of, 130
  Tayyibis of, 126–7
  Zaydi state in, 145, 160–3, 169, 171
Ya'qub b. al-Layth, founder of the Saffarid dynasty, 153
yatims (*aytam*), orphans, 188
Yazd, in Persia, 141
Yazid I, Umayyad caliph, 32, 33
Yusuf b. 'Umar al-Thaqafi, Umayyad governor of Iraq, 46
Yusuf b. Yahya b. Ahmad, al-Nasir, al-Da'i ila'l-Haqq, Zaydi leader in Yaman, 164–5

Zabid, in Yaman, 168
al-Zafir, Fatimid caliph, *116*
Zahid 'Ali, 21–2, 23
zahir, 7, 55, 80, 113, 114, 120, 127, 134, 211
  see also batin; *ta'wil*
al-Zahir, Fatimid caliph, *116*
Zahr al-ma'ani, of Idris 'Imad al-Din, 127
Zand dynasty, of Persia, 88, 141
Zanjan, in Persia, 153
Zanzibar, 103, 104
Zayd b. 'Ali b. al-Husayn, Zaydi imam, 46, 52, 145–6, 148, 151
Zaydis, Zaydiyya, 1, 145–62
  in Caspian region, 151–6
  against Ismailis, 111, 126, 160, 161, 162, 169
  and Mu'tazila, 159
  origins, 46–7, 146
  state in Persia, 153
  state in Yaman, 162–174
  and Sufis, 159, 168–9
  at war with Ottomans, 169, 170–1
Zayn al-'Abidin, imam *see* 'Ali b. al-Husayn, Zayn al-'Abidin
ziyara (pilgrimage), 61, 84, 186
Ziyarid dynasty, of Tabaristan and Gurgan, in northern Persia, 152, 157, 158
Zoroastrians, Zoroastrianism, 35, 93, 151, 170, 189
Zubayrid anti-caliphate, 35
zuhur (manifestation), 67, 126
  see also dawr al-kashf
Zurara b. A'yan, Imami scholar, 45